THE THIRD AFRICA

Eschel Rhoodie

THE THIRD AFRICA

with concluding chapter
by Professor Stefan Possony,
Director, International
Political Studies Programme,
Hoover Institution on War,
Revolution and Peace,
Stanford University, California.

Twin Circle Publishing Co., Inc.
in association with
Nasionale Boekhandel

Twin Circle Publishing Co., Inc.
1776 Broadway, New York, N.Y. 10019
In association with
Nasionale Boekhandel Ltd., Cape Town
Dust jacket design by Horst Walter
Set in 10 on 12 pt. Baskerville Monotype
Printed and bound by
National Commercial Printers Ltd.
Elsies River, Cape, South Africa

First edition 1968

Contents

Introduction

To most Americans *Southern Africa* is like the dark side of the moon. The bulk of our literature deals with Arab or North Africa and with Central or Black Africa. Because of the repercussions of the slave trade to the Americas and the many newly independent Black states there has always been an inclination to think of Africa as the Dark Continent although over the millennia of recorded history it has been the home of Egyptians, Greeks, Hamites, Berbers, Negroids, Arabs and, for more than three centuries, also "White Africans".

Of the three regions of Africa we know least about Southern Africa, i.e. Africa south of the Congo and the Great Lakes. This is the area which Dr Rhoodie refers to as the Third Africa. It is inexplicable that this should be so for the history of one of the countries in this region, the Republic of South Africa, is remarkably similar to ours. President Hoover, Alexander Hamilton, Will Rogers and other household names in America also march through the pages of South African history. In modern times Southern Africa enjoys a position of economic and technical pre-eminence in Africa similar to that which the United States exercises in the Americas. In addition Southern Africa is America's principal trading partner and the recipient of more than fifty per cent of all private American investments in Africa.

Southern Africa includes the independent Republic of South Africa, Rhodesia, Mocambique, Angola, South West Africa, Zambia, Malawi, Lesotho, Botswana and Swaziland – countries which have featured prominently in the press of the world for the past ten years; South Africa for its much condemned but little understood policy of apartheid; Rhodesia for its Declaration of Independence similar to that of the infant United States of America nearly 300 years ago; Angola for the gruesome terrorist attacks in the early 1960's; South West Africa for the marathon five year dispute over its international status before the World Court which ended in victory for South Africa (who administers the territory) only to see the United Nations General Assembly vote overwhelmingly to "take over" South West Africa – by force if necessary.

For years now the United Nations has declared the state of affairs in some of these countries a "threat to world peace". At the same time a great number of American and European visitors found the area to be the most stable, dynamic and prosperous region in all of Africa with a fantastic potential for development; an area in which Black and White are enjoying an increasingly higher standard of living unparalleled elsewhere in Africa. Every year thousands of people from Europe migrate to Southern Africa to start a new life in a new world. To distinguish between this "threat to world peace" and the true face of Southern Africa is one of the main objectives of this book.

Dr Eschel Rhoodie, whose forefathers came to Africa in 1659, brings a wealth of background to his subject. He worked as a journalist in Johannesburg, the bustling metropolis of South Africa which is today the youngest city of its size in the world, and studied at the University of Pretoria for his degrees. Later he travelled and worked for many years in Australasia, Europe and the United States where he has had first-hand experience of the activities of the United Nations and other international political organisations. He has written a book on South West Africa, one of the few current works on that country which exists in America today, another book on the legal and penal systems of the Commonwealth, one on world pressure on Southern Africa, and is completing a mammoth 1,000 page Political History of Africa.

As Dr Rhoodie rightly points out, tremendous changes are taking place in Southern Africa of which Americans have hardly heard. Precisely because the United Nations consider this area "a threat to world peace", we need to know infinitely more of this region.

For the first time independent Black states are rubbing shoulders with the White controlled Republic of South Africa, the home of 90 per cent of all White people in Africa. Instead of ideological sparks, a remarkable degree of co-operation is being evolved. The Black states of Botswana, Swaziland and Lesotho are linked to South Africa in a customs union; a trade pact between Malawi, Tanzania's neighbour, and South Africa has also been signed. Hydro-electric projects which will link several countries are under way. What is in

fact taking place in Southern Africa is the birth of a strong regionalism in which racial affairs are apparently taking a back seat. This is
an area twice the size of the whole of Western Europe with a population of over 40,000,000. It will have far reaching repercussions on
the entire political and economic future of Africa. There is a strong
movement under foot for the establishment of a Southern African
Common Market. The Black states in this area are eager to join in
this venture with South Africa and Rhodesia. Trade, scientific and
government delegations have begun visiting the land of apartheid
and have been warmly welcomed and publicly entertained. At the
Organisation of African Unity, the Black states of the South refused
to go along with talks of military action or boycotts against South
Africa, Rhodesia and the Portuguese provinces of Angola and
Mocambique.

All this has prompted journalists to take up the pen and in
magazines such as *The Reporter* and *Harpers,* and in newspapers such
as *The Observer* in London, the *Christian Science Monitor, The National
Observer* and others, lengthy reports have appeared referring to the
new sweet winds of change blowing from Southern Africa.

What is important about this book is that the author has set out to
inform us of the tremendous diversity of Southern Africa, both in
terms of the human population and the economics and geography,
and to explain how much this area resembles Europe in its early
stages of development, rather than other areas of Africa. The history
of the people, their cultural differences, the political and racial
problems in South Africa and Rhodesia, plus the southern continent's
struggle for understanding in a hostile world is all brought to light.
It is by far the most comprehensive work on Southern Africa and
probably the best researched book yet to appear in this country
dealing with past and future trends in Southern Africa. Much of it
concerns South Africa, a country which we have censured on many
occasions for its racial policies without really having a proper
appreciation of the underlying philosophy and objectives of that
policy, which is not really opposite to ours but different. Perhaps the
two greatest mistakes we make in regard to Southern Africa is to
regard the native Bantu as if they were Negroes from Pittsburgh or
Atlanta and the white people as if they were 20th century colonists.
The Negro and the Bantu have little in common except the colour
of their skin and even that is different. The Bantu's tribal languages

3

and customs make him much more like the American Indian of the early nineteenth century. The White people, on the other hand, are as much an African nation as we are an American nation.

The fact that Dr Stefan Possony has written a special chapter for this book is indicative of the importance of the subject of Southern Africa to us and the high regard in which Dr Rhoodie is held. Dr Possony has served as a special adviser to the French Air Ministry, and as psychological warfare officer for U.S. Naval Intelligence. From 1946-1961 he lectured in the graduate school of Georgetown University, during which time he was a special adviser to the Pentagon. He is visiting professor of the Foreign Policy Research Institute of the University of Pennsylvania, and since 1961 has been Director of International Studies of the Hoover Institute on War, Revolution, and Peace, at Stanford University.

The author of scores of books and articles, the scholarly Dr Possony has lectured widely on Communism, strategy, and international affairs throughout the United States and Europe. He is the Strategy and Military Affairs Editor of the American Security Council, and is a member of the Asian Speakers Bureau. His observations on Dr Rhoodie's thesis are particularly valuable.

DANIEL LYONS, S.J.

1. The Third Africa

It is said that when the late Dag Hammarskjöld visited Cape Town, Africa's southernmost metropolis, he stared at the 17th and 18th century Cape-Dutch architecture, the soaring office buildings, the mass of automobile traffic and the red-tiled roofs of magnificent houses marching up the side of Lion's Head and Table Mountain and exclaimed: "But this is not Africa! This is Europe."

Many visitors to South Africa's mother city have marvelled at the remarkable similarity between Cape Town's Clifton Beach and parts of the French Riviera. Mosterts Mill, situated on De Waal Drive, a dual carriage highway leading to Cape Town's suburbs, reminded them of Holland, while the magnificent Constantia Valley with its vineyards and lovely farmhouses brought into mind the valleys one encounters on the way from Geneva, in Switzerland, to Chamonix, in France. Not far from Cape Town is a valley aptly named Franschhoek (the French Corner) where Huguenot families, fleeing from France, found a new home.

Hammarskjöld's involuntary exclamation was recognition that not since the time of the Romans has a part of Africa been so Europeanised. The Romans eventually returned to Rome, but the White people in the south represented something new in Africa, something permanent.

The famous British statesman, Lord Balfour, observed some fifty years ago that the most remarkable development ever witnessed in Africa was the birth, for the first time, of a truly European nation within this ancient continent. Seven years ago in his famous "Wind of Change" speech, the British Prime Minister, Mr Harold Macmillan, referred to the *Afrikaner* as the first of Africa's nationalists.

Few people know or stop to think that Africa has never been the exclusive preserve of any one race. It may have been the "Dark Continent", a term with the same kind of meaning as "the dark side

5

of the moon", but it never was the "Black Continent", an image that has arisen abroad or that has been purposely developed at the United Nations by the militant Black African states as part of their campaign to eliminate every vestige of European presence in Africa.

The "Dark Continent" has, over the millennia of recorded history, been the home of Carthaginians, Egyptians, Greeks, Israelites, Hamites, Berbers, Negroids, Europeans, Arabs . . . and, if one wishes to speak of colours, it has been the home of Black, White, Brown and Yellow; these are *Africans*, all of them.

The White African, whose ancestors came from Europe centuries ago, only a few years after the first European pioneers arrived in America, is no less a child of Africa than is the Black man of Ghana or the Moslem in Algeria. There is no single African race . . . just as there is no Asian race, or Australian race or American race. Even among the copper skinned Bantu of East and Southern Africa there are differences as great as between the New Yorker and the Parisian. Between the Bantu and the tall West African Negro there are sufficient differences to serve as the basis for several anthropological or ethnological studies.

Until the founding of the United Nations in 1945, when the Afro-Asian states began their vendetta against the White controlled Republic of South Africa, people abroad had shown scant interest in the political affairs of the southern mass of Africa, i.e. Africa south of the Congo. Through their study of the history of the ancient world they had come to know intimately the *First Africa* which embraced Egypt, Libya, Tunisia and other Arab states and territories of the Mediterranean littoral. Through the slave trade and the 19th century "Scramble for Africa" by the British, French, German and Belgian empire builders, the *Second Africa* became more or less known to them and to the world, as Central or Black Africa. Not until the discovery of the world's biggest gold-fields, diamonds, a host of other valuable minerals and, later uranium, did the Western world show more than a passing interest in the socio-economic development of the *Third Africa*, the southern mass of the continent. Then in a matter of two generations the Republic of South Africa became one of the top markets for British and American exporters and the recipient of fifty per cent of all private American investments in Africa.

6

For the past decade the world had its eyes drawn involuntarily to the vociferous and, often, juvenile attempts, by the newly created African states to capture the international limelight and as many free handouts from both East and West. In all that time it either never really tried, or failed, to "discover" the *Third Africa*. Those who succeeded soon observed that while the states of Black Africa and North Africa were clamouring at the United Nations or the Organisation of African Unity[1] for the sword to fall on the White controlled countries of the *Third Africa* (Angola, South West Africa, Mocambique, Rhodesia, South Africa) their own people were being overtaken by the lot of Black dictatorships and economic ruin – such as in Ghana. In addition coups, military take-overs and civil war left a streak of deep tragedy because of the appalling loss of life. In less than twelve months seven governments fell to a military *coup d'etat* with the loss of thousands of lives. Frontier wars and skirmishes took place between several states in Arab Africa and Black Africa, again with considerable loss of life. In Rwanda and Burundi tens of thousands of the Watusi inhabitants were slaughtered by their former slaves, the Hutu – an example of what a Black "majority" can do to a Black "minority".

In 1966-1967 came the bitterest blows of all to those people in the West who had believed that once Black Africa had shaken off her colonial shackles the road forward to a better life would be cleared of all political obstacles. Sierra Leone held Black Africa's first free general election but in less than three weeks after the elections, three governments fell to a military take-over. Kwame Nkrumah of Ghana, the one man who personified the newly independent African states, was himself deposed in a military coup, while in Nigeria, the giant African state on which most of the West had pinned its hopes, disintegration set in when the Eastern region seceded and proclaimed an independent Republic of Biafra.

In the meanwhile, and in sharp contrast, domestic tranquillity, regional stability, remarkable economic co-operation and purposeful diplomatic effort in the south were contributing to a process whereby the various countries were slowly and peacefully being drawn in closer embrace. Given time and without outside interference a powerful alliance between these states may become possible, if not

1. Representing thirty-eight African States in North and Black Africa.

between all, then between the majority. Their combined influence, economically or politically, will be such as to command the attention of the world, particularly since the participant states will be Black *and* White.

At this stage economic, scientific and technical co-operation between some is not far short of that enjoyed by the countries of the European Common Market and in some respects is even more advanced.

The *Third Africa*, at the moment, can be said to consist of the Republic of South Africa, the sovereign Black states of Lesotho (Basutoland) and Botswana (Bechuanaland), the self-governing British protectorate of Swaziland, South West Africa, Angola, Rhodesia, Mocambique and may, *ultimately* also include Zambia and certainly Malawi.

It may well be that what people of these states are witnessing, is the germination of a regional structure which may one day bear out Dag Hammarskjöld's exclamation . . . the Europe of Africa.

Although informed people are conscious of the tremendous obstacles on the long road to such a goal, the very thought that such visions are being openly entertained by statesmen and advocated by economists and political scientists marks a decisive change in the direction of political and economic thought in Southern Africa.

In Chapter 3 (The Years of Change) is set out a mass of evidence which supports the thesis that new sweet winds of change are blowing in the south and that the attempts at closer diplomatic ties and economic co-operation are being made by both Black and White governments. The objective of a Southern African Economic Market is being openly canvassed and has the blessing of several states. Visits to South Africa by government representatives of independent Black states (on Cabinet level) have already taken place and a far reaching trade pact has been signed between Malawi and South Africa.

By their very antagonism towards the southern tier, other Black African states are contributing to the growth of the idea of "alliance" in the *Third Africa*.

This part of the continent is more than two thirds the size of the United States of America and twice as big as Western Europe. Its population, less than forty five million people, view with deep con-

8

cern the despair now blanketing so many of the artificially created Black states of Africa – the bloodshed, political turmoil and the plummeting standards of living. There are also too many educated Bantu in Southern Africa who can read newspapers for the bulk of the Black population, or those in the opinion forming group, to be unaware of what happened in so many of the independent Black states in the north. This justifiable concern is, therefore, *not* only confined to Whites or Asians.

To-day the southern tier enjoys a per capita income much higher than the rest of Africa as well as job security, educational opportunities and social services unparalleled in Africa. This applies as much to the Bantu, Asians and Coloureds as it does to the Whites. Generally speaking they also have more in common with each other, particularly in respect of the structure of government, judicial and educational systems, communications, commerce, etc. than any other group of African, Latin American or Asian states. In addition the political and economic forces generated by the presence of more than six and a half million non-Blacks in this area, the Whites, the Asians and the Coloureds, are rapidly increasing the gap between the "haves" in the *Third Africa* and the "have-nots" in the rest of Africa.

The wealth and vast potential locked up in this part of Africa is such that in a public address the now deposed President of Ghana, Kwame Nkrumah, called on the other African states to "liberate" South Africa in order to "regain *our* wealth and resources in this area for the rapid industrial development of the entire African continent."

It is a fact that the Black states in Africa have come to look upon the "liberation" of South Africa as the panacea to almost all of Africa's ills.

The south of Africa became known to the people in Europe five hundred years ago. As the Renaissance flowered on the western peninsula of the Eurasian landmass, the explorers of Europe, first the Portuguese, and then the others, set sail. In South Africa European men and women, the Dutch, French, English and Germans founded a nation which to-day is an established European society with all the attributes of a modern industrialised community; indeed, according to the United Nations it is one of only twenty-six developed states among the one hundred and fifty countries and territories of the world – and the *only* one in Africa.

In Angola and Moçambique, in South West Africa and Rhodesia as well as in the former British Protectorates of Bechuanaland, Basutoland and Swaziland, the Portuguese, Germans and British did not similarly sire a new nation but introduced western civilization to a society of warring, primitive Bantu tribes. Up to that stage these tribes had not generally progressed beyond the iron age and were completely illiterate. The wheel, the alphabet, paper, even the rudiments of sailing were unknown to them until the arrival of the Europeans. Not a single garden with planted flowers or shrubs graced the African veld. Not a single Christian prayed to the Almighty. The Almighty was the tribal Chief or the spirits of his forefathers.

The Europeans soon imprinted upon the entire southern landmass a pattern of life commonly referred to as Western, or Christian, civilization. This included the rule of law, freedom of religion, free enterprise, state aided education, modern communications, a monetary system, postal and telephone services, health services and a limit to the absolute powers of the Chiefs. The subsequent constitutional history of the various states also closely resembled the pattern which gave birth to the nations of Europe.

During the early 1950's and up to the present, the increasing interest which most foreigners abroad began to show in Southern Africa had fed almost exclusively on one source – race relations. For Britain the interest was fanned by her policy of one-man-one-vote in the many colonies she had decided to "free". The sudden influx of Black people from these ex-colonies to Britain brought the matter of Black-White relations closer to home.

Caught up in a maelstrom of racial disturbances the United States was also a ready market for news of racial conflict, but particularly conflict in other areas which they knew were also inhabited by Whites and Blacks, but of which they knew very little else. Even to-day one rarely finds someone other than a government official, teacher or industrialist who has more than the barest knowledge of the geography, sociology and socio-political forces which have laid the basis for, and are now active in transfiguring the structure of this part of Africa. *Angola* and *Moçambique* only became newsworthy after attempts to foster rebellion in those areas – and

10

even then few people were told that the insurgents directed their little war against the Portuguese across international boundaries, a gross violation of the Charter of the United Nations. *Rhodesia* burst into the news after a Declaration of Independence not because it was similar to the struggle of the American colonies to free itself from British rule but because of the seeds of *conflict* with Black Africa and Britain which the declaration carried.

Apart from newspaper comment of what may possibly happen, the general public in Britain, Europe or America know or care little about these territories. The few per cent who do care or who have made it their business to be well informed are government officials, political activists, professors at universities, industrialists, travel agents, businessmen, Communists and agitators – all for different reasons of course. The view of a country such as South Africa as entertained by the businessman and the politician is more often than not as wide apart as the poles. The impressions of political scientists are equally divergent.

The only people who sense a rebellion behind every kraal are the newspapermen, particularly the two-day visitor and the ones who do not even bother to leave New York or London.

The general uniformity of press reports on developments and events in the *Third Africa* would normally have been of little concern if the lives of people and the very destiny of nations were not thereby involved. Sensational reports in the press have often served as the only basis for an impassioned plea to the General Assembly of the United Nations. An egalitarian solution for Southern Africa is being strenuously advocated by uninformed editorial writers and parroted by the leaders of newly independent states. They seem totally unaware of the fact that the problems arising from multi-racialism and multi-nationalism, such as exists in the Third Africa, could also be resolved through some other if less simple method or approach.

While there are always at least two sides to any problem, on the subject of race relations there is generally believed to be only one valid criterion, namely, that numbers, irrespective of the differences which do exist between people, is the dominant factor in Southern Africa. The liberal-egalitarian philosophy of powerful political figures and newspapers dictate that five thousand Bushmen in the wilds of the Kalahari Desert equals five thousand students at New

York university; the wishes of the majority must be backed under all circumstances, irrespective of their capabilities to distinguish between political right and wrong and irrespective of their lack of the most fundamental requirement for the franchise – literacy. This is what is known as "the new humanism".

"Majority rule" has replaced "merit and only merit". No exceptions are to be tolerated even where the uncivilized and illiterate masses outnumber the civilized community – such as in Rhodesia.

This credo has been adopted and is being nursed despite the loss of freedom and human lives which occurred when independence coupled with majority rule was conferred upon people in Africa barely emerged from the iron age. Apparently the aforementioned politicians and editors are oblivious of the fact that between the mass of people in London and, for example, the villagers in Lesotho there exists a gap in social organisation of some 2,000 years. Alternatively they can only be clinging to this philosophy because they fear losing face if they admit their gross miscalculation of the factors which govern the growth of multi-racial and multi-cultural communities in Africa.

This miscalculation is largely due to the fact that theories and principles which are valid and practical in an advanced civilization such as the United States cannot be transferred to a continent where most countries are, for all practical purposes, less advanced than Britain was during Roman occupation.

Whatever the case, the objectives and policies of those responsible for acts of state in Southern Africa are ignored quite often because they simply do not conform to "majority" opinion. The mere fact that the *two hundred and twenty thousand White Rhodesians* controlled the government while the *four million Black* people had a lesser say was sufficient reason for Rhodesia to be wholeheartedly condemned by the majority of newspapers in the United States. All *other* considerations, which many Black Africans in Rhodesia support, were considered irrelevant.

The socio-historical and political basis for the policies of the governments in Rhodesia, South Africa, Angola, etc., have never been adequately presented, thoughtfully discussed or objectively and dispassionately analysed – no matter how idealistic, logical or economically sound these may be to their supporters. For example: up to the end of 1966 it was impossible to obtain a single hard cover volume in the United States which the White South Africans believed gave a reasonably fair account of their philosophy and objectives. In Britain, France and West Germany, Holland and Belgium the position was for all practical purposes hardly any better. Since 1964 perhaps half a dozen such books were published in all the aforementioned countries.

It is indeed ironical that a people who were good enough, clever enough, sufficiently idealistic and humanitarian to spill their blood in World Wars I and II and in Korea for the sake of civilization and Christianity, should now find that they are not clever enough or good enough to rule their own country or to defend that same western civilization and Christianity in Africa. Although the same policies were being implemented when South African pilots were being shot down in American aircraft over Korea, the government of the United States now refuses to sell arms to South Africa. The *rationale* is that the African states are threatening war against South Africa because of its domestic race policy and since South Africa is prepared to defend to the death its sovereignty, South Africa (not the African states) represents a threat to peace. In addition, so the American Government argues, these weapons could be used by South Africa to enforce apartheid – separate development. How ground-to-air-missiles and submarines can be used for this purpose is beyond mere human comprehension.

It has been said that the "international community" or "world opinion" was not interested in Rhodesia, Portugal or South Africa's point of view because it ran contrary to "world opinion" on the subject. Apart from the fact that Britain, the United States, Canada and other states do not recognise such a thing as "world opinion" when their own vital interests are at stake, those in power in Southern Africa have long grown cynical of the moral basis on which the views of the "international community" rests. While continually being advised, instructed and even threatened to toe the line in the name of "human dignity" and "the rights of man", they see their own dignity downtrodden at the United Nations and their own rights, such as the right to be heard, ignored and abused.

Being responsible for acts of state in Southern Africa the governments in question are convinced that they are acting in the only realistic manner. But their efforts and their ideas, whether it be gradual integration of the races in Angola or gradual political separation of the various communities in South Africa, have met with abuse in Black Africa and the United Nations, with scorn in Asia, or have been blandly discounted by politicians in the West.

Surely, if the threats uttered by two-thirds of the states at the United Nations fail to shift an opinion, held by no matter how few, or fail even to modify the views of the governments of the southern tier of Africa, that point of view, so firmly held, is worth examination?

To argue that those in power in Southern Africa have no valid point of view and are blind to the gravity of their problems, indeed blind to any real solution, is to take the easy way out. Even a very superficial analysis of the situation, particularly compared with the economic retrogression and bloodletting elsewhere in Africa, Asia, and Latin America, reveal that over the past fifty years those in power in Southern Africa have established conditions which have improved living standards faster and provided more opportunities to all their peoples than almost anywhere else in the world except in the United States, Australia, parts of Western Europe and Canada.

It is, therefore, logical to investigate whether the key to a proper appreciation of developments in Southern Africa does not lie in a more dispassionate examination of conditions, deep-seated beliefs, and socio-economic policies there. Of course, to do so requires a discarding of prejudices particularly those acquired through reading newspapers, and a greater reliance on the views of those who have actually visited these areas. This is not easy, but worth trying. Above all, Southern Africa should be viewed in an African context, not as if Johannesburg or Salisbury were suburbs of New York or London.

The questions which key individuals and organisations, governments and agencies in the West should ask themselves are not only whether they are thoroughly acquainted with the strategic and economic importance of the countries of the Third Africa, but how these compare with other African states; they should satisfy themselves whether they fully appreciate the stability, economic progress and the relatively high standard of living already achieved here, as well as the vast potential of these areas if left unchecked to develop according to their own proven formula.

As applied to their particular situation they, and they alone, are the true judges of what is best for their future development.

If the answers to these questions were in the affirmative, there would have been a proper appreciation of the domestic problems faced by each country and a sympathetic consideration of relevant policies without having to agree with all objectives or methods. However, in view of the pressures applied on government level against those in power in Southern Africa by for example Britain and America and the exceedingly hostile attitude of "neutral" countries such as Ireland, Sweden[2] and others towards an ally of two World Wars and Korea, the conclusion can only be that they have *not* considered the questions objectively or in detail. As the Editors of *Life* recently observed, the United States was wrong in its evaluation of the needs of Black Africa; it would be a tragedy and a disaster for the West if the same error is made in respect of Southern Africa.

It is ironic that a Black man, Mr Robert Gardiner, Executive Secretary of the United Nations Economic Commission for Africa should have put his finger on the spot when he said in Addis Ababa on March 21, 1967: "I returned from Southern Africa a week ago with the conviction that unless the rest of Africa approaches the problems of that part of the world with some knowledge of facts and an understanding of the current situation they may – even with good intentions – confuse issues." Later he also said that "any action towards alienating the people of Southern Africa is likely to affect adversely the vital interests of the whole of Africa." Mr Gardiner's approach is one not shared, for instance, by the Scandinavian countries who were once invited to visit South Africa and see for themselves how *apartheid* works, and again, in March 1967, to visit South West Africa. On both occasions the Scandinavian countries, without waiting for their reply to reach the South African authorities first, called a press conference and rejected the invitations out of hand. Obviously their criticism of policies in Southern Africa is not going to be taken seriously and their motives in doing so will remain suspect.

The purpose of this book is not just to unmask the indifference, cynicism, double standards and self-interest revealed by other countries. That alone will serve a useful purpose, namely to put

2. The Swedish government is so obsessed with apartheid that on March 30, 1967 it gave instructions that its annual contribution to Amnesty International be used only "for helping the victims of apartheid". It is clearly stipulated that the money may *not* be used for political prisoners suffering under Communist rule, such as those across the Baltic in Estonia, Latvia and Lithuania.

overseas attacks upon, for example, Rhodesia and South Africa, in their proper perspective.

If the nature of these attacks are known for what they really are, the people of, for example, Rhodesia and South Africa, will be able to react when and where these attacks *should* be repulsed, instead of wasting energy on criticism voiced by every vote hunting politician abroad or by newspapers whose code of moral conduct is set by their circulation figures.

The nature of these attacks upon Rhodesia and South Africa when stripped of their high sounding but generally false premises, is also such that people in the *Third Africa* would be less inclined to squabble over minor differences and build on those forces which unite them.

It is only after many years living abroad that one discovers how party political differences in, for example, South Africa, are of no concern, whatsoever, to the Afro-Asians. These political differences give no food for thought to their delegates at the United Nations, or even to the delegates of most white Western nations. To all but a handful the problem in Southern Africa revolves around the question of *race*. White opponents and supporters of the Government might as well always bear in mind that in Washington, Accra, Oslo, London and Moscow they are all lumped together as *Whites* and unless they favour majority rule as soon as possible or one-man-one-vote, they represent "an obstacle in the path of human progress".

To understand the nature of the foreign crusade against the white governments of Southern Africa and the barriers raised to prevent objective reports from reaching the masses of the people, will enable the people of the *Third Africa* to convince visitors, businessmen, students, tourists, that Southern Africa is as good a place to live in with an equally rosy future, as most other Western states.

Important as this aspect may be, the real purpose of this book is to introduce the *Third Africa* and all its nations to those people in all walks of life who have the courage and integrity to concede that they are uninformed or *may* be misinformed about many things in Southern Africa.

The objective is to draw attention to the achievements and philosophy of the various communities in Southern Africa; to explore the cultural and historical developments in this multi-national area and to analyse the various political and economic factors which not only made this the most developed area in Africa, but are also contributing to the extraordinarily amiable relations between the various Black and White states. It also examines the forces hampering development in this region such as Communism, Western indifference, the influence of the East-West conflict, Black extremism and the role of the United Nations.

It is hoped that consideration of prospects for the future, particularly in the light of Africa's record of political turmoil and economic decay, will spark a reorientation of thought about *all* three Africas. The political stability and socio-economic success which, for instance, the Republic of South Africa has achieved in the *Third Africa*, in contrast to failures elsewhere in Africa, certainly *demands* such a reappraisal.

The issues at stake in the Portuguese provinces of Angola and Mocambique, in South Africa and South West Africa and in Rhodesia, have time and again been raised in the General Assembly of the United Nations and even in the Security Council as "a threat to world peace". Common sense dictates that the world should be *thoroughly* acquainted with all threats to world peace. The *Third Africa* can be no exception.

The aforementioned objectives apart, there remains one very important matter which deserves attention. It concerns the future relations between the states of Southern Africa, who, as will be shown, are as dependent on each other for regional stability and economic progress as the nations of Western Europe are. In October 1966 two more sovereign independent states joined the cluster of self-governing countries in the south of Africa, namely Lesotho and Botswana. Rhodesia declared itself independent in 1965, Swaziland is earmarked for independence leaving only the international status of South West Africa somewhat undecided.

For the first time, however, independent Black and White states are rubbing shoulders in Africa.

Although this book should not be considered to be a blueprint for a regional "alliance" in the *Third Africa*, it will, hopefully, contribute to a better understanding of the underlying political and economic motives for closer co-operation and illustrate the first steps taken in that direction. (It was most unfortunate that when these steps were first suggested by statesmen in the *Third Africa*, their expressed views were either ignored, played down or, in some cases, deliberately misrepresented.)

South Africa has always been interested in regional stability and economic co-operation between countries of the *Third Africa*. Yet even South Africa was taken by surprise when the late Prime Minister, Dr H. F. Verwoerd in August, 1964, foreshadowed the establishment of a Southern African Common Market.

The proposed Market, he said, would embrace all the countries falling within the Third Africa and possibly the Congo. Elaborating upon the idea his Minister of Planning subsequently pointed out that it would differ from the European Common Market in only one important objective: where the ultimate goal of the European Common Market is also *political unity*, South Africa seeks economic co-operation as a means of assuring stability and maintaining or achieving meaningful *political independence* for all the states in Southern Africa. In January, 1967 South Africa's Minister of Economic Affairs stated in Vienna that South Africa was prepared to enter into a customs agreement with Malawi and Zambia to assist them in their economic development.

If common sense and reason (spelt with capital letters) prevail, Dr Verwoerd's proposal, particularly in the light of various other developments which will be set forth in the next chapters, clearly show the road ahead for Southern Africa in the coming decade.

2. Southern Africa and the West: Liability or Asset

To most informed observers, Dr Verwoerd was no dreamer when he forecast a "Common Market" for Southern Africa. Between (1) South Africa; (2) South West Africa; (3) Lesotho (Basutoland); (4) Swaziland; and (5) Botswana (Bechuanaland), an economic "common market" already exists with an easily converted decimal currency, postal union, shared customs, shared communications, etc. Add to this the 1965 trade pact between South Africa and Rhodesia and the groundwork is complete for a common market for the greater portion of the *Third Africa*.

It is natural that the Republic of South Africa should form the hub of this development. Her economic strength in Southern Africa can be measured by the fact that her Gross Domestic Product is 80 per cent of the total of the *Third Africa*,[1] while South Africa's share of the total inter-regional trade is more than 76 per cent.[2]

South Africa is the only nation in Africa which the United Nations considers as a "developed" country; in fact, South Africa is one of only twenty-six such industrially developed countries in the entire world. With only six per cent of Africa's population, she generates nearly thirty per cent of the continent's total geographical income. Her mineral production is forty-three per cent of that of the whole of Africa and she generates and produces twice as much electricity and six times as much steel as the rest of Africa *combined*. Nearly fifty per cent of all Africa's vehicles, telephones and radios are in South Africa. Thus by every yardstick she is undoubtedly the industrial giant of Africa.[3] Add to this the fact that Rhodesia,

1. "Economic Co-operation in Southern Africa", by J. A. Lombard, *Tegnikon*, S.A. Academy of Arts and Science, March 1967, p. 19.
2. South Africa Foundation, *Tempo*, April 1967.
3. Cf. "The only industrial complex south of Milan", *Fortune*, December, 1966, p. 180.

19

Lesotho, Botswana, Swaziland, South West Africa and even Malawi and Zambia are *dependent* in various degrees upon South Africa's risk capital, trade and investments and the proposal which Dr Verwoerd held out to these states and territories assumes a tantalizing and realistic character.

Dr Verwoerd's staunchest critics at the time conceded that there was much to be said for this idea. Some of the newspapers which opposed his racial policies even declared that when he responded to the Congo government's request for aid, back in 1963-64, this idea was already at the back of his mind.

Such a development would even now, after his death, be a natural outflow of what was building up before the Black African revolution took place, sweeping with it every vestige of common sense and political foresight. That revolution so befuddled the thinking of Black leaders that they have made their own people suffer in their crusade against South Africa – without harming the object of their wrath in the slightest. In Kenya for example, the government in 1963 forbade the export of soda-ash to South Africa as part of its trade boycott. As a result South Africa developed its own deposits providing work for several hundred Bantu and saving more than R1,500,000 ($2,000,000) in foreign currency, while the Kenyan factory almost had to close down at the sudden loss of her principal export market. Two thousand Black workers in Kenya were laid off – all for the sake of a few favourable headlines in the African and Communist press. It was only three years later that Kenya found a substitute market – Russia.

Fortunately common sense has prevailed so far in the states of the *Third Africa*. Zambia, Malawi, Botswana and the others would no doubt, for the moment, prefer to show solidarity with the boycotters, but they have been realistic enough to know that they stand only to gain by co-operating with South Africa.

South Africa's contribution to the development of other countries on the continent in the past has not been insignificant. South Africa has already furnished proof of its willingness and ability to co-operate by actively participating in various organizations for scientific and technical co-ordination in Africa. South African engineers have given freely of their skill and of their knowledge in the establishment of mining and engineering schemes, low cost housing projects and road and rail construction in other African territories. The fruits of South African research in the fields of veterinary and medical science are readily available to those in need and have indeed found their way into many African and Asian states. Serums and other medicines, particularly adapted to African conditions have on many occasions been and are in fact still being supplied. The World Health Organization looks to South Africa to provide many services for African territories and has established reference centres at South African universities. Fruits of projects conducted by the South African Council for Scientific and Industrial Research can be found in many African countries.[4]

In an editorial, the anti-apartheid, anti-Government *Cape Argus* said that it was not fanciful at all to compare Southern Africa to-day with Europe after World War II, when the threat of Communist aggression and subversion and the need to use rapid technical advances for the improvement of living standards brought the North Atlantic Treaty Organization and the Organization for European Economic Co-operation into being.

The Southern tier of Africa is already beginning to remould itself, the extent thereof and the supra-national form it may ultimately assume, will be analysed later[5]. Through their new approach and efforts to weld this part of Africa into an effective economic unit, the statesmen of this area are undoubtedly contributing to the kind of regional stability which Africa so desperately requires. Given time, it may become an insurmountable political and economic obstacle to Sino-Soviet imperialism in Africa.

The face of this new power is one of infinite variety. Geophysically it is the most blessed area in all of Africa. The extent and variety of its mineral deposits can only be described in superlatives.

The face of the *Third Africa* is also one of constant change as huge hydro-electric projects begin to make the desert bloom. Magnificent highways and railroads are beginning to spread in all directions. The world's longest stretch of electrified railway line (outside North America and Russia) is not to be found in Europe or elsewhere, but in South Africa. Here are also the world's biggest mines, some of the biggest manufacturing concerns outside the United States of America, the biggest dynamite factories, one of the

4. Cf. "South Africa Helps Emerging Black States", *Bantu*, Pretoria, April 1967, pp. 1-6.
5. [5]See Chapters 7, 8, 9.

most extensive railway systems and a communications system of telephones, teletype and an F.M. radio network overshadowed only by the United States, Canada, Britain and a few of the European powers.

Here one finds an infinite variety of cultures, the dominating ones which are clearly aligned with western and Christian civilization and almost uniformly anti-Communist. The personality cults and dictatorships of Black Africa or Berber-Arab socialism are alien to this region.

This huge territory twice the size of Europe is buttressed by stabilising and unifying factors of a kind which, properly developed, may withstand these crucial years of shifting alignments – even though some of these states are White, some Black and some of mixed population.

Because of their explosive nature and negative influence on the growth of regional co-operation in Southern Africa three factors should be continually kept in mind, namely, the widespread misunderstanding and unfavourable press coverage of developments in South Africa and Rhodesia; the foreign crusade to "liberate" the people of South Africa, Rhodesia, the Portuguese provinces and South West Africa from what is termed their "oppressive White settler governments" and, thirdly, the Communist threat to Africa.

Upon a correct and proper evaluation of all three, rests the future of the *Third Africa*; whether it will be permitted to live up to its tremendously impressive potential or sink into a morass of racial antagonism, tribal warfare and economic ruin.

To misjudge the three, to consider the views of people in Southern Africa on these subjects as either insincere or without reason, is to jeopardise the future of perhaps all of Africa.

Much of this book, particularly in respect of the issues mentioned above, evolves around South Africa. If at times the impression is obtained that the rest of the *Third Africa* is skimped, it is only because the situation in South Africa serves as such an excellent example of popular misconception and because the political and economic future of the *Third Africa*, as will be made abundantly clear in Chapter 9, does indeed ride with South Africa. It is not a question of belittling the status, achievements and future of the other states. South Africans have only admiration for the way in which the Portuguese, Rhodesians and the people, Black and White, in South

West Africa, Malawi, Lesotho, Swaziland, the Transkei and elsewhere are striving to improve their lot with a minimum of foreign
assistance. (The rest of Africa would do well to study their achievements in the absence of worthwhile foreign aid.) But just as the
disintegration of the United States or its non-existence would have
relegated North America to an impotent political and economic
region, so there can be no meaningful future for all of Southern
Africa without a stable, prosperous Republic of South Africa. On
that liberals, conservatives, idealists and, of course, the Communists
are all agreed.

It is generally accepted that the setback to Communism in the
overthrow of Ghana's President Nkrumah marks a continuing loss
of influence throughout Africa. What is important however is to
realise that the Communist record in Africa, both Russian and
Chinese, has been quite remarkable. They realise that setbacks are
inevitable but not irretrievable. It took the Communists twenty
years to conquer China and with mineral resources elsewhere in the
world being slowly but surely exhausted, it seems unlikely that they
are going to be put off by temporary setbacks in their efforts to
capture mineral rich Africa. At the time of writing there is still real
danger of a Communist take-over in four key African states: Guinea,
Burundi, The Congo (Brazzaville) and Tanzania.

Addressing the American Negro Leadership Conference in
Washington late in 1965 American Secretary of State Dean Rusk said
that the Russians and Chinese have funnelled some R700,000,000
in aid to new African nations since 1960 and have assigned 5,000
technical advisers in an effort to woo Africa's emergent states. In
addition some 6-8,000 African students are in Communist countries
while Communist Diplomatic and Consular Missions number some
150 in Africa. With an investment of this nature, he said, the Russians
and Red Chinese have no intention of abandoning Africa. "The
Communists remain a threat to African freedom", he said.

For those involved in the struggle against Communism in Africa
or who would like to believe that the Communist setbacks are of a
permanent nature it is therefore as necessary to appreciate Communism's remarkable record in Africa as it would be for the surgeon
in the operating theatre to understand the case history of a patient
suffering from cancer.

Great play has, for example, been made of the *new* peaceful attitude of the Soviets, but just their record after the Cuban episode is enough to rule out any moderation of Communist objectives. In November 1963 the Soviets inflamed the highly dangerous situation in North Africa by sending arms and equipment to Ben Bella and openly inciting the Algerians against the Moroccans. In the same month the Russians were expelled from the Congo for plotting to overthrow the Government; in South Africa the Rivonia and Fischer episodes are still vividly in memory. In November 1964 the official Russian mouthpiece *Izvestia* wrote in an editorial: "The condition of peaceful co-existence will assure the success of the struggle for liberation and the carrying out of the revolutionary task of the peoples." A similar editorial appeared in *Pravda* on September 18, 1964.

Undoubtedly there is a tremendous split between the Soviets and their counterparts in Red China, but does this really mean that people in Southern Africa, in all of Africa, can sit back and consider the Communist threat to Africa a thing of the past? This would be a mistake of the worst kind and people who suggest this should read the minutes of the so-called tri-Continent Conference held in Havana, Cuba, during January 1966. At this time the Soviet Chinese split was already a fact and the Russians and Chinese had already suffered their worst setbacks in Africa. Yet the chief result of the conference was to foster the Chinese thesis of Communist seizure of power, by any means, of the remaining pro-Western countries in Latin America, Asia and Africa.

The recommendations and statements coming out of this conference represent a veritable blueprint of Communist designs and aims throughout the world in the 1960's and 1970's.

The Soviet Union was represented at the Conference by a 44 man delegation and they voted to a man for Chinese style "wars of liberation" of the kind now being fought in Vietnam and attempted in Angola and Mocambique. The basic theme of the conference, a theme hammered upon by Russian and Chinese spokesmen, was a strident call for war on all fronts against the free world.

Another alarming aspect of the conference stems from the scope of participation. There were delegations from eighty-two nations, including thirty from Africa. These delegations also supported the proposals for an intensified campaign of subversion and political warfare against democratic regimes in the free world. The representatives of Egypt, Tanzania, Guinea, Ghana and so-called Black nationalist movements in Rhodesia, Mocambique, Angola, South West Africa, Lesotho, Botswana and Zambia (all represented individually at the conference) and others were unanimous in their support of the aggressive Communist designs.

The conference went much further than any similar meeting in recent years in spelling out the aggressive designs of international Communism.

The Communists' interest in economic sanctions against Rhodesia and Angola or South Africa is therefore at once obvious. As Dr Stephen Enke of the American Institute of Defence Analysis pointed out in an article in *Optima* in 1962, economic sanctions, to be effective, would have to be supplemented in time with an armed blockade. "But armed blockade, involving into war in other ways, could bring widespread war to the most economically developed and most staunchly anti-Communist nation in Africa." From such an adventure, Dr Enke pointed out, the anti-Communist countries which need a stable government in this strategic part of the world would ultimately emerge as the losers.

The scope of the Communists' grand design for Africa (particularly that of Red China) is as enormous as it is little comprehended. Peking's ambitions are not confined to the Congo or Zanzibar; they range from Lesotho (less than 200 miles from the massive South African gold-field) to the gates of Europe. American, British, French, Dutch and German observers have all pointed this out; many have written about it at length. If their observations are poorly noticed or not given prominence, it is largely due to the current fad of labelling anyone pointing to these dangers as either a "scaremonger" or "hard" on Communism and, therefore, an extremist of the wrong kind.

But Europeans, perhaps more than Americans, are at last beginning to sense the colossal danger of Soviet and Chinese inroads in Africa and are seeking ways of countering it. Major Stephen Foot of the British Army, writing in NATO's *Fifteen Nations*, has warned: "Today Africa is in the position that China occupied in 1926 except that few experts think the process of take-over will take twenty years."

Astute observers are beginning to look for a place where the line will inevitably have to be drawn.

Africa is Europe's hinterland and European (if not all Western) industries require the raw materials for the years ahead which only the markets of Africa can provide. One such crucial material is uranium, of which South Africa is the world's second biggest producer.

The 1964 Geneva Conference on the peaceful uses of atomic energy was told that the world's known uranium reserves are estimated at about 500,000 tons of which South Africa's known reserves constitute more than a quarter. World requirements up to the end of this century will be between 700–800,000 tons, and every ton of uranium reserves in South Africa must sooner or later become invaluable unless substantial resources are discovered elsewhere.

If Communist China or the Soviets were to become the dominant influence on the African continent it would be a disaster for Europe, as crippling a blow as the Moslem conquests of the seventh century that paralyzed Europe for several hundred years. For the new African nations themselves, Chinese or Russian supremacy on the continent would be a thralldom of an especially tragic nature and ruthless character.

In adding up the balance sheet on the importance of the countries grouped at the southern reach of Africa, the European statesman will be struck less by the fact that this area comprises almost thirty per cent of the African land (2,352,000 square miles), or by its forty five million population, than by its fantastic mineral wealth.

The *Third Africa* is not only strategically located but also contains resources of strategic minerals which must inevitably play a vital role in the Free World's efforts to maintain itself against the Sino-Soviet front.

Here is where 75 per cent of the gold of the Free World is mined; gold without which the monetary systems of every major power would be thrown into chaos, gold required for increasing international trade and liquidity.

South West Africa, Angola and South Africa are the principal diamond producing areas in the free world. Diamonds, apart from being decorative and valuable, are also essential for industry. They are used extensively for drilling everything from teeth to oil wells. Sales of industrial diamonds have boomed during the past two decades because of the increasing use of alloys and refractory materials which only diamonds are hard enough to cut. In 1939 five million carats of industrial diamonds were sold; in 1964 the total exceeded thirty million carats. A deficiency of diamonds today would cause the slowdown of the modern metal working industry in the West and would devastate mass production. The first countries to suffer from a loss of the diamond supplies from South Africa's Central Selling Organization would be the United States, Britain, France and West Germany.

When President Lyndon Johnson in 1964 announced a new, supersonic 2,000 m.p.h. interceptor aircraft for the United States Air Force, it was stated that the skin of the aircraft was made of titanium alloy. South Africa has the world's largest titanium-magnetite deposits.

The free world's principal source of germanium, the most vital element in the manufacture of transistors, is a mine in South West Africa. The importance of transistors in to-day's defence equipment and industries need hardly be elaborated upon.

The territories in the *Third Africa* contain reserves of many other minerals. South Africa alone – apart from her huge gold, diamond and uranium supplies – ranks among the world's leading producers of platinum, coal, iron-ore, chromite, manganese and asbestos.

But it is in military terms that the area, particularly South Africa, assumes even greater significance.

As space vehicles become more and more sophisticated (particularly those of Russia), the military significance of these space craft increases. When the head of the Jet Propulsion Laboratory of N.A.S.A. visited South Africa in 1964, he was careful to point out South Africa's significant contribution to the American space research programme. From America's point of view, he observed, the tracking station at Hartebeeshoek (one of two entirely manned by South African scientists) is a very important one since it is the first station to receive reliable information about the actual trajectory of many American space vehicles. What he did not mention was the fact that the American I.C.B.M.s fired down the Atlantic Range are aimed just off the southern tip of South Africa.[6] Without this base to operate from, a check on the accuracy of the missiles would have been seriously hampered.

6. Observers from Cape Town on one occasion actually witnessed the re-entry of a nose cone into the atmosphere. American aircraft and ships were stationed in and near Cape Town at the time.

The ports of Cape Town, Port Elizabeth and Durban in South Africa and Lourenco Marques in Mocambique are of direct military importance to the West. The United States, which looks to the establishment of an Indian Ocean fleet, needs South Africa's naval facilities in the event of *emergency*. At Simonstown the drydock is capable of handling heavy guided missile cruisers while Cape Town's Duncan Dock is the only one in Africa capable of servicing aircraft carriers of the United States. It is the only drydock in Africa capable of making repairs on the super oil tankers of up to 90,000 tons. Deepening part of the harbour would make it suitable for the 100,000 ton plus vessels.

In war time, ships would need protection against enemy submarines operating in the Atlantic and Indian oceans. South African naval facilities include fuel, ammunition and anchor facilities adequate for a large naval force in time of war. The naval menace in waters surrounding the African coast is increasing rapidly. During 1964 no less than thirty four submarine sightings off the coast of South Africa were logged officially. In this respect one need only cite the readiness of Russia to supply African nations, of which Egypt is an example, with submarines and crews making it possible for even small and technically backward countries, leaning towards Russia, to possess dangerous naval forces. There are many places on the African coast suitable for use as Communist naval bases. Zanzibar is a prime example but naval experts declare that even the port at the mouth of the River Congo is quite suitable.

The Middle East War of 1967, the threat to Suez and President Nasser's subsequent closure of the canal has underscored, as nothing else possibly could, the vital strategic importance of the Cape of Good Hope sea route around the southern tip of Africa to all engaged in world trade or concerned with the world's security. From the Naval offices in Washington to board rooms in London where shipping tycoons plan their future fleets, this is likely to be remembered long after the last shot was fired in Sinai.

At the time of writing the Cape route has become Europe's lifeline to the East as it was in 1956 when the Suez canal was also closed. The total ships diverted from the Suez around the Cape from August 1956 to June 1957 totalled over 2,650 of which 1,556 called at Cape Town and the rest at Durban, Port Elizabeth and

East London.[7] As a result of the closure of the canal, Europe is facing an immediate petroleum shortage of critical proportions and it is estimated that to meet the shortfall in normal supplies an additional 1,440 tankers or 22 per cent of the total free world's tanker fleet is required. In the past ten years with the conversion from coal to oil European oil consumption has trebled to the point that oil now supplies about 50 per cent of Europe's energy requirements. Within one month after the closure of the Suez Canal in May 1967 oil deliveries were down 30 per cent.[8]

There is a considerable body of Western opinion, notably in Scandinavia and America (and of course in the Afro-Asian world) which would like to see a non-aligned one-man-one-vote Black African state in South Africa rather than the present White government. But had there been a neutralist government in power with the economic woes and inefficiency which seem to go hand in hand with neutrality, instead of a strong pro-Western, highly industrialized country with modern shipping facilities and the know-how for servicing, refuelling and handling of the mass of ships which converged on South African ports in 1956 and now again in 1967, the resultant dilemma would have had incalculable consequences in the West not far short of an insurmountable crisis.

Even without the present crisis in the Middle East the importance of the Cape route was bound to increase because of the trend towards mammoth tankers and bulk carriers too big to negotiate the Suez Canal. Tankers of 250,000 tons have already been ordered to carry Middle East oil around the Cape of Good Hope to Bantry Bay in Ireland.

Now that the Suez Canal has been forcibly closed, twice in ten years (and there is the threat of permanent Arab resentment against the United States, Britain and the West in general) it might only be a matter of time before the major trading nations and the oil companies decide to secure their supply lines by building up their fleets of tankers designed for the Cape route.

A 1955 pact between the British and South African governments provided that South Africa would maintain the Simonstown naval base at the foot of the African continent for the unfettered use of

7. *South African Financial Gazette*, June 9, 1967, p. 778.
8. Statement issued by the United States Department of the Interior, June 28, 1967. Cf. *The Star*, Johannesburg, June 29, 1967, p. 1.

British and allied warships during times of war, *irrespective* of whether the Republic is a co-belligerent.[9] Under the terms of the Simonstown agreement, a strategic zone of 5,000,000 square miles of ocean was demarcated and South Africa is responsible for the patrolling of this area. The South African Navy, already the most powerful of the African continent, is in the midst of an expansion that will quadruple its strength in a few years. This includes the purchase of submarines and missile cruisers. At the moment it has modern anti-submarine frigates, supersonic naval strike aircraft, helicopters and long-range aircraft to patrol the coastal waters. A submarine wolf-pack operating unchallenged in Southern African waters could wreak havoc with allied shipping (as it almost did during the last world war). For this reason South Africa has concentrated on anti-submarine warfare; its naval personnel study abroad in England and Europe and naval units have held numerous combined exercises with units of the American, French, British and Portuguese navies.

The British move to acquire two Indian Ocean islands to serve as bases if Aden and Singapore have to be abandoned will increase the significance of South Africa in the Western global strategy, according to military experts.

Britain has acquired the Chagos Archipelago from Mauritius. This includes the coral atoll, Diego Garcia, which was of strategic importance in the Second World War.

The other island which Britain wants to retain is Aldabra, a dependency of the Seychelles.

But both Mauritius and the Seychelles are heading for independence.

Sir Francis de Guingand, Lord Montgomery's chief of staff during the Western Desert campaign, said in November, 1965, that the switch will certainly not lessen South Africa's importance but will probably increase it.

In Sir Francis' view, the new island bases would be "stuck out

9. At the high level talks between Britain and South Africa during January 1967, it was agreed upon that in future South Africa will assume full responsibility for the defence of the entire sea-route around the Cape from a point roughly opposite Lourenço Marques in Mocambique to the Kunene River on the west coast of Africa – a distance of some 2,600 miles. Britain would henceforth retain only a token force at the Naval base of Simonstown.

there" and would need South Africa as a back-stop, particularly in the event of the Suez Canal being closed to the West.

"It is easy to see the Suez Canal being closed under certain conditions, if, for instance, Afro-Asians decide that the Americans and British are taking some line in South East Asia they do not like", he said.

There would then be a repetition of the events at the time of the 1956 Suez Canal crisis and the war in the Middle East of 1967, when South Africa had to handle the traffic which normally used the canal.

Some observers tend to reason that the next war will inevitably be a nuclear war which would be over in a few weeks and which would mean that the Cape sea route is no longer of any importance. By using this argument one can prove that the Suez and Panama Canals are also no longer of any importance. The next war may as well be a land war in Asia, perhaps against Red China, without the use of nuclear weapons. The war in Vietnam despite the overwhelming air superiority of the United States Air Force is still largely a land war requiring the use of hundreds of troop and supply vessels and the Middle East war of 1967 proved this point over and over again.

That Sir Francis was right is evident from the latest information available on the emergency air route to the Far East now being developed jointly by the United States and Britain. This Allied defensive system evolving east of Suez also includes Australia, New Zealand and certain friendly Asian powers. Strategic planners of these countries looking to the 1970's when Red Chinese expansion may have to be contained, are working to build up a network of air staging and communications facilities across the Indian ocean. These are being designed to link their base areas and key relay points together with a series of well-sited and well-defended military stepping stones in the Atlantic, Indian and Pacific oceans. But no one knows better than Britain that in certain conditions their route to the Far East could be barred if Middle East states were to erect an air barrier by cancelling all overflying rights and facilities. (This has happened before and to this day and age British Air Force planes cannot overfly Egyptian and other Arab territories). Accordingly the need to develop secondary and tertiary air routes becomes vital and it is here where South Africa comes into the picture. For an alternative route British planes would have to fly over Africa to the Indian Ocean, for example from Ascension Island, and countries like the two Congos and Tanzania are not thought likely to provide overflying or staging facilities. But South Africa can be relied upon to do so and, in addition, has the know-how and paraphernalia to accommodate the sophisticated installations and electronic communications that would be needed.

A situation packed with irony is therefore shaping up since Britain and America at the moment refuse to sell any arms or other equipment for defence purposes to South Africa.

In the *Third Africa* the West has not only a tremendous reservoir of essential metals and minerals but also a rapidly developing manufacturing centre of world significance. South Africa is already among the first ten steel-producing countries of the world, excluding the Communist bloc. It has a well-developed automobile industry capable of manufacturing tanks, personnel carriers and a host of other ancillary military equipment. An aircraft industry, capable of manufacturing supersonic jets, is rapidly coming into existence. In the *Third Africa* sophisticated manufacturing complexes include petro-chemical, electronic and related industries, quite apart from shipbuilding facilities and manufacture of electric railroad rolling stock. Here are the largest dynamite factories in the world and armaments factories which can turn out rockets, bazookas, modern lightweight rifles, machine guns, high explosive bombs and grenades.

The gross *industrial production* of South Africa alone is currently about 80 per cent of that of the entire African continent. Its per capita consumption of electricity is on a par with that of Western Europe and it boasts one of the world's finest railroad systems with many hundreds of miles of electrified railroad completed and more under construction.

In terms of military potential (production of essential supplies, food, metals) South Africa is one of the most important countries in the West. Together with Australia, it possibly forms the bulwark of Western defences and supplies in the southern hemisphere.

In view of the pending withdrawal of British troops from Swaziland, a situation will arise in Africa where, outside South Africa, Angola and Mocambique, and perhaps Rhodesia, *the West will have no significant military staging areas or naval bases, airfields or troops in the whole of Africa.*

In the rest of the *Third Africa*, Rhodesia has a significant manufacturing potential while in Zambia the world has one of its greatest copper-producing areas. The remaining territories of the *Third Africa* are not of importance in manufacturing but they produce or contain huge reserves of copper, asbestos, silver, tin, cobalt, zinc, manganese, diamonds, and iron ore, all vital to the industries of the Free World.

Rhodesia has the world's largest deposits of metallurgical chrome, is the principal producer of Lithium minerals and the third largest producer of Chrysotile Asbestos.

Although many people live in this area, its contribution to the Allied effort during the two world wars (except that of the Union of South Africa) was rather limited owing to the undeveloped state of the Black majority in the area. South Africa's war effort, however, was considerable. Out of her small White population, then only a million and a quarter, South Africa eventually supplied nearly 150,000 men to the allied forces in World War I. They saw action in East Africa, Egypt and Palestine, Flanders, the Somme, Delville Wood, etc. Twenty-one years after the Peace of Versailles, World War II broke out. This time a White population of two million contributed no fewer than 280,000 soldiers, all volunteers, fighting in East Africa, the Western Desert, Italy (the battles of Casino, Monte Stanco, the valley of the Po) while some 45,000 air force personnel fought in practically every theatre of war. The country produced a fantastic amount of food for the allied nations while the manufacturing industries produced thousands of armoured cars, bombs, etc.

Currently South Africa is in a position to put perhaps 350,000 *trained men* in the field, the most powerful military force in Africa. Egypt can field a much *larger* force but the number of men under arms is not the criterion by which a military force is rated. Training, morale and leadership count for more as the war in the Middle East between Israel and the Arab states proved conclusively.

Apart from its naval forces, South Africa has several squadrons of supersonic French Mirage fighters, Buccaneer jets (low level naval attack aircraft) Canadian Sabre Jets, Vampire jet trainers, Canberra medium range jetbombers, Shackleton long-range aircraft, as well as helicopters, squadrons of Hercules and D.C.3 troop carriers, and sufficient mechanized equipment for the army. Airborne assault

33

troops have been trained and both troops and aircraft are equipped with modern ground-to-air and air-to-air rocket weapons.

Military research at South Africa's huge Council for Scientific and Industrial Research complex outside Pretoria has recently been stepped up with emphasis on guided missiles and rockets. During the last few years budgetary provisions for this research have been raised from some R29,000 ($42,000) to R10,000,000 ($14,000,000) according to a statement by South Africa's Minister of Defence early in 1967.

With available weapons and trained manpower, a complete radar network across the northern borders of South Africa and South West Africa, a sophisticated Decca navigation system to keep a watching brief over coast lines and shipping, South Africa's future is secure and she is enabled to play an important role as an ally of the Free World in any future conflict.

Above all, South Africa and Rhodesia have shown a willingness and an ability to play their parts in the cold war against Communism and in the defence of the Free World.

Few seem aware that when the United Nations called upon member states to oppose the Communist military invasion of Korea, South Africa was one of only fourteen countries (out of more than eighty) to heed this appeal. It is a sign of the morality of the times that, while South Africa sustained many casualties, killed, missing and wounded in defence of the Charter of the United Nations, the countries which then held back (including far more powerful nations) are now attempting to use the same Charter to bring South Africa to her knees because of a dislike of her domestic policies. Again, during the critical period of the Berlin airlift, South Africa contributed her share. During the 1963 Cuban crisis, South Africa was the *only* country in Africa to send a message of unqualified support to President Kennedy. (It is of more than just passing interest that the African National Congress of Nobel Peace Prize winner Albert Luthuli sent a message of support to Fidel Castro.)

There can, therefore, be no doubt as to South Africa's military alignment with the West. Because they form part of Metropolitan Portugal, (a N.A.T.O. member), Mocambique and Angola are automatically counted as pro-Western areas, the same is true of South West Africa which is administered as an integral part of

South Africa. With her record in World Wars I and II, Rhodesia has also proved herself a good ally of the West.

For all practical purposes the entire *Third Africa*, excepting perhaps Malawi and Zambia, can, therefore, be said to form a pro-Western region.

In Europe recognition of the situation set out in the previous pages is beginning to show. In a 1962 editorial, the British magazine *Time and Tide* considered the strategic importance of South Africa and her military alignment with Britain (and the West) and observed that "it would be against the most fundamental interests of Britain and the West" to irritate the Republic of South Africa.

The leading defence journal in West Germany, *Wehrkunde*, recently quite frankly discussed the possibility of a Southern African Treaty Organization (SATO) on the model of the Atlantic Pact.

Such an organization, said the magazine, would embrace most, if not all, territories considered part of the *Third Africa* and would specifically include South Africa, the Portuguese territories and Rhodesia. In line with this proposal, several members of the British Parliament in 1964 called for "a defensive partition" of Africa along the boundary of the Zambezi River which would thus embrace South Africa, Rhodesia and presumably Angola, South West Africa and Mocambique.

With Britain's commitments east of Suez diminishing, security planners face the danger of what they call "a power vacuum" in the Indian Ocean. This is heightening Western naval and military interest in South Africa and particularly in Simonstown. Commenting on this development in July 1966, Hanson Baldwin, the well-known military correspondent of *The New York Times* stressed the importance of including South Africa and Australia in a multi-nation defence scheme for the Indian Ocean.

Finally, of great importance is the fact that here in the *Third Africa* is concentrated 90 per cent of all White persons in Africa.[10]

In Africa to-day, trained White men – scientists, engineers, doctors and above all teachers – are invaluable to any country genuinely interested in bettering the lot of its people and in progress towards a self-sufficient economy. Every year South Africa's eleven

10. 4,000,000 persons (estimated end 1966).

universities and five university-colleges turn out more properly qualified doctors, engineers, draughtsmen and scientists of all races than the rest of Africa combined. It is, however, not only the attitude of the White people in South Africa which is uniformly pro-Western. It is borne out by the whole socio-political structure. South Africa is not only the country with the longest established two-party parliamentary system in Africa, but here is also one of the great capitalistic systems of the world where free enterprise is officially encouraged and protected.

This way of life has obviously made a tremendous impact on the twelve million Black men in South Africa.

The premise advanced by the Afro-Asian states at the United Nations that the Blacks are a bitter, maltreated, explosive element is belied by the simple fact that South Africa has had to invent the most stringent regulations to prevent excessive numbers of Black people from other independent African states from entering the country. In a single recent year, more than 10,000 Africans from the North crossed the border into South Africa – at the risk of imprisonment for unlawful entry. To-day there are close to a million inside White-ruled South Africa, attracted there by opportunities for work, higher wages, education and a better life in a law abiding society.

At the last mass escape of people from East to West Berlin, newspapers of the West called it "an occasion for rejoicing by humane and civilised people everywhere in the non-Communist world". The political significance of Black people walking hundreds and in some cases thousands of miles to go to White-ruled South Africa is equally enormous. Lenin had a phrase for it when he said of the Russian soldiers streaming home in 1917 that they "voted with their feet". Black men and women from a dozen African states (almost one-twelfth of the total Black population of South Africa) have voted with their feet for a country which is pro-Western, Christian and civilized, where the "rule of law" is not an empty slogan but firmly anchored in Roman-Dutch law and diligently applied by an independent judiciary.

Robert Ardrey (author of *African Genesis*) wrote in his *The Territorial Imperative* (1966) that if a White force were to invade South Africa for the purposes of taking over the country, the defence would be eighty per cent. "If the invasion force consisted of Blacks, the defence would be total."

3. The Years of Change

Enough has happened during the recent past to justify the fears of the Black African states and the Arab North that the principal countries of the Third Africa may consolidate their military power and establish such a powerful economic union that their efforts at the United Nations and elsewhere to oust the White governments in South Africa and Rhodesia, to expel the Portuguese from their overseas provinces and to end South Africa's administration of South West Africa, may be doomed to failure. It should also be noted at once that the territories involved here are not governed by one race. The Third Africa embraces not only White South Africa, Portuguese-controlled Angola and Mocambique and White-ruled Rhodesia but also five independent or nearly independent Black states.

The first indication that vast political and economic changes were due in Southern Africa was the 1964 proposal by the South African Prime Minister to the Conservative Government in Britain that South Africa be permitted to put its case of separate development (apartheid) to the then British protectorates of Bechuanaland, Swaziland and Basutoland. The two latter territories are totally surrounded by South Africa while Bechuanaland (now Botswana) is hemmed in by South West Africa on the west and South Africa and Rhodesia on the rest of its frontiers.[1]

South Africa's Prime Minister stated that "we could lead them (the Protectorates) far better and much more quickly to independence and economic prosperity than Great Britain can do". The South African Prime Minister also later added that, "a *greater* Basutoland, Swaziland and Bechuanaland could eventuate since consolidation could take place with the adjoining areas of the same ethnic groups from within the Republic . . . where desirable, the Republic would be prepared to help the Bantu of these Territories

1. Except for some 300 yards where Botswana adjoins Zambia.

37

to regain, by purchase or exchange, areas at present occupied by Whites."

If this plan became a reality, it would mean that Africa south of the Limpopo River, would again be divided roughly fifty per cent between Black and White, the situation which existed prior to the Anglo-Boer War and before Britain, just after the same war, arbitrarily partitioned Southern Africa into the three Protectorates and the Union of South Africa.

Botswana and Lesotho are now independent countries and Swaziland is on the eve of independence. It is also the avowed policy of the South African government to grant to the Black men within its borders (consisting as they do of several distinct Bantu nations of whom the most important are the Zulu, Xhosa, Tswana and Sotho) political independence in those areas of South Africa which are legally and historically theirs. It could well mean therefore, that within a matter of a decade or two there may be a White state (the Republic of South Africa) and a number of Black states; Zululand, Xhosaland (the Transkei) etc., as well as the states of Lesotho, Swaziland and Botswana; all politically independent but economically interdependent, joined in a Consortium or Commonwealth of Southern African states – South Africa's ultimate diplomatic objective.

Destined possibly to be the most significant historical and political development in sub-Saharan Africa since colonial disengagement, this new trend is still in its very early stages but is nonetheless clearly visible.

When just before his assassination in September 1966, Dr Verwoerd had a lengthy and cordial meeting with the Black Prime Minister of Lesotho, Chief Jonathan, in Pretoria, this objective came a step closer. And when Jonathan and the new South African Prime Minister, Mr Vorster, met in Cape Town in January 1967 for the first working discussion, a great step forward was taken.

Following hard on the heels of Prime Minister Jonathan of Lesotho was the first formal Cabinet level visit by representatives of an independent Black state *north* of the Limpopo River – *Malawi*. The visit had three most important results.

On March 13, 1967 the three man Cabinet delegation signed a trade agreement with South Africa – an agreement welcomed with equal warmth by *Die Transvaler* in Johannesburg and *The Malawi*

Times in Blantyre. (The Malawians received V.I.P. treatment accorded only to visiting statesmen and also had discussions with the South African Prime Minister. They stayed in the most elegant hotels and were always accorded the finest service.) The agreement is calculated to stimulate trade between the two countries and to assist in the acceleration of Malawi's economic development, but several other important matters concerning communications, technical aid, capital investments, etc. were discussed.

The *second* important result from the Malawi visit was the registration of a preliminary agreement with Malawi to send a permanent mission to the Republic which will be housed in Johannesburg with Consular status and be responsible for trade and labour matters. Malawi's current representative in Johannesburg, Mr F. B. Smith, a White Malawian government official, is already enjoying unofficial Consular status.

The *third* result was a public invitation by the Malawian Cabinet Ministers to South African investors and journalists to come to Malawi, while a Cabinet Minister also told the correspondent of the Johannesburg *Sunday Times* in Blantyre at the beginning of March 1967 that Malawi's President, Dr Hastings Banda, would welcome a visit by the South African Prime Minister.

One month after the visit by the Malawi delegation South Africa sent a top level mission to Lesotho to investigate the feasibility of the Oxbow hydro-electric project. This was the first time since Africa's headlong rush towards Uhuru in the late 1950's that an all White mission from South Africa had paid a visit to an independent Black state to discuss a project of mutual concern.

In the other neighbouring Black state, Botswana, the government is also intent on cementing relations with South Africa. Addressing Editors in South Bend, Indiana, on February 15, 1967, Professor Z. K. Matthews, Botswana's Ambassador to the United Nations, said that his country's relations with South Africa were a matter of practical politics. "A moral outlook is very important in international power politics," he said, "but it doesn't carry the day. Self-interest and pragmatism are what count."

Negotiations are now also underway for a visit to South Africa by Sir Seretse Khama, Prime Minister of Botswana, and by a delegation from the Malagasy Republic. South Africa and Malagasy have already reached agreement on a regular air service between

Tananarive and Johannesburg – which five years ago was thought impossible.

Dr H. F. Verwoerd's belief in the possibility of a Common Market or free trade association for Southern Africa which would include Black and White states suddenly no longer looks like an unattainable dream. This view is now generally accepted while the *Rand Daily Mail's* Laurance Gandar, long a bitter opponent of Dr Verwoerd's objectives, said on March 18, 1967 that the idea of a Southern African free trade area is now becoming a realistic target.

That South Africa (despite the hysterics by certain African states at the United Nations) has no territorial desires on the three Black states of Lesotho, Botswana and Swaziland was not only borne out by Dr Verwoerd's offer to cede South African territory to the Protectorates but by the basic philosophy underlying South Africa's political objectives. In a recent article in *The Diplomatist* the South African Ambassador in England reiterated that South Africa considers itself a multi-national country comprising a White nation and a number of Black nations, each with its own language, traditions and well-demarcated country. The establishment of the three British Protectorates of Bechuanaland, Swaziland and Basutoland was an embodiment of this fact of Southern African life.

Incorporation would thus be completely contrary to a belief in multi-nationalism.

Referring to the independent status then still to be conferred on the Protectorates, the Ambassador said: "We look with favour on their attaining independence. It is very much part of the process of separate development in South Africa . . . We join Britain, and for that matter the world, in upholding the right of self-determination of three of the nations that originally inhabited certain parts of South Africa, the Tswana, the Swazi and the Basuto. Their separate identity is recognised and their separate development guaranteed. We believe that at least the same should apply to other nations in South Africa including my own, the White Africans of South Africa, whose forebears over 300 years ago moved into uninhabited parts of South Africa."

While the British Government refused to grant South Africa the right to put its case to the people of the three Protectorates (although this was explicitly agreed to by the British and South African governments when the Union of South Africa came into being in

1910) it would appear from subsequent events as if the British Government has in any case made a meaningless political gesture by its blank refusal, intended only to placate the other more vociferous Black states of Africa such as Ghana and Ethiopia.

In October 1964 the leader of the Basuto National Party, Chief Jonathan, declared during a visit to South Africa that an independent Basutoland would have to maintain friendly relations with South Africa "if she wants to survive politically and economically". He added, "Those who say that after independence Basutoland won't have anything to do with South Africa and that the Whites will be driven out, are enemies of its progress." He also declared that his government would not allow Communists to seek asylum in Basutoland under the cloak of "political refuge" from South Africa.

Subsequently the Basutoland National Party stated that it would seek to exchange ambassadors with South Africa as soon as Basutoland becomes independent. It would seek close economic co-operation with South Africa and as a fully-fledged member of the United Nations would not become committed in advance to any set policy regarding South Africa.[2]

Early in 1965 the Basutoland National Party won the first free election and its leaders reiterated their declared friendship for South Africa. This was followed by Chief Jonathan's historic visit with Dr Verwoerd and his formal statement in Maseru in September 1966 that Basutoland would oppose any move which advocated sanctions against South Africa.

Since South Africa's attitude towards the Protectorates was made crystal clear by Dr Verwoerd's invitation to join South Africa in a Commonwealth of Southern African states, "in which no state will lord it over any other, but meeting on a basis of absolute equality" (as Mr Jonathan and Mr Vorster subsequently did), a shifting of alignments, even in the face of Afro-Asian pressure, is unlikely. As Chief Jonathan expressed it: "Basutoland is an integral part of Southern Africa". Soon after independence, the Prime Minister of Lesotho announced the appointment of a famous Afrikaner industrialist, Dr Anton Rupert, as the top economic adviser to the Lesotho Government.

2. The Maramatlou Freedom Party, one of the other political parties in Lesotho also stated at the time that its policy towards South Africa is broadly the same as that of the Basutoland National Party.

Lesotho's official attitude towards South Africa is made transparently clear in the historic joint statements issued by the late Dr H. F. Verwoerd and Chief Jonathan before the latter became Prime Minister of an independent Lesotho and by Prime Minister Vorster and Chief Jonathan after this event.

The first statement signed in Pretoria on September 2, 1966 stated inter alia: "The object of our meeting was to get acquainted and to establish how the good neighbourly relations and co-operation could be arranged on which both have already made favourable public statements. We are pleased to say that our meeting took place in a spirit of goodwill and that it is quite clear that there is no desire between our states to interfere in one anothers domestic affairs but that the friendly relations between these two independent neighbouring states will be preserved."

In the joint statement signed by Mr Vorster and Chief Jonathan in Cape Town on January 10, 1967 the key paragraphs read as follows:

"On fundamental issues we found ourselves in complete accord, more specifically on the fact that differences in political philosophy are no bar to fruitful co-operation. We both firmly believe in peaceful co-existence on the basis of equality, mutual respect and non-interference in another's domestic affairs.

"We agreed that our two countries should remain constantly vigilant against the dangers of international communism.

"Our examination of the problems affecting economic development of Lesotho revealed the close interdependence of our two countries and the need for continued close co-operation to promote, still further, our common weal. The Prime Minister of Lesotho put certain specific proposals for economic aid and technical assistance to the South African Government and the Prime Minister of South Africa has agreed to have these examined by his colleagues as soon as possible.

"Deeply conscious of the ardent desire of our respective peoples that friendly relations between our countries should be strengthened still further, we call upon men of goodwill throughout the world to join us in the pursuit of peaceful co-existence between countries, regardless of differences in size, race or national policies."

The extent to which Lesotho considers itself part of the Third

Africa and to which it was prepared to work with White South Africa was made crystal clear in May 1967 when the Prime Minister Chief Jonathan also suggested that White and Black states in Southern Africa should form "an economic community within the context of their political differences". Chief Jonathan did not make this suggestion while in South Africa but during a visit to another Black state, Malawi. In a specially prepared speech he condemned African leaders in the north who criticised those Black states already co-operating with White Southern Africa. He said he looked forward to the time when the Southern African states could sit round a table and work out an economic community for the whole southern region. He said that the prospective grouping would moderate the vociferous and doctrinaire left wing element in Africa now headed by President Sekou Toure of Guinea and President Gamal Nasser of Egypt.[3]

Much the same attitude prevails in Botswana and Swaziland.

At the last Swaziland general elections, the political party which swept the boards ran on a platform which included "close co-operation" with South Africa. Swazi leaders have made it clear that, in common with a statement issued by the Basutoland leaders who attended the independence talks in London, they would have no part in an Afro-Asian boycott against South Africa nor permit their state to be used as a base for subversion against South Africa.

In an exclusive interview with the Johannesburg *Star*'s Africa News Service, Prince Makhosini Dhlamini, leader of the majority party in Swaziland, the Imbokodvo National Movement, revealed details of his party's proposed foreign policy for the first time.[4] The future Prime Minister said that these principles brought Swaziland into line with the announcements already made by the Prime Ministers of Lesotho and Botswana. The basis of the policy, as approved by the Party executive, would be "a healthy good understanding with neighbouring states" and "non-interference in the internal affairs of other countries". Political refugees would be granted asylum but only on condition that they abstained from taking part in local politics and guaranteed they would not use Swaziland as a base for subversion against other countries. His party accepted the "economic

3. *The Rand Daily Mail*, May 16, 1967, p. 11.
4. Swaziland is due to become independent in 1969.

and geographical facts" of Swaziland's position in Southern Africa and would maintain close economic ties with South Africa and, to a lesser extent, Mocambique. Swaziland would exchange diplomatic representatives with South Africa provided they enjoyed the same privileges and facilities as other diplomats.

The friendly relations between South Africa and the then British Protectorates was the reason for catcalls and a motion deploring their attitude at the last conference of the Organization of African Unity in 1965. Dr G. L. Msibi, Secretary General of the Imbokodvo Party, the governing party in Swaziland, told a Johannesburg newspaper on November 9, 1965 that he and Prince Makhosini, the heir apparent to King Sobhuza of Swaziland, had attended the meeting at the personal invitation of the then President of Ghana, Dr Nkrumah, as observers. When the O.A.U. drafted a motion critical of the three territories, they prepared a joint statement wherein their attitude towards South Africa was made clear, namely: that the three territories believed in friendly co-existence with all their neighbours, which included South Africa, and that the economic ties between the three countries and South Africa are so close that they cannot afford to adopt an aggressive attitude towards South Africa.

After Swaziland's election for internal self-government in April 1967, Swaziland's leaders revealed their non-racial approach and absence of anti-White feelings by appointing four White persons to the state's first Legislative Assembly. Heading this group is a former Labour Party member of the South African parliament. Shortly afterwards the Prime Minister-elect Prince Makhosini Dlamini said that if after independence a meeting with South Africa's Prime Minister became necessary it would be organised "with pleasure". An independent Swaziland, he said, would strengthen its links with the "White South" as well as the organisation of African Unity where he hoped Swaziland would become a moderating influence.[5] Later in the same momentous month, Swaziland talks between representatives of Swaziland, Mocambique and South Africa got under way in Mbabane, Swaziland, on the subject of the future development of the common rivers such as the Komati, Msutu and Umbeluzi and with a view to signing

5. *The Star*, African News Service, Johannesburg, April 22, 1967, p. 1.

a formal agreement. The prospects for a common hydro-electric and irrigation system for this north-east border of South Africa were also under discussion.[6]

To the west of South Africa Botswana has also adopted a strongly pragmatic approach in its dealings with White South Africa. The most important action taken so far is Botswana's attempt to bring about a *rapprochement* between Africa's politically embattled White South and Black North. This was revealed by the President of Botswana Sir Seretse Khama in an exclusive interview to the Africa News Service of the Johannesburg *Star* on June 25, 1967. President Khama gave the interview just before his official visit to several other African states. He said it was his object to promote direct contact between these states and White South Africa "to break down a situation that is to some extent based on misunderstanding and emotionalism".

Botswana's independence has brought rapid changes. In May 1967 the first Black delegate from that state arrived in Johannesburg for the annual symposium of the South African Commission for the Conservation and Utilisation of Soil and mixed with White guests at the cocktail party in the posh Langham Hotel. Far away in Washington a prominent guest at the South African Embassy Republic Day champagne party on May 31 was Professor Z. K. Matthews – the Botswana Ambassador to the United States who was once *persona non grata* in South Africa for his political activities and at one stage arrested and accused of treason. But realism is the policy both countries stick to.

President Seretse Khama of Botswana (Bechuanaland) told John d'Oliveira of the Johannesburg *Star*'s Africa News Service on February 13, 1966 that he had to be realistic about his relations with South Africa and Rhodesia, his two big neighbours: "Our railways are Rhodesian, our ports are South African" he said. "We must trade with our neighbours and to trade with other countries our goods must pass through our neighbouring countries. To live in these circumstances we must be realistic, not emotional." The Prime Minister further observed that Botswana used South African currency and tens of thousands of his countrymen crossed the border to work in South Africa. They are sending back millions of Rand to their

6. *Die Transvaler*, Johannesburg, April 26, 1967.

relatives at home, he said. "We do not like South Africa's race policies but we must think of our own survival first. Without friendly relations with our neighbours we could be smothered."

The statements by the Presidents of Botswana, Lesotho and the Swazi leaders that they are willing and anxious to establish diplomatic relations with South Africa (both Malawi and Zambia had earlier voiced more or less the same desire but laced with a number of difficult provisos) *marks the first time Black African states had shown that they recognised the permanent nature of the White community in Southern Africa and, in particular, the status of a White government in Africa.*

The significance of this development, particularly in view of the Organization of African Unity's declared objective to wage a "war of liberation" against the south, is that any such attempt by the O.A.U. would, conceivably, meet objection from a completely new quarter, namely Black states working in close co-operation with South Africa.

Hitherto the only attempts to establish diplomatic relations between the southern White tier and Black Africa were attempted by South Africa, with Madagascar for example. The present state of affairs is, therefore, a far cry from the day when every ex-British colony which became independent immediately, with great fanfare, "severed relations" with South Africa, whether relations existed or not! At the Botswana independence celebrations, South Africa's Foreign Minister was a respected guest. The furniture in the Prime Minister's Office is a gift from South Africa. In Lesotho the Speaker of the House of Assembly sits on an elaborately carved stinkwood chair – also a gift from South Africa.

In September 1966 the dominant political party in Swaziland, which will almost certainly become the governing party after independence in 1969, publicly rejected the concept of *Pan-Africanism*, eliminating in one stroke one of the major obstacles to co-operation with South Africa and Portugal. Shortly afterwards the Botswana governing party of Sir Seretse Khama published a document which not only attacked the opposition for harbouring a Communist front organisation but rejected out of hand any proposal which smacked of "liberation movements" or which could bring Botswana into any kind of confrontation with the White South.

This is the first time that any Black government or party has taken an open stand against the kind of war talk made popular by the militant members of the Organization of African Unity while also rejecting Communism. Up to now the O.A.U. had permitted its members to be openly pro-Communist but never openly pro-Western.

The economic ties between the three states and South Africa are virtually inextricable with the advantages mostly on the side of the former Protectorates.[7] In fact, without South Africa the very existence of the people might be seriously imperilled and economic development permanently retarded. While Lesotho, for instance, has great resources for hydro-electric projects, its development would be useless unless South Africa was prepared to buy the power thus generated.

In 1962 the *combined* Gross Domestic Product of the three territories amounted to only one per cent of that of South Africa.

It is, therefore, clearly illogical for the former Protectorates (comprising of an area larger than France, Belgium and Holland) to antagonize their powerful neighbour. For sheer economic survival, they must seek the closest possible relationship with South Africa.

The most important change is not the increasing economic co-operation between these states, which has been building up steadily the past decade, *but the fact that Black leaders are primarily interested in economic progress and the welfare of their people rather than an ideological, anti-white, anti-colonial crusade.* They now recognize the permanent nature of the White nation in Southern Africa.

The new Black states which South Africa is now in the process of establishing for its various Bantu nations will also be economically interdependent with South Africa for decades to come. The relationship between a future independent state such as the Transkei (homeland of the Xhosa speaking people) and White South Africa would be no different to that existing between South Africa and for example Botswana and Lesotho.

It is therefore, no surprise to informed people in Africa that leaders of the Transkei, the first of these Black states in South Africa to achieve internal self-government, should have wholeheartedly endorsed the Government's programme of separate development.

7. See Chapter 7.

Geo-politically the Transkei cannot be compared with South Africa, nor should this be attempted. It should be seen for what it really is, an African state. In *African* terms the Transkei's geo-political statistics assume new importance. The area of the new state exceeds that of a dozen other countries of the world currently represented at the United Nations, and it has more citizens (and voters) than fifteen other member states. The economic interdependence between the Xhosa nation and the three and a half million Whites of South Africa is perhaps even greater than between Lesotho and South Africa. The same applies to the three million Zulus and the two million Sotho.

South Africa's declared policy to proceed with political independence for its Bantu states should not be doubted. In the first place there is no turning back and, secondly, in view of the independence for Lesotho, a country with little more than one quarter the population of the Xhosa nation, the latter will no longer be satisfied with anything less. A second state (for the Tswanas living in South Africa) is now in the process of being established. The considerable power the Black Transkeian government wields (control of finances, justice, education, agriculture, commerce, the right of taxation, etc.) indicates the autonomy which it already enjoys.

To talk of the Transkei state as an "experiment" in race relations in South Africa is not only erroneous but behind the times.

It is unlikely that any *future* government would or could stop this pattern of political division of South Africa.

The multi-national situation clearly calls for internal decolonization by re-establishing the pattern of Bantu homelands in Southern Africa which existed before the creation of the multi-national Union of South Africa in 1910. Apart from this the Zulu and Xhosa nations in South Africa, numerically more powerful than many other African nations, are the most educated Black group in Africa *per capita* and have as much a right to the dignity of nationhood as Lesotho, Chad, Liberia or Ghana. It is unlikely that they would become the one exception in Africa to accept anything but a policy of self-determination for their own people – which South Africa's policy of separate development can and will provide.

A quick calculation (even allowing for the amalgamation of some of the potential Bantu states in South Africa) shows that within a lifetime there could conceivably be a consortium of at least seven states[8] in Southern Africa joined by such close economic ties and common geo-political interests that they would not consciously pursue policies detrimental to their neighbours' interests.

To this group one can, of course, also add *South West Africa*, the huge territory lying to the west of South Africa and immediately south of Angola, whose international status was the subject of a five year dispute before the International Court of Justice (the World Court) at the Hague during 1962-1966. South West Africa was a German colony until World War I when German forces surrendered to South African troops who had invaded South West Africa as part of the Allied war plan. In terms of the Peace Treaty of Versailles the government of South Africa as Mandatory was endowed with the right to govern the territory as an integral part of South Africa. When the League of Nations, which conferred the Mandate, collapsed, South Africa adopted the view that the Mandate had also elapsed but continued to administer the territory in the spirit of the Mandate. The Afro-Asian states however, adopted the view that the United Nations was heir to the League of Nations and that they could censure South Africa's administration of the territory.

The World Court's decision on July 18, 1966, came as a stunning surprise to the Afro-Asians. In its judgement the Court found that Liberia and Ethiopia, who instituted the proceedings against South Africa *on behalf* of the Black states of Africa (their legal costs were paid by the O.A.U.) had no legal right or interest in South Africa's administration of the territory. Legally the effect of the decision is to give South Africa a free hand to administer the territory as it sees best. The Court also found, in effect, that only the League of Nations as an entity previously enjoyed any "watchdog" rights. The Court virtually indicated that there is now *no* entity, not even the United Nations, which is *entitled* by law to act as a watchdog over South Africa's administration of the territory. *Legally speaking* the relationship between the people of South West Africa and the Republic is no longer of international concern.

Since the decision, the South West Africa case has again become a hot political issue at the United Nations. The same allegations which Liberia and Ethiopia had to withdraw before the World Court

8. The Republic of South Africa, Lesotho, Botswana, Swaziland, the Transkei (Xhosa), Zululand, Tswanaland.

in the face of South African evidence to the contrary, are being bandied about. The African states and their supporters who had previously carried the World Court on their shoulders (and who even arranged conferences, such as the one in London presided over by Mr Ronald Segal, to decide *how* they would go about breaking South Africa's hold "once the World Court's ruling is handed down") have now decided that it is after all "only a White man's court" and that the decision was a "slap in the face of world opinion". Having further disposed of the five year battle by abusing the judges, the African states urged the United Nations to "take over" South West Africa by force of arms if necessary. The World Court and the 5,000,000 words of written and spoken evidence and pleadings which the case took up might just as well not have existed. The General Assembly decided at the close of 1966 and by an overwhelming majority that because South Africa had "violated" its "Mandate", the territory was no longer under South African administration.

Thus for the first time in its history the General Assembly of the United Nations consisting largely of Afro-Asian states purported to direct control of a territory (almost the size of France, West Germany, Holland and Belgium) which has had internal self-government for thirty years. The facts indicate that this action was politically motivated without any consideration of the merits of the case – the merits having been abundantly illustrated during the protracted dispute before the World Court, unfortunately, not in favour of the Afro-Asian powers. The facts also indicate that the General Assembly's action is unconstitutional and illegal. However, without South Africa willingly abdicating from its responsibilities in South West Africa, there was little the Assembly could do and after two months of intensive campaigning fourteen countries were found, the United States included, who were willing to serve on a Committee which was to investigate ways and means of getting South Africa out of South West Africa. In April of 1967 the Committee reported to a special session of the General Assembly that it could offer no solution and the Israeli-Arab War saved the delegates from further senseless discussions.

To-day the half million people of the territory (of whom some 80,000 are White) are South African in all but name. The territory elects six members to the South African Parliament and its Administrator (local Governor) is appointed by the South African Government. While the territory has its own system of taxation and a local Legislative Assembly, the Parliament of South Africa is the supreme legislative authority. Its status is thus not much different from any of South Africa's four provinces, viz., a provincial (state) authority with control over such matters as roads, taxes, hospitals, municipal affairs, education, etc.

Linguistically and ethnologically the non-Whites of South West Africa are people of the most divergent origins, customs and traditions. Between the Nama and the Hereros for example, there is an age-old history of friction and war and any policy concerned with self-determination of the people which loses sight of this multi-national pattern is doomed to failure. Because the Ovambo number almost half the total population the other races such as the Bushmen, Damara, Okavango and Namas would never consent to a policy of one-man-one-vote in a unitary state.

South Africa's policy for the territory is clearly not one of annexation. In line with its policy of self-determination for each of the different Black nations within its own borders, it has proposed a similar policy of separate development for South West Africa's different nations. This calls for a number of autonomous states, economically interdependent, with, in the end, only such matters as defence and foreign relations likely to remain with the South African Government. However, even independence is not ruled out.

As in the case of the Transkei, the self-governing state established for South Africa's 3.5 million Xhosas, South Africa is also prepared to accede to a request from the people for full independence. In March 1967 the government offered to the Ovambos of South West Africa self-government in Ovamboland plus substantial economic assistance (running into millions of Rand annually) with a prospect of complete independence at a later stage. Whether Ovamboland would elect to remain as a self-governing state as an appendage of a greater South Africa or elect to become a sovereign independent state in close association with South Africa (or the consortium of Southern African states now taking shape) is at this stage mere conjecture and of academic interest only. But a landlocked Ovamboland, surrounded by countries who are committed to the new deal in Southern Africa and without any source of power such as coal would in any event find it difficult to adopt an attitude different to that taken by landlocked Lesotho.

Whatever the future of South West Africa, the fact that it is hemmed in between South Africa and Portuguese Angola, its complete reliance on the South African market, communications, capital power supplies, etc., makes it fairly certain that its political and economic destinies are *permanently* tied to South Africa.

Geographical and other factors make it impossible for any other state or states to provide just the electricity required by South West Africa.[9] In fact, it is inconceivable that any other country would be able to administer South West Africa if this function should somehow be taken from South Africa. The United Nations, for one, would like to do just that. Yet, the world organization, which can hardly maintain itself financially and has virtually to beg for funds to maintain a token force on Cyprus (after having withdrawn from a chaotic and dangerous situation in the Congo because of money troubles) would not even be able to furnish a fraction of the amount required to maintain the current pace of development in South West Africa.

South Africa's five-year plan for the political and economic development of the territory calls for a *yearly* outlay of capital sufficient to finance the *entire* United Nations administration for a full year.

In short, within the Third Africa, south of the Limpopo River and Angola, the territories are economically so interdependent and subject to the influences radiating from South Africa that political leaders of all colours have come to recognize the common sense of harmonious co-operation with the Republic.

South Africa's attitude has been to stress the prosperity which increasing trade and economic development can bring, particularly for those Black states heavily dependent on agricultural exports which are subject to price fluctuations. Her goal is stability and peaceful co-existence in Southern Africa. The South African Minister of Planning made it crystal clear in a major address to the National Conference on a Common Market for Southern Africa, in Johannesburg in March 1965, that South Africa has neither the wish nor the power to build up an economic empire in Southern Africa. Materially the lesser developed states stand to gain far more from any re-

9. See Chapter 4.

gional economic alliance whether on a bilateral basis or under a common market programme.

North of the Limpopo River and South West Africa lie the Portuguese (overseas) provinces of Angola and Mocambique.

The Portuguese and South African alignment has never been formally acknowledged, such as in a military pact, but in official statements of goodwill towards each other (on occasions of state visits, or after consultations between foreign ministers) this "alignment" has lately assumed a far less nebulous character.

In Lisbon in October 1964, the two foreign ministers signed an important economic pact, consisting of several different agreements. South Africa's Foreign Minister, Dr Hilgard Muller, termed this a sound formal basis for existing good relations: "It was a positive fact which nobody could deny and which would contribute highly to the peace and welfare of the African continent."

The two most significant agreements concerned South Africa's use of the Port of Lourenco Marques in Mocambique and the development of the mighty Kunene River between Angola and South West Africa. Dr Muller added that in the disturbed world of to-day, both countries share the same problems and ideals. Both have the same attachment to Africa in an unbreakable determination to remain there for the welfare of the population and in defence of the West.

The Portuguese Foreign Minister, Dr Alberto Nogueira, in his reply said: "The ways and methods of the two countries are certainly different. That fact has never been concealed by either of them. That, however, does not prevent us from collaborating, as we have done and are doing, for the common welfare of all. Because, indeed, the two countries have in common great extensions of frontiers, important problems of transport and large possibilities of technical and economic utilization of natural resources for the progress and development of the respective populations. All this imposes a collaboration within a determined spirit." He then added these significant words: "As a matter of fact it is a case of defending and expanding in the African continent what the two countries consider to be the values of the West, despite all the lack of understanding shown by that same West."

South Africa and Portugal have not (yet) signed a military pact but in the words of the Portuguese Foreign Minister, "defending the values of the West in collaboration with each other does not imply a completely independent action on the part of each country."

Despite its failure, the "invasion" by terrorist groups of Mocambique during October 1964 was of tremendous importance to South Africa. *Die Burger,* probably South Africa's leading Afrikaans daily newspaper, observed in this respect that, as a neighbouring state, Mocambique can fill one of two roles; it can either be a buffer against the aggressive forces that are planning the downfall of Mocambique and South Africa, or become a gateway for invasion which would make it much easier for those forces to strike at South Africa. "South Africa should have no illusions about what the situation would be if the plans against Mocambique should ever succeed," *Die Burger* said, "over a distance of between two and three hundred miles, South Africa would then border on a state that could be used as a basis for constant attack and raids onto its territory."

It has already become evident in other parts of the world what enormous problems can arise from such a situation. One tiny state, Zanzibar, has provided the Red Chinese with a gateway to the whole of East Africa.

It has been proved beyond dispute that the leaders of the so-called "liberation movements" in Angola and Mocambique are either self-confessed Communists or heavily in debt to the Russians and Chinese.

A terrorist regime in Lourenco Marques is quite likely therefore, to become openly Communist-orientated within a matter of months (as the Russians and Chinese set-up shop with their hundreds of embassy "officials" and "advisers") and would provide a deep water harbour for the Communists some 400 miles from the world's major gold-fields and the huge industrial complex of Johannesburg and environment.

The outside world is inclined to view Portugal in its continental context only. Her overseas territories are usually referred to as "colonies". The Portuguese rightly reject this view. The word "colony" is foreign to their way of thinking and they speak instead of their overseas provinces. Despite geographical discontinuity, Portugal is to them the mother country plus the overseas provinces, in the same way as Alaska is regarded not as a colony but as an integral part of the United States.

The Portuguese Prime Minister had the following to say about Angola and Mocambique: "Angola is a Portuguese creation and does not exist without Portugal. The only national conscience rooted in the province is not Angolan but Portuguese, even as there are no Angolans but Portuguese of Angola. This is also applicable to Mocambique. If the ties which bind her and make her part of the Portuguese nation are destroyed, there will be no more Mocambique either in history or in geography."

Because Angola borders on South West Africa and Mocambique borders on the Transvaal and Natal, Angola, Mocambique and South Africa are neighbours. However, since the two provinces are really part of metropolitan Portugal, most people think in terms of *Portugal* and South Africa as being neighbours.

The two neighbours to-day face the same challenge – the efforts of the African states, egged on by the Red Chinese and the Russians, to "liberate" Angola, Mocambique and South Africa by force of arms. They face the same abuse at the Afro-Asian dominated United Nations – the same barrage of misconceptions in the popular press. Their efforts to combat the damaging actions of terrorists whom they can prove beyond doubt to have been financed and trained in Russia, East Germany, Cuba and Red China have made them friends in need and in deed.

The old *Central African Federation* of North and South Rhodesia and Nyasaland, which Britain established when it believed that multi-racialism between an established White community and a burgeoning Black nationalism could still be made to work, forms a most interesting triangle in the Third Africa.

The Federation shattered to pieces when Black nationalists in Northern Rhodesia and Nyasaland declared what White South Africans have always maintained; viz. that nationalism is exclusive and cannot be placated by paper formulas such as "partnership", the official policy of the Federation. Despite the fact that racial integration (based on what Mr Harold MacMillan called "merit and nothing but merit") was progressing more rapidly here than in any other place where similar mixed societies were grouped together in one state, the Black people clamoured for only one thing: government *by* Black people *for* Black people. In the light of developments elsewhere on the continent, this was to be expected. They were unlikely to be the one Black group in Africa prepared to settle for anything less.

"Merit and nothing but merit" became an empty slogan as the Black nationalists pressed for immediate universal franchise – regardless of whether or not the voters could read or write – not even mentioning the political sophistication required in electing qualified representatives.

The net result can be seen on the maps of the mid-1960's. On December 31, 1963, the 10-year-old Federation of Rhodesia and Nyasaland officially ceased to exist and the three territories that had comprised it – Southern Rhodesia, Northern Rhodesia and Nyasaland went their separate ways.

Since then, Northern Rhodesia and Nyasaland (now known as Zambia and Malawi) have become sovereign, independent states. And the third territory – Southern Rhodesia?

To future historians it may well present itself as an astonishing piece of irony that Rhodesia (as the country is now known), which voluntarily surrendered a strong claim to independence in 1953 in order to become a partner in the now defunct Federation, should be the one country denied the right it could have had so long ago, while the two other former partners have long since been granted their independence.

And those self-same historians will surely find something grotesque in the fact that various territories which, not so long ago, could never have put forward anything like the same claim as Rhodesia for independence, should now, as sovereign states, be threatening to "quit the Commonwealth" if Britain recognises Rhodesian independence.

Rhodesia's claim to independence is frequently represented as a conspiracy on the part of White Rhodesians to perpetuate their political domination. From what has been said about the 1961 constitution, which is the basis on which Rhodesia claimed her independence, this is demonstrably absurd. This constitution must lead to a Black majority as inevitably as night follows day but only when that majority is politically mature. Nor is it valid to claim, as many of Rhodesia's critics do, that White Rhodesians are only bidding for independence in order to give themselves a point of vantage from which to erode Black political rights.

The independence claim is based on totally different considerations. Primarily, it is a demand for the recognition of 43 years of capable and responsible government since Rhodesia was granted full self-government early in 1923. During this period a territory the size of the Cape Province, Transvaal and Natal has been developed into one of the most productive and economically advanced areas on the African continent with no foreign assistance; has dramatically improved the standards of living of all its peoples; has made a major contribution to the defence of western values in peace and war; has faithfully met its international obligations and in all respects demonstrated its capacity for good and efficient government. Rhodesia has a proud record of accomplishment.

If Rhodesia should yield to parrot cries of "one-man-one-vote" and "majority rule now", they know that they would be condemning the country to one-party, totalitarian rule: the most notorious African nationalist leader in Rhodesia is on record as having stated that he rejects Westminster-type democracy, with its insistence on Parliamentary Opposition, as being "unsuitable" for Rhodesia. As with other nationalist leaders in different parts of Africa, he has taken the line that any parliamentary criticism of "My" government will come from within.

Even before its unilateral declaration of independence, Rhodesia had indicated in no uncertain terms that it is consciously and purposely aligning itself with South Africa. Rhodesia's Prime Minister, Ian Smith, put it this way: "Tshombe's Congo and Zambia could be considered buffer states but if all else fails (Southern) Rhodesia is truly South Africa's buffer state." He also stated in an interview with South African newspapers in September 1964 that he had not the slightest doubt his country would move much closer to South Africa once it wins its independence. He emphasized the close relations which have always existed between the two countries and stressed the many common factors such as trade, culture, the defence of Western civilization in a chaotic Africa, etc., which made close co-operation even more essential.

Significant of the trend on the economic side is the pre-independence trade pact between Rhodesia and South Africa under which, for the first time, most South African-made goods will enter Rhodesia on the same terms as British goods even if Rhodesia succeeds one day in obtaining Commonwealth membership. Conversely, the South African market will be opened wider for Rhodesian products.

In Pretoria and Salisbury the agreement was seen as the first step towards Dr Verwoerd's objective of a Southern African "Common Market".

The situation which arose after independence when Britain declared an economic war on Rhodesia led to the Rhodesians openly inviting South Africa to step in and grab the R55 million represented by British exports to Rhodesia.

To-day White Rhodesians are unanimous that South Africa is the friend in need, and that Britain is among the enemies. *Even if Rhodesia and Britain somehow manage to settle their differences*, the Wilson government has left such a legacy of hate, because of its handling of the Rhodesian crisis, that "British influence" in Rhodesia has suffered a fatal blow.

It would take pages to list the various fields in which South Africa has taken over from England as the "Mother Country" but it includes capital, technical advice, higher education, military staff courses, supplies of essential materials etc.

Politically the growing pressures from the United Nations, Britain and the Commonwealth to hand over power to the Black Africans immediately – and the Rhodesian Whites will fight this to the end – are forcing Rhodesia into an embattled camp with South Africa. (Saboteurs infiltrate into Rhodesia and South Africa from the same training camps in Tanzania . . . A common underground pipeline brings southwards Russian grenades, plastic bombs, manuals of sabotage and guerilla warfare and other offensive materials.)

As far as the independent Black African states are concerned, they have no doubt that Rhodesia will closely align itself with South Africa and, even worse from their point of view, become a member of the proposed Commonwealth of Southern African states. These states, such as the Transkei, would be politically autonomous but would, as a consortium, certainly have a largely common foreign and defence policy. If South Africa can extend this offer to the Black states of Lesotho, Swaziland and Botswana (with which it has less in common) it would certainly not hesitate at the right moment to extend a similar offer to Rhodesia.

Inevitably White Rhodesia is moving away from Britain and the Commonwealth and stretching out both arms to South Africa, its rich and powerful neighbour. Ideologically, spiritually and economically the two countries have never been closer than now, not even in the days when Rhodesians held a referendum on whether or not to become South Africa's fifth province.

Because of its strategic position in relation to Mocambique, a closer alliance between Portugal and Rhodesia also seems to be in the making. In fact, Dr Kenneth Kaunda, the President of Zambia, charged at a Press conference in August 1964 that a secret military and defence pact had already been signed. Although this was subsequently denied by both Salisbury and Lisbon the co-operation between Rhodesia and Mocambique after independence has not only been of the highest order but the plans for a direct natural gas and oil pipeline and other projects seems to indicate that it will be of a permanent nature.

Certainly Mr Smith of Rhodesia does not seem to doubt the trend towards an alliance. Asked by a reporter of *U.S. News and World Report* whether there was such a trend in the economic and political fields he replied: "Yes, I believe that this is probable and natural, because, after all, this is what is happening everywhere else in the world – not only economically but also strategically – and this has been proved in Europe and South East Asia." Pressed on the question of a military alliance, Mr Smith said that he did not want to commit anybody else but that he believed it was "a logical line of thinking" and that "the chances . . . are high".

Hitherto the signs of growing co-operation between Southern African states were largely to be found in countries either under White western government or, as the critics will point out, countries and territories economically dependent on South Africa, for example, Lesotho, Botswana and Swaziland.

Black nationalists in the North, in Nigeria, Ghana, Ethiopia and East Africa, however, are now disturbed at the signs of a *re-appraisal* of attitudes towards "White Africa" on the part of two other Southern Black states, namely Zambia and Malawi; at one stage even the Congo before Moise Tshombe was deposed as Prime Minister. This re-appraisal, or evidence of "trying to live with South Africa", is in stark contrast to the attitude of leaders of other Black states who would rather see their own people die of hunger than co-operate with South Africa. That the average Black man in his state may not share this view probably never occurs to the educated handful who run the government.

When the leading Afrikaans newspaper, *Die Burger*, published an editorial in October 1964 congratulating Zambia on its independence, it observed pointedly that of all the African states which have been granted independence thus far, Zambia has the most important relations with South Africa in investment and transport.

Quite apart from the fact that investments from South Africa running into many millions of Rand have contributed vastly to the overall development of Zambia, this observation is not a one-sided view. Perhaps because of the developments which South Africa had made possible, President Kenneth Kaunda was spared the necessity of going hat-in-hand to ask for outside economic aid even before the independence day bunting was taken down. It did not surprise South Africa, therefore, when the Prime Minister observed (*Newsweek* October 26, 1965) that "Zambia must get along with South Africa".

Earlier that month the President also had bluntly and quite courageously told the conference of "non-aligned nations" in Cairo that his nation's very existence depends on getting along with South Africa. "These are our seaports" he said, "and our economic dependence on South Africa becomes even clearer to you when I say that even the smallest village store in Zambia holds stocks of South African goods." Zambia of course, also has more than 77,000 White people living in the new state, less than 4,000 of whom chose to move out before independence. Their goodwill towards the new Black regime (and many of them are White South Africans and Rhodesians) will probably not needlessly or recklessly be jeopardized. In August 1964, less than two months before independence, 200 White railway workers went on strike in the new state. Kaunda saw the entire transportation system grind to an agonizing 15-day halt while the dispute with the Whites was settled. As a result the country lost R1.15 million per day in copper exports.

Since the brutal stoning of a young White mother on October 30, 1966 during industrial riots, some 500 White mine workers have left Zambia – all for Rhodesia or South Africa. Their resignations were all due to anti-White actions on the part of Black officials and workers. Production of copper for 1966 was expected to be down some 100,000 tons over the figure for the previous year – representing a loss of some R50,000,000 in revenue – and this exodus of skilled workers is certain to push production figures for 1967 down even more.

This is a development which President Kaunda must view with grave concern. Without revenue from copper, Zambia might as well close shop. Without the White people, copper production will plummet, communications will grind to a halt, factories will close down and the income of the Zambian government be slashed to a pittance.

Zambia's only rail links with the outside world also run through Rhodesia, Angola and Mocambique. The chances of a line being completed from the copper fields to Dar-es-Salaam are very remote, despite claims that the African states would build it themselves. The World Bank turned down the project flat. Intelligence sources declare that the Red Chinese are willing to construct the line for Zambia but this would, according to the same sources, lead to immediate retaliatory steps on the part of Rhodesia and Portugal. By the time such a line could be completed, even allowing for a crash programme, Zambia's whole economy would have fallen in ruins. And if this is not enough to sober up Mr Kaunda, Zambia's main sources of electricity are in White hands – on the other side of the Zambezi River in Rhodesia.

All this was probably at the back of Mr Kaunda's mind when he stated flatly that he would not permit Zambia to become a staging place for a "freedom march" against South Africa or Mocambique. "I do not intend to encourage armed uprising," he declared.

Zambia's Kenneth Kaunda will undoubtedly have to put up with heavy pressure from other governments in Black Africa and North Africa – and of course outside Africa – to take a more active part in the "War of Liberation" against South Africa and Portugal. If common sense and a desire for stability and prosperity for his people is of first importance to him, however, the pressure will fail. *This is the key to Zambia's presence in the Third Africa.* If he succumbs to the White haters in the North and lets his emotions override his common sense, Kaunda may become popular at the O.A.U. and the United Nations, but he will probably also live to see turmoil and misery fall upon his land.

The practical value of Kaunda's attitude towards South Africa, Angola and Mocambique is best exemplified by South Africa's official attitude that, despite the differences between Rhodesia and Zambia, South Africa would continue normal relations with both countries. This has meant that Zambia could count on (and actually received) vital stocks from South Africa, Angola and Mocambique, including coal, which she lost as a result of her economic war against Rhodesia. *During 1966 South Africa became the principal source of Zambia's imports from abroad.* While the Zambian Government on the one hand has moved to stop the flow of thousands of Zambian work seekers to South Africa it has, on the other hand, been extremely active in recruiting skilled White workers, professional and advisory personnel, for Government projects and services.

At the beginning of 1967 President Kaunda stepped up his verbal attacks on "racialism" in South Africa and following his visit to Red China in May 1967 these attacks assumed a more belligerent note. The most important question now is whether this is the real thing or chest-thumping blasts merely to impress neighbouring Tanzania and the O.A.U. But certainly Kaunda's attitude towards South Africa in the economic sphere is becoming far more pragmatic.

Similar indications of a re-appraisal of the general political situation in Southern Africa are to be found in *Malawi.*

At the General Assembly of the United Nations of 1966 Malawi was the only African state which refused to join the Afro-Asian walk-out when the South African Foreign Minister addressed the General Assembly and, despite the pressure of the entire African block, Malawi rejected all Afro-Asian proposals to wrest the control of South West Africa from the Republic of South Africa.

What makes Malawi's stand at the United Nations all the more significant is that the majority of the White Western states had privately described the Afro-Asian proposals as unlawful and unrealistic but left it to Malawi to show the courage of stating it from the rostrum.

At a special press conference in Zambia on March 29, 1967 Dr Banda pointed out that Malawi has had relations with South Africa since the British established Malawi as a protectorate in the previous century. The first African preacher and the first African teacher came from South Africa and since that time Malawians have gone to work in South Africa in their tens of thousands. "It was impossible for Malawi to cut itself off from South Africa", he said. Dr Banda said that there was another very important reason that should not be overlooked: "South Africa is here to stay," he said. "It is no use we African leaders deceiving or deluding ourselves about it. South

Africa is also militarily the strongest power on our continent." He added that no single state or combination of states in Africa can ever hope to expel South Africa or obliterate her from the face of Africa. This attitude on his part is, of course, not new, for at the 1964 African summit conference at Addis Ababa he had already informed Heads of State that he and his country would not support any economic or diplomatic sanctions against Portugal or South Africa.

Dr Banda also warned other African states on November 9, 1965, that they should not plan any attack on Rhodesia or attempt to bring the country to its knees by economic sanctions. He pointed out that he knew the real strength of Rhodesia's armed forces and that these could shatter any army the Black states could raise. His remarks coincided with a statement in Rome by Diallo Telli, Secretary General of the Organization of African Unity, who said that the African states would themselves finish off Rhodesia militarily if the United States or Britain cannot do so.

Dr Banda ridiculed the threats by other African states to withdraw from the British Commonwealth and to close their bank accounts in London if Britain did not speedily act against Rhodesia. "What bank accounts", he asked, "their overdrawn accounts?" He said that demands for British troops in Rhodesia was childish and inhuman while sanctions would fail in the same way as they failed against South Africa.

Since Rhodesia's declaration of Independence, President Banda has maintained a largely neutral attitude while the relationship with South Africa and the Portuguese in Mocambique, particularly in the economic field, have continued to improve. A South African firm has even been awarded the contract to plan and design Malawi's new capital at Lilongwe, a project which will mean paying millions of Rand into White South African coffers. The contractors must also provide for air services to the new capital, electricity, telephone services, etc.

While South Africa has been making a major breakthrough in her relations with Black Africa by having three Malawi Cabinet Ministers as guests, Malawi has not neglected its relationship with Portugal and the Portuguese territories. At the beginning of March two Cabinet Ministers from Malawi also visited Lisbon and had discussions with the Portuguese Prime Minister, Dr Salazar.

Towards the end of 1966 it became evident that South African exports to Africa would be up by a spectacular thirty per cent. Since not all of this was due to increased trade with Rhodesia and the Portuguese provinces it can be assumed that exports to both Malawi and Zambia were up by an appreciable amount. For tactical reasons the South African export figures in respect of individual countries in Africa are not made available but according to figures released by Zambia on October 11, 1966 imports from South Africa are expected to reach R55 million at the end of 1966 as compared with R40 million the previous year ($77,000,000 and $56,000,000 respectively).

It is also significant that the Presidents of both Zambia and Malawi have publicly declared the necessity for exchanging diplomats with South Africa and their willingness "to sit down and talk over" mutual problems. Problems in the implementation of this exchange of diplomats and talks of "guarantees" are in the long run less important than the *desire* and *intent* of co-operation.

This expression of intent of co-operation sent a shudder through the ex-British colonies in East Africa. These are the states in the vanguard of the run-the-White-man-into-the-sea school, aided and abetted by the dictatorships of Ghana, Algeria, Egypt and Ethiopia. The attitude of Ethiopia (which serves as one of the training grounds for the "army of liberation" which is supposed to march south one day to "liberate" South Africa) is extremely ironical because of the all important role South African troops played in "liberating" Ethiopia from Italian occupation during the last world war!

Finally there is the Congo.

It is not part of the Third Africa but at one stage it did appear as if the Congo and South Africa would get along. As in so many other Black states in Africa, however, even matters of basic policy towards neighbouring countries depend entirely on the personal beliefs of the man who is Prime Minister. With Tshombe no longer in power any hope of co-operation is, for the moment, wishful thinking.

It could, however, change.

The Congo as a unitary state is, at the time of writing, safe and sound, due to the victories over the rebels by White "mercenaries" from South Africa and Rhodesia. It is said that these were "soldiers of fortune", drifters, etc. who would fight anywhere for money. This may be so but the fact is that Tshombe's government advertised for hiretroops in South African newspapers and the recruiting offices were set up openly in public buildings. Had the government of South Africa (and Rhodesia) wanted to, they could have put a stop to the recruiting immediately. In much the same way thousands of Jews from South Africa were permitted to travel to the Middle-East to fight in the Israeli war of Independence. (South Africa was the only country in the world which permitted this.) The White mercenaries were, therefore, in the Congo with the consent of South Africa. To have sent in troops would have given nine-tenths of the United Nations and the United States Government a heart attack, besides which it would have been illegal since South African troops cannot be dispatched abroad at will. Even during World War II the entire body of 250,000 men who fought overseas were volunteers.

Mr Tshombe, therefore knew very well at the time that without official blessing the White mercenaries would never have materialised.

Tshombe's victory over the Chinese backed rebels came at a time when the United Nations and the O.A.U. refused to support the legitimate government of the Congo in its efforts to put down the rebellion. Until that time the entire West, with the rather surprising exception of the United States, sat back and watched (finally caught in the web of their own political expediency) how the Chinese-backed rebels achieved one victory after another, threatening to turn the Congo into a huge Zanzibar.

When Katanga had a secessionist government fleetingly "recognised" by the United Nations, South Africa received two of its Black Cabinet Ministers and furnished Katanga with much needed supplies. When Katanga was no longer recognised as a state, South Africa told its "mercenaries" that they would endanger their citizenship by serving what was no longer a legitimate government.

To-day South Africa still has an interest in the legitimate government of the entire Congo. As South Africa's late Prime Minister, Dr H. F. Verwoerd pointed out, it was obviously in the interests of the African states and the world at large that the unity of the Congo now be preserved, for, if the country fell to the rebels, the Congo would immediately become a threat to the entire Africa and the Southern tier, first to Zambia and eventually South Africa, apart from opening up the whole of Central Africa to the Communists.

South Africa, he said, was therefore prepared to aid the Congo government in every sphere short of direct military intervention.

If *a political realist* such as Moise Tshombe should come into power again, the chances are good that he will look south to the White controlled states for aid and comfort.

A political realist in Black Africa is of course a man who is primarily interested in eradicating poverty, illiteracy and disease in his country and who believes that co-operation with White people (and the West) is the surest way of achieving this in the shortest possible time.

Mr Tshombe told Milt Freudenheim of the *Chicago Daily News* that he had to be realistic about Angola, Mocambique and White South Africa. "The Congo", he said, "needs the assistance of these countries, their communications, etc. in order to survive economically."

Whether the Congo's present leaders will eventually realise that the country's current turmoil and economic stagnation can at least be alleviated by adopting a realistic policy towards the South, only time will tell. However, in Zambia and Malawi, in Lesotho and Swaziland and the other Black states in the South, *the question of personal attitudes does not arise*, nor does the growing evidence of closer co-operation reflect this.[10] For some it is simply a question of economic realities, for others one of survival. Unless it is a completely Leftist government under Chinese or Russian influence such as in Zanzibar, or a small clique and dictatorship, such as existed in Ghana and still exists in Liberia, caring not a whit for the welfare of their people, these states are unlikely to cut their vulnerable throats by joining the crusade to "liberate" South Africa and the Portuguese provinces, *no matter who is in power*. Of all the states in Africa these countries know best that such a move would imperil their very existence or lead to serious economic retrogression. In Africa economic hardship is invariably followed by greed and corruption and, finally, dangerous political unrest. The Black leaders in the south will probably bear this in mind particularly after what happened to so many other leaders elsewhere in Africa.

These developments have duly impressed the foreign press corps in South Africa and articles summarising this new trend in Black White relations ("a new sweet wind of change" wrote one correspondent) have appeared in magazines such as *The Reporter*

10. See Chapter 7.

(U.S.A.), *U.S. News and World Report*, and newspapers such as *The National Observer* (U.S.A.), *The Christian Science Monitor* (U.S.A.) and *The Observer*, London. What most correspondents have not stressed is the scope and depth of this change. News of the latest developments and the benefits which have accrued to Lesotho, Botswana, Malawi and Zambia as a result of co-operation with South Africa have even penetrated the closed minds of newspaper editors in Ghana. On June 6, 1967 *The Pioneer* in Accra, Ghana, advised African leaders not to spurn the friendship with Black Africa that was being offered by South Africa. In a lengthy editorial on South Africa's Foreign Minister's statement that the Government intended to open diplomatic missions in some African states the newspaper said: "After all, is it not repugnant that the wealth of South Africa should not be enjoyed by all Africans, but by only a handful of descendants of poor Dutchmen?" This is hardly the sort of friendly co-existence any country would be looking for but it shows that the editors have been *thinking* – a process which has so far been almost totally absent – and the rest of the editorial did suggest that White South Africa's presence in Africa should be accepted.

4. Face of a New Power

Physically the Third Africa is an area of great extremes and contrasts.

There is the solitude and mystery of the desert; the noisy bustle of sophisticated cities with elevated highways and mile long traffic jams; there is the warmth of golden beaches stretching endlessly along the shores of False Bay at the southern end of Africa and the iciness of the snowfields in Basutoland. The vast featureless plains of South West Africa and Botswana is as striking as the upthrusting Drakensberg with its 11,000 feet high peaks. The roaring and awe inspiring majesty of the Victoria Falls in Rhodesia and the roar of the surf pounding the Skeleton Coast in South West Africa is in contrast with the absolute silence of night in South Africa's Valley of Desolation. On the West coast, the Namib Desert has sand dunes as high as the Empire State Building. On the East coast, however, the high and rolling green hills of Zululand are covered in soft green grass.

It is this endless variety and contrast which provides the subcontinent with its fascinating characteristics – sundrenched plain, enchanting forest and animal haunted bush; magnificent farms, immense irrigation projects and glittering cities.

Visitors who have flown direct to Salisbury, Lourenco Marques, Luanda, Johannesburg, Durban or Cape Town have been astounded by these modern cities which can hold their own in sophisticated life, amenities, communications, size and modernity with those in most other parts of the Western world. There are, for instance, only a dozen cities in America or England with a bigger population than Johannesburg, whereas for modern architecture Cape Town and Pretoria need take no second place.

Cape Town reminds one of San Francisco but of the two, Cape Town is the more striking because of its magnificent mountain backdrop. "This Cape is a most stately thing and is the fairest Cape

68

we saw in the whole circumference of the earth" – said Sir Francis Drake.

Here South Africans built a city that is part oriental (the Malay quarter), part Riviera (Clifton), part Parisian, part Dutch and part English. Add a mediterranean climate, valleys cloaked in vineyards planted 300 years ago, some of the loveliest sandy beaches one could imagine plus a cosmopolitan population of close to a million and one realizes why Cape Town ranks with Rio de Janeiro as the most beautiful city in the world.

It was here that the late Dag Hammarskjöld exclaimed: "But this is not Africa, this is Europe."

Visitors who stop off in other parts of Africa (the Sudan, Egypt, Ethiopia, Mali, Togo, Gabon, etc.) appreciate this remark by the late Secretary General of the United Nations far better than those who fly into Johannesburg and Cape Town and back to London or New York without really seeing Arab and Black Africa. It is only when one visits other African states – whether newly independent like Gambia, Gabon or Guinea or an ancient empire such as Ethiopia – that one is struck with the tremendous difference between Black Africa and the Third Africa. All of a sudden projects and cities in the Third Africa assume new proportions. After sidestepping camels and goats in the streets of Khartoum and potholes in the dirt roads of Conakry, it is almost like receiving a physical jolt to get caught up in a mile-long traffic jam on a dual carriageway in Johannesburg.

Geographically, of course, the Third Africa is inescapably part of Africa. It has Africa's climate, its soil, its diseases, its lack of navigable rivers, its lack of rainfall. However, what the people in the Third Africa, particularly those in Rhodesia and South Africa, have made out of this raw continent is unlike anything elsewhere in Africa.

They have tamed the land.

In doing so they gave it a future which is so promising that it may indeed one day become the Europe which Mr Hammarskjöld thought he saw in Cape Town. Except it will be Euroafrican.

Travelling by air, the visitor enters the Third Africa either at Salisbury airport in Rhodesia or Luanda, Angola. By ship it may be through Beira or Lourenco Marques in Mocambique, Luanda in Angola or Cape Town and Durban in South Africa.

Angola, Portugal's largest overseas province, contains a total area of 481,000 square miles, slightly bigger than the Republic of South Africa, but with a population of only 4.8 million people of whom 173,000 are White. It has a land border of over 3,000 miles and frontiers with the Congo (Leopoldville) in the north, Zambia to the east and South West Africa to the South.

Viewed from the Atlantic Ocean on the west coast, Angola embraces a narrow semi-arid coastal plain with broken terrain rising sharply eastward. In the north it rises direct into vast inland tablelands up to 5,000 feet in elevation. In the southern portion, a high plateau region separates this broken terrain from the tablelands.

Numerous rivers flow through the province; the Rio Dande, Rio Cuanza, the upper reaches of the mighty Zambezi, the magnificent Kunene River, the Rio Cuvo and others, but few are navigable owing to the precipitous nature of the terrain. On the other hand the river system offers excellent conditions for hydro-electric utilization, for example the 400 foot high Ruacana Falls on the Kunene River.

This is one of the sites which the South African and Portuguese Governments are now jointly developing into a huge hydro-electric project.

Angola's climate is generally very humid, particularly the coastal areas and the north. The interior tablelands, however, almost as far north as Malanje (on a latitude only ten degrees south of the equator) are temperate with little humidity and an average rainfall of from 50 to 60 inches. Here one finds excellent conditions for agricultural development and for human occupation, in fact, for an area so close to the equator the climate and environment is one of the best in Africa.

The most striking features of Angola are the great virgin forests, the waterfalls such as the Braganza, the Chela mountain ridge, the rolling plains of Cameia and its many white tropical beaches. The towns of Luanda, Lobito, Benguela and Mocamedes rank amoug the most beautiful towns on the West coast of Africa.

Much of the customs, dress and beliefs of simple Portuguese towns are to be found in many little villages in Angola, their colourfulness enriched by the more accentuated multiracialism.

Compared with other far more populous African states to the north with smaller land areas to serve and despite its great manpower shortage, Angola has built up a good road system of over 23,000 miles. The total railway network is about 2,000 miles of which the Luanda line and the Benguella railroad is the most important.

The latter connects the port of Lobito with the interior highland zone and with Katanga for whose materials it is the principal route to the outside world. From Elizabethville it continues on through Zambia via Lusaka and Livingstone to Wankie in Rhodesia. Luanda, Lobito and Mocamedes are the principal ports while Luanda is now served by international airlines flying from South Africa to Europe, from Leopoldville in the Congo and from Salisbury in Rhodesia and Lourenco Marques in Mocambique. The internal airlines, D.T.A.,[1] an agency of the government of Portugal, serve some twenty five towns in the interior, most of them on a scheduled basis. Communications by telephone, however, are still inadequate, made even more difficult by the unpretentious economic boom which the country is currently enjoying. Television has not yet made its appearance but there are some nineteen radio broadcasting stations in Angola of which eighteen are privately owned.

Luanda is the oldest town in Central Africa dating back to 1576.

This beautiful city with its crescent shaped bay and palm trees, its modern buildings and air of tradition seems almost out of place in Africa. It is also the only sizable town in Angola with a district population of over 500,000 or almost seven times that of the next important towns of Nova Lisboa and Lobito. It is the scene of frantic activities – extensions to the harbour, new roads, a twenty four storey skyscraper for the Commercial Bank of Angola and other buildings.

Flying into *Salisbury*, one is struck by the hustle and bustle and modernity of the Rhodesian capital. With a population of 327,000 it reminds one mostly of Pretoria, with its tree-shaded suburbs and the sudden upthrust of new buildings – even if on a much smaller scale. But to the four million people of Rhodesia, Salisbury is the Johannesburg of Rhodesia.

The country is extremely rocky, most of it granite which here and there has pierced the topsoil as balding mountains and smooth granite hills. It is a rugged country, arid and gaunt in the dry season but virile, green and beautiful when the rains come. About one-third the size of South Africa, it is bounded by Zambia to the

1. Divisae de Transportes Aêros.

North, Botswana to the West, Mocambique to the East and South Africa to the South and is thus surrounded by states of the Third Africa.

The natural vegetation is primarily treeveld varying from open grassland with scattered trees to almost closed forest. The high central plateau has an altitude of over 4,000 feet with a rainfall of 24 to 44 inches while the potentially rich lowveld has a rainfall of less than 20 inches. Along the eastern border is a high mountainous region of great beauty.

Before the White man came to this territory the Black man adjusted himself to the rhythm of nature. The White man set about bending it to his uses. Massive irrigation schemes conserve the abundant river flow of the rainy season. Kariba Dam in the North (damming the Zambezi below the Victoria Falls) has created the largest man made lake in the world. A chain of dams is now under construction in the South already carpeting thousands of acres of undeveloped lowveld in green. A new railway line has linked this new developing region with Lourenco Marques, the first branch line to be built in Rhodesia in thirty three years.

The development of this barren 30,000 square mile area, which is to Rhodesians what the lowveld is to South Africa or the Mid-West to Americans, has always been held back by lack of water. But the eight huge new dams now being built or already completed promise to change all this. The political significance is also tremendous. Caught up in a constitutional and economic struggle with Great Britain over the question of independence, the country desperately needs to become self-sufficient as soon as possible. The big lowveld project will bring new homes to thousands of people, opportunities for individual settlers, etc., but more important, it will send the country's production of citrus and sugar soaring, as it is already doing, earning precious foreign exchange. It is also destined to produce large quantities of meat, cotton, Burley and Turkish tobacco and even winter wheat and soybean.

In a continent crying out for food, the political bargaining power which the lowveld will hand to Rhodesia is not insignificant as is the economic value to Rhodesia itself. Furthermore this development is only part of the Sabi-Limpopo Irrigation project destined to represent 750,000 acres of irrigated land growing both summer and winter crops and capable of supporting an *additional* 1,500,000 people.

For its size and population, Rhodesia is second only to South Africa as the most developed region in all of sub-Saharan Africa. Its cities, Salisbury, Umtali, Bulawayo, Gwelo and Fort Victoria are clean, modern and attractive. Bulawayo has a population of over 236,000 with over 50,000 White people; Salisbury's population of 327,000 include about 90,000 White people. Umtali, only 184 miles by good road from Beira in Mocambique is the third largest city with a population nearing 50,000.

By African standards the road, rail and airways systems are excellent and reach to all parts of the country. Rhodesian railways operate 1,616 miles of route mileage while the road system includes some 5,000 miles of first class roads and 14,000 miles of secondary roads. Rhodesians enjoy television and the broadcasting system is modern and efficient. At the beginning of 1967 there were also some 100 periodicals including 30 newspapers (four dailies) which is exceptionally high for Africa – far more for instance than Morocco with a population three times that of Rhodesia or Ethiopia with a population five times that of Rhodesia.

If modern cities, planned housing projects for the lower economic classes, first class communications, a working telephone network, modern communications, roads, railways, newspapers, irrigation projects, schools, a wide variety of agricultural and industrial products, a postal service, a stock-exchange and a sound currency can be used as a yardstick, Rhodesia together with South Africa, are perhaps the only really "developed" countries in the Third Africa. Most of these facilities and services also exist in several other African states but as experienced travellers in Africa will wryly observe these facilities are not only in poor shape but operate rather erratically. In trying to telephone a number in the capital of a neighbouring country one often has to go via London.

Rhodesia is also one of the few states in Africa which is making a determined effort at wild life conservation. The fourteen National Game Parks and Game Reserves include the famous Wankie wild life sanctuary. This, too, in Africa, has become symbolic of a civilized community.

Together with Angola, *Zambia* is the most northern of territories in the sphere of the Third Africa. Outlined on maps in the shape of a butterfly, Zambia is a country of over 290,000 square miles. Great stretches of bushland interspersed with huge forests cover most of the region. Large inland lakes and numerous rivers give the land rich water resources while the Victoria Falls is on its southern border. The watershed of most of the mighty Zambezi river lies within Zambia. With the exception of the valleys of the Luangwa, the Kafue and lower Zambezi river, the whole of Zambia lies at an altitude of 3,000 to 4,000 feet above sea level. Because of this altitude most of the territory is suitable for human occupation. The rainy season extends all the way from November to April with an average fall of sixty inches in the North.

Zambia (formerly Northern Rhodesia) has Malawi (ex-Nyasaland) as its neighbour on the east with Rhodesia and Mocambique on the south and south-east. On the south-west, for only a few hundred yards, it touches the newly independent state of Botswana. On the north-west and north-east it has the Congo and Tanzania and in the west, Angola as its neighbour.

The few hundred yards at the northern end of South West Africa's Caprivi Strip provides militant Black Africa and the Communists with their only route to South Africa. Zambia has been loath so far to stop terrorist traffic across its soil while prior to independence the British in Botswana have looked the other way.

Twice as big as Rhodesia and six times as big as Malawi, Zambia is inhabited by only three and a half million people (1964).

The country has enormous potential but except for the rich copper belt with its scattering of towns, light industries, television, and cities like Kitwe and Ndola, it is poorly developed compared with either Rhodesia or South Africa. There is only one railroad which runs from Livingstone through the capital, Lusaka, to the Congo and then swings west to Angola and the Atlantic coast. The country has less than 3,800 miles of main or principal roads, only a small percentage of which are sealed, but is well served by the air services of Central African Airways. (Whether the services will remain as good, once the C.A.A. is divided up between Zambia, Malawi and Rhodesia, remains to be seen.) Its cities of Lusaka (population 75,000), Ndola (85,000) and Kitwe (92,000) are a mixture of modernity and shanty town and are the only towns well served by postal communications, telephone services and transport in the whole country.

In most other respects, Zambia has attained only half the stature of Rhodesia. It has less than half the number of trucks and automobiles; only one broadcasting studio, one third the number of present at all altitudes. This, however, is also true of Zambia and telephones and only five newspapers (compared with Rhodesia's thirty), only one which is printed as a daily. But it is in the general economic sphere and the administration of the country that Zambia sorely lags behind its former Central African Federation partner. This aspect is dealt with more comprehensively in Chapter 8.

Malawi (formerly Nyasaland), the third ex-member of the now dissolved Central African Federation, is only 36,686 miles square, smaller than the Orange Free State. Although it is six times smaller than neighbouring Zambia it has about half a million more inhabitants.

The country consists of a very narrow strip of land lying only on the west and south of Lake Nyasa. In some places it is only fifty miles wide. The whole territory lies within the tropics. For this reason roughly fifty per cent of the population lives on the Southern highlands where it is less humid. The most closely settled areas are the Shire Highlands in which the old capital, Blantyre and also the satellite town of Limbe is situated. The total population for the two places is only 45,000. A new capital is now being built at Lilongwe.

The landlocked territory is bordered on the north by Tanzania (Tanganyika-Zanzibar), by Zambia on the west and encircled by Portuguese Mocambique on the southern half. Except for about 200 miles, it is therefore geographically wholly within the Third Africa.

It has a strikingly varied topography. About twenty per cent of the land is covered with a great variety of forest comprising all the main vegetation types. In the high mountain areas are isolated patches of evergreen rain forests of cedars. On the floor of the Great Rift Valley, which runs north to south through the country, are fine groves of palms. Because it is such a beautiful country with breath-taking mountain scenery, the Malawians have high hopes that their new relationship with South Africa will lead to an influx of tourists from the Republic.

Compared with Rhodesia and even Zambia or Angola, Malawi is a classically undeveloped country. Water supplies are inadequate as is its telephone and postal service and communications. The dreaded tsetse fly is common in all the low lying areas while malaria is present at all altitudes. This, however, is also true of Zambia and parts of Rhodesia. In fact, of all of Africa the only country which has established a regular supply of pure water to all its towns and cities, and even the more populated rural areas, is South Africa. It is also the only one in which the tsetse fly and malaria have been virtually eradicated.

Communications in Malawi are particularly poor. The country has a mere five hundred miles of railroad which penetrate only about one third into the interior and about 2,800 miles of useable but unsealed road. Rhodesia alone has ten times as many motor vehicles and trucks and fifteen times as many telephones. Overseas air services to Malawi connect with Central African Airlines at Salisbury and Nairobi. There is also a weekly service via Dar-es-Salaam, while C.A.A. fly scheduled flights between Blantyre and Lilongwe, calling at half a dozen different towns.

In comparison with most other *Black* African states, however, Malawi shows up in a much better light. Its towns are modern in comparison, all parts of the country can be reached either by rail, bus, car or air; postal services operate as do the telephone networks. Economically it has a better future; it enjoys a stable currency and local administration is not in complete decay as in some African states. *The Nyasaland Times*, although only published twice weekly, appears on time – no mean feat in Black Africa.

South and east of Malawi lies the remaining Portuguese territory, *Mocambique*, which is also Portugal's second largest overseas province.

Stretching for over 1,430 miles along the south-eastern seaboard of Africa, it appears on the map to be virtually all length and little breadth. In fact its boundaries, which were finally drawn only after the 19th century "Scramble for Africa" tend to compress and expand the territory into a somewhat odd shape, although there are natural delineations. In contrast to the long coastline the relatively narrow hinterland varies in width from a mere thirty miles in the south to almost four hundred in the north. Malawi pokes a long finger of territory into the northern half of the province and the Zambesi virtually divides the total land area of 315,000 square miles into two equal halves. Most of the country's seven million people live in the southern half.

Unlike Angola, Portugal's other great overseas province in Africa, Mocambique has little topographical diversity. The whole territory is relatively flat and bush-covered. The land rises gradually from the coast to the hills and mountain ranges which form the natural frontier with Rhodesia in the west and around the area of Lake

Nyasa in the north. There are none of the dramatic escarpments, deserts and equatorial forests, which make Angola so full of scenic variety. Nevertheless, Mocambique has a charm and distinction of its own, and although many parts of the interior appear to lack interest, the long coastline with its palm-fringed white beaches and sweeping bays is of great beauty.

In the hinterland between the Limpopo and Zambezi river basins the land tends to be sandy bushland, which is unproductive on account of the low rainfall but which is well suited to cattle raising because of the quality grasses which grow there. South of the Limpopo River and stretching down as far as the Zululand border are the rich, fertile lands, which are highly suitable for agriculture and cattle raising. This is the area which to date has been the most heavily developed and populated.

Annual rainfall averages fifteen inches and is heaviest in the north, particularly in the tea-growing area near the Malawi border. Here, where the monotony of the landscape is broken by weird rock outcrops (some rising to over 8,000 feet) and blue-smudged mountain ranges, is potentially one of the most attractive areas for settlement and development. The climate is healthy and temperate and the open country with its rich soils is ideal for agriculture.

Unfortunately Mocambique (as in the case of virtually all countries of Africa, except Rhodesia and South Africa) suffers from lack of good communications.

A glance at the map of Mocambique shows that the problem of communications is basically one of linking a very extensive seaboard with a relatively narrow hinterland. From the first, therefore, development has been limited to the coastal ports giving direct access to the interior.

The length of the province's seaboard makes the question of harbours very important. Luckily nature has been very kind in this respect and there is a whole string of excellent deepwater harbours with good anchorages along the coast.

Of these the two most important are undoubtedly the ports of Lourenco Marques and Beira. The former is one of the best equipped and safest harbours in Africa and it serves as a natural if not vital outlet for the trade of South Africa, Rhodesia and Swaziland. A new seaport is now being planned at the mouth of the Zambezi. It involves dredging a five-mile canal, about 300 yards wide, through a giant sandbar, one of four which has closed the Zambezi delta from the Indian Ocean for centuries. The new seaport will form part of the long term Zambezi Valley Development Plan.

Mocambique's railway network forms an essential complement to its port installation and together they constitute one of the province's major economic assets to-day. There are six separate railway systems in operation, all running inland from the seaports. There is no north-south railway link as yet, although one is projected in the near future to run between Lourenco Marques and Beira.

Of these six systems, the one running up from Lourenco Marques to the Transvaal in South Africa is naturally the most important. Freight carried on this line in 1965 amounted to approximately 7,800,000 tons per year. It is run by the Mocambique Transport Commission in close co-operation with South African Railways.

The railway, which runs inland from the port of Beira, provides an important link with Rhodesia and carries some three million tons of freight annually to and from this part of Africa. As a result of Britain's economic war against Rhodesia, this has become a veritable life-line for the people of Rhodesia.

Roads in Mocambique have a total length of 25,000 miles although only some 3,000 miles of these can be considered first class (1,900 miles asphalted). Portugal is, however, now developing its communications in Mocambique under a crash programme that has tremendous economic and tactical significance, not only to the Portuguese, but also to South Africa and Rhodesia. The newest link in an intensive study of road, air and bridge problems in Mocambique will be a bridge over the Zambezi River at Ville Fontes. The bridge, which will cost two million Rand ($2,800,000), will be two miles long and thirty feet wide with a double traffic lane. It is scheduled for completion in about two years.

This bridge and roads leading from it will not only open up the whole of northern and north-eastern Mocambique to all-weather road traffic, but will be sealed to provide all-weather communications between Lourenco Marques in the south and the provinces of Zambesia and Niassa in the north. It will not only mean that the rich tea, coffee and sugar-bearing hinterland is linked with Beira, but will also expedite the movement of security forces if they are needed.

Because of the size of the province, air communications play an important part in Mocambique. There are three major airports and twelve smaller ones. A government-owned airline (DETA) runs regular services to all the important centres in the province as well as to Zambia, Rhodesia and South Africa.

With the exception of Dar-es-Salaam in Tanzania, and the east coast cities of South Africa, Lourenco Marques (population 200,000) and Beira (population 70,000) are the two most modern cities on the entire 7,000 mile east coast of Africa. Lourenco Marques is a particularly beautiful city with garden suburbs and modern office buildings. Like Cape Town, it is a truly European orientated city in spite of its multi-racial population of Chinese, Arabs, Indians and Bantu.

In general, Mocambique lags behind Rhodesia and South Africa in development and as a modern state. For the size of its population the country is indeed just on the threshold of development. Nonetheless, in most respects it outstrips the majority of countries in Arab or Black Africa.

Of all the countries in the Third Africa, except Botswana, the most difficult terrain and the most hostile elements are to be found in *South West Africa.*

Bounded on the north by Angola, on the east by Botswana and on the east and south by South Africa, this huge territory of over 317,000 square miles has one of the most inhospitable environments one can imagine. For the most part it is desolate. Here every hour of every day, man has to pit his ingenuity against nature – his principal enemy being lack of water, lack of rain, of rivers and even of underground water. The rainfall is the lowest in Africa, south of the Sahara.

The forbidding Namib desert, eighty miles wide, edges the western coast; the huge Kalahari Desert, home of the Bushmen, slices into the eastern section. In the flat featureless terrain in the north, tribes still navigate by stars over the waterless plains. In the centre is a broken highland sandwiched between the Namib and Kalahari deserts.

From the Kunene River in the north, where it abuts the Portuguese overseas province of Angola, the territory runs some 900 miles down the coast of the South Atlantic where the Orange River separates it from the Cape Province of South Africa. Its average width is 350 miles, but no physical features mark its eastern border.

The border consists of two of the longest fences in the world, some 800 miles in all, cutting through the Kalahari desert, dividing it from South Africa and newly independent Botswana – formerly Bechuanaland.[2]

For many years people referred to the territory as "the Nameless Land" for this remote place does not have a name – only a rather cumbersome geographical designation – South West Africa. Outside South West Africa, even in South Africa, its big and prosperous neighbour, people know or care little about this deeply fascinating and, despite its generally cruel exterior, hauntingly beautiful land. In fact, most people know as little of this territory, which has often been the subject of discussions in the General Assembly of the United Nations and mentioned in connection with a threat to world peace, as they do of the surface of the Moon.

On closer examination there appear to be all the reasons in the world for politicians, botanists, students of archeology, historians, ethnologists, economists and even the man in the street to find South West Africa a most fascinating subject for discussion or study.[3]

Unlike the myth which has grown up at the United Nations, South West Africa is not a rich country and is, therefore, not being coveted by South Africa for its wealth. For many decades it was thought utterly unlikely that the territory could yield anything of use to mankind. The very face of the territory contributed to this belief. It is harsh and forbidding, bleak and hostile. Vast expanses of desert and blasted rock hills, scrub-bush country and desolate plains unroll below the wings of the plane flying to Windhoek from Cape Town. Here and there endless sand dunes stretch in parallel lines for miles on end with only a few thorn trees and melon like creepers to be seen. Other areas resemble a cosmic strip mining operation with fissures and canyons gouged out of the earth. Along the coast giant dunes are cloaked in fog and frequently torn by fierce and blinding sand storms. Inland there are ranges of barren hostile mountains devoid of any tree cover or vegetation and extinct volcanoes. One, a non-active gas volcano, the Geitsigubib as it is called by the Nama people, was used by America's Smithsonian

2. Because the maps of mid-1966 do not indicate the state as *Botswana*, map references elsewhere in this book are still given as *Bechuanaland*.

3. Cf. Rhoodie, E.M.: *South West: The Last Frontier in Africa*, Voortrekkerpers, Johannesburg, 1967.

Institute as a heliometric station for many years until shortly before World War II.

The big rivers in the North lie on the boundaries of the territory and while there are some grassy plains to be found as well as hidden valleys and gorges where fountains of water flow from the earth, the fact remains that the area is geo-physically poor and arid. Except for the boundary rivers, the Orange, Kunene and Okavango, there is not a single flowing river in an area not much smaller than South Africa.

Under the generally appalling surface, much of which enjoys a rainfall of less than two inches a year and sometimes none at all for several years, does lie some wealth. Like the Sahara Desert now giving up its hidden treasure of oil, the desolate and waterless plains of South West Africa also contains deposits of minerals, but it is exceedingly difficult to develop because of the inhospitable climate, the lack of water and the vast distances from railheads and ocean ports.

The Caprivi Strip which juts out from the north-east corner of South West Africa to within a few hundred yards of Rhodesia, was named after Count Caprivi, the German Chancellor who obtained its secession from Great Britain in 1893 on the grounds that German South West Africa needed an outlet to the Zambezi River. However, direct access from South West Africa is barred by trackless desert and two large rivers. Owing to the resultant difficulty in control, direct administration of the territory was taken over by South Africa at the outbreak of World War II.

Walvis Bay, the only real harbour of the territory, embraces 434 square miles, but although it is administered by South West Africa, it has constitutionally and lawfully been part of the Cape Province for almost a century, long before South West Africa became a German colony. The significance of this fact is that an independent South West Africa under United Nations supervision, would have no outlet to the rest of the world except through Portuguese or South African territory.

The three ex-British protectorates within the Third Africa, *Lesotho, Botswana and Swaziland*, have widely divergent topography and living conditions.

Within an area of only 11,716 square miles of mountainous territory, *Lesotho* (Basutoland), has often been called "the Switzerland of South Africa", and indeed, during many past winters, the mountains have been covered under feet of snow for as long as five months. (In sharp contrast, Botswana is flat, featureless and dry.) The western region is a continuation of the high plateau in the Orange Free State province of South Africa and has an average altitude of over 5,000 feet. The eastern part of Lesotho is exceedingly mountainous and consists of the Maluti Mountains with peaks rising to over 11,000 feet. The mountains of Lesotho form the chief watershed of Southern Africa.

Taking into consideration the small habitable area, Lesotho (population 976,000) is the most thickly populated territory in the Third Africa and every square mile of arable land is under cultivation. However, even by low African standards Lesotho is physically an "undeveloped" state, not only because of its lack of economic development but its general backwardness. The British record in aiding Lesotho to build up the semblance of an economy is one which the British would like to forget as soon as possible. Lesotho has only one mile of railway line connecting Maseru, the capital, with South Africa – and this line is run by South African Railways. The country has only some 1,000 telephones (less than an average skyscraper in New York City) and about 560 miles of second grade roads, mostly along the western border with exits to South African towns. More than ninety per cent of the interior is inaccessible to automobile traffic and can only be reached via bridle paths, by trucks with four wheel drive and light aircraft using improvised strips of bare earth as runways. Its capital, Maseru, has less than six thousand people with one newspaper – published weekly.

Lesotho, which is entirely surrounded by South African territory, achieved sovereign independence from Britain during October, 1966, which is somewhat like having a sovereign French speaking state complete with its own army, secret service and Ambassador in Washington, right in the heartland of America.

Botswana, the biggest of the former protectorates, is over 220,000 square miles in area (about the size of Natal, Transvaal and the Orange Free State combined), yet it has a population of only 576,000 or some 2.5 people to the square mile. With the exception of a few hundred yards where it joins Zambia at the north-east corner of the Caprivi Strip, it is surrounded entirely by South West

Africa on the west, South Africa on the south and east and Rhodesia in the north-east.

It is a dust-swept land of poverty and thirst. Most of the territory is bone dry except for the north-western part which is served by the Okavango River. Even in this river, which carries a great volume of water, the water evaporates so rapidly that it is called "the vanishing river". Immense quantities flow into the vast Okavango swamps north-west of Francistown, a 6,500 square mile inland delta with a fantastic irrigation potential. Severe malaria is prevalent particularly after the brief but heavy rains during December to April.

The eastern part of the state is hilly. The western portion is more undulating, largely sandy and waterless but with stretches of grass, trees and bush with many traces of old river courses. Despite the apparent waterless state of affairs the major part of the country abounds in game of almost every known species, particularly the north-eastern corner adjoining the Wankie Game Reserve in Rhodesia. With the deterioration of game in other major areas of Africa, notably East Africa, Botswana has already attracted a large number of safari firms and many believe that this north-east corner has the world's biggest concentration of plains game.

As in the case of Lesotho it is in almost every respect a hopelessly undeveloped region.

There is one major through road from south to north with branch-roads running about fifty miles in either direction before petering out into desert country and bushland. The only railroad is the Cape Town-Rhodesia run which traverses the country for 394 miles along its eastern frontier and is operated by Rhodesian Railways.

The principal "towns" are Francistown, Serowe, Lobatsi, Gaberones (the new capital), Molepolole and Kanye but they are little more than villages. Lobatsi has a population of 25,000 but the other towns all have a population of less than 10,000. For many years Botswana was simply referred to as "bushland" and even the capital was located not in Botswana but in Mafeking, South Africa. In 1964, the new government began moving its affairs to Gaberones and since then frantic building activities before independence have given the town some semblance of a national capital.

Of the former protectorates, *Swaziland* has the least hostile environment for human occupation.

Bounded on the north-west and south by South African territory and on the east by Mocambique, the 6,704 square mile country consists of towering green hills, fertile valleys and plains with an ideal climate except for a few warm months in summer. While bilharzia and enteric fever are widespread in the territory, malaria has been almost entirely eradicated.

The territory has three physiographic provinces running north and south in roughly equal breadth. On the west the land rises to altitudes of over 6,000 feet; the middle region has an average altitude of only 2,500 feet while the lowveld is some 1,000 lower. The lowveld is bounded east by the Lebombo Mountains and is the only area not well watered. It is also covered in bush, mostly hardwoods, while gums, wattles and pine thrive in huge forests in the western and north-western areas. There are numerous small rivers and streams in the territory.

For a country with a population of only 390,000 in a relatively undeveloped state, communications, though far from being adequate, are much more satisfactory than in more populous Lesotho, Botswana and several other African states.

There is some 204 miles of trunk highway, most of it sealed, and an additional 900 miles of main and district roads. Telephone and telegraph connections are in operation between the principal towns and villages, Mbabane (capital), Manzini, Piggs Peak, Emcembe, Stegi and others. A railway link from the vast iron ore deposits at Ngwenya near Mbabane to Lourenco Marques was completed in 1964, giving the landlocked territory a short rail outlet to the sea – something which many Black African states do not enjoy. A tar-sealed runway near Manzini can take twin engined aircraft and from here charter flights operate to and from Johannesburg and Durban.

Swaziland's future appears to be bright, for the small, thinly populated country not only has a friendly environment and diversified resources, but some large scale industries. This could mean a well-balanced economic development programme which so many other African states seek but are unable to achieve because of the absence of one or both of these elements.

In terms of physical environment, geography, rainfall, climate and in the essential field of communications the territories of the Third Africa, excepting South West Africa, Lesotho and Botswana, are therefore well off compared with other newly independent African states.[4] In addition, if some standard of "development" *based on a truly African yardstick* could be agreed upon, all of the territories in the Third Africa except Malawi, Botswana and Lesotho, would fall into the category of "developed" states in Africa.

In terms of health services, social welfare, education, per capita income, communications, not to mention agricultural development, irrigation projects and economic development, the average Black man in these states is notably better off than his counterpart in the thirty other states such as Ethiopia, Mauritania, Upper Volta, Niger, Togo, Mali, Dahomey, Gabon, Chad and others. In fact *only* Egypt, Tunisia, Algeria, Morocco and the Ivory Coast would also qualify as "developed" *African* states.

The outstanding country in the Third Africa both in terms of its environment, its location and general development, is the *Republic of South Africa* – listed by the United Nations as the only "developed" country in Africa and one of only twenty-six developed nations among the 132 principal countries of the world.

South Africa is perhaps forty years ahead of the next African state in overall development while its economic and industrial development, communications and capital structure overshadows that of the rest of the Third Africa combined. Since the South African economy in relation to *The Third Africa* will be more fully discussed in Chapter 4, some brief comparisons with the rest of the African continent and Europe would give the best indication of the Republic's position of pre-eminence in Africa.

With only six per cent of Africa's population, South Africa generates almost thirty per cent of the continent's total geographic income; the per capita income of all South Africa's people (Bantu, White, Coloured and Indian) averages about 4.5 times higher than the average for Africa. In the case of many other African states such as Ethiopia, Chad, Dahomey, Niger, Upper Volta, the Central African Republic and Somaliland, it is between *ten* and *twenty* times higher.[5] South Africa's mineral production represents forty-three per cent of the entire African continent; she also generates and

4. The economic development, mineral riches and other resources and systems of government are discussed in Chapter 9.

5. Source: Africa Report, Africa-America Institute, Washington, September, 1963.

produces twice as much electricity and six times as much steel as the rest of Africa combined. The Republic's communications system is the most modern and comprehensive in Africa; nearly fifty per cent of all Africa's automobiles, buses, tractors, trucks and telephones are in South Africa; the A.M. and F.M. network of Radio South Africa is comparable to that of France and broadcasts in nine different languages. Per capita use of electricity is on a par with that of Western Europe; per capita expenditure on social services is six times more than the next highest in Africa; there is one doctor for every 1,800 people while in Africa's largest and most populous state (Nigeria) it is one for every 50,000 and in the oldest independent African state (Ethiopia) it is one for every 105,000 people.[6]

This phenomenal development has been achieved despite the country's disastrous population loss in the Anglo-Boer War (ten per cent of the total population of the Transvaal and Orange Free State) and loss of manpower in World Wars I and II.

It has never asked for nor received a cent in foreign aid from any country at any time, while it is still one of only three countries in the world which have repaid their war debts to the United States in full.

South Africa is the southernmost country in Africa, bounded on the north by South West Africa, Botswana, Rhodesia and Mocambique. It lies almost wholly within the South Temperate Zone. South, east and west and for most of its surface it is bounded by the Atlantic and Indian Oceans which meet at Cape Agulhas, the southernmost point of Africa.

In area it is 472,000 square miles – five times the size of Britain and larger than Germany, France, Italy and Portugal put together – but it has a total population of 18,000,000 people as against England's 46,000,000 and a combined total of 158,000,000 in the four European countries mentioned above.

The topography of the country, the invigorating climate and the relatively large population for Africa, have contributed in no mean way to the country's overall development. Only Ethiopia, Nigeria and the United Arab Republic has a bigger population.

By the end of this century South Africa will probably have some forty-two million souls.

In at least a few important aspects, namely communications, city

6. Cf. *South Africa – A History of Great Achievements*, Trust Bank, Cape Town, 1967.

and suburban life and industrial and economic development, South Africa strikes the visitor as being generally no less developed and modern than say Canada, Britain, France or West Germany.

South Africa's ten principal cities all have a population in excess of 150,000 people and if the top three (Durban, Cape Town and Johannesburg) were transplanted to the United States, they would rank among the first fifteen cities in terms of population. There are also at least another dozen cities and towns with populations between 50,000 and 150,000.

But there is more to these cities than the size of their population; it is the modernity of construction, the skyscrapers, city layout, planned growth, sophisticated municipal government, modern amenities, well-stocked shops and dual carriage highways, including freeways, which strike the eye.

The visitor who knows Africa will find the massive complex of the Council for Scientific and Industrial Research outside Pretoria, the country's eleven universities, the nuclear reactor at Pelindaba outside Pretoria, the three satellite tracking stations (two American, one French), observatories in half a dozen cities and the huge hospitals[7] particularly impressive. These projects and such commonly expected services (by United States standards) as direct dialing for long distance, weather forecasting and daily newspapers in virtually every town of any consequence is tangible evidence of the decades by which South Africa has outstripped the rest of the continent, in fact, outstripped all but some twenty-five other countries of the world.

There are some one hundred and fifty-one daily, weekly and Sunday newspapers in South Africa, nineteen news magazines and periodicals and some three hundred and eighty journals of educational, professional, legal, religious, scientific, medical, technical, industrial or financial character plus an additional forty periodicals catering for sports and hobbies.

The grand total of five hundred and ninety publications exceeds that of the rest of the African continent put together.[8]

The most astounding aspect of South Africa's development is the fact that virtually all of this was achieved during the past sixty years

---

7. Baragwanath just outside Johannesburg is the biggest specialist hospital in the world.

8. Cf. *Blue Book of Advertising in South Africa*, P. N. Barrett Co., Johannesburg, 1967.

(the Union of South Africa was only established in 1910) and largely through the sweat, endeavour and know-how of a little over three million White people. There is no denying the contribution of Black labour to this development but it has always been a guided contribution. The Black man in South Africa has, so far, been shy of creative achievements, and not because of lack of opportunity. Considering that the vast majority lived in the iron age only half a century ago, this is understandable.

Historically speaking South Africa is only a child compared with Europe but the lusty infant has in some respects already surpassed older countries in Europe with much bigger populations.

In South Africa the land has been thoroughly tamed; it has been occupied, cleared and developed. By every standard it is a modern industrialized and civilized community – the only one in Africa. It will probably be another twenty to thirty years before even Egypt with its twenty-six million people and massive doses of foreign aid, will reach a similar stage of development.

In terms of its topography and environment, the Third Africa (except South Africa) is more hostile to human occupation than most of Europe, less well endowed with navigable rivers, rich soil or a sufficient rainfall – yet it is better suited for human occupancy than any other area in Africa and it is sparsely populated, with room for millions more people. Compared with Europe, Asia and Latin America, this is an asset of tremendous importance.

5. Mosaic of History and Culture

If in its physical characteristics the face of the Third Africa does not generally resemble that of Europe, Asia or America, its history reveals the far reaching influences of Europe, particularly Britain, Portugal, France, Holland and Germany. At the same time the parallels with North and South America are striking.

In terms of early history, it is remarkably similar to that of the New World but completely different in respect of historical developments with a direct bearing on current political affairs.

A knowledge of the history of the various states in the Third Africa is imperative for an appreciation of to-day's socio-political problems, for nowhere in Africa, or in the world, does the dead hand of the past weigh so heavily on the shoulders of those trying to sort out and plan its political future.

The history of the industrial revolution in Britain has little bearing on Tory-Labour differences or on Britain's present world status. The American Civil War, even its War of Independence, has little direct bearing on its present racial problems or its position as leader of the West. In South Africa, however, history still plays a role. The settlement of the country by Black and White three centuries ago, both late comers with none having a prior claim to the country except in those areas which each settled by right of first occupation, is still of utmost importance. The Boer War and its aftermaths, the division of British South Africa into Black states and a White controlled Union of South Africa, *all* have a direct bearing on current racial and political problems and the country's "image" abroad.

The same is true in the case of Rhodesia. It is certainly true in the case of Angola and Mocambique. Five hundred years of history as part of the Portuguese nation cannot be ignored in Portugal's present struggle to maintain those provinces as an integral part of its national life.

Similarly, to judge the political situation in South West Africa

89

without knowing the history of the territory, particularly its conquest in 1914 by South African troops and its subsequent status as a mandated territory, is an impossible task. Nor can South Africa's separate development programme which aims, *inter alia*, at restoring to the Bantu people self-government in their respective homelands (the situation which existed prior to the heyday of British imperialism) be appreciated without a perspective of its history.

The fundamental geo-political factors indicate that in most areas the Third Africa is a *multi-racial* community living within largely artificially created boundaries. In the case of the Republic of South Africa the multi-racialism is superceded by its *multi-national* character.

The comparisons with Europe or Africa as well as the seemingly irrelevant detail of environment, history, population diversity, etc., presented here and in other chapters, will assume far greater significance in that chapter dealing with the political future of the Third Africa. If this amount of background seems nonetheless superfluous to some readers, it should be remembered that without a detailed background of the historical-ethnological patterns in Africa, the present geo-political problems will defy the most astute and discerning observer.

The reluctance of the university student, government official or journalist to delve into Africa's past or its topography, ethnological diversity and backwardness compared with the United States or Europe, is perhaps one of the main reasons why there is such gross misunderstanding and often hostile attitudes expressed in respect of all three Africas.[1]

The history of European contact with South Africa (Angola, Mocambique and South Africa) is as long as that with America – just under 500 years. Five years before Columbus undertook his voyage across the Atlantic, which led to the discovery of the new world, the

1. The survey of the history of Southern Africa and its cultural development in this chapter is based largely on the following works: G. P. Murdoch, *Africa; Its History and Peoples*, McGraw Hill Book Co., New York; Eric Walker, *A History of Africa South of the Sahara*, Longmans, London, 1964; Lord Hailey's *African Survey*, Oxford University Press, 1957; I. Schapera, *The Bantu Speaking Tribes of South Africa*, Maskew Miller, Cape Town, 1962; James Duffy, *Portuguese Africa*, Harvard University Press, 1959; Van der Walt, Wiid & Geyer, *Geskiedenis van Suid-Afrika*, Maskew Miller, Cape Town; F. Skeen, *Prelude to Independence*, Van Schaiks, Pretoria, 1966 and other works.

Portuguese navigator, Bartholomew Diaz sailed southwards round the unknown tip of Africa with a similar objective – to bring the rich merchandise of India, China and the East to Europe by a quicker and more direct route.

Diaz sailed from Portugal in 1487 and returned with the news that it was possible, after rounding the southernmost point of Africa, to return northward again and reach the Indian Ocean. Ten years later another Portuguese, Vasco da Gama, achieved what men had hoped for – the return trip from Europe to India by sea. The Portuguese were soon rivalled by the French, British and Dutch. Before the 16th century had drawn to a close, there was a regular and highly profitable traffic around Africa in spices, silk and other Eastern produce.

The first Portuguese settlers arrived in Angola in 1491 and Luanda, the capital, was founded in 1575. The other Portuguese province, Mocambique, was discovered by Vasco da Gama's fleet on the first day of March 1498 and the first houses were built near the port of Beira and Lourenco Marques in 1505.

Thus the Portuguese were living in Africa for nearly a century before the first settlements of North America – the colonies of Virginia in 1608 and Plymouth in 1620.

Da Gama's ships threw anchor off the coast of Mocambique more than a year before Amerigo Vespucci reached the mainland of Central America.

The Portuguese had been living in Africa for a score of years before Cortez began the conquest of Mexico and only thirty years after the fall of Constantinople and the ending of the Eastern Roman Empire.

The man who truly laid the foundation for Portugal's huge overseas provinces was Prince Henry, whose genius lay in an insight into the significance of the emerging science of long-range sea navigation as an instrument of statecraft. His policies were pressed forward by succeeding Portuguese kings and between them they nourished the vision of a Greater Portugal. The Portuguese who settled in Angola and Mocambique a century before the settlers went to America, did not live there as traders but as colonists. The Portuguese kings did not think of the sea as a body of water separating men but as a road that unites them. A demonstration of this fact can be found in the very extraordinary maritime history of Portugal.

It is, therefore, evident that the Portuguese concept of a common nationhood, shared by the people of the overseas provinces and metropolitan Portugal alike, and the status of their lands as overseas provinces, is not an expedient political slogan of the moment developed because of the pressure of "world opinion" to "liberate" its provinces. This concept was developed over a period of five centuries starting with the Age of Discoveries and it has lost none of its validity.

It is in South Africa, however, that the historic parallel with the United States of America is most fascinating and striking.

After the Portuguese rounded the southern tip of Africa, the Cape of Good Hope had been considered merely as a landmark showing that half the distance to India had been covered. Before long, however, it assumed a more important character – that of a refreshment station where crews went ashore for fresh water and to gather vegetables to cure scurvy. No attempts at settlement were made for a century although in 1620, when the Pilgrim Fathers sailed to the new world, two British sea captains formally "annexed" the Cape.

As shipwrecked sailors told of their success in raising crops in this area, the Dutch East India Company began to make plans for using the Cape as a permanent victualling station. In 1652, Jan van Riebeeck arrived with a fleet of three ships and the history of a White nation in Africa began.

Many of the settlers of North America were English Puritans and in only a few points did their theological doctrines and stern habits of life diverge from those of the Calvinist Dutchmen who settled the Cape. People from the Netherlands followed in the footsteps of the new world Puritans and soon little Dutch settlements dotted the countryside of New York, New Jersey and Delaware. This was about the same time the Dutch in Africa began to move inland from their victualling station and settled the lovely valleys of the Cape. French Huguenots migrated to the Cape just as they followed, although in much larger numbers, the English and Dutch settlers to North America. And scattered through both the South African and North American colonies were a considerable percentage of Germans, adding to the European origins of both populations.

New Amsterdam from which the city of New York grew, and the settlement at the Cape, were founded in the same period of colonization, the former by the Dutch West India Company and the latter by the Dutch East India Company. The original forts were similar in layout as was the layout of the two towns. In each, the principal street was the Heerengracht. New York had its Wall Street, the Cape its Wale Street.

Intermarriage inevitably followed among the settlers. In North America the fusion slowly led to the emergence of a new American nation with one language. In South Africa a new nation also emerged but two languages survived.

There is one difference which has historical and political significance of the utmost importance to-day.

In North America the settlers immediately clashed with the permanent indigenous people resulting in the massacre of the Red Indians, the original inhabitants of the country. Thus the American settlers became in modern political terms, "conquerors", "late comers", "colonists" or whatever term is used to indicate that the land was forcibly taken from an already indigenous population. *In South Africa this was not the case.* It was more than a century later and over 600 miles inland that the White men first met the vanguard of the Black nations migrating in wave upon wave of internecine warfare from the Great Lakes area, southwards.

By co-incidence the American War of Independence began in the same year the first boundary between Black and White was declared in South Africa, namely that on the east coast. Hereafter followed years of frontier war between an already established White society and that of the Xhosa, one of the many Bantu nations.

In the modern Black-White relationship in South Africa this history is of vital importance and forms the basis of the White man's claim to his part of South Africa.

In one other important aspect do the histories differ. The settlers in America, particularly after the importation of Black slaves, made strenuous attempts, still continued to-day, to *force* upon the Red Indians and the West African Negro an alien European civilization. In South Africa this never occurred and Bantu languages, customs, traditions and way of life, even in modernity, remain largely different from that of the White nation and respected as such. The Bantu also still largely own the land they had occupied at the time of contact with the White man, whereas the Indians lost all but the desert. The Negro slave lost all his cultural heritage – language, customs and ideals.

93

As the European populations in Africa and America grew, political and economic causes led to a natural spirit of frontier restlessness in what seemed a wild and limitless land. The result was epic migrations in both continents. In America the covered wagons went westward. In South Africa the covered wagons pushed eastward and northward.

Politically both regions felt the impact and pressure of the endless European wars of the 18th century and the struggle of European empires for mastery over the newly populated overseas areas. In America the result was the important and concerted national reaction against the colonial dominance of Britain. This led to the formation of the United States of America. In South Africa there were abortive attempts to break away from the rule of the Dutch East India Company and when the British occupied the Cape the White farmers and frontiersmen soon thereafter packed their wagons and began the epic Great Trek.

Pressing northwards the pioneers opened up the largely uninhabited central highlands and plains bringing civilization and the rule of law to a continent that had known the wheel only along its Mediterranean littoral. The two Boer republics of the Transvaal and Orange Free State were firmly established in the north when British imperialism again showed its hand. Britain and the two republics clashed in the Anglo-Boer War of 1899-1902. The two men who epitomized the struggle were Cecil John Rhodes, who dreamed of an Africa "painted Red (British) from the Cape to Cairo" and the Boer President Paul Kruger, who stood for the independence and self-determination of his small nation.

The Boers fought for their independence in a bitter war that saw more Boer women and children perish in British concentration camps, proportionately, than Jewish people killed in the German concentration camps in World War II.

After the unequal struggle in which the British Empire, then at its mightiest, put more troops in the field than there were Boer men, women and children, the Boers lost their freedom. However, they won the distinction, although little appreciated then, of becoming the first African nationalists who fought for their freedom by force of arms.

In the interior and at the Cape, the amalgam of Dutchmen, French, German and English gave birth to a new nation, a White

African nation – the first time a White nation had established itself on the African continent. *This occurred, moreover, in territory unoccupied by an indigenous Black people.* Then followed a linguistic wonder, the birth of Afrikaans, the language of the majority of the people of this new White African nation. An Indo-Germanic language it is spoken by White men of European descent in South Africa but nowhere else in Africa or Europe: It became symbolic of the extent of the White man's roots in Africa.

The Americans had won their battle of independence, the Boers lost theirs and from there on their histories also lost resemblance, except in the economic sphere.

Up to that time and for a while afterwards, the American influence in South African history is one little known to people in South Africa, yet some of their most famous citizens have walked on South African soil. The very spirit of the new world was reflected in early South Africa. In view of the leading role which America is now playing at the United Nations to discredit White society in South Africa, American influence in early South African history is of more than just passing interest.

The American War of Independence (1776-1783) had its repercussions, direct and indirect, at the Cape of Good Hope. The American struggle for freedom was a cause of jubilation on the part of the opposition Patriot Party in Holland, and from 1778 onwards its ideas were transmitted to the Cape, imbuing townsmen and the dwellers in the outlying districts with those ideas of political freedom and personal liberty then being turned into reality in America.

As early as 1780 a Dutch advocate could write to the mayor of Rotterdam: "In accordance with my promise I am forwarding to your honour a copy of the rebellious paper which has been circulated among the burghers (free farmers) of the Cape and to which in the first instance I attribute the unrest which has lately taken place there. Your honour will find that they are inspired by an American spirit."

Then five years later, when the Cape burgher spokesmen appeared before the Government in Holland, they invoked the American example and dwelt on how the North American Congress had been created as the instrument of liberty.

At the close of what is called the "Cape Burgher Movement of 1779-1786", the burgher representatives were using the American

Revolution as "a living example of the way in which free colonists, tired of endless oppressions and having poured out in the lap of their sovereign their righteous and reasonable grievances", had decided to achieve their liberty. "We ask", they said, "in what respect does this picture (of the English Americans) differ from the Dutch Cape Colonist?"

Implied recognition of the United States of America as a sovereign nation is seen in the formal resolution of the Cape Council of Policy, on 13 April, 1784, to admit the Boston craft *Harriot*, "just as those of all other states and powers with whom our Republic lives in peace and friendship".

From roughly 1820 onwards American ships were bartering with the Zulus along the East coast of South Africa. One of the pioneers, Nathaniel Isaacs, became friendly with many of the American skippers and suggested that the United States declare the area a sphere of American influence. In 1835 American missionaries began their labours in Natal, and before long the inhabitants of the Cape actually became alarmed at the intensity of American activities in Natal. They were, however, reassured by the United States consul, Isaac Chase, who said at a public meeting in Cape Town in 1847: "You may quiet your fears about the American Government's desire to have anything to do with Port Natal. The Government of America has no ambition to possess territories abroad."

The American mission to the Zulus took its printing press from place to place and it was probably the first press to be used in the interior of South Africa. By 1883, the entire Bible had been translated into Zulu by the American Bible Society. Mormon missionaries arrived at the Cape in the middle of the 19th century. They made converts, and nearly a hundred men, women and children sailed from Table Bay in 1852 to join Brigham Young's settlement in Utah.

Most South Africans sympathized with the Southern Confederates during the American Civil War. On August 5, 1863, Cape Town forgot about its lunch when the greatest raider of the war, the Confederate *Alabama*, sailed into Table Bay and captured the Federal merchantman *Sea Bride*, which had entered the Cape road shortly before.[2] Crowds gathered to watch and, as the excitement mounted, the Coloured people began a spontaneous chant:

2. During these raids in the neighbourhood of the Cape of Good Hope, Captain Richard Semmes of the *Alabama* captured no fewer than fourteen northern vessels.

"Daar kom die Alabama, die Alabama
Daar vêr oor die see . . ."

The catchy song and tune has never been forgotten and to-day it is still a rollicking number at Coloured and Malay picnics.

Americans were much to the fore in the turbulent period of South African history that marked the last quarter of the 19th century. "Nowhere on this continent", it has been said, "has the American been more in evidence than in the opening up of those gigantic deposits of diamonds and gold which have become synonymous with the name of South Africa."

A striking visual sign of the American influence in opening up South Africa at this period, was the American stage coach. At first second-hand coaches, and then new coaches, were imported almost exclusively from the firm of Abbot-Downing in Concord, New Hampshire. Having proved their worth in the American West, they preceded the railways to Kimberley, Barberton, the gold fields of the Witwatersrand, and were even used to get to Rhodesia.

Of the personalities on the diamond fields, one of the most picturesque in the early days was the American Stafford Parker, a "forty-niner" who for a few exciting months was the "president" of a "diggers republic".

When Cecil Rhodes amalgamated the various diamond interests in one great company called De Beers Consolidated Mines, he chose as his general manager, Gardner F. Williams of Michigan, a man of vast and varied experience in mining.

Americans in increasing numbers quested for gold in the Tati fields and Mashonaland, as well as in the Transvaal at Lydenburg, Pilgrim's Rest, and Barberton. An American, E. Woodford, was appointed the first Government Mining Engineer of the Boer Republic of the Transvaal. The mere catalogue of the names of these American engineers would fill pages. Johannesburg's finest technical library was endowed in honour of one of them who gave his life for Britain in the Anglo-Boer War, Louis Seymour. The world's largest single gold property, the Crown Mines, was laid out by another, Ruel C. Warriner.

In 1904, Herbert Hoover, later President of the United States of America, visited South Africa and did experimental work for John Ballot, a South African of Scottish descent, who made his fortune with methods of extracting copper from lowgrade ores.

At the outbreak of the Anglo-Boer War, American public sympathy, led by the Irish, was largely on the side of the Boers. About 3,000 Irish-Americans left for South Africa to fight with the Boer forces, joining the Irish Brigade. The Irish Brigade fought in two sections, one commanded by Arthur Lunch and the other by J. Y. Filmore Blake. A photograph is extant showing President Kruger in top hat before his Pretoria home, wishing god-speed to the Chicago Irish-American volunteers, a body of some forty men commanded by Captain O'Connor of the Clan-na-Gael Guards.

Operating separately from the two sections of the Irish Brigade were the American Scouts under Captain John Hassell. Hassell lived in Vryheid, Natal, but was a native of New Jersey. His scouts, some fifty American volunteers, helped cover the Boer retreat in the Orange Free State in 1900. Among them were Texan cowboys and several journalists who, as they put it, "had come to write but had stayed to fight".

At home in the United States, prominent among champions of the Boers were Andrew Carnegie, General James Obeirne, and some Dutch Americans such as George van Siclen and C. van der Hoogt.

At the turn of the century, President McKinley and his Secretary of State, Hay, were pro-British, so that the Government of the United States remained strictly neutral in the war between the Boer Republics and Britain. Nevertheless, a visit to the United States by A. D. W. Wolmarans, C. H. Wessels and Abraham Fischer evoked great popular enthusiasm for the Boer cause, though the efforts made were unco-ordinated and, therefore, somewhat fruitless. For all that, pro-Boer activity persisted throughout the States until the end of the war in 1902.

Among the earliest measures for the rehabilitation of the devastated areas was the importation from Texas and Colorado of long-horned cattle. Among the cowboys who accompanied the shipments of these animals was one who, in later years, became a celebrity under the name of Will Rogers.

The ideas of Alexander Hamilton, whose brilliant legal mind was one which shaped the American Constitution, had a profound influence on the constitution drafted for the Union of South Africa. Sir Walter Hely-Hutchinson, last Governor of the Cape of Good Hope at the time of the unification of the four colonies, wrote to Allen McLane Hamilton, a grandson of Alexander Hamilton and author of his biography, that the delegates at the National Convention "went about, so to speak, with a copy of Alexander Hamilton's life in one pocket, and a copy of the "Federalist" in the other, preaching unification and advising their friends to read . . .''

Not one of the other countries of the Third Africa was so profoundly influenced by events in Europe and the United States as South Africa.

By 1576 the court of Portugal had already assumed control over the area now known as *Angola* and the first plantation owners moved in. At the Treaty of London (1600) the European powers recognized Portuguese title to both Angola and Mocambique. Thereafter the flow of Portuguese from Europe to Angola was never more than a trickle until after 1900 and particularly after World War II, when development in Angola was accelerated. Following on terrorist attacks in the early sixties, Portugal moved thousands of troops into Angola, encouraging them to settle in the new land. Military activities on a massive scale contributed vastly to the province's overall development.

The history of *Mocambique*, often referred to as "the land of the friendly people"[3] is similar to that of Angola. Trade, Portugal's desire to expand its influence across the globe and to develop its newly settled overseas territories, were the driving forces.

The Portuguese connection with Mocambique goes back to the days of Vasco da Gama and the early Portuguese expeditions which set out in search of the legendary world of Prester John. When Vasco da Gama visited the East African coast on his pioneer voyage to India and back (1497-98) he found that the region was dominated by a string of Arab and Arab-African (Swahili) settlements stretching from Somaliland to Sofala, the great gold entrepot in the South near present-day Beira.

Portuguese control was swiftly established along this coast and in 1505 King Manuel, rightly surnamed "The Fortunate", ordered forts to be constructed at Sofala and the island of Mocambique in the North, which soon became an important refueling and watering-place for Portuguese ships *en route* to and from India.

Through Sofala the Portuguese could control much of the rich gold trade coming down from the interior. The pattern of their

3. See Volkmar Wentzel's article in *National Geographic*, August, 1964.

99

trade along this part of the coast followed that of their Arab and Swahili predecessors, and was based on the bartering of Indian beads and textiles for gold-dust, ivory and slaves. Although the Portuguese did not succeed in supplanting the Swahili traders who travelled in the interior, many of their own men likewise ventured far into the bush in search of gold and ivory. They were particularly eager to establish contact with the legendary "empire of Mono-matapa" which was believed to be fabulously rich in gold and silver mines. Monomatapa was in many ways the Portuguese equivalent of the Spanish dream of El Dorado, and, as with the South American mirage, many lives and much energy were spent in pursuit of it.

One of the results of the quest for Monomatapa was that the Portuguese early established themselves along the Zambezi Valley, which was the main highway into the interior. In the 1530's they founded settlements at Tete and Sena. Later they pushed up the river as far as Zumbo near the present-day frontier with Rhodesia.

The depth of this penetration by way of the Zambezi Valley contrasted markedly with the shallowness of Portugal's hold along the coast and it was not until the last quarter of the 19th Century that effective occupation of the territory was completed.

Enormous strides have been made since then, particularly in the last two decades and to-day the 16th Century Portuguese dream of finding an African El Dorado in this part of the world has been realized in the more prosaic form of agricultural settlement schemes and industrial expansion.

The history of *South West Africa* has a direct bearing on the current conflict over the country's international status. Efforts on the part of the Afro-Asian states to establish a United Nations presence there with the idea of making South West Africa independent under a one-man-one-vote programme, reveal abysmal ignorance of the territory's history.

South West Africa was originally inhabited by only the nomadic Bushmen and Hottentot, the former a relic of the stone age. Later came the Namas, Hereros, Ovambos and others, including the White man. The Herero who believed that all lands on which his cattle had grazed (no matter whether it was tribal grazing land of other peoples) are forever to be considered Herero land, by this action precipitated a century of bitter tribal warfare during which tens of thousands of people perished. (It was only in 1907 that Germany was finally able to bring under control the various warring factions and tribes and to establish its own authority over the territory).

Towards the end of the previous century when the European scramble for Africa was at its height, Germany's Otto von Bismarck proclaimed the territory to be under German rule. Meanwhile, however, the British had proclaimed Bechuanaland (now Botswana) a protectorate and consolidated its hold over southern Africa by overpowering the independent Boer republics of the Transvaal and Orange Free State, adding this to its expanding empire in Africa. The outbreak of the World War I in Europe in 1914 found German South West Africa a firmly entrenched island in a sea of British influence.

On July the 9th, 1915, soon after the outbreak of the war, German forces in South West Africa surrendered to South African troops led by General Smuts. Thus South Africa's presence was established in the territory by military conquest, part of the Allied effort against Germany. At the end of hostilities the Principal Allied Powers allocated the Mandate over South West Africa to the then Union of South Africa.

Following the initial military administration (the League of Nations confirmed the Mandate on December 17, 1920) the Union of South Africa established local autonomy for the territory in terms of the Mandate, the operative article (Article 2) being: "The Mandatory shall have full power of administration and legislation over the territory, subject to the present Mandate, as an integral portion of the Union of South Africa and may apply the laws of the Union of South Africa to the territory subject to such local modifications as circumstances may require."[4]

The sorry eclipse of the League of Nations is now history and the question of whether the mandate continued to exist afterwards, did not arise immediately. It only became "relevant" when the Afro-Asian campaign at the United Nations against the White Government of the Union began to pick up steam after 1948. Then the African, Asian and Communist states began to suggest that the

4. In 1943 the Legislature of S.W.A. expressed a formal desire for incorporation and between December 1945 and April 1946 the non-Whites voted overwhelmingly for incorporation. In a 70% poll, 208,850 out of 244,370 voted "Yes".

United Nations was the legal successor to the League of Nations and that the United Nations had, therefore, taken over the supervisory powers of the mandate. However, when China suggested this on April 18, 1946 the suggestion was promptly dropped because of lack of support; the United Nations itself agreed that the United Nations could only take over mandates and treaties when the parties concerned *requested* the General Assembly to do so. In the years following the establishment of the United Nations, not *one* of the thirty one members who had also been members of the League of Nations suggested that the mandate was now subject to the control of the United Nations. In 1947, fourteen states, including America, Pakistan and India took part in the discussion of South West Africa and not one raised this point. On March 19, 1948, in the Palestine debate before the Security Council, the American delegate stated: "The record seems to us entirely clear that the United Nations did not take over the League of Nations mandate system."

The uncertainty about South West Africa's international status and the mandate was thus deliberately fostered at the United Nations by the Afro-Asians. This was followed by years of mudslinging at South Africa in the General Assembly of the United Nations, culminating in the five-year dispute before the World Court to which reference was made in Chapter 2.

South Africa put at the disposal of the Court complete records of the struggle to get the country on its feet; of the struggle to find a home for each of the different races where they could live in peace; of the political development of the territory and the socio-economic progress made up until the Odendaal Commission's Report in 1964.

A careful analysis of the detailed history of South West Africa brings to light several points of overriding importance. Not one of the tribes in South West Africa has a claim to the whole territory. Except for the Bushmen and related races they were all "settlers" or late-comers; the various races were continually at war with each other until forcibly subdued by the Germans; the enmity between the tribes was such that thirty years after becoming a colony, Germany still had to use troops to put an end to tribal warfare; South Africa's presence in South West Africa can be traced to military conquest; her presence there and her administration was agreed to by the Allied Powers, confirmed by the League of Nations and was never disputed until the Afro-Asians launched their ideological war against South Africa; the United Nations is not the legal successor to the League of Nations; when the mandate was given to South Africa everyone, including the United States Government, who now want to get rid of South Africa, envisaged South West Africa's incorporation into the Union; South Africa has a fine history of betterment of socio-economic conditions for all the people of the territory.

For the Afro-Asian states at the United Nations, obliquely supported by Western countries such as Canada and the United States, to labour for the "liberation" of South West Africa and to arrange for independence under a policy of one-man-one-vote is to totally ignore the preceding factors and is so unrealistic as to be absurd. The consequences of such a step could only bring another century of chaos and turmoil, genocide and misery to South West Africa.

What the world should learn from this history of South West Africa is that a policy of differentiation between the various races is not only historically just and moral, but socio-politically sound and realistic.

Hemmed in between South Africa and South West Africa and surrounded by South African territory, are the former British protectorates of *Botswana, Swaziland* and *Lesotho*.

The history of these three protectorates is closely allied to that of their big neighbour, the Republic of South Africa. The British take-over of these countries towards the end of the last century as part of its imperialistic expansion in Southern Africa has had repercussions which will bedevil relations between the countries of Southern Africa for decades to come.

Botswana (Bechuanaland) was declared to be in the British sphere of influence early in 1880 and proclaimed as a "protectorate" in 1885 without a referendum on the subject. In 1895 the southern part of the territory (including Mafeking) was constitutionally embodied in the Cape Colony. It was ruled by a resident British High Commissioner until independence in 1966.

Until about 1820, *Swaziland* was largely empty country. Driven northwards by the warlike Zulu, the Swazis led by their Chief Sobhuza, fled into the high Swaziland hills where they were ruled by a succession of Swazi Kings and, later, Paramount Chiefs. In 1894 under a convention between the South African Republic (the Transvaal) and Britain, the Boer Republic was given power of protection and administration over Swaziland. The territory continued to be governed under this form of control until the outbreak of the Anglo-Boer War. After the cessation of hostilities, the British High Commissioner became the head of the Swaziland administration and this colonial control has remained up until 1966 when Swaziland became a self-governing state. It is set down for sovereign independence in 1969.

Lesotho (Basutoland) is the mountainous homeland of the Basuto people. Here they found excellent protection against other marauding Bantu nations. It was here that the various feuding families and tribal units were welded into one nation by the wily Moshesh whose profile adorns the gold coins of independent Lesotho. At the request of Moshesh, who was Paramount Chief at the time, Basutoland received a promise of "protection" from Britain in 1868. By 1884, however, this "protection" had been discarded and Basutoland was proclaimed a protectorate under the direct control of the British Government through its High Commissioner in South Africa.

In this way Britain consolidated its hold over all of Southern Africa barring the two Boer Republics of the Transvaal and the Orange Free State. Within a matter of a few years, from about 1890 to 1892, Britain also expanded its control over what later became known as the Central African Federation so that only the two Boer Republics stood between her and complete dominance of the southern continent. The war directed against the Transvaal and the Orange Free State was, therefore, from a British point of view, inevitable – even if it had to be "manufactured". After the Anglo-Boer War, Britain of course restored to the defeated Republics internal self-government and in 1909 consented to the formation of the Union of South Africa.

The territorial partitioning of British South Africa as it was then known, recognized what Britain refuses to concede to-day, namely, the multi-national character of Southern Africa. Basutoland, Swaziland and Bechuanaland were carved out as homelands for their respective peoples and set on the way to self-government.

This form of *territorial apartheid* created a pattern of development which is quite likely to be repeated in homelands for the Xhosa speaking people, the Zulus, Tswana and other Bantu nations in South Africa. It has also bedeviled political thinking in South Africa since pressure is now being put on South Africa from all quarters of

104

the globe, and within South Africa, to increase the size of the remaining Bantu homelands in South Africa. Whatever merit there may be in this argument it is historically and constitutionally not justifiable, for no country in the world has ever willingly ceded part of its land to other nations in order to promote good neighbourship. In any case, the division of British South Africa between Black and White was more or less on a fifty-fifty basis.

By creating a sovereign state within South Africa which is economically wholly dependent on South Africa, the British action forced hundreds of thousands of Basutos to make their way to South Africa for a livelihood. The same applied to work-seekers from the other two territories. This in turn added to the racial imbalance in South Africa and is still continuing to do so.

It is evident that the history made by Britain at the turn of the century is not going to take a back seat in political affairs in South Africa. Only after the sub-continent has been fully divided into sovereign homelands for the various nations, as it existed prior to Britain's adventure in Africa, will the various races be able to proceed with their business in a more normal and less constricted way.

In the early 1960's Britain, riding the winds of change, agreed to constitutional talks with Basuto, Swazi and Bechuana national leaders. A constitution was agreed upon for each state and the first elections held. Six years later independence was granted to two of the Protectorates and the sovereign states of Lesotho and Botswana came into being. Swaziland will become autonomous by 1969.

The remaining area of the Third Africa constitutes what was known until a few years ago as the *Central African Federation* of Southern Rhodesia, Northern Rhodesia and Nyasaland.

Whereas Angola and Mocambique historically fell in the Portuguese sphere of influence and South West Africa in the South African sphere, the Central African Federation was cast in typical British colonial mould – as in the case of the three Protectorates discussed earlier.

The 19th century expansion of the British Empire in Africa led directly to the formation of the Rhodesias and Nyasaland. Livingstone's discoveries north of the Limpopo River and later that of Stanley encouraged Britain to move into these vast new territories.

Cecil Rhodes, the British Prime Minister of the Cape Crown Colony, also dreamed of a British Empire that would stretch from the Cape to Cairo.

When the scramble for Africa was at its height, and Colonialism fashionable, Britain led the scramble just as it later led the race in decolonization. By 1891 Nyasaland was "made" a British Protectorate although unlike the Basutos under Moshesh, the people of this region never requested British "protection". In 1907 it was renamed British Central Africa. In 1911 two territories to the north-west of Nyasaland were joined to become Northern Rhodesia, named after Rhodes and his dream of a British Empire in Africa.

Southern Rhodesia was occupied by White people from about 1890 after which it was administered by Rhodes's British-South Africa Company, operating under a Royal Charter, until 1923. In this year Britain granted Southern Rhodesia a Constitution and it became a self-governing colony within the British Empire.

When the White pioneers arrived in Rhodesia in 1890, they found an untamed land sparsely settled by tribes that had driven out the Bushmen whose original hunting grounds this had been. Only thirty-seven years before their arrival there had also been a massive invasion by the Matabele (from Natal) who had imposed their will on the numerically superior Mashona and other tribes. The early pioneers faced the same difficulties and endured the same hardships as the White farmers in South Africa on the frontiers of the Transkei and Ciskei in the 18th century and the early American settlers. Much of the lands which they occupied were uninhabited and never tilled. There was no sign of permanent residence. Largely by the enterprise and industry of the Rhodesian pioneers the wilderness was tamed and converted into one of the most highly developed and productive areas in Africa. As in the case of South Africa, the pioneers put an end to tribal warfare (between the Matabele and Mashona) and as their efforts in this field and in the supply of medicine and the eradication of disease began to bear fruit, the Black population grew from a mere 400,000 in 1900 to over four million in 1966.

The possibility of closer political association with South Africa was first officially raised by the British-South Africa Company but it was opposed by the Rhodesians who feared that amalgamation with South Africa would defer responsible government. In the 1922 referendum 8,774 voters chose responsible government for Rhodesia while 5,989 voted for incorporation in the Union.

Independence was offered to Southern Rhodesia prior to World War II but the feeling in Rhodesia then was that the war had first to be won.

In the early 1950's, after a referendum in Southern Rhodesia (but not the two other territories) the Federation of Rhodesia and Nyasaland was launched with great fanfare. It was to be Britain's answer to the world's multi-racial problems and their programme was diametrically opposed to that of the National Party government in South Africa which advocated not fusion between the different people of Southern Africa but separation – apartheid.

In 1963 the Central African Federation disintegrated after a referendum (this time in Northern Rhodesia and Nyasaland) which revealed that the Black nations of these states preferred government by Blacks for Blacks to "partnership" with the Whites in the Federation. It was the end of Britain's multi-racial dream for Central Africa and the end of "partnership" between Black and White in Africa. It also greatly influenced political thinking in South Africa to the extent that the public rejected hopes of self-governing Bantu areas linked with the White area in a Federation. Instead, Dr Verwoerd's thesis of politically independent states and economic interdependence with consultation on equal terms at the highest level, became the dominant theory.

In October 1964 Northern Rhodesia became the independent Republic of *Zambia* (named after the Zambezi River) and Nyasaland followed shortly afterwards to become the Republic of *Malawi*.

Southern Rhodesia alone was refused independence by Britain on the grounds that its government would not be directly and immediately representative of all the people – this despite the fact that the constitution which empowered the Rhodesian government to act as it did, was of Britain's own making and was supported by all political parties, Black and White, when it was introduced in Rhodesia.[5]

With the exception of the Portuguese provinces of Angola and Mocambique and South West Africa, this review of the history of

5. Chapter 2, page 19.

the states falling within the Third Africa has one recurring theme – the artificial and arbitrary demarcation of states, now countries, on the part of Germany and Britain, which cut right through tribal and language groups leaving for example more Tswana speaking people in South Africa than in the independent state of Botswana – their natural homeland.

The *dominant* forces in the history of the Third Africa were however, either Portuguese or British. In its way this influence contributed to unifying factors in the Third Africa – not only through trade, common currency and postage, but also through forms of administration, local government, training methods, types of institutions, procedures of government, the rule of law, etc. Whether of Portuguese or British origin, public administration inevitably required methods and procedures generally followed by the democracies of Europe. The same applied to transportation problems, methods of communications, etc.

The one field in which the British left a legacy of bitterness and complications was in political and constitutional development as it affected the various races.

Britain created the almost impossible situation of the British Protectorates surrounded by a sovereign independent Republic of South Africa and, as a sop to "world opinion", doomed the Central African Federation to an impossible future by insisting on "amalgamating" different nations and people under the cloak of multi-racialism. Idealistic, political experiments such as "partnership" between Black and White added to the Federation's burdens. This was undertaken despite the fact that all over Africa the trend had clearly been towards government *by* Black people *for* Black people in an independent Black state.

By this foolish and politically expedient experiment it doomed Rhodesia to a constitutional struggle it never sought of its own. It recognized Rhodesia as its child but refused it maturity in the form of self-government.

The British influence in the history of the Third Africa has, therefore, been both a blessing and a curse.

6. The People of the Third Africa

It can be said, and quite rightly so, that one who has no knowledge of the people of Africa, cannot possibly claim to understand its problems or its requirements for stability and progress.

Despite the fact that people make news, Americans and Europeans generally know very little of the races and nations of the sub-continent. It is quite possible and very probable that even the average university graduate knows as much of the people of the Third Africa as he does of the population of Outer Mongolia.[1]

Perhaps because they constitute so many disparate communities, speaking several dozen languages and dialects, most foreign journalists and observers have tended (and still do) to employ only two categories in describing the people of Southern Africa – so as to make it easier for the listener or reader back home to follow his reasoning. Thus in South Africa most reporters refer to the "Blacks" and the "Whites" as if the Bantu (Black) people constituted a single homogeneous nation with a common loyalty and speaking one language. But though they are all Black, they are as different from each other as the Scandinavians are different from the French. This immediately distinguishes the South African population complex from that of the United States for example, where there is a nation of one hundred and ninety million people of whom some are White and some Black. There are also millions of individuals of Irish, Italian, Polish and German descent living in America but the countries of Ireland, Italy, Poland and Germany are still in Europe to-day.

The United States is, therefore, *multi-racial*, but South Africa is

1. Much of the detail in this chapter is based on information obtained from N. J. Rhoodie, *Apartheid and Partnership*, Academica, Pretoria 1967; Lord Hailey's *African Survey*; I. Schapera, *The Bantu Speaking Tribes of South Africa*; Rosenthal's *Encyclopedia of Southern Africa*, various issues of *Lantern*, Journal of the Department of Adult Education, Pretoria and other works previously quoted in this book.

multi-national, for here the *entire* Zulu, Xhosa and Sotho nations are still to be found.

Oversimplification of what is really an intricate population structure is one of the main reasons for the misconceptions about the racial issue in Rhodesia and South Africa.

Since there are different *races* and *nations* living in South Africa, more or less akin to the old multi-national Austrian-Hungarian Empire, it is obvious that to try to force upon South Africa a simple formula of "integration" is to ignore every lesson of history as well as being a dangerous form of idealism.

History abounds with examples of how disparate *communities* (not groups of *individuals*) living in one area or country continually experienced disturbances, strife and even war as a result of their conflicting ideals, religions and beliefs. A good example is India and Pakistan, also Sweden and Norway, Ireland, Cyprus, the Congo, the old Central African Federation, the Sudan, Burma, Ceylon, Malaysia and Singapore and others.

A thorough knowledge of the population is obviously required to grasp the issues at stake in Southern Africa or to evaluate the aspirations of the different races, nations and communities. For anyone to actively propagate a system of one-man-one-vote for say, South West Africa, without realising that the Black Ovambos, who are in majority, would gladly chase the Black Hereros (who are a small minority) into the sea, is not an expression of liberal thought; it is merely making it unnecessarily difficult for those responsible for the orderly development of South West Africa. Such a crusade lends support only to the Communists who realise that such a system, if forced upon South West Africa, would result in the chaos on which Communism thrives. Yet this is precisely what several important British and European newspapers have been doing. Although apparently completely *au fait* with the almost insurmountable obstacles facing the march towards a politically unified Europe, they blandly suggest (and often urge) that such a policy can be made to work in the far more difficult and complicated situation in Southern Africa.

This chapter deals only in very general terms with the people of the Third Africa but it is sufficient to show that their *diversity* is even greater than that of Europe.

As a result of their history they are *familiar* to each other in a degree not shared elsewhere in Africa. The Matabele of Rhodesia once lived in South Africa; the Tswana speaking people of South Africa are linguistically part of the Tswana group resident in Botswana; tens of thousands of Black men from Malawi, Zambia and Mocambique are familiar with South Africa, having travelled to the Republic as migratory labour.

The traveller entering Zambia in the north or any of the states of the Third Africa except perhaps Angola, is likely to meet many Black and White men who have, at some stage or another, studied in South Africa. The Prime Minister of Malawi, Dr Hastings Banda, worked and studied in South Africa as did several senior members of the Foreign Service of other independent Black African states. The Prime Minister of Lesotho once worked in the Republic. To-day tens of thousands of Black men from virtually every state in the Third Africa still work in South Africa. Some estimates put their number at more than a million.

White people from South Africa work and live in considerable numbers in all of the Third Africa, except Angola. They are engineers, industrialists, professional administrators, doctors, miners, scientists, teachers, businessmen, etc.

All this has contributed to a greater understanding between the various peoples compared with for instance, Algerians and Moroccans. In modern times they have lived in far greater harmony with each other than the Black men of, say, Ethiopia and Somali, who have lately been using tanks and aircraft against each other. By word of mouth knowledge of the economic prosperity and the conditions of law and order in South Africa has spread far and wide among the average Black man in Southern Africa.

In the beginning only the Bushmen and later the Hottentot were to be found in the Third Africa.

The Bushmen themselves have a saying "in the beginning the only people were Bushmen and baboons". In Bushmen folklore there are long incomprehensible passages purporting to be in baboon language which the little yellow skinned hunters claimed to understand very well. The Bushmen at one stage lived in every part of the Third Africa. There is little evidence of *permanent* Bushmen abodes or Hottentot villages anywhere in Africa. They were always on the move. In caves and rock shelters from Rhodesia to the mountains of Basutoland and South Africa's Drakensberg, one can still see the paintings which they left in glorious colours.

Until the 16th century no clearly demarcated boundaries or homelands existed anywhere in Africa, not even in the ancient Ethiopian empire and in the south the Bushmen and the Hottentot remained in undisturbed possession of their ancient hunting lands. Then almost simultaneously a massive immigration of quite divergent racial groups from the north and the south began.

From the south came the European and from the north the Bantu in wave upon wave of warring tribes.

Considered by anthropologists to be the hybrid offspring of Negro (i.e. West African Blacks) and a Hamitic people who intermarried in the area of the Great Lakes, the Bantu (clearly distinguished from the true Negro by his dark copperish skin and shorter stature) brought with them primitive agricultural and mining skills. In Rhodesia and in overlaps into the Transvaal province of South Africa, one of the groups, the Mashona, is said to be responsible for the establishment of the romantic Kingdom of Monomotapa and the erection of the great stone walls of the Zimbabwe. However, other anthropologists believe the Zimbabwe was built by a Persian race who finally integrated with the numerically more powerful but intellectually inferior Hottentot and Bantu, thereby destroying their creative power.

The Bantu were a warlike people and once they crossed the Zambezi River and moved into the pleasant valleys and fields of South Africa, they overran the Bushmen and drove them into their last sanctuaries in the most arid portions of Southern Africa where the Bantu dared not follow. From the south the Hottentot and Bushmen were pressed northwards by the White man, also into the arid areas. Disease, smallpox and fever introduced into the continent from Europe and from the East by seamen resulted in disastrous epidemics among Bushmen and Hottentots.

To-day the Bushmen are extinct in Basutoland and all of South Africa except the north-west part. Dr P. V. Tobias, Professor in Anatomy at the University of the Witwatersrand (Johannesburg) recently estimated the total number of Bushmen still alive in the Third Africa (Botswana, South West Africa, Angola, Rhodesia and Zambia) at 55,000. Of this the greatest number, some 31,000 live in Botswana.

112

The traditional record of Bantu migration southwards into Zambia, Malawi, Rhodesia and South Africa is one of ceaseless warfare and bloodshed. No *written* records exist of their movements into the sub-continent, although references occur of encounters with shipwrecked sailors and ivory hunters. As far as can be ascertained, by 1775, the surviving Mashona and Makalanga had settled in Rhodesia and Mocambique; the Barotse, in what is to-day Zambia and the Bavenda and Tswana had overrun warmer portions of the northern part of South Africa. The north-western portion and Botswana were settled by the Batlapin and Barolong. During these years the Ovambo and cattle breeding Herero had streamed across the continent roughly along the Zambezi into what is now the northern part of South West Africa.

In the vanguard of the southward moving Bantu were the Nguni group, cattle farmers and warriors, who between the 17th and 18th centuries regrouped in what is now Zululand and finally became separated as the Zulu, Swazi, Xhosa, Tembu and Pondo nations.

It was at this stage that they met the northward moving White man.

Concurrently with the first conflicts between Bantu and European in the south-eastern part of South Africa a much greater conflict was raging among the Bantu nations of the interior. By this time missionaries, traders and ivory hunters had been on the scene long enough to record notable events and tales of refugees. According to the most eminent historians such as Eric Walker, Theal and others, the entire south-eastern half of the lower continent was ravaged by savage Black military despotisms.

An aspect of *overriding importance* in this period of genocide and pillage which bears repeating, was the fact that none of the lands south of the Zambezi were in any way *permanently* occupied, permanently settled or marked by boundaries when the White man began pushing northwards. The arrival of the White man brought an end to this internecine warfare. The Whites established law and order and those territories which they did not occupy by right of first settlement were obtained either through concessions or outright purchase. By 1880 the conflict between Black and White on the eastern frontier and elsewhere had virtually come to an end. Since by the end of the century the Tswana, Basuto and Swazi territories were demarcated by Britain, it can be said that the area of occupation had actually drawn to a close by 1880.

Since then no Black nation (or the White nation) had lost any territory either by conquest or conflict with the White nation or in conflict amongst themselves.

From the preceding survey of the early history of the people of Southern Africa spring the determining considerations for South Africa's policy of separate development. Briefly these are as follows: Between the 17th and 19th centuries different parts of South Africa were settled by different races and nations by right of first occupation; the only people who had a prior claim to South Africa, the Bushmen and the Hottentot, were virtually exterminated; all other peoples were late-comers or migrants from other homelands; the division of and occupation of land was established well before the turn of the century and was not the making of the present generation; the people of Southern Africa would never have achieved permanent abode in any area of Southern Africa nor would many of them have survived the tribal wars if the White man had not brought stability and order to the sub-continent.

Southern Africa ended up as British domain in 1902 (excepting South West Africa) but this domain consisted of different Black nations and a White nation, living largely in separate areas or homelands. Separate development or apartheid was evolved to provide for each of the nations a sovereign homeland even if this should ultimately lead to the fragmentation of the existing Republic of South Africa into several independent African states.

The idea of inalienable homelands for nations who are as different from each other as the nations of Europe is, therefore, deeply rooted in the history of South Africa.

When the Bushmen and most of the Hottentots fled northwards from contact with the White man, the labour force for the Cape of Good Hope was recruited largely from the East; from Java and Malaya, from the island of Madagascar, whose people were largely of Eastern stock, plus a few hundred Negroes imported from West Africa. This mixed group was the forefather of the present *Coloured* population of South Africa, numbering some one and a half million.

South Africa's remaining racial group, the 500,000 Indians (Asiatics) were the last to arrive in the country. In 1860 after the Cape Colony had voted against the entry of Asiatics, Natal, under tremendous pressure from the British and Indian Governments, opened its doors to Indian immigration. After working for five years as indentured labourers, mostly on the sugar estates, the Indians, under the then existing arrangements, could choose to become free labourers and after ten years they could decide whether they wished to stay in Natal or be given passage back home. The majority were agricultural workers from Madras and southern India, untouchables for whom the long journey to South Africa meant freedom from caste and semi-starvation. Small wonder that few chose to return to India. On their heels came traders and craftsmen from Bombay, most of them Mohammedans.

The Indians, through sharp trading practices, made themselves most unpopular, to such an extent that they became virtually unassimilable. The worst racial riot in the history of South Africa occurred in 1949 when the Zulus turned upon the Indians at Durban, killing some one hundred and forty and injuring over two hundred. The Government finally called in White troops to stop the massacre.

During the previous years, South Africa had made every effort to get the Indians to return to India, but all to no avail. Since the Indian delegation at the United Nations first introduced a motion criticising South Africa for its "inhuman treatment" of people of Indian descent, several thousand Indians actually migrated to South Africa. Almost none left. In 1962 the South African Government finally declared the Indians to be a permanent part of South Africa with all rights of citizenship.

It has been calculated that the *per capita* income of South Africa's Indians, particularly the urban Indians, is the highest of that of any Indian group anywhere in the world. In terms of housing, education, literacy, social welfare and health and hospital services, their standard of living is probably also unmatched.

South Africa, with its more than eighteen million people is by far the most populated state in the Third Africa and for this reason a more detailed survey of its population structure is required.

What has been presented so far, reveals a few outstanding characteristics: The country is populated by diverse national groups who come from vastly different backgrounds and with great differences in language, culture, history and tradition. They find themselves in South Africa not by their own choice but as a legacy of the country's colonial history. The population of eighteen million people includes not only different races (Negroid-Bantu-Asiatic-Caucasian) but also, and more important, different nations; the White nation, the Zulu, Xhosa, Sotho, Venda, Tswana and others. The Xhosa number some 3.2 million, the White nation 3.5 million (est. 1967), the Zulu 2.8 million, the Cape Coloureds 1.5 million, the Bapedi 1.2 million, the Sotho 1.2 million, the Tswana 900,000, the Asians 500,000 and smaller Bantu nations some 1.6 million.

In ethnological terms the White people are the *majority* group in South Africa. Population statistics which refer only to the Bantu, Indians, Coloureds and Whites are misleading and erroneous. No Tswana would, for example, consider the Zulu and Tswana as belonging to the same group.

South Africa's population complex projected on the United States would mean a population in the United States of some forty million Whites and one hundred and thirty-five million Red Indians, of whom forty-five million would still be primitive, speaking six major and several lesser languages other than English.

While South Africa's principal languages are English and Afrikaans (the two official languages of the country) Xhosa is now also an official language in the state of the Transkei. This is the homeland of the Xhosa nation and the first self-governing Black state set up by South Africa under its programme of separate political development for the country's disparate Bantu nations. As the other Bantu homelands attain a similar status, Zulu, Tswana and Sotho may join the list of official languages. In the schools of South Africa, children are taught in Zulu, Xhosa, Sotho, Afrikaans or English as the case may be.

At any given moment more than forty per cent of the Bantu can be found in the Bantu homelands, while the rest sell their labour in the White areas of the country. Their numbers fluctuate considerably since so many are employed temporarily on farms while those in the urban area are often migratory labour. Even those who have been absent for many years retain strong links with the homeland.

The development of the Bantu in South Africa has been phenomenal. There are scores of top flight foreign journalists, statesmen and students who have found (and so reported) that in terms of every tangible socio-economic yardstick, the Bantu in South Africa are far better off than any other Black people outside the United

States. Better off, in fact, than some of the East European countries and all the Latin American and Asian countries with the exception of Japan and the Argentine.

Fifty years ago the Bantu could neither read nor write, lived in mud huts and wore animal skins. In 1962 some R30 million was spent on advertising in newspapers in South Africa which also circulate among the Bantu. Radio Bantu, staffed by Bantu, broadcasts in seven languages while thirty newspapers and eight periodicals now circulate among the Bantu.

Considering the *centuries* it took the European nations to achieve a ninety-five per cent literacy rate, it is remarkable that Bantu in the age group ten to twenty, already enjoy a literacy rate of over sixty per cent.

To quote statistics of Bantu education, housing, health and welfare services, per capita income, etc., in comparison with other African countries would only take up space. In South Africa the school attendance figures for the Bantu in the age groups seven to fourteen, is eighty-five per cent compared with only twenty-nine in Ghana, eighteen in Ethiopia, seventeen in Liberia, eleven in the Sudan and five per cent in Somalia. Sufficient to say that the Bantu own four times as many cars per capita than the Russian people and that there are more Bantu university graduates in South Africa (some 2,600) than in all of the African countries south of the Sahara with a combined population eight times that of South Africa. *The income of the Bantu in South Africa equals the gross national product of fourteen African states with a total population of thirty-three million.*

Bantu development has been rapid for three very understandable reasons. *Firstly*, because the government in South Africa believes in the potential of the Bantu to administer to the need of their people. *Secondly*, the Government is anxious to develop a competent Black administration; consequently the uplifting and development not only of the exceptionally gifted group in the leadership class, but also of the mass of people is given high priority. This calls for an overall programme of development of considerable proportions. *Thirdly*, the Bantu, because of their lower income, relative to the White man, could not afford this programme. For the most part, it has been financed by South Africa's Whites. The average White *family* unit contributes R200 per annum in various ways to betterment services for the Bantu. At cost of services in the United States and relative to the number of people and income, this is equivalent to about R860 ($1,204) per American family per year.

South Africa need not, therefore, defend itself against allegations of "White superiority" or "White supremacy". Had this been their real attitude, outlays on Bantu development would have been infinitesimal.

The parrot cry often heard is that while Bantu development has indeed been impressive, for example in education, it is less than that enjoyed by the lowest income groups among the Whites. This should not cause any embarrassment to South Africa. In the ultimate analysis it is extremely unfair to the Bantu, not to the White man. Since the Bantu had not developed much further than the iron age at the time both came under one administration (1910), one could hardly expect them in the space of a mere fifty-five years to reach the stage of development achieved by the Whites over 3,000 years. That they have developed so rapidly speaks volumes for the civilizing ability of the White nation.

While it is true that Whites are holding the skilled and better paying jobs, this state of affairs belongs to a dynamic setting in South Africa. The increase of monthly wages for the urban Bantu has been far more rapid than in the case of the White worker, both skilled and unskilled. As Professor Richard Logan of the University of California also points out it is fallacious to compare non-White wages with wages earned by Whites "because of the totally different nature of expenses incurred by the two groups". Such a comparison if made, is vastly favourable to the non-Whites. Professor Logan rightly points out that "the housing costs of the native are largely subsidised by the employer and the municipality; medical treatment is essentially free; transportation costs, etc., are greatly reduced; there are no taxes to be paid; and custom dictates that very substantial gifts of clothing and cloth must be made by the employer on a number of occasions". Professor Logan was referring to South West Africa when he made these remarks in testimony before a subcommittee of the American Congress, but it is equally applicable to South Africa. Professor D. C. Krogh of the University of South Africa and a witness before the World Court, also pointed out in a recent article in *Africa* that the distribution of income (as represented by wages) is less unequal in South West Africa than in other

African territories where the ratio of Whites to non-Whites in the total population is far less favourable.

The important point to remember is that there is no ceiling to Bantu development, no maximum level on his education, no maximum level on his wages. There are enough Bantu university graduates and businessmen paying super tax to prove this point. The nearly one-million foreign Bantu working in South Africa (one out of every twelve South African Bantu) is testimony of the material welfare of the Black man in South Africa.

South West Africa's population at the last census count (1960) was only 530,000. Of these the Bantu groups numbered 427,000, Coloureds 24,000 and Whites 73,000.

South West Africa is a kaleidoscope of racial types. No less than twelve different groups speaking as many languages and several dialects can be counted among the inhabitants. Of the twelve, six (the Ovambos, Whites, Namas, Okavangos, Hereros and Damaras) constitute almost ninety per cent of the total population.

The remaining groups which include the Caprivians, Coloureds, Bushmen, Basters and Kaokovelders are numerically insignificant. The Caprivians total some 16,000 souls but the other groups vary from only nine to about twelve thousand people.

Ethnologically the people of South West Africa span the millenia of recorded history. The recently arrived and highly developed White man lives here as does the most ancient and primitive race on earth, the Bushmen.

Linguistically and otherwise the non-Whites are people of the most divergent origins.

A very determined effort has been launched by the Afro-Asian states at the United Nations to wrest control of South West Africa from the Republic and to establish a United Nations presence there, which would prepare South West Africa for independence within twelve months. This is as good a reason as any to take a look at the principal groups in South West Africa in terms of this Afro-Asian plan which also has the support now of a number of Western countries such as Canada, Sweden and America and the mass of the liberal newspapers of the world. The latter disagree with the Afro-Asians only on the methods by which the control of the territory can be taken away from South Africa.

Among the "native" groups, the 42,000-strong *Hereros* are the most vocal advocates of independence. Although they are a minority among the Territory's non-White population, they are a closely knit nation whose traditions reinforce their bellicose demands. For several decades during the latter half of the 19th century, Herero chieftains held a tenuous authority over much of the central part of South West Africa. The descendants of these pastoral nomads, imbued with the spirit of "herrenvolkism" which is their national trait, feel that despite their relative insignificance in numbers, *theirs* should be the paramount voice in the councils of an independent South West Africa.

They remain one of the most unique peoples in all of Africa. With the exception of one other obscure tribe in Central Africa they are the only people with a matriarchal as well as a patriarchal family structure. No one can ever become a Herero through marriage. As one student observed: "one can only be born a Herero".

Co-operation between the Hereros and the other Bantu nations of South West Africa is, therefore, impossible, simply because their social organisation and tribal customs are incompatible. The Herero's way of life urges him to be different. Not all the foreign aid in the world or the unanimous opinion of the United Nations will convince the Herero that it is liberal and democratic to live together under a system of one-man-one-vote with the Ovambos – who out-number them by six to one. This is one of the prime reasons why South Africa's policy of separate development is considered to be the only solution – because it recognises and accepts the deep-rooted difference between people and races and their fervent desire to retain their identity.

Belatedly, perhaps far too late, even the United Nations, which is *the* great champion of the amorphous mass, recognise the desire of smaller nations and population groups to safeguard their identity – the birthright of all peoples. This was made abundantly clear at the Seminar on the multi-National Society held in Ljubljana, Yugoslavia in June 1965 and organised by the United Nations.

By historical fact, the Hereros' chief competitors for the position of dominance in a potentially independent South West are the *Namas*, a clever and intensely individualistic nation of Hottentot derivation.

Roughly comparable in numerical strength to the Hereros, the Namas were also once masters of the central highlands of South

West and thus have an equally valid claim to authority. A "yellow" people who consider themselves superior to the Black Bantu peoples of Africa, the Namas could be expected to resist strenuously any effort by the Hereros to exert dominance in South West Africa.

Herero petitioners at the United Nations (their pockets lined by funds from Ethiopia, Ghana and Algeria) and the activities of a British Minister of religion, Michael Scott (currently *persona non grata* even in New Delhi because of his role in the Naga rebellion for independence against India), have created the impression that the Hereros are the only people worth any consideration in South West Africa.

In point of numbers, the northern Bantu nations – the Ovambo and their cousins the Okavango – are by far superior to the other non-White groups. The Ovambo (239,000) scoff at the thought of a South West Africa "dominated" by Hereros. And, indeed, any constitutional government based on universal (or even representative) franchise would certainly find Ovambos in all the key governmental positions.

Historically, their claim is weakened by the fact that they have never ventured far south of "Ovamboland", the northern quarter of the territory, in any great numbers. Even to-day, the Ovambo and Okavango (28,000 people) are largely content to enjoy a facile and unhurried life on the stoneless plains of the Kunene watershed, reaping a leisurely existence from the abundant grazing lands and fertile, well-watered banks of the mighty river. Their traditional and emotional roots reach north among the Angola Bantu and east toward the lands of their origin in Central Africa.

A reasonably well-organized social structure provides the peoples of these two nations with a firm basis for the development of constitutional government, but delegating to them the responsibility of governing the southern portions of South West Africa would be something like placing Tai Wan Chinese in authority over Alaskan Eskimos.

One of the cruelest of the many ironies that afflict South West Africa is the fact that the people with undoubtedly the best historical claim to political pre-eminence, the Bushmen, are certain never to achieve it. By reason of their scanty numbers and primitive social organization, they are the most gullible candidates for potential exploitation.

It was not until the assumption of control by South Africa that a serious effort to lead the Bushmen to a settled life was conscientiously instituted. And even to-day, they are so far below the level of the territory's other inhabitants on the scale of civilization, that they would be easy prey for any group seeking to exploit them.[2]

Their very existence creates an acute moral problem for the South African authorities who must decide if they should be "protected" and allowed to pursue their stone-age nomadic lives or be induced to settle on agricultural plots where they can be "civilized" and initiated into the social and technical skills of the 20th century.

It must, therefore, be apparent to anyone with even a superficial knowledge of the territory that there is no single unified indigenous group of "native" South West Africans to whom the central authority, even over a protracted period of time, could be transferred.

The differences between the various groups in customs and culture and in numbers is arid soil for the application of a policy of one-man-one-vote.

"South West Africa for the South West Africans" – the simple solution of the sloganeers – thus becomes a mockery of well-intentioned ignorance. And the withdrawal of South Africa from the territory would constitute an abdication of a moral responsibility to its peoples and the abandonment of them to political chaos and civil strife (of the kind that killed the Congo) that would mean a reversion to the bloodshed that marked the history of South West Africa in the 18th and 19th centuries.

The only group of people who pledge prime allegiance to the territory which they occupied and developed – rather than to a chief or a tribal group – are the Whites. They are the second strongest group (after the Ovambos) in the territory. They, or their fathers and grandfathers, came to South West Africa as soldiers, missionaries or farmers to open up the land and they have succeeded to a remarkable extent in the face of seemingly insurmountable hardships.

The Bantu people of South West Africa are less developed than the Bantu resident in South Africa, but their housing developments, health and educational services, educational attainments and per capita income still puts them ahead of most of the Black people in

2. Some idea of the Bushmen's code of existence can be gathered from the fact that if a woman should die in labour, her living child is buried with her.

sub-Saharan Africa. Abundant evidence in support hereof was submitted by South Africa to the World Court during 1962-1966.

Diametrically opposite South West Africa, on the Indian Ocean, lies the Portuguese province of Mocambique.

When the last census was taken in 1960, the total population of *Mocambique* amounted to just about six and a half million people. Of these the vast majority are of Bantu stock. There are nine main ethnic groups subdivided into innumerable tribal groupings. While most of the Black population are of Bantu extraction, there are communities of Arab and Swahili to be found along the coast, particularly in the north. Although the tribal unit continues to play an important part in the native social structure of the country, there has been an increasingly marked trend away from the tribe to the urban centres, particularly to the two great ports of Beira and Lourenco Marques and also to seek work in the Republic of South Africa and Rhodesia.

The 1960 census shows that the European population of Mocambique numbers just over 160,000. Most of the European population are concentrated in and around Lourenco Marques, the Zambesi district and the north.

Apart from the European community, there are also some 20,000 Portuguese of Indian descent living in Mocambique and they play an important role in the territory's commerce; a 2,500 strong Chinese community (mainly from the Portuguese province of Macao) also adds to the racial mixture which is so clearly apparent in every walk of life in the Portuguese territories overseas.

The multi-racial background, which has been such a marked feature of Portuguese expansion overseas, is as noticeable in Mocambique as in the other Portuguese territories in Africa, although it does not reach the proportions to be found in places such as the Cape Verde Islands where over ninety per cent of the population are of Coloured origin. There are an estimated 50,000 mulattoes in Mocambique; that is to say, first-generation off-spring of mixed marriages. But a far higher proportion of the population have some degree of coloured blood in their veins. Multi-racial societies are particularly evident along the Zambezi Valley around the old town of Quelimane, as it is in this area that the Portuguese have been settled the longest. Many of these people of mixed descent play an important part in government, professional and technical work.

Perhaps the most striking description of the people of Mocambique appeared in the August (1964) edition of the journal of the *National Geographic Society* in Washington. Written by Volkmar Wentzel it illustrated the remarkable degree of multi-racialism attained by the Portuguese in the land despite the enormous differences in background and in civilization between Portuguese newcomers and the sixty ethnic native groups. Wentzel found striking evidence of Portugal's desire to improve the lot of the people through education, health services and programmes of self-help. "The way in which the Portuguese have identified themselves with the every-day lot of the native has been quite remarkable", he observed.

The expansion and development of educational facilities in Mocambique has been one of the main concerns of the provincial government in recent years and some promising progress has been brought to bear on this problem, which is one of great importance throughout Africa. There are approximately 3,500 educational institutions in Mocambique to-day with a total of 432,552 pupils.

Religion in this land is as varied as it is in South Africa and the other areas of the Third Africa. There are literally hundreds of sects and splinter groups and hundreds of thousands of people who, for lack of a better word, can only be described as primitive pagans. However, what the Portuguese have achieved here and what they are busily achieving in Angola, is something which neither South Africa, Rhodesia nor any other land in the world has managed, and this is a seemingly stable truce between Arab, African and Indian.

Livingstone first wrote of the Portuguese hospitality in Africa which has rubbed off on a Bantu people known for their inter-tribal clashes and hostility to newcomers. The late Robert Ruark wrote that he could walk from one end of Mocambique to the other during night or day "with nothing but a big stick to keep the snakes away".

From these and many other sources it is apparent that the differences in civilization, in education, in income and way of life, between primitive Makonde, wily Arab, work-shy Makuans and industrious Portuguese, as well as in languages (varying from Swahili to Chinese and Arab) will not be the spark of any "unrest" or "disturbance" in Mocambique.

Any "liberation" movement or "nationalist uprising" is sure to be an imported or, rather, exported product, emanating from Black Africa or the Arab north.

The third most populous state in the Third Africa after South Africa and Mocambique is *Angola*. Portugal's largest province is also one of Africa's biggest territories – greater than South Africa, Mocambique, Nigeria or Tanzania and only slightly smaller than the Congo. For its 480,000 square miles, however, it is considerably under-populated. At present the 4,832,000 inhabitants are irregularly scattered over the territory. In ninety per cent of the area the density is only between one and two persons per square mile, although the average works out at about nine. The most densely populated regions are those of the highlands and of the north near the Congo border while the only concentrations of people are in the regions of the capital, Luanda, and Lobito and in the plateau area in the vicinity of Nova Lisboa. Large areas in the south-east are virtually unpopulated.

Because of its relatively small population, Angola has to rely on immigration contingents to complete its deficiency in labour, especially with regard to skilled labour which is largely recruited in metropolitan Portugal. The people in the north and coastal portions are considerably better educated than those further south, particularly in the south-east near the triangle made by the borders of South West Africa and Zambia where some of the Bantu tribes have remained virtually uninfluenced by western civilization. Here, as in most parts of the country, the great majority of the people live by agriculture and particularly by a system of economy-in-substance.

The dozens of tribes resident in Angola are all members of the Bantu group. Their original homeland seems to have been the Cameroon Mountain and environments, somewhat east of the Great Lakes area where the majority of the southern and eastern Bantu nations, the Tswana, Sotho, Zulu and others came from. Almost nothing is known about their early history but evidence suggests that near the first century A.D. they began pushing southwards together with a host of other Bantu tribes and nations. By A.D. 500, Bantu had occupied most of the Congo basin which had been predominantly pygmy. In the next few hundred years, together with the Bantu from the immediate vicinity of the Great Lakes, they spread southward but whereas the bulk of the Bantu moved eastward across the continent in their march south, the Angolan Bantu moved mostly along the coast and later through the interior driving southwards the Bushmen and Hottentot tribes then living in Angola.

By 1576 the court of Portugal had already assumed control over the area now known as Angola and the first plantation owners moved in. At the Treaty of London (1600) the European powers recognized Portuguese title in both Angola and Mocambique. Thereafter the flow of Portuguese from Europe to Angola was never more than a trickle until after 1900, and particularly after World War II, when development in Angola was accelerated. To-day the permanent White population number some 190,000 – estimated for 1967.

Up to 1964 there was no university in Angola. Bantu requiring higher education had previously gone to Portugal where some ten per cent of the 15,000 students attending universities were from Africa. Now universities are to be found in both Luanda and Lourenco Marques. In Angola and Mocambique illiteracy is decreasing at the rate of some two per cent per annum and by the end of 1967 some sixty per cent of the school age population in Portuguese Africa will be in schools.

Because of the dozens of dialects spoken in Angola and Mocambique, the Portuguese have chosen Portuguese as the one medium of instruction. In this way they have also contributed to the sense of unity in Southern Africa. The primary and secondary schools are identical for both Black and White Portuguese and on the whole, closely modelled after the educational system in Portugal.

Malawi and *Zambia*, the two independent Black African states to the north-west of Mocambique and immediately north of Rhodesia, together account for only about 7,600,000 people (1965) or less than one seventh of the population of the Third Africa.

Of the two *Malawi* (ex-Nyasaland) with a population of 4,000,000 is the most populous. Though its White community is small, only some 10,000, it is still one of the largest – and most committed – in Black Africa. The majority of the European people are settled in the southern highlands. Some fifty per cent of the total population lives in the southern half of the territory. As in most of the African states on the east coast, there are also several thousand Indian traders in the area. The Europeans are mostly British settlers or colonial administrators who elected to stay on after the dissolution of the old Central African Federation. There are also several hundred South Africans – mostly professional men, engineers, technicians and scientists working in Malawi either out of free choice or under contract to the Government.

The inhabitants of this part of the world are also of Bantu stock. First to reach the area were the Nyanja. A docile and unwarlike people, they suffered much at the hands of the Yao who came into the Shire Highlands area at a much later stage. The Ngoni were formerly members of the mighty Zulu Confederation under Chaka but sometime after 1825 they were driven northwards by the main Zulu body and settled the area around Lake Nyasa. During the present century large numbers of the Lombe and kindred tribes have crossed from Portuguese territory into Southern Malawi. By the end of 1960 they numbered more than 400,000 or roughly the same as the original inhabitants – the Nyanja. The most numerous tribe (almost wholly resident in the Central Province) and also latecomers are the Achewa, who number nearly three quarters of a million. Other lesser tribes are the Tonga, Henga and Nkonde.

The predominant venacular in all but the Northern Province is Nyanja, although English is widely used and understood. In the field of education progress has been painfully slow and the percentage of the total population enrolled in school only one third of that of South Africa.

Because of its huge copper deposits, *Zambia* (formerly Northern Rhodesia), has long been held to be one of the "newly emerged" African states with an exceptionally bright future. It was estimated that in 1964 the population of 3,650,000 contained no less than 77,000 Whites – a sizeable proportion for a Black African state – attracted by this future. In addition there are about 100,000 other non-Bantu peoples, mostly Asians. The White population is predominantly English speaking, as in the case of Malawi, but here too a surprisingly large number of White people from South Africa (some estimates run as high as 6,000) are to be found.

The Black native population consists of a large number of Bantu tribes. English is widely used and understood all through the territory but the principal Bantu languages are Chinyanja and Lunda.

Rhodesia, population wise, is a most important member of the Third Africa, not only because of its big population (4,259,000) (estimated 1966) but also because of its relatively big White population of 220,000 people. Of the Black population consisting mostly of the Mashona, Makelanga and Matabele nations, only about half a million are resident anywhere near the urban areas. The larger element is spread over the state's 150,000 square miles, mostly bushland, in small communities.

Of the White people the greater majority are English descendants but a sizeable percentage are Afrikaans or English speaking people from the Republic of South Africa.

The White people in Rhodesia enjoy a standard of living equal to that of South Africa and superior to that of the majority of western nations in Europe. The Bantu population, while far below the Whites on the scale of per capita income (and in their degree of civilization) are nonetheless substantially better off than the vast majority of people in other African states – in both Arab and Black Africa.

Considering that Rhodesia was a primitive bushland, a wilderness without a single road, railroad, paved highway, irrigation canal, a brick building, hospital or secondary school a bare eighty years ago, its White population must rank as one of the most industrious in the world. Alternatively, they have shown themselves remarkably adept at organising the services of the lethargic Black population in carving a modern state out of virgin bush in the space of one lifetime.

The Rhodesian Bantu are said to include some of the laziest people on earth. Whether this is true or not cannot be vouched for but one finds less drive among them than in the case of the Black men in Swaziland or in South Africa. There are fewer examples of Black businessmen who have made good than in South Africa where there are already a number of non-Whites paying millionaire income tax and a surprisingly large number in the super tax class.

The remaining territories in the Third Africa are the trio of former British protectorates, *Botswana, Swaziland and Lesotho*.

Lesotho, with a total population of 685,000, has the most homogeneous Bantu society of any African state. It is true that at any one time there are always about 180,000 to 200,000 Basutos out of the country, working in South Africa, but of the remaining total only some 2,000 are European, mostly British subjects (administrators, teachers, engineers) and South African Whites, while the Asiatic population numbers less than 800. The people of Lesotho (Bantu) are descendants from the remnants of various tribes that were broken up during the internecine wars between the Matabele and Zulu and who, between 1815-30, were united by Moshoeshoe I.

Taking into consideration the habitable area, Lesotho is the most thickly populated territory in Southern Africa. English is the "official" language but Sotho is the popular language. With the exception of South Africa and Rhodesia, Lesotho also has the highest school enrolment in all of Africa and the ratio of pupils to teachers in the secondary level (17:1) is also one of the ten best in Africa. In the *primary* standards the rate of literacy is about 85 per cent, the highest in Africa, and some 75 per cent of the total population are considered Christians, mostly Roman Catholics. The University of Lesotho at Roma was also founded by the same Church.

Botswana has a population of only 543,000 (1964 census) and its density (roughly one person per square mile) is about the lowest in Africa. The non-Bantu population is less than 6,000 of whom 4,000 are Whites – traders, civil servants, professional men – virtually all resident in the so-called "White areas", all border areas, known as "blocks".

Prior to independence the state was really just a collection of Bantu tribal areas, crown lands and White farming areas held together by a common administration. The White areas or "blocks" consisted of the Tati district in the north which was recognized by the British and South African governments as a "White area" even before the Protectorate was proclaimed. The Tuli "block" along the Limpopo river, together with the smaller Lobatsi and Gaberones blocks were formed from land ceded by the native chiefs to the British-South Africa Company. The Ghanzi block was established by Cecil Rhodes to forestall German expansion eastward from South West Africa.

Of the Bantu there are eight major tribes, descendants of refugees from the Zulu impis of Chaka. The largest tribe is the 200,000 strong Bamangwato, to which President Khama belongs. The Bamangwato and other tribes such as the Bakwena are all part of the Tswana speaking people of whom about 800,000 actually live within the borders of South Africa. In addition some 25,000 – 30,000 people from Botswana work in South Africa on a full time basis.

This newly independent country is now a wonderful example of the completely illogical Africa policy followed by Britain. Botswana which should have been part of South Africa, and therefore, the homeland of all the Tswana people, is now in the position Belgium would have found itself in had seven of its ten million people lived in, say, Holland, or better still if 12,000,000 of Mexico's 25,000,000 people lived in America. Up until 1965 even the capital of the state was outside Botswana – in Mafeking, South Africa.

Enrolment of school children in Botswana is only half that of Lesotho and only one fifth that of South Africa. Its pupil teacher ratio in secondary education is 11:1, primarily because of the small number of schoolchildren in this grade. In 1961 UNESCO reported that there were only thirty teachers employed at *secondary* education so that the number of children in secondary schools at that time was a mere three hundred and thirty. Most recent official statistics (1966), however, put this figure at 1,409. Botswana has no university of its own.

Swaziland, with its population of 275,000 is also a remarkable homogeneous nation. The non-Bantu population is quite large for so small a population. There are nearly 10,000 Whites. They include not only engineers, civil servants, doctors, skilled labour and teachers, but also quite a number of permanent residents, mostly traders, farmers and small entrepreneurs.

The Swazi are mostly a pastoral people, most of them living in small scattered communities while the Whites tend to gravitate towards the towns. The important thing is that they all consider themselves members of the Swazi nation (a Zulu offshoot as explained earlier in this chapter). As in the case of Lesotho, this accounts for the lack of tribal tensions.

One potentially dangerous situation is that the Whites own nearly half the land. The Swazis are now buying back properties, taxing themselves to raise the money. So far there has been no confiscation of property and confiscation is also thought by the Whites themselves to be unlikely. The fact is that because of a sound economic policy and a moderate as well as modern outlook, King Sobhuza II enjoys tremendous personal prestige among Black and White and is more than likely to be the executive head of State when independence comes in 1969.

Education is one of the limiting factors in the country's development. Presently sixty-five per cent of the children of school age are said to be in school which is a hundred per cent improvement on the situation ten years ago. But there is a great shortage of Swazis with secondary school qualifications and Swaziland as yet has no university of its own.

There is an exploding realization of the importance of education in all of the Third Africa.

Few scholars would quarrel with the contention that without basic education and technical education, there can never be any hope for stable, progressive communities in Africa. History has taught two lessons on which all ideologies are agreed – that the nation with the greatest percentage of educated individuals has the best chance of becoming a stable political community or a viable economic unit, and, that a true democracy, such as exists in America, can only survive if practically the entire population is educated.

The important point is that *only* in the Third Africa does it appear as if these lessons have made any impact. Elsewhere in Africa politics, ideology and other people's affairs are accorded far more time and money – mostly foreign aid.

Rhodesia, for example, was always considered to be a country with a sound future, not only because of the stabilising influence of its big White population on the economy but because of the tremendous progress made in Bantu education. In 1965 some eighty per cent of *all* children of school age were enrolled in schools. This ratio is bettered only in South Africa. Bantu education has for the past few years invariably been the largest item appearing on Rhodesia's financial estimates. In 1965 it was nine per cent or *four times* the comparable figure for Algeria and Ghana. Schools include primary and secondary education, industrial and technical schools and teachers' colleges.

Ethiopia, Gambia, Guinea, Mali, Upper Volta and other states with big Embassies abroad, high spending diplomats, overpaid officials (the few educated men in the country) and outrageously expensive government buildings and conference halls may enjoy good publicity overseas, and even play a disproportionate role in world affairs during this decade of African history, but their future is bleak.

Take Mali, for example. Its envoys play an important role at the International Labour Organization, the United Nations and the Organization of African Unity. Rhodesia, on the other hand, has become, with South Africa, the whipping boy of "world opinion". But there are proportionately *seventeen* times more children at school in Rhodesia than in Mali. In a matter of years, Mali will probably become a forgotten Republic living on handouts from Communist and Western countries while Rhodesia will be nearly self-sufficient both in production and food and in educated manpower.

Education has become the key to success in Africa.

The strength of South Africa does not lie in its soil, its gold or its diamonds, but in its educated manpower.

In terms of political prestige at the United Nations, neither Rhodesia nor South Africa enjoy anything near the "respect" and "popularity" which Mali (or Ethiopia) command, but if the bulk of the population of Mali and Ethiopia could live in South Africa for one year, they would probably fight rather than return.

The Indians in Natal are a tangible example. Despite the massacre of so many of their people by the Zulu and despite a doubling in government compensation to get them to return to India, they refused to budge.

To the Black élite and its feudal monarch, Haille Selassie, Ethiopia is an African "power"; to the world at large it is a "progressive" and "pro-Western" African state. In terms of the realities by which the common Ethiopian lives, however, it has barely changed in 2,000 years and is one of the most backward and primitive regions on earth.

The main reason for this lies in the ninety-five per cent rate of illiteracy in Ethiopia.

In Mocambique and Angola the school enrolment expressed as a percentage of the population is still low but the programmes instituted to overcome this overshadow that of Mali, Ethiopia and Guinea. The latter's leaders choose to spend money and effort, manpower and knowledge on the training of guerillas for "liberating" areas to the south, on guns for rebels in other countries, on high living and playing at politics. On the other hand the Portuguese, South African and Rhodesian leaders are far more conscious of the *real* needs of the Black population and are bending their backs to get the mass of the people uplifted.

The battle for Africa, if one is permitted to coin a slogan, will be won on the school benches and not in an army training camp.

7. Alliance Prospects South of the Limpopo

It is impossible within the space of one or two chapters to analyse *all* the relevant factors which contribute to a closer alliance between different countries. In some cases such an alliance or co-operation in various fields is even forced upon the parties concerned, usually by circumstances beyond their control, for example Lesotho and South Africa.

If it is impossible to pin-point all the *relevant* factors, it is even more difficult to isolate any single factor which serves to *promote* closer co-operation, particularly where the Black and White controlled states in southern Africa are concerned. An alliance or co-operation is certainly not brought about only by a common ideological outlook for sometimes there is a spirit of unity and closeness even when this outlook is at opposite ends of the scale. Portugal, for instance, believes in a policy of assimilation of the races – as an evolutionary process of course, and not as a forced programme – while South Africa believes in separate freedoms, separate development between Black and White, between Black and Brown and between Black and Black. Yet the Portuguese provinces in Africa enjoy the most cordial of relations with South Africa.

Similar cultures or a common heritage is also no guarantee of cordial relations. To that the Irish Republic and Britain, or Rhodesia and Britain, can testify.

In actual practice almost everything which may affect the daily lives of the people and the authority of their governments can contribute to closer co-operation. This could mean common frontiers, trade, investments, communications, history in so far as it affects circumstances of the moment, tourists, migratory labour, matters of defence, fear of a common enemy, similar institutions of government, law and religion and, finally, self-interest – euphemistically termed "statesmanship".

"Statesmanship" means, no more, no less, that which in the final analysis will benefit your own people and its government more than it will benefit someone else's. By whatever name it is called it is nonetheless naked self-interest.

National self-interest applied so as *not* to weaken your allies but to strengthen your own position and thereby also that of your neighbours, is not synonymous with "political expediency". When a country adopts a certain attitude at the United Nations, for example on race relations or colonialism, not because it intends to apply that standard to its own population but to protect its own "image" then it is a case of "political expediency". When Iran signed the universal declaration of human rights at the United Nations and agreed to abide by the rules of the International Labour Organization, children of four years of age were working in its carpet factories. Today, years later, children of between four and five years of age still toil in the carpet factories. Signing the articles was an act of "political expediency" on the part of Iran.

Russia signed the United Nations anti-colonial resolution, calling for all non-self-governing areas to be "free" and "independent" by 1970. This was an act of political expediency for Russia never intended that her satellite states and the enslaved East European countries would be freed, nor did she make any attempt in that direction.

The United States of America signed a United Nations resolution stating that the backwardness of a country (e.g. the Congo) should not be an "excuse" to withhold independence. This also was an act of political expediency for in the light of what this has brought to Africa, no intelligent American observer could ever accept its premise. Agreeing to the resolution was rather a transparent example of "me-tooism" on the part of America so as not to be classed as "pro-colonial" even though colonialism, by then, was beginning to look quite respectable in the face of Black Africa's post-independence record.

On the other hand a healthy form of national self-interest has much to commend. South Africa can, in the spirit of national self-interest, build up a strong defence force. By doing so it adds to the security of neighbouring states with whom it enjoys good relations and who may share South Africa's concern at the disintegration of law and order all over Africa. In such a case self-interest can lead to regional security.

National self-interest also means that a country is primarily interested in the lot and development of its own people. This is a healthy attitude since it precludes undue concern with the domestic affairs of neighbouring states and, by improving the lot of its own people, their economic development and systems of communication and government, contributes to regional stability.

Earlier in this book Professor Z. K. Matthews, Botswana's Ambassador to the United Nations was quoted as saying that while a moral outlook on these things are all very well it simply does not carry the day. "Self-interest and pragmatism is what counts," he said. Professor Matthews is not the only Black African who now shares this view. Dr Hastings Banda, the President of Malawi, is also on record as saying that his relationship with South Africa and the Portuguese territories is dictated by the realities of Malawi's domestic situation. Dr Robert Gardiner, the Head of the United Nations Economic Commission for Africa also observed in Addis Ababa on March 21, 1967 that the attitude of Lesotho, Botswana and Swaziland towards South Africa is a natural outflow of the realities of the situation and an expression of self-interest on the part of these three states. He did not believe that there was anything wrong in their economic interdependence and co-operation "provided the governments are serious in their belief in non-intervention in the domestic affairs of each other". Remarkable words about the White South coming from a Black African. Dr Gardiner's observations were followed up by the Lesotho High Commissioner in London who said at a press conference on March 29 that Lesotho and South Africa were parts of a socio-political economic system which could not be tampered with. He added: "So far South Africa has treated us with the utmost propriety and respect."

The past five years have brought forth abundant evidence that those countries which have the most to say about the affairs of other nations are usually experiencing serious problems at home. Take for example Ghana, Nigeria, Algeria, Red China, Cuba, Mali, Tanzania, Indonesia, etc. While civil strife, chaos, corruption, economic ruin and starvation are causing misery and havoc in these countries their leaders are constantly in the press or on Television urging the "liberation" of other prosperous and peaceful countries. If Indonesia or India had been subject to a healthy form of national self-interest its leaders would have concerned themselves far more with the day-to-day lot of the average Indonesian or Indian (who is generally hungry, uneducated and suffering from disease) than is the case at present. Nor would they have had time to pry into the affairs of a dozen other countries in the world or be concerned about the fate of people of Indonesian or Indian descent in Malaysia or South Africa.

If the half dozen African heads of state deposed in military coups in 1965-1966 had practised national self-interest rather than political expediency they might still have been in power, and, in some cases, alive.

President Nkrumah of Ghana was so intent on "liberating" the people of South Africa that he woke up in Red China one morning to discover that his own people had been "liberated".

It is not the contention that there are *no* governments in the world capable of lending genuine assistance to other countries or of expressing *bona fide* interest in the welfare of other nations. However, if that interest or assistance is only indirectly related to the welfare and future happiness of their own people, such "interest" and "assistance" should be viewed with suspicion.

This is also not a plea for a lull in "international co-operation" or a belief in isolationism – on the contrary – it is simply that in the long run "international co-operation", "mutual assistance" and even "internationalism" would best be served by a thorough job of individual house-cleaning. If governments were dedicated first of all to the betterment of the lot of their own people and to developing their natural resources and human material the "small" countries would have no fear of "big" countries, and big countries would end up having more money for assistance to those less well endowed in natural resources and human material.

This thesis can be faulted on grounds of technical expression but as far as the Third Africa is concerned the increasing co-operation between different nations and states and between people of widely diverging ideologies has shown it to be true in practice. They have found co-operation easier because of a healthy form of self-interest. By diverting all energies to house-cleaning they have also improved their own internal situation and thereby contributed to regional stability.

The countries of the Third Africa are to a large extent the victims of a United Nations and Communist sponsored ostracism, but they are not isolated in terms of each other nor is their common cause one of "political expediency". This is one of the less tangible but, nonetheless, recognised factors contributing to the concept of regionalism in Southern Africa today.

Though it believes in multi-racialism, Portugal has never taken it upon herself to lecture South Africa on her domestic policy of separate development of the races. The countries are getting on with the job at home, Portugal in Mocambique and Angola and South Africa in South West Africa and its various Bantu homelands. There are no attempts by either state to set itself up as arbiter of differences elsewhere, to create turmoil elsewhere, to boycott each other's trade or to act as a staging ground for quasi-military expeditions against other states. In one way or another virtually every Black African state has been guilty of these offences, notably Mali, Ghana, Tanzania, Ethiopia and Tanganyika. It is no co-incidence that the internal situation in these countries leaves much to be desired. The same, of course, is true of Egypt, Algeria and the Sudan. By mutual respect for each other's difficulties and programmes Portugal, Rhodesia and South Africa found that in matters of truly mutual concern such as postal communications, trade, tariffs, science, health services, research, tourism, etc. co-operation comes easily.

The entire southern mass of the continent is moving towards a situation of increasing economic and political alliance – sufficient examples of which will be held up in this chapter – while the other two Africas, Black Africa and Arab Africa, are faced with increasing dissension.

The Arab States are experiencing disunity in respect of Israel, the war in Yemen, the role of Egypt and Algeria in the Congo, and in frontier matters. Tunisia and Egypt have broken off diplomatic relations; Syria accuses Jordan of being an imperialist puppet; Jordan says Egypt is trying to settle brotherly arguments by force, and so forth. The Organization of African Unity (after the Congo episode and the eclipse of Nkrumah) belies its name. On the question of the Congo the O.A.U. was split right down the centre. Not only was there disunity on how the Congo situation should be handled but also on the Pan-Africanist attitude towards economic boycotts and the part to be played by so-called "freedom movements" in Africa. In addition the last full conference was hampered by the unspoken awareness of all its delegates that they have been playing the international stage to such an extent that economically and politically their countries have hardly made any headway since independence. Ghana and Nigeria, the Sudan and the Congo, Somalia and Ethiopia have all been at loggerheads. Following Nkrumah's departure from Ghana, open war threatened between Ghana's new rulers and Guinea.

Individually the leadership class seems to suffer from an overdose of personal self-interest. In addition they cannot give a real lead in the conduct of African affairs if individually they are experiencing difficulty in conducting their own affairs. There cannot be Pan-African orderliness if the separate states subscribing to this ideal do not maintain proper order within their own borders, for example the Sudan, Tanzania, Algeria and Nigeria. This is what places Southern Africa in a position of political pre-eminence as far as *future* developments in Africa are concerned. While the constituent elements of independent Black Africa are drifting further and further apart (for example, Togo accuses Ghana of planning its overthrow, while Ghana is seeking military assistance from Nigeria – its erstwhile critic – to defend itself against "invasion" from Guinea) there are plenty of signs of a steady consolidation of policies and opinions in Southern Africa in spite of the Rhodesian-Zambian set-up. Some of these developments have been described and listed in Chapter 3 of this book.

On the part of the Whites of the sub-continent there is a growing determination to retain that to which they are rightly entitled as a consequence of history and hard work. At the same time one can, by referring again to the statements of the Black leaders quoted in Chapter 3, observe a growing determination among the Black nations of the Third Africa not to be misled by their would-be saviours from the north who are regarded as free with advice which they fail to follow themselves.

The Third Africa, except perhaps Zambia and Malawi, has one advantage the rest of Africa lacks. This is the interaction of established western democratic principles and practices (as practised by the White community) upon the traditional tribal laws and customs of the Bantu. This interaction of one way of life upon another, without the one being *forced* on the other (as happened in the case of the Red Indians in America or the Negroes in the Sudan), tends to produce vital conditions of tolerance particularly when the dominant legal system honours and recognises essential laws and customs of the other community, as is the case in South African law.

The many people in Lesotho, Black people, who believed at the time that their state should have seriously considered joining up with South Africa in the establishment of separate states for its different Black nations, did so not only because they realised that South Africa could have led them to meaningful independence and economic stability at a faster rate than Britain, but because of the safeguards to their identity as a people, their language and customs in a programme of separate development. The best proof of this is the South African government's dedication to safeguarding the identity of the White nation *and* that of the other Bantu nations. It is anxious to prevent the clash which inevitably follows when different races and cultures are forced together. In fact, South Africa and the three former British Protectorates, as well as the Bantu homelands in South Africa, provide the two political elements of interaction so sorely lacking in the rest of Africa. It is accepted in Southern Africa that the White nation is there to stay, just as it is accepted that the Black man is there to stay and to administer his own affairs. *That* is the major distinguishing feature of the sub-continent and it makes the Pan-Africanist ideals of Black Africa politically unrealistic.

The Black people in Southern Africa are politically more mature – in the sense that they are politically more realistic – than the Black man in the north. To a large extent this is a result of their being more closely associated over a longer period of time with the White man and the values which he has introduced in Africa. With almost no exception the political leaders of the Black states in Southern Africa (Kaunda, Khama, Banda, Jonathan, Mantanzima and others) plead for greater economic responsibility and less Black racism. There is nothing strange about this. It is a natural result of the history described in the previous chapter and forms part of a process of political evolution which is only now beginning to bear fruit.

The Bantu leaders in the south have also seen the results of political outbursts directed against the White man elsewhere in Africa as well as the fruits of Black racism and economic irresponsibility. They are taking careful note of what they have seen. They are far more aware of what the White man has meant to them in the past and what he could mean to them in the future than given credit for.

This is one of the reasons why Moise Tshombe made a success of Katanga's development. When he said that he depended on the goodwill of Angola, Mocambique and South Africa to get the copper and cobalt of Katanga to seaports he was expressing a healthy form of national self-interest.

Having experienced and observed the economic development in booming, prosperous South Africa, the economic fantasies of Nkrumah and others appear to these leaders in even worse light.

The countries in the Third Africa have certain obvious fields of close contact, some abstract some concrete.

In the *abstract* field there is, for example, what Professor Hans Morgenthau, Professor of Political Science at Chicago University, discerns as "the quality of government" as an element of national power. This is probably also what F. H. Hartmann means in *The Relations of Nations* when he speaks of "administrative and organizational ability".

This is a great source of strength to South Africa, Rhodesia, Mocambique, South West Africa and Angola, both internally and in foreign policy. In the case of South Africa it distinguishes her in Africa and in this respect she is on a par even with the great powers. Some observers believe that except for her powerful position in the gold mining industry it is this quality of government, more than anything else, that enables South Africa to speak on equal terms with America and Britain despite the huge differences in size and power.

In the case of the countries of the Third Africa their "quality of government" is superior to that of the other African states. Their administrative and organizational ability is such that the maintenance of proper relations with neighbouring states presents less of a problem than, say, between Ethiopia and Somali where trained government officials experienced in the ways of international relations could easily eliminate the prevailing attitude of "shoot first and talk afterwards".

In a more *concrete* form, it is the simple question of geography.

The Third Africa has no countries to the west, east or south whose attitude it needs to consider, only to the north and in this case it borders on the Congo for almost two thirds the distance.

During Premier Moise Tshombe's reign of power the Congo's

attitude towards White and Black states of the Third Africa was one of common sense. Tshombe said that the Congo "needs" Angola, Mocambique and South Africa for its economic well-being. In view of other considerations expressed in Chapter 3 it was not anticipated that this attitude would undergo any radical change. The success of White mercenary troops, most of them from Rhodesia and South Africa, in keeping Tshombe in power for so long may rankle in the memory of other militant Congolese. Since General Mobutu ousted both President Kasavubu and Premier Tshombe in 1965 an uneasy quiet has settled on most of the Congo and it is too early to judge the new strongman's attitude to the countries of the Third Africa.

Taking South Africa as a focal point, the Republic has frontiers with Mocambique (300 miles), Swaziland (200), Lesotho (360), Rhodesia (150), Botswana (850) and South West Africa (600). South West Africa, administered by South Africa as an integral part of the Republic, has a 950 mile boundary with Botswana, 800 with Angola and 120 with Zambia.

If South West Africa is included there is a total of some 3,760 miles of frontier for South Africa – all with territories of the Third Africa.

A brief glance at the map will show further factors of common interest.

Territories under White or European control lie in a horseshoe shape round the southern part of the continent from between 5° and 10° latitude to almost 35° south, while Botswana, Lesotho and Swaziland (Black states) are virtually hemmed in by territories under either South African or Rhodesian control.

The matter of *control* itself is not important here, except for those who foolishly believe in a form of White imperialism. What is of vital importance in the sphere of contact and co-operation are such matters as customs, communications, overflying rights of aircraft, water rights, control of agricultural and livestock diseases and research.

Several major rivers run through a number of states in the Third Africa or their catchment areas are located in other states. For example the *Zambezi* begins in Angola and wanders through Zambia and Rhodesia to enter the sea on the east coast of Mocambique. The *Orange River* has its catchment area in Lesotho and flows through South Africa to the Atlantic Ocean. Over the last few hundred miles it serves as the boundary between South West Africa and South Africa. The *Limpopo* has its catchment area in Botswana and South

Africa but later becomes the boundary between Rhodesia and South Africa and flows through Mocambique to the sea.

The proposed development of the incredibly vast inland delta of the *Okavango River* where it becomes the Okavango Swamps in Botswana could boost the progress of that country in ten years to heights which no amount of foreign aid can do in thirty years. But the project, which involves the construction of dams to generate hydro-electric power and a huge pipe-line to carry water to South Africa's industrialised north, will never get off the ground unless Angola, Botswana's neighbour to the north, guarantees a regular flow from the upper reaches of the Okavango and unless South Africa, and South West Africa, is prepared to purchase water and electricity.

In the use of the waters of these rivers for irrigation and hydro-electric purposes or for industrial use, the countries must obviously co-operate closely. (The Arab-Israeli dispute on the waters of the Jordan is a good example of what should *not* happen). Lesotho is another case in point. Where the Orange River rises in the Lesotho mountains, there are wonderful sites for generating hydro-electric power, but unless South Africa purchases the electricity, the Basutoland government might just as well not build the dams. It is, incidentally, the *only* potential earner of foreign currency for Lesotho of any real significance. In the case of the hydro-electric power station now to be built on the mighty Kunene River which forms the boundary between the north-western area of South West Africa and Angola, South Africa has agreed to purchase electricity from the Angolan station for use in South West Africa.

A common bond which also exists in the countries of the Third Africa is a healthy respect for the law. Each territory has produced its own variation of major European systems, whether Roman Dutch (South Africa), English Common Law (Rhodesia) or the Portuguese model (Mocambique), but at the same time incorporated or recognized to a greater or lesser degree "native law and custom". This interaction of legal systems has maintained and strengthened the rule of law in all of the Third Africa. The process of replacing "native law and custom" in which principles of right and justice are differently conceived and supplied – depending on the tribe to which one belongs – has also been evolutionary and not revolutionary.

142

Salisbury, Windhoek and East London form a triangle of some 4,000 miles but within that triangle, covering five different states, the procedures of arrest, provisional hearings, trial, appointment of a jury or judge and assessors and the right of appeal are generally alike and firmly established. A similar triangle in West or East Africa touching a dozen states would turn up perhaps one or two states where the right of counsel, trial by jury or *habeas corpus* is acknowledged but certainly not generally applied. In other African states a sound legal system respecting the rights of the accused and the interest of the convicted offender in prison is non-existent. The recent military trial of ex-Cabinet Ministers in the Congo on charges of high treason which lasted only 48 hours and their public execution is not an isolated case.

The *personal* attitudes or outlook of statesmen in the Third Africa, as reflected in the many statements quoted in Chapter 3 of this book, is therefore not the first contributing factor to a closer alliance. Their attitudes, apart from a more realistic appraisal of the broader aspects of African politics and the attitude of their people, are not derived from a vacuum. There are many other factors and aspects of life in the sub-continent which influence their thinking. Perhaps the most important individual factor is the realization that the Republic of South Africa dominates the military and economic scene all the way from the southern boundary of the Congo to the Cape of Good Hope – clearly and decisively. For this reason a discussion of other unifying factors in this region can best be done by considering the countries in their individual relationship with South Africa.

In the sheer scope of its industrial development in Africa, its employment opportunities, domestic and export market, financial resources, technical know-how (atoms to transistors and aircraft to ships) as well as its mineral and other natural resources, South Africa acts as a stabilising factor in the southern tier of the continent and generates considerable opportunities for closer co-operation.

Foreign investment in South Africa to-day is to the tune of R3,200,000,000 ($4,500,000,000) of which R500,000,000 ($700,000,000) is from the United States. The country's exports in 1966 (including gold) exceeded R1,810,000,000 ($2,520,000,000) and her imports approximately R1,750,000,000 ($2,430,000,000).

This makes her one of the fourteen great trading nations of the world.

Projects already commenced involve capital investment of more than R2,100,000,000 ($3,000,000,000) for the next ten years in iron and steel, electric power, gasoline-from-coal, transport, hydro-electric projects, copper mining, etc. In May 1965 the Electricity Supply Commission announced construction plans for building the world's two biggest conventional power stations at a cost of nearly R320,000,000 ($450,000,000). The power stations (as in the case of the R500,000,000 ($700,000,000) Orange River Hydro-Electric project) will attract tenders and labour from all over the world and Africa.

The country also has a mushrooming consumer market and in a matter of ten years the income of the twelve million Bantu has doubled. In fact, the *income* of the twelve million Bantu through wages and business alone is nearly twice the total gross national product of *fourteen* other African states with a population in excess of thirty million.

In a relatively undeveloped region of the world, the influence and attraction of a country in an advanced stage of industrial development with a big population is quite significant. Take the question of employment. In his authoritative survey of the position of the foreign Bantu workers in the South African economy Dr G. M. Leistner of the Africa Institute pointed out that by the end of 1964 there were some 497,000 foreign Bantu employed in the Republic of which 294,000 were mine workers under contract. Their total annual earnings exceeded R133,000,000 ($186,000,000) out of which cash and goods to a total value of R24,000,000 ($23,600,000) are estimated to be remitted to their countries of origin.[1] In American terms these amounts may seem small but their total earnings exceed the total gross national product of countries such as Upper Volta with a population of over 4,500,000 people (nine times the number of foreign workers in South Africa) or Guinea with a population of over 3,000,000 people.[2]

Lesotho's Information Service recently reported that Lesotho labour in South Africa earned the territory some R13,000,000 ($18,000,000) in wages and *in natura*. If wages represented only fifty

1. *South African Journal of Economics*, March 1967, pp. 42-43.
2. *Africa Report*, September 1963.

per cent of this sum it is still considerably more than the total Lesotho budget and almost twice the value of all its exports.

Of greater importance than the cash earned is the dissemination of new ideas on health, social welfare, feeding schemes, hygiene, education, labour saving devices, mining methods and safety care by those foreign workers throughout Southern Africa.

In some cases the foreign worker arrives in South Africa without knowing how to use a fork and knife or a spade and hammer. The workers are taught safety measures, how to read and write, first aid, elementary construction techniques, operation of mechanical equipment, etc. This knowledge is taken home where it would have cost the home government thousands to give them the same schooling or where, in some cases, the facilities for such training simply do not exist.

An industrially and technically developed state such as South Africa does not only provide work for labourers from surrounding countries. It provides assistance in many other fields and can render services in a dozen other directions. During the past few years, aid in agricultural technology was extended to virtually every country in the Third Africa and even further afield. Millions of doses of vaccine were dispatched from the huge Onderstepoort Laboratories (107 full time scientists) to countries such as Mocambique, Rhodesia, Malawi, Zambia, Kenya and Tanzania, the three former British Protectorates, as well as to the Middle East and Asia. In May 1965 six Southern African veterinary experts and over 100 stock inspectors assisted by three mobile fencing units helped to combat an outbreak of the dreaded foot-and-mouth disease in cattle-rich Swaziland. A considerable amount of analytical work in biological specimens and soil and water samples was also undertaken in Mocambique, Kenya, Angola, the Congo, the Protectorates and other states in the Third Africa. In many cases experts from South Africa's Department of Agricultural Technical Services undertook field trips to give technical assistance in connection with specific agricultural problems such as stock diseases and insect control.[3]

This is an example of what has already been done in only *one* important field.

3. Cf. "South Africa Helps Emerging Black States", *Bantu*, Pretoria, April 1967, pp. 1-6.

In other fields, the Bureau of Standards, the Council for Scientific and Industrial Research, the National Chemical Research Laboratory, the Fuel Research Institute, the Bureau for Personnel Research, Medical Research Institutes at various universities, the National Mechanical Engineering Research Institute, etc. have made contributions of equal importance to a developing continent. Experiments in low cost housing by the National Building Research Institute alone have saved some African countries millions of dollars.[4] The scientists in these laboratories and workrooms are men trained not only at South African universities, but in the United States, in Germany, Italy, England and France.

There is still a vast field in which South Africa could play an important role. South Africa could be of great assistance to the other African states in the use of nuclear energy to solve problems indigenous to Africa. The information presented in papers at the third International Conference on the Peaceful Use of Atomic Energy (South Africa has two atomic accelerators and Africa's only *working* nuclear reactor) has shown that nuclear explosions as applied to civil engineering can become an important factor in the development and construction of harbours, canals and open pit mining. The use of nuclear methods in the desalinization of water is another example.

Because of the size of its domestic market and its ability to generate capital, South Africa has and will play an important role in the industrial and economic development of most of the countries of the Third Africa. South African capital has been behind much of the big projects in Malawi, Zambia, Rhodesia and Swaziland.[5] Many of the engineers and scientists also came from South Africa.

According to the latest information total South African investment in Southern Africa is about R650,000,000 ($910,000,000).[6]

On a government to government level South Africa, because of her advanced stage of development, can in many ways afford to render assistance to other states. In 1964 South Africa undertook to provide a loan of some R6,000,000 ($8,000,000) and a direct part-

4. See "South Africa has made a Great Contribution to The African Continent" by W. Marshall Clark, O.B.E., B.Sc., M.Inst., C.E., in *Africa*, May 1965, Afro Publications, Johannesburg.

5. See the later discussion on individual countries.

6. South Africa Foundation, *Tempo*, April 1967.

contribution of R3,000,000 ($4,000,000) for the expansion of the hydro-electric project at Matali, Rhodesia. This was the first direct loan of its kind and has been widely publicised in South Africa and Rhodesia. Early in 1965 South Africa extended another loan of some R5,000,000 ($7,000,000) to Rhodesia for the Chiredzi Dam, electric power supply and airport construction.

The scope of government and private financial assistance to territories of the Third Africa has never been fully analyzed but there is no doubt in informed circles that as the territories respond to the growing signs of peaceful alignment South African assistance and investments, whether in the form of long term credits for payment of imports or private investments, will be made on a more appreciable scale. In May 1965 South Africa's Industrial Development Corporation announced that long term loans have been made available to enable South African companies to build a sugar mill of more than R5,000,000 ($7,000,000) in Mocambique and another of nearly R2,000,000 ($3,000,000) in Malawi. The latter plant is designed to produce sufficient sugar to supply the entire internal market in Malawi and its total cost is set at over R6,000,000 ($8,200,000).

Commenting on this, the Johannesburg *Rand Daily Mail* said: "This new development brings South Africa into line with procedures which have been successfully adopted in recent years by several highly industrialized countries for exporting capital goods and technical know-how to underdeveloped countries. These new African states desperately need help in their development and we are uniquely well placed to provide it. Political attitudes on both sides have been the major hindrance up to now, but the Industrial Development Corporation's new venture is an important step forward in this sphere."

Because of its big imports, South Africa will forever be an attractive partner in any regional economic alliance, particularly in Africa. The trading position of the Republic is such that it completely dominates the character of the sub-regional pattern, its trade representing more than 80 per cent of the sub-regional total. Of the roughly R550,000,000 ($770,000,000) inter-territorial trade within the sub-region that is the Third Africa, trade with the Republic counts for more than 70 per cent.[7]

7. J. A. Lombard: "Economic Co-operation in Southern Africa", *Tegnikon*, March 1967, p. 18.

Producers in Rhodesia, Swaziland and the Portuguese provinces will also try to get a stake in the rising Bantu consumer market referred to earlier. In plain figures the Bantu in South Africa, at the present rate of development, will have a spending power of some R5,000,000,000 ($7,000,000,000) in half a life time. (At present their buying power is some R1,200,000,000 ($1,700,000,000). By any standards a market with a potential growth from R1,200,000,000 to R5,000,000,000 ($1,700,000,000 to $7,000,000,000) in thirty years or so deserves a very close study indeed.

There is another field in which South Africa can render "assistance" to countries of the Third Africa, namely in educated manpower and tourism. In the case of Malawi and Zambia the Black governments have openly recruited personnel in South Africa and have advertised in the Afrikaans language press for White tourists. These states realize that while countries may differ over their ideologies they can never, in this intractable continent, afford not to co-operate in the practical business of living and better living.

The situation and factors in other countries which promote a closer alliance notably in the economic field or which could serve to prevent an irreparable political rift, are particularly significant when those factors are analysed in their relation to South Africa's economic strength. The three former British Protectorates of *Lesotho*, *Botswana* and *Swaziland* form an outstanding example.

When South Africa's top financier, Mr Harry Oppenheimer, formally inaugurated the R4,500,000 ($6,255,000) Edwaleni hydro-electric project in *Swaziland* in 1965 he observed that without South Africa's help the present economic development in Swaziland would have been impossible. The new hydro-electric project marked an important stage in the state's programme to provide the power needed to transform the country into an economically potent neighbour of South Africa. Swaziland has now also acquired an iron ore mine which would earn some R12,000,000 ($17,000,000) in the next year and has constructed a R22,000,000 ($22,000,000) railway line to transport the ore to Lourenco Marques. The money came from two sources – a private loan raised in South Africa and a loan from the International Bank for Reconstruction and Development. Speaking at the inauguration of the hydro-electric project, Mr Oppenheimer, Chairman of South Africa's giant Anglo-American Corporation (total assets measured in billions) said: "Free access to

148

the South African capital market is of incalculable value to the country. Without it the iron ore mine could not have been opened nor the railway built." The railway line was built by three large South African companies. A South African company provided the first hundred iron ore wagons and the company operating the iron mine is part of the Anglo-American set-up. Japan is buying the iron ore and the Swaziland Government will thus be earning much needed foreign currency.

The fact, of course, is that South Africa's geographic and constitutional relationship with the former Protectorates and Swaziland has everything in favour of close co-operation. South Africa, Swaziland, Botswana and Lesotho already enjoy a measure of economic interdependence which probably exceeds that of the European Common Market. By agreement with the Union of South Africa in January 1910, Swaziland (and the others) united with South Africa in a customs union and receive a *pro rata* share of the customs dues collected. For Swaziland the estimated figure for 1966-67 is R470,000 ($650,000), about 5 per cent of the Budget. The telegraph and telephone systems are "integrated" with that of South Africa. South African banks operate in the former Protectorates. A monetary union also existed between the four states up until independence but South African coins and bank notes are still valid and freely used after independence. Bank rates are those in force throughout South Africa as are rates for loans by the building societies. As Mr Oppenheimer pointed out, the development of many African countries is inhibited by the small size of the internal market and the difficulty of securing risk capital from outside. Swaziland is therefore, fortunate in two respects – its natural resources are making it possible to develop an overseas trade and, secondly, it is in the same currency area as South Africa.

Of course, all three territories derive benefit from the internal and external monetary stability which the Republic maintains as custodian of the monetary area, and thus their economic development has been singularly free from balance of payments difficulties which so often hamper the advance of small sized developing economies.

The former British Protectorates also enjoy the benefit of an almost free flow of capital within the monetary area, while the Republic provides employment for a large portion of their labour force, as well as a ready market for their produce. The products of these territories are to a very large extent marketed as an integral part of those of the Republic. For example, the South African Citrus Exchange handles the citrus crop of Swaziland as part of the South African crop and markets it under the trade-mark "Outspan". Similarly, in handling wool the South African Wool Board and Wool Commission do not distinguish between the domestic and Lesotho wool clip, while wool from Lesotho also enjoys the benefit of the South African wool stabilisation scheme. Slaughter-stock from Swaziland and beef carcases from Botswana are exported to controlled markets in the Republic, i.e. the major urban areas, subject to veterinary restrictions and administrative considerations to regulate the flow of supplies. They also enjoy the advantage of minimum prices per grade and weight which the South African Meat Board guarantees.

More such examples can be quoted, but these few will suffice to illustrate the extent of co-operation which already exists between the Republic and those territories.

If Botswana, Lesotho and Swaziland should endeavour to develop their economies as separate and independent entities, it is likely that there will be a drastic reduction in their rate of development. At present these territories produce *for* the South African market and not merely for their *own* internal markets. Directly and indirectly they share in the South African infra-structure such as transport, communications, marketing and financial institutions, etc., which they otherwise would have had to establish at great cost.

It is necessary to bear in mind that in 1965 the combined Gross Domestic Products of the three territories amounted to only *one per cent* of that of South Africa.

The Republic also extends a wide range of technical assistance to Botswana, Lesotho and Swaziland. Owing to a lack of trained manpower, such as technicians, medical practitioners, administrative personnel and entrepreneurs, the United Kingdom and South Africa render a variety of technical assistance to them. On account of the great similarities in the climatic and agricultural conditions in the countries concerned, South Africa is in a favourable position to make a substantial contribution towards solving some of the problems which they have to face.

South Africa often offers advice and information to these territories in regard to the application of fertilizers, diagnosing of stock diseases and parasites, advice on citrus, cotton, tobacco and maize production, crop and plant diseases, irrigation and soil conservation, etc.

This close economic relationship between the former British protectorates and South Africa is to the mutual advantage of all parties. Owing to its geographical location, the Republic understands and appreciates the problems of her neighbours and is in a better position than any other country to assist these territories in their economic development.

It is natural that the promotion of their prosperity will also benefit the Republic. These close economic ties with the states in question also extend the scope of South Africa's domestic market. Owing to their proximity and economic interdependence each party is enabled to specialize in those directions where it has a comparative cost advantage.

In this relationship with South Africa, *Swaziland* is fortunate in having a diversified economy, even if on a small scale. It is rich in minerals. Apart from asbestos and iron there is gold, kaolin, tin, barytes and massive coal deposits. Geologists are intensively prospecting other resources. Its agricultural and livestock produce include sugar, tobacco, citrus, maize, cotton and slaughter cattle.

Because of the 1910 customs agreement there is a free interchange of goods between Swaziland and South Africa. This means that Swaziland can export without tariff barriers to South Africa – a huge consumer market on her doorstep.

Swaziland is part of the South African controlled marketing area for most of its essential cotton, citrus and vegetable production.

The country still operates on a deficit of about R7,000,000 ($9,700,000) per annum. For this reason the money sent home by Swazis working in South Africa is of considerable importance. By mid-1964 there were some 18,000 Swazis out of a population of 271,000, a sizeable proportion of the Swazi manpower, working on South African farms and in the mines. In 1964-65 the Swazi labour force in South Africa sent home cash and goods to the value of R766,000 ($1,072,000) an amount equal to government expenditure on education.[8]

Small wonder that with such a degree of economic inter-

8. Cf. *South African Journal of Economics*, March 1967, pp. 49-52.

dependence, Britain warned the United Nations that any boycott of South African trade by the United Nations would have "disastrous consequences" for the (then) Protectorates. In its report to the United Nations Committee which studied the feasibility of sanctions (it was subsequently found extremely unfeasible) Britain pointed out that 70 per cent of Lesotho's imports came from South Africa and 95 per cent of its exports go to South Africa. For Botswana the corresponding figures are 80 per cent and 40 per cent and for Swaziland 83 per cent and 43 per cent. Consequently, says the report, the effect of cutting off trade with South Africa would be disastrous. It would lead to a severe economic crisis which "the United Kingdom would be powerless to avert". The prohibition of irreplaceable breeding stock would have a most serious effect on Swaziland's cattle industry and sanctions would cripple the country's timber, rice, cotton and citrus industries. All three countries would incur serious balance of payment losses. Summing up, the report said that for at least one state, Lesotho, the strain would be such as to lead to "total political and economic collapse".

Lesotho, surrounded by South African territory, has many good reasons for desiring the customs union with South Africa to be continued and for seeking even closer economic and political relations.

The economy of Lesotho is intimately tied up with South Africa. Its mohair and wool, the only major exports, are shipped through South African markets. As much as a quarter of its population and the bulk of its able-bodied manpower (some 150,000 men) work in South Africa at any given time. In 1965, a year before the substantial wage increases for most Bantu labourers in South Africa, mineworkers alone sent home to Lesotho some R4,900,000 ($6,800,000) in savings assistance to families and in the form of back pay. (Their total income in South Africa exceeded R7,300,000 or $10,000,000.[9]) This meant that in 1965 money sent home from South Africa was twice the amount earned by the Government through tax receipts and equal to the revenue from customs and excise. In addition thirty-five per cent of the revenue raised by Lesotho from internal sources will come from customs under the custom union agreement with South Africa.

After a 100 years of British administration, the little mountain

9. Ibid, Table III.

country is pitifully undeveloped. No effort has been made by Britain to make the economy independent of South Africa and the economic interdependence which has been allowed to develop (the shared customs, common market, migratory labour, currency, telegraph system, etc.) is a further indication that *some* people in Britain had serious hopes that incorporation of Basutoland into the South African body politic would one day become a reality.

With South African assistance meaningful political independence and an infinitely better economic basis would have been achieved much earlier. Today secondary industry is virtually non-existent. Farming methods are as rustic as they were in the days of Moshesh. South Africa's first Bantu state, the Transkei, is infinitely better off. Small wonder that the Basutoland National Party at the time showed so much interest in Dr Verwoerd's proposal to lead Basutoland and the other Black homelands in South Africa, such as the Transkei and Tswanaland, to political self-realisation in a framework of political independence and economic interdependence.

On its own, Lesotho will never be able to feed its population, while agricultural, mineral and industrial development is possible only with the aid of South African private companies and the Republican government's blessing.

The hard facts are that even with massive financial aid from abroad Basutoland *must* trade with or import from South Africa to survive.

Leabua Jonathan, leader of the Lesotho National Party and now Prime Minister, expressed Basuto feelings in October 1964 when he told a 10,000 strong rally that if his party is elected (as it subsequently was) it would give South Africa first preference in establishing industries in Lesotho. Lesotho, he said, on its part had "white gold" – water, to build dams for irrigation purposes and for generating electricity (The Oxbow hydro-electric project). They would have to think first of those who would buy this commodity. "Neither Russia nor Communist China could buy Basutoland's water, only South Africa," he said; but to be able to win South Africa over to buy these commodities, Basutos must first plan to develop friendly relations with the Republic.

It is irrefutable proof of South Africa's *bona fides* that it has not made any attempt to force closer co-operation on the Lesotho people. South Africa has made it doubly clear in recent years that it has no desire whatsoever to incorporate Basutoland. Because of its unique geo-political position it would of course have advanced South Africa's programme of separate development if the country had voluntarily joined in this programme. However, the ultimate objective then, as it is now, remains political independence coupled with economic inter-dependence. Speaking to the press after his first two hour conference with South Africa's Prime Minister in Cape Town in January 1967, Prime Minister Jonathan said he was convinced that Lesotho and South Africa could work together in complete accord on the basis of this fundamental objective.

For *Botswana*, trade with South Africa is the country's life blood. Sixty per cent of Botswana's chief source of income, cattle exports, depends on South Africa and even if this was not the case she would still be dependent on South African ports for exports of any other kind. South Africa is the market for more than 40 per cent of all Botswana's exports, totalling R11,319,000 ($15,700,000) in 1965.

Sir Seretse Khama, now President of independent Botswana, told reporters in New York in 1964 that there were some 37,000 able-bodied people from his country working in South Africa out of a total labour force of only 320,000. In 1962 this migratory labour brought Bechuanaland some R500,000 in back pay from South African employers, an amount sufficient to pay for the running of the central administration and the country's entire educational programme at the time. In 1965 cash remittances and value of goods sent home to Botswana had risen to R2,280,000 ($3,200,000) and the labour force to 52,000.[10] In addition, the country also receives an income from the customs union with South Africa. The estimated amount for 1966-67 is R850,000. Considering that the 1967-68 Budget estimates revenue at only R5,200,000 the income derived from the customs union is most important.

There are no industries of any importance in Botswana and about 98 per cent of the people make a living through raising livestock. The number of people who receive salaries or regular wages number less than 13,800 and of these the majority are employed by the Government.

Here again, despite South Africa's overwhelming economic might, it has studiously refrained from entertaining any ideas of power

10. Ibid., Table III.

politics. Seretse Khama observed: "I think South Africa knows very well they stand for one thing – apartheid – while we stand for the exact opposite, therefore we can never agree on ideology. But they have not tried to intervene in our affairs or to influence us in any way, and we have no reason to expect that they will try to do so in the future."

Three other important factors tend to increase the inter-dependence of Botswana and South Africa. *Firstly*, the people in Botswana are all of the Tswana speaking group and just across the border, in the Transvaal province of South Africa, live some 800,000 Tswanas, almost twice the number of Tswana speaking people in Botswana itself! *Secondly*, education in Botswana is only in its infancy. The lack of teachers is serious. South Africa turns out thousands of Black teachers, many of them Tswana speaking, every year. There is an opportunity here for cementing the ties between the countries even more strongly. *Thirdly*, Botswana desperately needs water and electricity if she is to develop any sort of industry or to expand her agricultural production. The Orange River which forms the southern boundary of Botswana with the Republic of South Africa, will be harnessed for its entire length under the R500,000,000 ($700,000,000) programme already under way. Irrigation and power for South Africa are the main objectives but the southern portion of Botswana stands to gain from any extension of this programme northwards.

Shortly after his election as Prime Minister in March 1965, Seretse Khama said in Gaberones, the new capital, that he would also like to see South Africa extend her financial investments and risk capital to Botswana. Botswana uses South African currency and there is also extremely close co-operation in trade, agriculture, health services and most important, transport. The country's only railway line is the South Africa-Rhodesia line which runs from Mafeking in the Cape to Bulawayo in Rhodesia. This line which carries *all* of Botswana's imports and exports is operated by Rhodesia Railways.

Perhaps the key to improving the country's economic position as far as agriculture is concerned, rests with cotton and water.

The Director of Agriculture recently observed that if all of the 100,000 farmers in the state of Botswana planted one acre of cotton, the country would produce cotton exports worth over R5,000,000 ($7,000,000) every year. This amount would wipe out, overnight, the grants from the United Kingdom which have been keeping the country together up to now. Here again South Africa could provide an ideal outlet, for up to recent times the Republic produced only 30 per cent of her own cotton requirements and could almost provide Botswana with an assured market.

Harnessing the Okavango River system, a major river which dissipates itself in a vast swamp in Northern Botswana, on a massive scale, could produce enough water for the development of Botswana, northern areas of South Africa and also South West Africa. But this would have to be a massive regional project in which the various countries would share equally. According to South African scientists this project is entirely feasible. The water would be utilised for hydro-electric projects, industrial and agricultural purposes. To make this a payable proposition however, requires the whole-hearted co-operation of South Africa who would have to buy the bulk of the water supply.

The first tri-partite talks between the governments of Botswana, Portugal and South Africa, at a technical level, on the utilisation of the Okavango River took place in Pretoria on May 9, 1967 and further talks were then scheduled on the same subject.

Botswana also has sizeable deposits of coal, asbestos, manganese, copper and soda ash, but the full development of these potential riches would be almost impossible without the know-how, capital and management which only the big South African mining companies can readily provide – as they did in the case of Swaziland's iron mine. If soda-ash production can be made possible, Botswana can also take over part of the market left when Kenya stopped producing this export commodity in 1963 – because her principal market was South Africa.

No territory in the Third Africa, not even Lesotho, is so thoroughly economically and politically integrated with South Africa as *South West Africa*. For all practical purposes it can be said to be a fifth province of South Africa.

Up until five years ago the backbone of South West Africa was cattle farming, even though diamonds and base metals were of major importance as tax producers. Increased production of minerals and the fantastic rise of the fishing industry at Walvis Bay, have left agriculture more or less in the background now. The fishing industry had a gross production of nearly R50,000,000 ($70,000,000) in 1966, while minerals realized R115,000,000 ($161,000,000). In Africa these are impressive figures, equal to Liberia's gross national product in 1961. The total income from livestock farming in 1965 amounted to about R44,000,000 ($61,600,000) and the gross national product was more than that of several West African countries combined with a population *five* times that of South West Africa.[11]

Without the air services which South Africa provided, without the railway network which it built virtually from scratch, without the risk capital and other sources of financial assistance provided by South Africa,[12] plus the advantages of a customs union with the Republic and the use of its currency, the territory would never have enjoyed the development and prosperity it is currently experiencing.

On top of this little boom, a completely separate layer of prosperity has been added. This is provided by the massive Odendaal Plan under which South Africa is to invest millions of rand in roads, highways, airports, water resources, electricity, etc. in South West Africa. For the first five year phase the Government plans to spend some R156,000,000 which is like turning the present economic fire into a bonfire. In terms of South Africa's budget, this is equal to the United States pumping some R9,000,000,000 ($12,500,000,000) into, say, Indian reservations in Nevada over a five year period. The Commission also proposed a second five year plan calling for expenditure of R91,000,000 ($127,000,000) on the part of South Africa bringing the total for the ten years of development planned for South West Africa to R247,000,000 ($346,000,000). No estimate of expenditure was made for the third five year development programme envisaged by the Commission.[13]

The main reason for this involvement is, of course, the fact that South West Africa is administered as an integral part of South Africa according to the Mandate (now elapsed) granted South Africa by the League of Nations.

11. *South West Africa Survey*, Government Printer, Pretoria, 1967, pp. 63-70.

12. Between its assumption of the Mandate in 1920 and the case before the World Court in 1962, South Africa has contributed financial aid to its mandated charge of R300 per capita – the most consistent and valuable "foreign aid" programme of this century.

13. *Report of the Commission of Enquiry into South West Africa*, Government Printer, Pretoria, No. 12/1964.

It requires little schooling in geography and economics to discover that South Africa is the *only* country suited to assist South West Africa in her economic development. Even if the territory were not administered by South Africa, the Republic is the closest major economic market and industrial state within a radius of some 6,000 miles.

Since South West Africa has no coal at all the fuel used to power its industries (coal) comes from South Africa – hauled over a distance of 1,500 miles in South African trains. Even more important is the electric power situation. The 318,000 square miles of South West Africa would be without electricity were coal supplies from South Africa cut off. And electricity not only provides vital communications, but, what is most important, runs the water pumps essential for life in a semi-desert country.

If South Africa were forced to cut off the railroad, South West Africa would have a famine in fourteen days and all industry would halt.

South Africa's de Beers group control the diamond mining operations in South West Africa; South African fishing companies, the fish canning factories. Finally, Walvis Bay, the only good harbour on the entire South West African coast south of Luanda in Angola belongs to South Africa and is constitutionally a separate entity within the territory.

Ray Vicker, the eminent correspondent of the influential *Wall Street Journal*, recently wrote after a visit to the territory: "Like it or not, South West Africa now is economically integrated with South Africa after forty-three years of government by the latter country. Separating the two would be like separating Alaska from North America." The parallel is a good one for South West Africa is strategically and economically as much part of South Africa as Alaska is a part of the United States.

Geo-political realities dictate a policy of moderation for Botswana, Lesotho and Swaziland. Perhaps in less constricted circumstances the policy of Botswana, particularly, would be more in line with the policies of White-baiting states of Central and West Africa. But in the foreseeable future its actions will be moderated by its position between South West Africa, South Africa and Rhodesia and its dependence upon South Africa for economic survival. Political independence and economic co-operation, as forecast by the late Dr Verwoerd (also in respect of the future relationship between the Bantu states of South Africa and the White Republic) has already become reality as far as the former British Protectorates are concerned.

In time the people of these states and, hopefully, their governments will come to realise that the geo-political situation was not of South Africa's making and that her desire for regional co-operation and stability has nothing to do with apartheid. Apartheid will survive and continue even if Botswana and the other ex-British territories were on the other side of the globe. It has also nothing to do with a secret South African plan to incorporate these new states. Apart from now being impossible and illegal, incorporation would place a financial and administrative burden on South Africa which it simply cannot afford today – apart from adding to the racial imbalance in the Republic. Assisting them in their development is one thing, running these countries is something entirely different.

In time they will also come to realise that there is nothing sinister about South Africa's expressions of goodwill and that its hopes for their orderly development and prosperity are as sincere as that of their own leaders.

Such a realisation would immeasurably contribute to the ties which bind the southern states.

In the case of South West Africa the ties which bind the territory with South Africa are both ideological and economic and the roots go back into history. The geo-political factors which are of vital importance to *all* the people of South West Africa are of such a nature that even if the territory were to become independent neither the United States nor Britain, and least of all the United Nations, could keep South West Africa on its feet without South African co-operation. Whatever progress there would be, would be completely artificial or so heavily subsidised that a rapid change in international affairs, necessitating the withdrawal of this support, would lead to economic chaos in a very short time.

It seems assured that a strong economic alliance with a powerful influence on positive political attitudes will indeed come to be realised in Africa south of the Limpopo and the chances of a common market being established in this part of Africa must, therefore, be rated excellent. Indeed, south of the Limpopo and the Kunene such a common market exists for all practical purposes.

Barring massive outside intervention such as in the South West Africa dispute, the chances that this situation must sooner or later also bring about a political alliance, at least on questions affecting the basic interests of the five different countries and territories, cannot be rated any *worse* than for the western European countries where the geo-political and economic factors are basically the same as in Africa south of the Limpopo.

8. Factors Promoting Alliance: North of the Limpopo

In the preceding chapter, some principles in the field of regional attitudes and positive relations between sovereign countries were examined, together with the factors which may promote even closer economic and political alliance between those states in the Third Africa whose geo-political relationship is inextricable and whose economies are heavily dependent on South Africa.

What is the situation in the rest of the Third Africa?

North of the Limpopo and the Kunene Rivers are the Portuguese Provinces of Angola and Mocambique, Rhodesia, Malawi and Zambia.

There is good reason for presenting their relationship with South Africa in a separate chapter. In all five territories there is a determining factor present which may vitally affect their relationship with other countries of the Third Africa, including South Africa. No such factors are present in the countries discussed in the previous chapter, not even for South West Africa, for even if the territory is "liberated" by some means or another, the future of the territory, whether under its own steam or United Nations subsidy, remains largely in the hands of South Africa.

In the case of *Rhodesia*, the determining factor is its struggle for recognition as an independent state; for *Zambia* it is her blind dedication to bring Rhodesia to a fall, even if it means destroying the Zambian economy in the process; for *Malawi* it is the political tight-rope with, on the one side, her sound economic approach and co-operation with South Africa and Mocambique and, on the other mounting Pan-Africanist pressures to cut these ties; for *Angola* and *Mocambique* it is either their protected status as provinces of Metropolitan Portugal with whom they are locked in a common market or the undisguised attempts by rebel forces of the Organisation of African Unity to foment a guerilla war of sufficient magnitude to bring in the United Nations.

These considerations apart, the factors contributing to even closer co-operation with South Africa and each other are increasing both in number and in magnitude, so that the current situation favours the Republic.

In the early twenties *Rhodesians* voted by a narrow margin against integration with the then Union of South Africa. To-day a majority of the people would consider a political and even a military alliance both wise and farsighted and an act which would relieve the country of some of the international pressures to get it to hand over government to the Black majority immediately. However, whether a Black, mixed or White government is in power would really be immaterial, for in the *long run* close co-operation with its big southern neighbour (and Mocambique) is the only certain formula for sustained economic growth and political stability in Rhodesia.

At the moment there are many good reasons why the White Rhodesian government will and should remain in power (see next chapter and Chapter 3) and excellent reasons why a common market agreement with South Africa cannot be ruled out for the near future. As for a political alliance with South Africa, such a development is enacting itself without a conscious effort on the part of Rhodesia. Britain and the militant Black African states are forcing Rhodesia in this direction.

Recent developments reveal exactly how rapidly and smoothly this transition from a British colony to an independent state in close association with South Africa is taking place.

In December 1964 the Rhodesian Broadcasting Corporation announced that the general overseas news of the B.B.C., up until then relayed from London, would cease to be broadcast in Rhodesia. In its place would be the South African Broadcasting Corporation's news relayed by Radio South Africa. Three months later Rhodesian Railways in association with South African Railways introduced a new express service between Salisbury and Johannesburg. The service, known as Railstar South, was introduced to help manufacturers make use of the market opportunities in South Africa following the recently signed trade agreement. Two weeks earlier a proposal had also been made in the South African Parliament that the Minister of Transport negotiate with the Rhodesian Government on the matter of an entirely new link between Rhodesian Railways and the South African system. The proposal was for the link to be established between Beit Bridge (South Africa's main gateway to Rhodesia) and Rutenga on the so-called Pafuri Line (significantly, also the main line between Salisbury and Lourenco Marques in Mocambique) which would shorten the distance between Johannesburg and Salisbury by over 150 miles. Since then the Rhodesian Government has appointed a Commission of South African experts to investigate the practical aspects. The commission completed its work at the end of 1966.

But perhaps the most important development of recent years has been the trade pact signed between the two countries towards the end of 1964. The agreement regulating trade between the two countries specified that goods originating in South Africa are guaranteed Rhodesian customs tariff treatment equal to that accorded to imports from the British Commonwealth countries except Great Britain. (British dutiable goods are generally liable to lower rates than those of other "most favoured nation" countries.) Rhodesia has also undertaken to grant certain South African goods equal treatment to that accorded to goods from Britain. A third category of goods can enter the Rhodesian market at tariffs slightly higher than those of Britain but lower than those of any other country. South Africa on her part has undertaken to grant specified Rhodesian goods unrestricted free admission at a margin of preference subject to quantitative control.

This agreement was signed more than a year *before* U.D.I., a certain indication that as far as economic ties are concerned, Rhodesia was then already setting its sights on a closer orbit with South Africa.

The agreement will greatly stimulate two-way trade through the lowered tariff barriers. Rhodesian exporters should now be able to compete on a far more favourable basis with other overseas suppliers of the South African market. *Even if British-Rhodesian relations return to normal*, South Africa will for the first time be able to compete with Great Britain for Rhodesian purchases in machinery, textiles, foodstuffs and a wide range of manufactured goods. The Johannesburg *Star* pointed out that the new pact will allow South Africa to compete for the R70,000,000 ($98,000,000) British share of the Rhodesian import market, for, although tariff margins on these items will be equal, transport costs from South Africa will be considerably lower than those from Britain, 6,000 miles away.

South African industrialists will thus be able to push British exporters off a large portion of the Rhodesian market.

Exporters in South Africa observed that, because the South African market is opened up still further for Rhodesian manufacturers, the new arrangements should provide a stimulus for Rhodesian secondary industry at a time when that country's manufacturing economy is in need of some bolstering.

In view of Rhodesia's struggle with Britain over independence the timing of the pact had a strong psychological effect on a people-to-people basis.

Since Rhodesia's declaration of independence from Britain, South African goods have, of course, dominated imports as the British economic boycott precluded any exports to Rhodesia.

Even if Britain and Rhodesia manage to patch up their differences the trade situation is likely to remain heavily in favour of South Africa in the foreseeable future. Should Rhodesia be "victorious" and obtain recognition of independence within the Commonwealth, the pact would still favour South Africa.

Observers in Pretoria rightly hailed the pact as a concrete step in the direction of the Common Market of Southern African States proposed by the late South African Prime Minister, Dr H. F. Verwoerd.

At the time when most Western States submitted to Britain's demands of an all-out economic war against Rhodesia, South Africa and Portugal continued their normal relations with Rhodesia including trade. More than that, through stupendous gifts varying from tennis balls to thousands of gallons of gasoline to the people of Rhodesia daily, South Africans demonstrated the strong links of kinship with Rhodesians.

There are numerous examples of how South Africa's official stand of "business as usual" and non-interference in Rhodesian affairs and her refusal to join the boycott club have aided the Rhodesian population, Black and White. On her part, Rhodesia responded by sending barrels of sweets as gifts to South African orphanages and tons of fodder to the drought stricken farmers in South Africa.

There are, however, many other factors which tend to make Rhodesians and South Africans feel closer together. Many thousands of South African citizens live in Rhodesia. The bulk of Rhodesian travellers aim for the holiday resorts near Durban and Cape Town in South Africa. When a South African national football or cricket side is elected to tour Britain, Australia or New Zealand, the chances are good that a Rhodesian will be in the side. Hundreds of Rhodesians, Black and White, have graduated from the University of South Africa – the world's first correspondence university – with a current enrolment of 19,000, or studied at one or more of South Africa's ten other universities.

The overriding factors, of course, are the common ideals of western civilization in Africa, the rule of law, a two-party political system, free enterprise, etc. and resistance to irrational and militant Black nationalism and Pan Africanism. This factor will be fully dealt with in its broader aspects in the next chapter. Sufficient to say here that Rhodesians learned a bitter lesson with the dissolution of the Central African Federation which they and Britain naively believed would contain or somehow satisfy the aspirations of the militant Black nationalists. Here, according to the belief of the former British Prime Minister, Mr Harold MacMillan, "merit and only merit" would have been the keystone for development. There would have been gradual political integration between Black and White with power ultimately passing into the hands of the educated majority whether White or Black. The determinant was the logic (and in retrospect also the logical mistake) of numbers, viz. 4,000,000 Blacks and 220,000 Whites.

Most White people in the Federation thought the government was going far too rapidly with its programme of integration and Africanization. The Blacks on their part felt that no progress was being made – their impatience later further encouraged by the British Prime Minister's "winds of change" speech in Cape Town. When given the chance, the Black people in Northern Rhodesia and Nyasaland proved conclusively (through the ballot box) that the only thing which matters is *not* merit but whether you are Black. They settled for Black government by Black people in a Black country.

So ended the dream of a multi-racial state in Africa.

Subsequently chaos in the Congo, the Zanzibar Communist take-over, mutinies in Britain's old East African colonies, the establishment of one-party dictatorships or military governments in virtually every ex-British colony further helped to convince the Rhodesians that the South Africans in advocating a policy of

165

political separation between Black and White were not spouting racial hatred, but were merely being realistic.

It was realised that a political alignment with South Africa did not mean that one must shout the merits of apartheid from the rooftops. As with Portugal, the Rhodesians realised that differences between domestic policies are no bar to co-operation in many other spheres. This was also the attitude taken up by Prime Minister Jonathan of Lesotho.

In a matter of two years, Rhodesia also became convinced that a policy of one-man-one-vote immediately would only lead to turmoil and chaos similar to what happened elsewhere in Africa. What they chose was a policy embracing a qualified franchise and which did not exclude a Black majority in time to come.

Under the policy of one-man-one-vote, or "majority government" as it is called, there would have been a brief struggle by the White minority, a one-party state in which the Black man would have complete control, then a Black dictatorship and finally, a collapse of law and order and economic decay.

This has happened in virtually every ex-British colony.

Britain would be no more able or (under a Labour Government) willing to protect the White minority in Rhodesia than she was able to protect the Whites in her other ex-colonies. The United Nations would consider the rights of the White minority as non-existent – being, in terms of the Afro-Asian bloc, the remnants of a colonial set-up. Finally property rights and the safety of life and limb of White Rhodesians would have taken the same road as that of the Turkish minority in Cyprus, the Indians in Burma or the Chinese in Malaysia. Britain, America, the United Nations, the world, would be powerless to prevent a classic example of cultural geno-cide.

The result of these deliberations and the developments that led to the collapse of the Federation, and Britain's betrayal of her pledge to the White man in East Africa, have led Rhodesia to aligning herself with South Africa – ideologically, culturally and politically. Differences in domestic policy are accepted, but, in terms of the bigger issues such as maintaining Western Civilization, protecting Christianity, facing up to the threat of the O.A.U., opposing the dangerous ideologies which the United Nations majority are advo-cating for Southern Africa and so on, there is now as little difference in opinion between Rhodesia and South Africa as there is between the Republic and Portugal.

After the first year of U.D.I., the year in which Britain, with the help of the Commonwealth, launched an all-out economic war to force Rhodesia back into the fold, the situation is far from critical. In fact considering the efforts to crush the Rhodesian economy, 1966 can be described as quite a successful year. National income was down about eight per cent, exports down about thirty per cent (but because imports were held down there is still a visible trade surplus), employment is still high, industrial activity down by some ten per cent but the property market firm – more so than for several years – while share prices are for the most part higher than the year before U.D.I. In effect this means that Rhodesia is, economically, far from being in the state of crisis which the British Government had predicted would follow "within weeks". The trade surplus was still a healthy R41,000,000 ($70,000,000) and the industrial index higher than the year before U.D.I. Cost of living was up 2.2 per cent but so were building activities.[1] The Rhodesian Government's revised three year plan for 1967-70 calls for capital investment of some R146,000,000 ($204,400,000) in the public sector – a greater programme of development expenditure than at any previous time.[2]

Unable to crush Rhodesia, Britain passed the matter to the United Nations where the Security Council voted for mandatory sanctions proposed by Britain – the first time the world body has ventured to take such action in its twenty-one year history. What the effect of mandatory sanctions will be is examined more closely in the next chapter.

To-day Rhodesia, after South Africa, is probably the most developed country in all of Africa. Economically (complete with Stock Exchange) industrially and in terms of education and communication as well as agriculturally, technically and administratively, her development and quality of government is superior to that of any other African state.

During 1964 and 1965, Rhodesia became one of the few countries in Africa to achieve a favourable trade surplus; by African standards,

1. South African Press Association, April 14, 1967.
2. *Public Sector Investment*, 1967/1970, tabled in Parliament, Salisbury, 30.5.1967.

the figure of nearly R90,000,000 ($126,000,000) is extremely impressive. Rhodesia's *surplus* alone matches the *total* exports of a *dozen* Black states. Exports for 1965 were valued at R284,000,000.

Mining in Rhodesia is on a moderate scale but an inflow of capital from abroad after the present constitutional crisis has been overcome, could result in Rhodesia developing a major mining complex. Gold, asbestos, chromite, copper, iron ore, limestone, lithium minerals and tin are there in commercial quantities. The manufacturing industry is also becoming increasingly diversified (glass, steel and metal products). A new refinery is capable of producing large quantities of sulphur, gasoline, aviation turbine fuel etc. Agriculturally the country is becoming increasingly self-sufficient with tobacco, maize, sugar, cotton, groundnut and tea, deciduous fruits, etc. being produced in substantial quantities.

After South Africa, it is the only country in Africa producing sufficient steel for her own building requirements.

The Rhodesian Declaration of Independence and Britain's imposition of wide ranging sanctions has had the effect of estranging Rhodesia's closest economic partner, Zambia, formerly Northern Rhodesia.

Zambia and Rhodesia both have strong economic ties with South Africa. The outcome of Rhodesian independence in so far as it affects Zambia is hard to predict, but it must be assumed that at some stage the almost insane economic war waged by Zambia against Rhodesia will come to an end, if for no other reason than the realization that the economic war against Rhodesia is Britains' responsibility and that Zambia could do absolutely nothing to Rhodesia which would not cause infinitely more damage to her own economy. In trying to break up the jointly owned Rhodesian-Zambian railway by refusing to pay for freight, Rhodesia for a time simply retained Zambian copper exports at a loss of some R36,000,000 ($50,000,000) to Zambia.

President Kaunda has already taken other steps which, if continued, must ultimately leave Zambia's economy in ruins. The question is whether he will realise his mistake in time.

President Sukarno of Indonesia was as intent to destroy Malaysia and in the end his unreasonable and emotional attitude almost destroyed his country. It has certainly destroyed his own political future.

South Africa has maintained a strict neutrality in the Rhodesian-Zambian question and both countries continued to expand their trade with South Africa. For this reason too, an analysis of Rhodesian-Zambian ties prior to the declaration of independence is in order.

The development of Zambia originally stemmed from the South, i.e. Rhodesia. The railway line from the south opened up the main agricultural and mining centres at the beginning of the century when it was diverted through the Wankie coalfields of Southern Rhodesia, across the Zambezi at the Victoria Falls and on to link up with the Copper belt. The most successful agricultural projects have also been developed by European farmers along the line of rail.

Apart from the railway, Zambia and Rhodesia of course, shared a single hydro-electric power project at Kariba and a common airline. The electricity for Zambia is generated by the Kariba plant which is on the Rhodesian side of Lake Kariba. The plant produces ninety per cent of all the electricity used in Zambia.

The relationship which existed between the two countries was one of far reaching economic interdependence, and a very promising one at that. *In fact, when the British Government decided to dissolve the Central African Federation under pressure from extreme Black nationalists it decided to destroy one of the strongest economic units in modern Africa.*

Northern Rhodesia's (Zambia) copper wealth combined with the diverse agricultural, mining and industrial complex in Southern Rhodesia (Rhodesia) produced a viable economic unit of great promise which has proved its value to the whole of Central Africa during the preceding ten years – to the benefit of Black and White. Since 1953 there had existed between the two countries a common market for goods, services, capital and labour with a common currency and a common system of taxation applied to the best interests of both territories – much the same as the customs union and free market arrangement existing between South Africa, the former British Protectorates and South West Africa.

The internal markets of Zambia and Rhodesia were also complementary to the development of each country. Zambia supplied thirty-three per cent of the old Federal market for consumer goods and forty per cent for producer goods. In terms of wages and employment, Zambia's contribution was much smaller, based as it was on the small but highly productive area covered by the Copperbelt and the line of rail centres. Zambia currently employs thirty thousand Europeans and 238,000 Blacks and pays wages amounting to less than R132,000,000 ($185,000,000) per year. Rhodesia again, had been the main centre for secondary industry in the Federation because its economy was more diversified and because higher wages and employment provide a larger market. Rhodesia employs 86,000 Europeans and 624,000 Blacks and pays wages amounting to more than R330,000,000 ($464,000,000).

If Zambia establishes secondary industries on a large scale, she will have to look outside the territory for other markets in order to survive. Her best and nearest customer will still be Rhodesia, where wages are higher and where there is more general employment than in the countries to the north. On the other hand if Rhodesia loses the markets of Zambia, limited as they are, many industries, especially the textile industry, will receive a severe blow from which they might take some years to recover. (In 1964 Zambia took some twenty-three per cent of all Rhodesian exports.) However, Rhodesia has a very much wider spread of industrial, agricultural and mining operations to absorb the shock of such an event. Eighty per cent of the now defunct Federation's secondary industry was based in Rhodesia. Most of these industries are capable of quick expansion and are geared to adapt themselves to changing conditions.

Zambia, is as much dependent on the more mature and developed resources of Rhodesia as the latter's industrial complex is dependent on the market in Zambia for a ready outlet of its products. The loss of the Zambian market would be a severe blow to the industrialists of Rhodesia but the loss of Rhodesia's highly developed communications system and access to seaports could strangle the Zambian economy.

Zambia's leaders have been seeking an alternative source for exports and imports since 1962 with the latter being almost as important to its economic survival as exports. With the substantial development in Zambia's economy during 1962-1965 the closest and least expensive markets for imports of vital supplies was Rhodesia which supplied forty per cent of all imports, followed by South Africa with little over twenty per cent.

Lately Zambia has focussed attention on the controversial plan for a railway through Tanzania to Dar-es-Salaam, but the survey (by Canada and England) is not expected to be fully completed until January 1967 and the railway (assuming that the vast financial backing can be found) will take at least four to five years to complete. Thereafter it will, according to World Bank estimates, run at a substantial *loss* for some twenty years until 1990. *The project has little relevance, therefore, to Zambia's immediate needs.* Portugal, a silent ally of Rhodesia, controls Zambia's nearest points of egress on both sea-boards. This increases Zambia's vulnerability. In addition it is not expected that President Banda of Malawi will be very helpful because of his hostile attitude towards the militant O.A.U. policy on Rhodesia, which is fancied by Zambia. Apart from that, the nearest point of the Malawi line (which runs to the Portuguese port of Beira) is 450 miles by dirt road from Zambia.

Zambia has made every effort to make use of truck-transport in order not to use Rhodesian Railways. Trucks have been used extensively on the roads through Tanzania and Malawi. However the onset of the rainy season renders the existing roads virtually impassable. In October 1966 (according to Zambian figures), the roads carried 31,000 tons of copper out of Zambia, about half the full production, and brought in 16,000 tons of oil and 3,000 tons of general merchandise. Rhodesian Railways, despite limitations, carried 100,000 tons of coal and merchandise into Zambia in the same month. In addition overall Zambian transportation costs have risen by nearly 15 per cent.

Whatever the circumstances after another year of Rhodesian independence may be, both Rhodesia and Zambia are economically interdependent and must look to industrially developed South Africa if they are to become economically viable and stable countries.

If the two countries would one day again co-operate in the economic field and pick up the threads of their association after the present animosities have been buried by political common-sense, it could lead to a degree of prosperity for both states which neither could dream of individually.

Zambia recently announced a R700,000,000 ($1,000,000,000) four-year development plan. By 1970 the planners hope that the country will have diversified its economy, trade patterns and transport system and that it will be manufacturing most of its own needs. In the light of its confrontation with Rhodesia, which is costing

Zambia more than it could possibly afford, the chances are good that it will end with most of the targets little more than a distant dream. In addition the success of the entire project depends heavily on White skills and the "importation" of a sufficient number of technical and professional men from "other countries" such as South Africa. In view of President Kaunda's recent anti-White diatribes hope of obtaining this skilled manpower must be faint. However, if Zambia abandons her war on Rhodesia and turns to the industrially developed south, the chances are infinitely better that this well-planned project can achieve a great many of its laudable objectives.

Zambia still has a mono-economy based on copper production. More than fifty per cent of the Gross National Product comes from copper production. A slump in the copper price (similar to the near disastrous drop in the world price in 1957) would be equally disastrous to-day.

In the long term, Zambia's future will depend more on agricultural development. The mainstay of the country's agriculture are the 1,009 licensed White farmers who have close links with their colleagues in Rhodesia and upon whose institutions they depend for most of their marketing.

Up until now, the leaders of Zambia have tended to look towards the East African states for their country's development. The East African states, however, are hardly in a position to provide Zambia with a foreign aid programme or to spur its development. Not only are the African leaders tight-fisted when it comes to "foreign aid" but in view of their own state of economic decay they are far more in need of help than Zambia. As an expanding consumer market the East African states present a dismal picture. The rest of the Third Africa, particularly Rhodesia and South Africa and to a lesser extent the Portuguese provinces and South West Africa are the only markets worth cultivating in Africa south of the Sahara. The situation in Zambia's other neighbouring states, the Congo, Rwanda, Burundi, Gabon and Uganda is even worse than in the East African states.

In these two cases therefore, unifying factors or factors tending to promote closer co-operation between the two states individually and South Africa is complemented by their almost inextricable economic ties.

Quite apart from the preceding considerations, there are other developments which seem to indicate that the south is exercising a counter-influence to Pan Africanism in Zambian government and economic circles. In the first place there are her geographical ties with countries of the Third Africa. Zambia has frontiers of many hundreds of miles with Angola, Mocambique and Rhodesia, some of it most important rivers. Secondly, there are most important financial and economic ties and this, plus a certain amount of political realism, is beginning to make itself count.

First indications of a re-assessment on the part of the Black government towards the White South, came when Dr Kenneth Kaunda, the Prime Minister, refused to go along with the other African states in their boycott of South African trade. To what extent he was influenced by the White people of Zambia is not known but they are a vital force in keeping the country going. Only a handful of Black Zambians are trained in technical and financial fields. More than eighty per cent of the people live off the land as subsistence farmers. Cash crops for exports are largely the work of White farmers.

The existence of a solid asset in the copper mines moreover, has further sweetened Mr Kaunda's attitude to the White dominated south. It would be economic suicide for him to sever all relations with South Africa in an ideological dispute. The Zambian mining industry is almost totally dependent on coal supplies from Wankie, the vast Rhodesian deposits which are owned by South Africa's Anglo-American Company, while Zambia's principal source of explosives, clothing, mining and farming machinery, at prices which she can afford, is also South Africa.

Zambia also relies heavily on imports from South Africa to stock stores and supply manufacturing industries with metals and spare parts. It has become clear from statistics of the post Rhodesian independence period, that South Africa is becoming the top exporter to Zambia leading all other countries including Britain. South African exports to Zambia for 1966 are expected to total about R60,000,000 ($84,000,000) or twenty per cent of all Zambian imports.

On February 12, 1965 the Zambian Government Gazette contained the announcement that Zambia is to drop all customs duties on raw materials and component parts coming into the country *from all sources*, including South Africa. South Africa therefore, finds herself on the same trading basis as Britain. With steep sea transport charges facing the majority of Commonwealth countries, this puts South Africa in a strong position to improve trade relations with Zambia.

Observers now believe that Zambia's statement to the Economic Commission for Africa in Nairobi that it was studying steps to cut down trade with South Africa is merely a smokescreen.

Chronic unemployment (only 223,000 of the more than 3,650,000 people have steady jobs) has led to as many as 750 Zambians departing for South Africa *every week* to work in the gold mines of South Africa. It is estimated that they bring back some R3,600,000 ($4,200,000) in wages to Zambia annually. The Zambian governments "decision" to prohibit South African mines from recruiting labour is not expected to have a noticeable effect on these figures since they can easily cross the border into Mocambique or Botswana to join work seekers from these states.

All the preceding factors would weigh heavily on the mind of the most nationalistic statesman, although Kaunda's willingness to sacrifice his own country's economic interest for the sake of an unrealistic Black ideology in the form of Pan Africanism is an uncertain element. It nonetheless came as little surprise to people in Southern Africa when Zambia began advertising in South Africa not only for tourists but also for White technicians, scientists and engineers. With the break-up of the jointly owned Rhodesian-Zambian railways more than six hundred White Rhodesians have been asked to be transferred to Rhodesia. Without these workers, more than one third of the skilled workers on the Zambian part of the railways, the system is likely to be seriously affected. A special recruiting drive to find replacements has been launched in South Africa and East Africa, but because of the lack of skilled workers in East Africa Zambians are hoping that the White South will provide the necessary help.

The poorest relation of the old Central African Federation was Nyasaland, now *Malawi*.

Geo-politically, Malawi is firmly tied to the other states of the Third Africa. It has no railroad or first class road connections with any of the militant Black African states. The country's rail outlet to the sea is via Beira in Portuguese Mocambique and for two thirds of its borders it is surrounded by Mocambique. Its closest port city is also Beira and the city of Lourenco Marques in Mocambique.

The President of the new state, Dr Hastings Banda, who has had a battle on his hands with pro-Red Chinese factions in his country, realises that Malawi is extremely short of trained personnel and has been forced to invite a considerable number of White civil servants back to Malawi after Independence Day to man key posts in his administration.

Dr Banda, who has a shrewd eye for economic realities, has also insisted, despite bitter criticism from the militant Black states, on keeping the rail line to Mocambique intact. He has consistently condemned the militant attitude of Black Africa towards the South and has also stuck to his policy of non-interference in South Africa's household problems. At the United Nations in 1966, his delegation refused to join the boycott of South African speakers and rejected the Afro-Asian plan to wrest control of South West Africa from the Republic.

In March 1967 Portugal and Malawi signed an agreement which will make it possible for Malawi to enjoy a second railway outlet to the sea. From Mpimbe, north of Blantyre, a line will branch off from the existing line to Beira and connect at the town of Nova Freixo with the Mocambique railway line which leads to the thriving new port of Ncala, north of the town of Mocambique on the most eastern extremity of the province. The agreement included the use of the port of Ncala by Malawi. The Portuguese are to build the 50 mile section from Nova Freixo to the Malawi border and President Banda's Government will complete the 70 miles inside Malawi to Mpimbe. The agreement also included the outright sale of the world's longest railway bridge over water – the Sena bridge over the Zambezi linking Beira and Malawi – to Portugal and cost the Portuguese R7,000,000 ($9,800,000). The agreement is calculated to provide a far better service to Portugal's hinterland and to Malawi and is a further indication of President Banda's willingness to tie the future of his country to that of his southern neighbours.

Malawi is desperately in need of outside aid for development to keep pace with her growing population. The R7,000,000 ($9,000,000) sugar mill now being built in Malawi was financed by South African aid and is being built by South African engineers. It will not only employ 1,500 people but will meet the domestic demand for sugar and provide some 16,000 tons for export. In addition the mill brought with it a bank, post office, police station, airfield and hospital.

Of the considerable range of minerals in Malawi, only a few are known to occur in sufficient quantities to justify large scale mining. Rice and coffee has a limited future but the country's primary requirements are simply to step up general agricultural and food production and to increase employment.

The chronic unemployment has driven thousands of Malawians southwards to South Africa and into Rhodesia. The salaries which they bring home now run into R2,000,000 per annum. It was for this reason that Dr Banda wrote to an unofficial representative in Johannesburg urging migratory labour from Malawi to abide by and respect South Africa's laws. "Those who get into trouble," he said, "must not expect any sympathy from Malawi."

Dr Banda is primarily in quest of a better economic future for his people and country and to stabilise his government. Nothing tangible has been achieved in the economic field so far and the fact that the country's exports of some R39,200,000 or $54,500,000 (estimated 1966) were only R5,000,000 ($7,000,000) less than imports, was largely the result of production (tea, tobacco, cotton, groundnuts, tung oil, etc.) in the hands of non-Blacks – Asians and Whites.

The establishment of a Polytechnic Institute at Blantyre was financed by the United States Agency for International Development and the biggest single development project in Malawi's history, the Nkulu Falls hydro-electric scheme, is being financed largely by Barclays Bank and the British Commonwealth Development Corporation. However, Malawi officials realise and admit that the country's geographic location and its largely agricultural basis makes it imperative to maintain cordial relations with Mocambique and industrial South Africa.

Dr Banda himself told the Organisation of African Unity that he does not intend to boycott South Africa since his country's economic development depends on South African interest in industrial development and trade in Malawi. South Africa is also the only country which can provide much needed textiles and medicines, hardware and industrial machinery as well as motor vehicles and electrical supplies at prices which Malawi itself can afford.

Exactly how much closer to South Africa Malawi has moved during the past year is evident of course from the new trade pact signed between Malawi and South Africa during March 1967. The pact will greatly stimulate two way trade and also help to bolster the Malawi economy. South Africa indicated that it was much interested in the exploitation of Malawi's pulpwood potential on the Vipya Plateau where about 25,000 acres of softwood have already matured. South Africa is the only ready market in sub-Saharan Africa for softwood.

Malawi's tourist potential is considerable because of the great natural beauty of the countryside and massive Lake Nyasa. The visit of a three man Cabinet delegation from Malawi should be a boost to the lagging hotel industry there as they now expect more visitors from South Africa. Malawi's Minister of Development and Planning, Mr Aleke Banda (no relation to Dr Hastings Banda, the Prime Minister), told the representative of the Johannesburg *Sunday Times* during the week of March 5, 1967 that Malawi would welcome investments by South Africans in hotels, roads, housing projects and industry. (In return he hoped South Africa would buy more of Malawi's tea and cotton which are the country's two main exports.) This invitation is a clear indication that Malawians, at least, no longer fear the bogeyman of "neo-colonialism" which for so long has been held to be synonymous with "White capital investment".

Economics apart, the roots of friendship between Malawians and South Africans are deeply imbedded in their past association. For nearly 80 years more than 100 South African missionaries at a time, all White, have been working among the people of Malawi. For many years also the outstanding young men from Malawi travelled to South Africa for work, training and education. Dr Hastings Banda was baptised by a South African Minister and later worked in the town of Benoni, near Johannesburg. Today the activities of South Africans, particularly the White missionaries, are everywhere noticeable. The entire staff of the secondary school at Kongwe consists of South Africans. The school has an outstanding scholastic record and this is where the future leaders of Malawi are being educated. The Principal (President) of the biggest Teachers College in Blantyre is an Afrikaans speaking mission worker from South Africa, Miss Marion Liebenberg. Except for the government hospitals, the only surgeon and eye specialist in Malawi are both South Africans.

Most important of all, although many missionaries were ousted from Malawi after independence because of alleged political activities, this lot did not befall a single missionary from South Africa.[3]

Relations between *Angola* and *Mocambique*, the two Portuguese provinces in Africa, and the *Republic of South Africa*, the focal point of development in the Third Africa, have always been cordial. This springs as much from the belief in Western Christian civilization as from the conviction that developments in the rest of Africa, which are now taking such a grave turn, were due to a distortion in values (and political expediency) on the part of Britain and the West, which neither Portugal nor South Africa ever shared.

Portugal and South Africa have always maintained that it will take generations of hard work on the part of the Black population before African states are in any way equipped to maintain a modern state in the face of ideological pressures from abroad and the stresses thrown up by tribalism. The fact that a few qualified individuals went about agitating for independence "or else" made no impression on them since they believed that history had left them with a sacred trust over the underdeveloped and often primitive Black *nations*, not just over a few *individuals*.

The educated Black African in New York or London may sneer at this point of view, or the liberal newspaper editor may term this a very convenient outlook for maintaining White supremacy, but it nonetheless remains a strong point of agreement between Portugal and White South Africa.

Both countries believe firmly in a policy of evolutionary political development for the Black man, backed up by wide ranging educational programmes and the development of a substantial Black middle class. This, they maintain, is a formula for lasting success. In contrast the "liberal" recipe of revolutionary development (change = progress) calls for instant solutions. This includes one-man-one-vote immediately, irrespective of whether the country is economically viable and irrespective of its educational achievements. This attitude which has been adopted almost unanimously by the United Nations

3. A. S. Labuschagne: "Ons Vriendskapsbande met Malawi", *Tegniek*, Stellenbosch, June 1967, pp. 12-13.

178

has, of course, brought only misery, strife, civil war, hunger and economic ruin plus outright dictatorship to most of Africa.

Portugal has no intention of sacrificing five hundred years in Africa for the sake of an ideology and formula which has failed miserably in Africa, while South Africa's White nation, which has no homeland in Europe to scuttle back to, has an even stronger point here. Consequently they both energetically and sincerely seek stability, prosperity and a broadly based economic programme for the sub-continent – an atmosphere in which the gradual political development of the Black man will be meaningful – not only to the elite but also to the mass of the people.

Signs of ever increasing co-operation between South Africa and *Angola* in the economic field have multiplied over the past four years.

The South African Government agreed in 1965 to finance the building of a R5,000,000 ($7,000,000) dam on the Kunene River in Angola in return for which the Portuguese Government would supply power to South West Africa.

In early 1966 the Bank of Lisbon and South Africa was established by three Portuguese banks and a big financial company in South Africa. The General Manager of the Bank said that one of the major aims of the new bank was to promote a common market between South Africa and the Portuguese provinces in Africa, an objective shared by the South African-Portuguese Economic Institute.

South African Airways and the Portuguese Airline T.A.P. have agreed to operate their air services between Johannesburg and Lisbon in pool partnership. This service will also include Luanda in Angola.

The Portuguese Government, concerned at the slow development of the oil industry in Angola, decided in 1966 to step up production to help meet the rising demands for oil in the entire Southern Africa. The oil company, Companhia dos Petroleos de Angola (Petrangol) signed an agreement with the Portuguese Government in 1966 whereby it would invest close on R27,000,000 ($37,000,000) in expansion and further exploration of the Angolan oil field. The agreement permits Petrangol to take eight partners in the programme. Two are South African, two Portuguese and the others French and Italian. If production could reach two million tons per year, the Angolan oil fields will be able to meet over a quarter of the entire Southern African demand. Oil men believe the Angolan fields will eventually be able to meet all the requirements of Southern Africa. In 1966 production of crude oil totalled 600,000 tons and the estimated production for mid-1968 is set at 1,000,000 tons.

Oil has also been found in commercial quantities off-shore in Angola – opposite Cabinda the tiny Angolan enclave north of the Congo River mouth. By June 1967 the Cabinda Gulf Oil Co. (a Portuguese concern which is a subsidiary of America's Gulf Oil Company) was certain that the eventual off-shore production would far exceed that of the existing wells in Angola. However, in view of the fact that South Africa's consumption alone is expected to top the 7,000,000 ton mark by 1969 observers believe that a much greater strike will have to be made before Southern Africa will become independent of other sources.

Angola's economic potential is exceptionally good. The economy is based at present on the production of agricultural commodities, particularly coffee of which Angola is the world's third largest producer (after Brazil and Columbia), maize and sisal, the latter worth about R6,800,000 in 1965. With the exception of diamonds which brought the country R22,000,000 in 1965, minerals are not yet an important factor in the gross national product simply because of lack of development and exploitation. However, significant expansion in the production of iron ore (from virtually nothing in 1957 to 900,000 tons in 1966) and manganese is now under way. The iron ore reserves of the country are over 200 million metric tons and a consortium of companies headed by Germany's Krupps have invested R42,000,000 with the objective of raising production to 3,000,000 tons by the beginning of 1969.

At present, coffee and diamonds account for over fifty per cent of the total value of exports but with industrial development up fifty per cent from 1960 to 1964 and the increase in iron and oil production, this pattern is, of course, rapidly changing. Angola's total external trade (imports and exports) for 1966 should pass the R300,000,000 ($400,000,000) for the first time.

Terrorism in Angola has had the effect of shaking Angolans from their sleepy existence. There are still some 40,000 troops in the country and their operations have made it necessary to improve roads, railroads, airfields and telecommunications. Demands on local manufacturing and construction companies have been heavy and the large scale operations against the terrorists together with a new awareness of Angola as a home, a country and not just a province of Portugal, has given a considerable impetus to the country's economic and industrial development.

In 1964, Portugal's second National Development Plan for Angola involving an amount of over R115,000,000 for dams, transportation, colonization, forestry, agricultural and power projects was completed. This was followed by a Transitional Plan for 1965-1967 catering for expenditure totalling R180,000,000 ($252,000,000). A new six-year plan for 1968-1973 is now on the drawing board.

Probably the outstanding example of the investment, planning and faith the Portuguese are putting into Angola is the Cambambe Dam about 125 miles south-east of Luanda. When fully completed, this will be the second largest hydro-electric project in Africa with a first phase output of 1.25 million kilowatt hours. Although primarily constructed for power, it can also irrigate nearly 200,000 acres of land suitable for growing cotton and possibly rice.

There are many industries that could be developed in Angola such as ceramics, rubber, wax and tanning, textiles, footwear, foodstuffs, marble, mineral extraction, synthetic plastics and fibres, etc. provided the know-how, educated manpower and risk capital can be supplied. The development of sufficient communications, roads and railways is also a prerequisite.

Taking a long term outlook, the possibility that South Africa will be able to provide some of this assistance in the next decade, after its own almost run-away boom has levelled off, is a distinct possibility.

Anglo American of South Africa is one of the three or four big international companies involved in the search for copper in Angola. (The Nippon Mining Co. of Japan is planning to invest R17,500,000 ($25,000,000) in the development of copper deposits in the northern Angolan area of Mavoio-Malange. A German Norwegian group is operating in the Cassinga area.) The Anglo American search in co-operation with a Portuguese group, the Sociedade de Exploracoes Mineiras Afrikanas, is confined to the Alto Zambeze region in the east.[4]

4. Cf. Business Letter published by the Banco Portugueso do Atlantico, Lisbon, June 8, 1967.

Angola's principal trading partners have been metropolitan Portugal, the United States, Great Britain, Holland and West Germany and these are not likely to change in the foreseeable future unless the South African concept of a Southern African Common Market materialises. Because Angola is considered part of Metropolitan Portugal, their budgets and economies are also integrated. There is no chance therefore, of Angola or Mocambique *joining* in such a common market, but an associate membership is a distinct possibility. In that case some of Angola's imports of textiles, wines, industrial machinery and equipment, railroad stock, iron and steel and medicines are likely to come from Rhodesia and South Africa while a considerable proportion of its exports of coffee, sisal and cotton will go to South Africa and other states of the Third Africa.

Whatever the prospects may be of Angolan and Mocambique partnership in a Southern African Common Market, the fact is that the Portuguese and South African authorities are making a determined effort to improve existing ties between the two provinces and South Africa. What is probably the longest road building project undertaken anywhere in Africa is now underway in Southern Africa where a road is being driven northwards from South West Africa to Angola. When completed in 1971 one will be able to travel on a sealed (tarred) highway all the way from Cape Town to Luanda, capital and main port of Angola. The South West Africa stretch alone will run for about 1,000 miles from Vioolsdrif on the Orange River to Oshikango on the Angolan border. About 350 miles of the road remains to be tarred. The importance of the Cape Town–Luanda road is obvious – it opens up areas, particularly in South West Africa, which, because of poor communications, have been left to lie undeveloped. But the road has an international significance beyond its national importance – by opening up an economic transport road to Angola, the way is cleared for traffic in a vital commodity to South Africa – oil. This road has the same importance to the people of the Third Africa as the Trans Canada Highway to Canadians and the Latin American highway, which will link North and South America, to countries such as Guatemala and Costa Rica.

The other Portuguese province of *Mocambique* enjoys a very close relationship with South Africa, Rhodesia, Swaziland and Malawi.

About 135,000 Mocambique Bantu work in South Africa under

a special agreement between Portuguese and South African Governments; the bulk of exports from the massive mining and industrial complex around Johannesburg in South Africa is shipped through the port of Lourenco Marques; iron ore from Swaziland is exported by rail through the same port; agricultural products from Malawi pass through Mocambique's two principal ports, Beira and Lourenco Marques; Salisbury, capital of Rhodesia, has its closest port by rail in Beira. In addition Mocambique shares common borders with South Africa, Rhodesia, Malawi and Zambia.

The bulk of Mocambique's tourist trade also comes from Rhodesia and South Africa.

The same realistic outlook which now binds Angola and South Africa also binds South Africa and Mocambique. The attitude of the average Rhodesian and South African towards the Portuguese in Mocambique and vice versa is friendly and the relations between the governments extremely cordial. There is a regular exchange of visits by government officials (and military officers) and when the President of Mocambique's new university recently visited South Africa he was unexpectedly presented with over six hundred highly valuable books by the University of South Africa, the Republic's Information Department and the South African Association for the Advancement of Knowledge and Culture.

The question of Mocambique's big migratory labour to South Africa (mentioned earlier) requires some amplification.

A large number of labourers from Mocambique seek work in the South African gold mines every year. The recruitment for this labour force is regulated by terms of the so-called Mocambique Convention, which was signed between Portugal and South Africa in 1928, and is organized by the Witwatersrand Native Labour Association which provides all the necessary free transport and food for the miners. About eighty thousand Mocambique workers go to the mines each year on a contract for one year. Quite apart from the advantages to be accrued from the good pay and working conditions, this stint at the mines has become something of a status, if not a virility symbol to many young men in Mocambique. It has certainly greatly increased the purchasing power of the natives in the south of the Province, which is the area where most of the workers are recruited. One has only to see the twice-weekly arrival and departure of Mocambique miners on their way to and from "Jansburg" (as

Johannesburg is known) to note this enormous difference in economic status. Those leaving Mocambique take little but the clothes they stand up in; whereas those coming back after their year's stint in the mines return with a veritable caravan of sewing machines, bicycles, new suits and radio sets.

The total Mocambique labour force in South Africa remits some R7,400,000 ($10,360,000) in cash and goods to the mother country every year. By African standards this is an enormous income.[5]

As is the case in Angola, the bulk of Mocambique's wealth comes from the land and most of the population of the province lives by farming. More than 80 per cent of the total exports of R77,000,000 ($107,000,000) for 1965 consisted of eight agricultural commodities of which cotton, raw cashew nuts, sugar and tea are the most important. Nevertheless the vast agricultural potential of the territory still remains virtually untapped and only a small percentage of the total land area is at present under cultivation.

Mocambique offers tremendous scope for agricultural enterprise. Within its borders one can produce almost every known crop because of the country's topography and climate. With increased instruction in modern methods of farming and the development of irrigation and hydro-electric potential it is hoped that this rich potential can be developed and expanded.

One of the most interesting developments in the agricultural sectors in all of Africa has been the organization of *agricultural co-operatives* in both Angola and Mocambique, in which peasant immigrants from Portugal and Black native farmers work together in a multi-racial "Colonato". Volkmar Wentzel (*National Geographic Magazine*) and Thomas Molnar (*Africa a Political Travelogue*) both spent some time at these co-operatives and commented most favourably on the influence which this has had on the Black population.

It is most surprising that this excellent aspect of Portuguese planning in Africa has had so little publicity abroad.

Although the old Portuguese dream of finding an El Dorado in this part of Africa has never been realized, the potential mineral wealth of Mocambique remains tantalizingly apparent. Deposits include coal, gold, petroleum, iron, graphite, uranium, silver,

5. *The South African Journal of Economics*, March 1967, p. 52.

copper, chrome, tin, tungsten, lead, perlite and several semi-precious stones, but total production in 1965 was only some R1,000,000 ($1,400,000).

The rate of industrial development in Mocambique, particularly in the last decade or so, has not been insignificant (1965 production about R75,000,000 or $104,000,000) but there remains much to be done. Two of the reasons for the relatively slow rate of industrial development are inadequate communications (which was dealt with in the previous chapter) and insufficient power supply. The major hydro-electric project on the Revue River near Vila Pery only supplies power to local industries and to Beira and the Rhodesian town of Umtali.

Surveys have now been completed to tap the industrial and agricultural potential of the mighty Zambezi River in the Zambezi Valley which contains the greatest latent wealth of any area in the country. Over a third of the river's total length runs through Mocambique, forming a rich fertile alluvial basin. One of the proposals which now seems destined to be carried out is to dam the river at two places, Laputa and Cabora-Bassa. This would provide sufficient water to irrigate over 1,700,000 acres (later to be raised to 3.7 million) and would realise some 17,000 Kwh. a year in electric current -- *more than twice that of Kariba and considerably more than Egypt's Aswan Dam.*

Cabora-Bassa itself is planned as a five-hundred foot high dam creating a lake one-hundred and fifty miles long.

The Zambezi project has staggering dimensions. When all the dams have been completed some 45,000 Kwh. a year can be generated, or twice South Africa's output of electricity for 1965. At less than 0.1 cent per unit it will be the cheapest in Africa. The blueprints foresee a settlement of one million immigrants in the valley, farming all kinds of crops. Ultimately as much as 8 million acres could be irrigated from the Zambezi. About 600,000 acres of new forest are to be planted. The Cabora-Bassa gorge is in the heart of the most mineralized part of the country where both cokable coal, iron, copper, titanium magnetite, manganese, chromium, nickel and asbestos deposits are to be found. As a beginning some four million tons of magnetite will be processed by electro-fusion to produce iron, titanium and vanadium.

Also on the drawing boards is a plan to make the Zambezi navigable from the sea as far inland as Tete, a distance of two hundred and seventy-five miles.

It is obvious that in terms of irrigation and the generation of power the project, even in its initial stages, will dwarf projects such as the T.V.A., Kariba and Aswan. Lest the Zambezi Cabora-Bassa project be considered as grandiose and a paper-giant it can be pointed out that the company responsible for the surveys and planning have already spent some R5,000,000 ($7,000,000) on the project.

In March 1967 the World Bank agreed to provide up to half the R250,000,000 ($350,000,000) required for the first phase of the project. The South African government also confirmed in the same month that it had taken the scheme one stage further by agreeing to talks with the Portuguese government on the subject. Technical and feasibility discussions between a number of international financial and industrial groups headed by South Africa's Industrial Development Corporation have already taken place.[6]

When the project is completed, it will undoubtedly become the most important economic asset of the country. It could ensure a sustained growth of mineral, agricultural and industrial production. In fact, it is potentially one of *the* most important assets of the Third Africa and it could benefit virtually every state of the south.

More will be said about the Cabora-Bassa Zambezi project in the next chapter.

The total value of Mocambique's foreign trade in 1965 amounted to just on R200,000,000 ($280,000,000) with imports representing R124,000,000 ($152,000,000). About thirty per cent of this trade is with Portugal, the remainder with foreign countries, particularly South Africa (thirteen per cent) and Great Britain. The province's gold reserves are maintained at around R30,000,000 ($42,000,000) or one third of the province's annual exchange requirements. This amount has been built up by means of an agreement with the South African Government concerning the system of deferred payment for emigrant Mocambique mine labour.

The need to attract foreign investment is clearly apparent.

The R90,000,000 which Portugal earmarked for the period

6. H. J. van Eck. "A Central Scheme for the Supply of Electric Power in Southern Africa", *Tegnikon*, Pretoria, March 1967, pp. 37-42.

1959-1964 was hardly adequate for the development of essential services and the application of essential programmes such as communications, health and education. (The same situation exists in Angola.) There is a general awareness of Portugal's long term incapacity to provide sufficient capital and manpower required to develop these two immensely rich territories as they deserve. For 1965-1967 some R135,000,000 ($187,000,000) has been budgeted for Mocambique, but this too is far from adequate.

The Portuguese Government has for decades been loath to allow foreign interests to aid the development of Angola and Mocambique. Consequently the two territories have remained hamstrung, not for lack of natural riches as in Malawi or Botswana but through financial caution imposed by Portugal's limited capital resources.

The official attitude, for years, has been that if foreign enterprise is allowed too much freedom of action (particularly in two such potentially wealthy states as Mocambique and Angola) the possession will in the end lose its Portuguese character.

There are many reasons embedded in Portugal's national character and history for Dr Salazar's dogged determination that Portugal should go it alone as investor and financier in the two huge provinces in Africa. However, the recent revelation of the long suspected and real mineral wealth of Angola (oil, gold, bauxite, wolfram and iron) and Mocambique (iron, uranium, titanium-magnetite and copper) has brought the government face to face with reality. *If Portugal is to achieve a future for its people in Africa, it can no longer go it alone.*

Since 1962 there has been an appreciable increase in foreign investments in Angola and since 1964 Portuguese Embassies abroad have been issuing glossy, high quality brochures extolling the virtues of investments in Angola and Mocambique. With the rise of a strong middle class in both provinces, businessmen and entrepreneurs aware of the tremendous potential of the territory and impatient to get going, the pace has been accelerated. In April 1965 the Portuguese government relaxed the restrictive measures previously placed on direct investments of non-Portuguese origin.

This changed outlook can best be seen in the provinces' reaction to the extension of South African capital and expertise into Angola and particularly Mocambique. Some of this activity has already been presented but it also includes South African co-operation in the construction of a large and impressive wharf at Matola, opposite Lourenco Marques, to handle the export of Swaziland iron ore to Japan; the fusion of South African and Portuguese interest in a large scale canned and frozen sea-food industry along the coast of Mocambique and, of course, in Angola joint plans to harness the Kunene River, aid in the construction of hydro-electric projects, etc.

The latest project is the construction of a two-hundred and twenty mile pipeline from Moambo in Mocambique to Johannesburg for the supply of natural gas to the Witwatersrand. The total cost, including main and subsidiary pumping stations, is expected to exceed R100,000,000 ($140,000,000) and is to be financed partly by the Mocambique Gulf Oil Company and partly by long term loans to be raised in the Republic. Commercial Banks in South Africa are expected to figure prominently in the financing operation.

These developments, and the sense that there is more to come, have caused a marked strengthening of public confidence throughout Portuguese Africa, where they are interpreted as a mark of South Africa's political, as much as economic, faith in the territories.

The desire for solidarity with South Africa, of which this reaction is expressive, and the long range implications – a Southern African Common Market – is the topic of much discussion in the hotels and business clubs of Luanda and Lourenco Marques. The late Dr Verwoerd's speech on the subject of a Southern African Common Market which would include Angola and Mocambique aroused great interest in both provinces and is still the topic of much discussion in the press.

Writing in *Optima*, Austin Coates (a leading writer on contemporary Asian and Portuguese history and social influence in Asia) stated that he found a very perceptible veering towards what may be called South African thinking in both provinces on the subject of Southern Africa's political future. "A sense that with so much at stake Europeans in Southern Africa, in defence of their own civilization, must put themselves and their children first, and never mind the outside clamour if to do this is regarded as an admission that all men are not quite equal . . . there is a fundamental belief that the only Europeans who ever understand Southern Africa are those who live there."

9. Political and Economic Prospects

It is a rash man who *predicts* the future of any state or area in Africa. The realistic and cautious individual will mull over it. Most people's "predictions" on Africa, from Professors of great universities to school teachers in little villages, have taken a shattering blow except, of course, those who predicted that instability and turmoil must inevitably follow when a conglomeration of immature, uneducated and economically backward tribes are cast into the role of nation states with a major voice in the councils of the world.

Those who "predicted" after 1945 that the world at large would be a better place to live in and that man would no longer find himself in the dark days of the late thirties have, of course, been equally wrong. In all the centuries of recorded history the world has known only two hundred and ninety-two years of peace and since 1945 the world has experienced twenty-six fair sized wars and some thirty-nine revolts, coups d'etat, civil wars and other serious conflicts within or between independent states.

"Peace in our time" is, apparently, a fable. Therefore to make any firm predictions about Africa where, to quote a reliable source on the subject, "the prospects of revolution are excellent"[1] is to let oneself out on a limb which has probably already been cut halfway. On the other hand permitted certain assumptions (based on immediate past history) and certain exceptions (based on current trends) one can nonetheless indicate in very general terms the direction in which a specific part of Africa, in this case the Third Africa, appears to be moving, economically and politically.

For more than half a century the states of the Third Africa have experienced neither war between each other nor fatal domestic strife. This compares with the two World Wars, the Spanish Civil War and other conflicts in Europe since 1910. Elsewhere in Africa the

---

1. Chou en Lai, Premier of Red China, Africa, 1965.

pattern has been the same, war and revolution, in the Congo, in Algeria, in the Sudan. Only in the Third Africa did the countries continue to live at peace with each other. The "uprising" in Angola was inspired not from within the country but was directed from across the northern borders of this Portuguese territory in the same way as the riots and uprisings in South Vietnam were and are directed from the north. In the same way domestic strife was "exported" from Cuba to Venezuela and Colombia. The defeated enemy in South West Africa in 1914 was a European power, Germany. The economic war against Rhodesia in 1966-67 was and still is being directed by Britain.

Of course, the future does not only include the possibility of war and revolution or economic and political collapse, but everything, from prospects for the arts and science to water conservation and education. However, the day to day existence of all human beings are so inescapably tied up with political developments and economic policies that they are, within available space, the only matters worth discussing.

Politically the Third Africa has experienced a period of stability of government not equalled anywhere else in Africa, Europe, Latin America, Asia and the Far East. In South Africa the governing National Party has been in power for eighteen years[2] and every indication, as amplified in surveys by such reliable institutions as the Carnegie Endowment for Peace, is that nothing short of military conquest of South Africa by a major power is going to change the pattern of government. And the repercussions of such an act would shake and perhaps shatter the very foundations of the West.

In Lesotho, Swaziland and Botswana there has been a notable absence of strife and riots prior to self-government. Two of the territories, Lesotho and Botswana, advanced rapidly and peacefully towards political freedom in 1966. Swaziland will be independent before the end of 1969. At the same time, in terms of South Africa's Bantustan policy, the Black homelands within the Republic are also moving peacefully towards autonomous status as, for example, in the Transkei.

This *regional* political evolution represents recognition of the full

2. The General Election of 1966 assured them control of government for another five years.

and separate title of the Black nations to the various regions which they settled in the course of their respective migrations into Southern Africa.

The Portuguese territories, from all reliable accounts and from on-the-spot reports, are now enjoying a greater measure of political harmony than ever before. For more than a year there have been no terrorist attacks in Angola. Black Africans from Mocambique who fled the country after the bitter little brush war against infiltrators from Tanzania are returning to Mocambique in droves. Sallies by "freedom fighters" into Mocambique from Malawi have been decreasing. Prime Minister Hastings Banda of Malawi personally put the squeeze on the so-called "freedom-fighters" around Milange. It was not only to contribute to stability in Southern Africa but because Banda's arch enemy Henry Chipembere (who is now in America) considered the Milange area in Malawi, adjoining Mocambique and the base camp of the "freedom fighters", as his personal province. Weapons entering Malawi and Zambia from the north have been confiscated by the authorities despite the fact that they were destined for "freedom fighters" trying to infiltrate Rhodesia and South Africa.

In both Portuguese territories there has also been a marked up-swing in economic development and, politically, more and more Black Africans are being taken up into the administration of the territories. In both countries army patrols now sometimes consist solely of Black men, a sure sign that the Portuguese are absolutely confident of the allegiance of the Black population. Portugal and Malawi have signed an agreement on a new railway link. Swaziland and Mocambique have made new and improved arrangements for speeding up two-way trade between the countries. Both Dr Banda of Malawi and Dr Kaunda of Zambia have reiterated their opposition to boycotts and militant actions against Mocambique or South Africa.

The permanent nature of Portugal's presence in the Third Africa is nowhere better illustrated than in Zambia and Tanzania, where frantic efforts have been made in the past two years to make a start on the proposed Zambia-Tanzania railway. The British-Canadian survey team completed their field work during mid-1966. If the northern Black states had any hope of seeing the Portuguese leave, the plans for the one thousand mile multi-million dollar line which will run at a deficit until 1990 effectively disproved it. The line which will not only cost a fortune but take five years to build would not even have been contemplated if the Black states thought there was a reasonable chance that the Portuguese might pull up stakes.

In the South a major characteristic of the constitutional development of the two former British Protectorates, and a feature of public debate in parliament and in the press, has been the open recognition by political leaders – whatever their ideological preferences – of their countries' dependence upon South Africa. Indeed, as the independence roots go down, the stronger appear to become their advocacy of harmonious relations with their developed and rich neighbour.

In Botswana the government is cracking down on anti-South African elements which had been permitted a free rein during the last five years of British administration. The latest under the whip is the South West Africa Peoples Organisation (S.W.A.P.O.). Eight members of S.W.A.P.O. whose leader, Sam Njomo, is based in Tanzania, were declared prohibited immigrants soon after Botswana's independence celebration. Sir Seretse Khama who was alarmed by the capture of Communist trained terrorists in northern Botswana, is said to be afraid of being blamed for harbouring people who could harm South Africa. Botswana has also declared certain members of the banned African National Congress (A.N.C.) from South Africa as prohibited immigrants.

Early in 1966 the governing Democratic Party of Sir Seretse Khama also issued a remarkable political document attacking the Botswana National Front as "a Communist front organisation". The Democratic Party not only completely rejected Communism but also any proposal which bore the earmarks of a "Liberation movement" or which could embroil Botswana in an armed or political confrontation with "the White South". It is possibly the most outspoken criticism of Communism made by any Black government and a clear rejection of the war cries of the Organisation for African Unity.

In *Swaziland* the Nqwane National Congress, the dominant political party, publicly repudiated Pan-Africanism in September 1966 thereby removing another stumbling block in the road towards open co-operation with South Africa and Portugal's provinces in Africa, notably Mocambique.

In Lesotho, Prime Minister Jonathan accused newspapers overseas and certain governments, of deliberately misrepresenting and distorting developments in White South Africa. "Their goodwill and human understanding are conveniently ignored and any disagreement and conflict is exaggerated and distorted," he said. Jonathan was received in Cape Town with all the courtesies due to a visiting statesman. The protocol arrangements were impeccable in accordance with the policy of treating heads of all friendly independent states on the basis of equality and goodwill. As Prime Minister Jonathan pointed out, his visit proved that there is only one formula on which a sound relationship between different states can be made politically feasible – non-interference, co-operation without commitment to each other's policies and a common dislike of Communism.

Between Rhodesia and South Africa the ties that bind the two states are being drawn tight and secure as a result of Britain's myopic economic war against her own Kith and Kin. South African Cabinet Ministers have visited Rhodesia on several occasions during recent times; a new and more direct railway link has been forecast; trade has improved as a result of new trade pacts and at all levels there is an acute awareness of the need for closer co-operation in all spheres of public life.

Rhodesia and the Portuguese territories have improved communications and trade. The Rhodesian Government has publicly stated its satisfaction with the ever closer co-operation between Rhodesia and Mocambique. Malawi, while disapproving of Rhodesia's unilateral declaration of independence, has refused to be drawn into a boycott of Rhodesia and its President has warned fellow Black states against rash military adventures.

Between South Africa and the Portuguese provinces of Angola and Mocambique, there have been new and favourable trade pacts, capital investments, banking arrangements, etc. while South Africa has increased her aid to South West Africa by millions of Rand.

Southern Africa is beginning to show the semblance of a *united front* against hostile United Nations and hostile pressures from individual countries. It has closed its ranks against the international boycott brigade and is pressing ahead with its own projects in Rhodesia, South Africa, Angola and Mocambique to find, refine and stockpile oil. Offshore exploration and drilling is underway. In Angola a major effort is being made to increase supplies of oil, not to Portugal, but to Southern Africa. In Mocambique gas deposits are being harvested principally to serve industry in the Republic. Rhodesia and South Africa are building up stockpiles of oil at strategic places. South Africa is proceeding with the purchase of its own oil tankers to carry crude oil to various ports in the Third Africa.

The death of Prime Minister Verwoerd, the architect of South Africa's policy of friendly co-operation with all the states of Southern Africa, did not dampen hopes for closer ties with other states. On the contrary, in a recent interview with *U.S. News and World Report*, Mr John Vorster, the new South African Prime Minister, said: "It stands to reason that all states in southern Africa will and must work as closely together as possible because it is in the interest of each and every one of us to do so. As far as South Africa is concerned, we want good relations not only with Rhodesia and Angola and Mocambique but also with Zambia and Malawi, and also with the British protectorates which have just become independent.

"While we are on that point, I may just as well add that we do not at all fear those developments – the establishment of African governments in these states. It is a natural development as far as we are concerned. So these new states – the former British protectorates – hold no danger for us. We want to work with them as independent Black states, to their advantage and to our advantage.

"There is no reason whatever why the closest of ties should not exist between them and us, as you would expect between good neighbours. So we do have close working relationships with Rhodesia, Angola and Mocambique, but our relationships with Lesotho (formerly Basutoland), Botswana (formerly Bechuanaland), and Swaziland are in many respects even closer, as we share with them a common customs union. There is no doubt in my mind that co-operation among all the states and territories of Southern Africa will continue to grow on a basis of mutual respect for each other's independence, and mutual recognition of the advantages to be derived from economic and technical co-operation without strings or interference."[3]

The *economic* pattern in the Third Africa is the single most important development of the sixties. The vital role which economics play in shaping relations between sovereign states and in buttressing the

3. *U.S. News and World Report*, November 14, 1966, p. 95.

respective governments cannot be over-emphasised. All over Africa, in Latin America and Asia, lack of economic development, unbalanced economic development, unsound planning and extremes in riches and poverty as a result of artificial economic patterns (the haves and the have-nots) have led to poverty and strife (India), poverty and revolution (Latin America), and poverty and economic ruin (Ghana and Guinea) so that its importance for the Third Africa cannot be overrated either.

The pattern in all of the southern continent, except in South Africa and, perhaps, Rhodesia, is that of a large country, underpopulated and economically undeveloped but with vast potential both for domestic consumption and for exports.

The countries, furthermore, are geographically closely aligned; in some cases communications (river traffic and rail) must be shared; there is a constant movement of unskilled labour across boundaries; a universal lack of sufficiently educated manpower, technicians and engineers, a lack of risk capital.

The overall impression one gains is that of an area of vast potential, rich in minerals and human resources.

Institutions of government and methods of local administration are largely similar as is law enforcement and education.

In the case of five of those countries a customs and monetary union and free trade area is actually in operation, viz. South Africa, Botswana, Swaziland, Lesotho and South West Africa. The economic interdependence of all the territories, however, is as great as between any two countries or group of countries in the European Common Market. Between two other states, Rhodesia and Zambia, there is an economic interdependence which will for years dictate the pace of development in each country. Between two others, Portugal's two biggest overseas provinces, Mocambique and Angola, there are, of course, not only tangible political and administrative ties but also a free trade area, both being politically and economically part of metropolitan Portugal.

A similar degree of interdependence on economic grounds and close co-operation between governments, does not exist anywhere else in Africa or Latin America. In addition the attitude of the people towards each other, despite the differences in civilization and the differences in colour, is in a remarkable state of change. In South Africa the average White man's attitude towards, for example, Lesotho or Swaziland has undergone an almost complete change in the past decade, while Portuguese and Rhodesian relations with South Africa on a people-to-people basis could not be better.

In all three areas newspapers are bending over backwards in their efforts to educate the people about the necessity of stable and prosperous Black governments in Malawi and Zambia and to appreciate each other's problems.

Finally there is the much discussed question of a military alliance.

A lot has been said at the United Nations and in the newspapers of the world about the embargo on sale of armaments to South Africa. South Africa requires these weapons not for internal use (as alleged) but for defence against external aggression, particularly now that the Organization of African Unity has officially created, at least on paper, an "army of liberation". The arms question is fully discussed elsewhere in this book.[4] It will suffice to say that South Africa is self-sufficient as far as the production of armaments for an "African" war is concerned. Speaking in Bloemfontein on May 1965, the South African Defence Minister said that South Africa could also supply all the neighbouring states with weapons and could even export certain arms to Western Europe if those countries wanted to buy armaments from the Republic. Numerous offers, he said, have also been received from foreign countries who wanted to build warships in South Africa. Tanks, heavy artillery, bazookas, machine guns, mortars, bombs, field mines, all types of military vehicles, etc. are *locally* produced. In addition the manufacture of jet aircraft and certain missiles went into production stage during mid-1966.

The countries of the Third Africa recognize that in Africa, South Africa presents by far the most formidable military power on the continent. It is also inconceivable that an armed insurrection will ever succeed in Rhodesia or the Portuguese provinces, no matter if the guidance and supply of arms and equipment comes from outside as it does in the case of Mocambique. There are many reasons for this which are not now relevant to the point to be made, mainly that a successful military campaign can *only* be launched against Rhodesia, Angola or Mocambique by a consortium of African states

4. See Chapter 2.

heavily backed by Russia, Red China or even India.[5] The strategic importance of the Third Africa, particularly South Africa, was discussed in Chapter 2, as well as the similarity of views between the Portuguese and South African governments concerning the defence of the vital interests of the West in Africa.

According to the most informed military circles in Britain, the United States and France, a Black African attack on Southern Africa *without any foreign assistance* would be doomed – logistically and for other military reasons. For this reason the possibility of a military alliance in the Third Africa must be rated as very slim and, at the moment, close to nil.

South Africa's military might, in African terms, contributes to the public confidence and stability in the entire region.

All in all, and apart from the aspects discussed in the chapters dealing with unifying factors south and north of the Limpopo, the past five years have seen a measure of co-operation between the Black states of Malawi and Zambia and the European controlled states of Mocambique, Angola, Rhodesia and South Africa hardly expected five years ago. Opening Africa's first nuclear reactor at Pelindaba, near Pretoria, in 1966 the late South African Prime Minister, Dr Verwoerd, again emphasised that South Africa was holding out the hand of friendship to the Black states in the north and that if they could bury their animosities, they could share in South Africa's vast pool of technical knowledge and economic know-how. His remarks were meant to include not only Malawi and Zambia but also states such as Malagasia and Kenya. This offer of co-operation with Africa was repeated by his successor Mr John Vorster who said in an interview with *U.S. News and World Report:* ". . . we are willing and anxious to assist other African states in coping with the tremendous problems of economic and social development that confront them . . . And we recognise against this background that in many ways we have, with respect to much of Africa south of the Sahara, a responsibility for assisting in development – comparable to the responsibility which the United States has undertaken on a much larger scale with respect to the un-

---

5. India's interest in African affairs and the tens of thousands of Indian citizens all over the east coast of Africa is a tale all on its own.

developed areas of the world as a whole. Although we do not publicise it, we are in fact already doing quite a lot in this field."[6]

South Africa's attitude is already paying dividends. During the 1967 session of Parliament the South African Foreign Minister said that missions were being sent to African states and representatives of African states are now also being received in South Africa for discussions. Malagasia has agreed on a new air link; Ghana is quietly permitting increased trade with South Africa and prominent Black economists such as Dr Robert Gardiner of the United Nations are publicly urging the Black African states to adopt a more pragmatic attitude towards South Africa.

The pattern of race-relations in the Third Africa has also improved. Relations between White and Black in South Africa, contrary to popular opinion abroad, have shown signs of great improvement in the area where for the moment, it mattered most – the political future of the Bantu. The Zulu nation has now indicated through their acknowledged leaders that they are prepared to accept the Government's plans to establish for them a self-governing state. The Zulus initially opposed the programme of separate development firmly, but now appear to have rejected the views of their erstwhile leader, Nobel Peace Prize winner, Albert Luthuli, who advocated political integration between Black and White in South Africa. The Paramount Chief of the Zulus has also given the policy his blessing.[7] In the North the Tswana are also rapidly heading for statehood.

The only two areas where there appear to be troubled waters ahead are South West Africa and Rhodesia. However, the important point is that it is not of the making of the inhabitants of these states, but the result of a situation forced upon the two administrations from London and the United Nations.

The status of South West Africa and its administration by South Africa as an integral part of the Republic, was first challenged by Liberia and Ethiopia before the International Court of Justice. When the Court threw out the case, the Afro-Asian states launched an all-out political campaign which rapidly escalated into a naked ideological battle. They demanded that the United Nations declare South Africa had forfeited its right to administer South West Africa

6. November 14, 1966, p. 105.
7. Statement made at Umzinto, Natal, February 10th, 1967.

because it applied a policy of separate development to the various racial groups and at the close of 1966 the General Assembly acceded to their demands. There was, as even liberal newspapers in America and Britain pointed out, *no legal or political basis for such a step*. But what mattered was that a negative vote on the part of any White state would have been interpreted as condoning "apartheid" in South West Africa.

It was a simple strategy on the part of the Afro-Asians but since the world is now dominated by simple formulas (for example Black-is-right and White-is-wrong, or one-man-one-vote, irrespective of whether the one voter is a nuclear scientist and the other a witch-doctor) the strategy worked.

What the vast majority of states in the United Nations have now voted to see in South West Africa is an independent, "one-man-one-vote" state represented at the United Nations. They adopted this attitude despite the fact that the most vehement opposition to such a state of affairs would come *not* only from White people but from the non-White inhabitants, the Namas, Damaras, Hereros, etc. They fear that under a United Nations programme of "one-man-one-vote" their lot under the majority rule of the numerically stronger Ovambos, would very likely be the same as the Turkish minority in Greece or the Watusi in Burundi. The Ovambo chiefs and headmen, on their part, petitioned the South African government in the beginning of 1965, saying that they fully accept the recommendations made by the Government appointed Commission of Inquiry into South West Africa (the Odendaal Commission) as being in their best interests.[8] Under the plan, the area of Ovamboland would be increased (at the cost of White farmland) and receive internal self-government with universal franchise similar to that granted to South Africa's first Bantu state, the Transkei, plus liberal economic aid. The same advantages would accrue to the other groups in their traditional homelands, thereby eliminating the possibility of internal political conflict and violence of the kind that is shattering Nigeria.

What has been made abundantly clear to visitors by people of various backgrounds in South West Africa is that there should be no foreign interference in its orderly development, not from the

8. See Chapter 7.

United Nations or any other international organisation or state.[9] "Foreign administration" is really purely of academic interest, since the development of the territory is so utterly dependent upon South African resources and because other industrially developed states which could lend a hand are *all* more than 6,000 miles away. Moreover, the United Nations criterion which, inter alia, presumes that an integrated homogenous society can be artificially spawned by means of a United Nations endorsed constitution, is not applicable in practice. Anyone who doubts this view should merely cast his eye over the history of the past ten years in Africa and Asia to see that the desire for genuine self-determination by disparate and distinctly different communities, such as exist in South West Africa, cannot be placated or contained by artificial formulas of partnership – of which Cyprus is as good an example as the old Central African Federation.

In the previous chapters it was pointed out that an "independent" South West Africa would suffer grievously under a one-man-one-vote policy because of the vast differences between the major population groups and their incompatibility – particularly the Herero. It was also shown how an independent South West Africa would become such a heavy burden on its would-be benefactors that it may well become impossible for them to maintain just the current standard of living in South West Africa. In fact, for all practical purposes a politically stable and economically viable South West Africa is impossible if its ties with the Republic are cut.

One of the other "solutions" mentioned in academic circles has been the concept of partition between the north, where over sixty per cent of the Bantu population live, and the south, where virtually all the White people, the Coloureds and the Rehoboth Basters (all non-Bantu) are resident.

On social and political grounds, it is arguable as to whether the northern groups of the non-White population are (even in this Age of Uhuru) capable of establishing and maintaining the machinery of sovereign government. There is no cadre of leaders or even a single messianic leader to offer magnetism around which the

9. Cf. Molnar, Thomas: *South West Africa: The Last Pioneer Country*, Fleet, N.Y., 1966; Jenny, Hans: *Südwest Afrika, Land zwischen den Eêtremen*, Kohlhammer, Berlin, 1966 and Rhoodie, E. M.: *South West: The Last Frontier in Africa*, Voortrekkerpers, Johannesburg, 1967.

organisation of statehood could be formed. Internal cohesion in the potentially northern "independent" sector is almost totally lacking outside the tribal allegiance which exists among the individual national groups.

Humanitarian considerations regarding the Bushmen (who reside principally in the northern areas) and the provision for their welfare under an independent government constitute an additional factor.

The concept of partition would undoubtedly be violently opposed by the Communist, African and Asian nations, in that it would involve granting a large measure of the total land area to South Africa. Any North/South partition must necessarily allot the fabulous "Diamond Coast" to the southern sector and this would be objectionable to the advocates of "Africa for the Africans".

But the major and most readily obvious disadvantage to a split is the economic one. The north is principally supported by its mining activities (the Tsumeb complex) with the subsistence agrarian activities of the resident non-Whites, while the southern sector provides mechanized farming and commercial activities as well as an outlet for what surplus produce exists. The northern areas rely heavily on the South for consumer products and for markets for its goods and labour.

Although an amicable interchange of goods and services could conceivably be expected after partition, it goes without saying that the southern portion would look more to the Republic for its economic exchanges, where better advantages could be obtained. The north would thus be gradually but effectively frozen out and would have to seek new markets and suppliers, with the long-term expenses involved in the search.

While the southern portion would reap economic benefits from a liaison with South Africa, the northern area would suffer an acute shortage of development capital. Without expenditure on a major scale, the achievement of anything like a balanced economy would be impossible. The projected Kunene scheme to supply both power and water to the north would almost certainly suffer from atrophy in the event of partition. The Republic of South Africa – already engaged in a R500,000,000 ($700,000,000) development plan for the Orange River – would be understandably reluctant to participate wholeheartedly in a programme to benefit only an independent north. It seems equally unlikely that the United Nations could be persuaded to advance capital on such a grand scale (an estimated R50,000,000 or $70,000,000), and no single nation – not even the ever open-handed United States – could reap sufficient economic, political or propaganda value to justify such a massive investment for a northern "nation" of perhaps 300,000 people. The only remaining possible source of funds would be a consortium of Iron Curtain countries. But since the Kunene is an international river, whose development would necessarily be carried out in conjunction with Portugal, help from Communist nations also seems to be ruled out. The Soviet Union has been articulate in its criticisms of Portugal's Africa policy and Lisbon's avowed anti-Communism makes such an alliance completely unlikely.

If independence and partition are eliminated, what other possibility exists? Since South Africa cannot gracefully withdraw from its responsibilities in South West Africa – responsibilities called by the late Prime Minister, General J. C. Smuts "a sacred trust of civilization" – what is to be the future of the territory?

The obvious solution would seem to lie in continued and even closer association with the Republic of South Africa.

South West Africa has already been substantially integrated into the Republic's economy. All phases of its development – its rail and other communications networks, its power supplies (upon which vital water resources depend), and the major proportion of its consumer goods – have been inextricably woven into the fabric of South Africa's own. Political order and continuity will be maintained and each of the diverse national groups will be led to self-determination in their homelands or states, according to plans already blueprinted by the Odendaal Commission.

The *ultimate* status could be a Commonwealth of self-governing states, such as in Australia, with the powers of the Central Government in respect of customs, defence, foreign affairs, etc. vested in the Parliament of the Republic of South Africa. In all probability the people themselves will elect to enjoy such a constitution.

This view is shared by some of Africa's most prominent scholars. Writing on the economic change and political deadlock facing South West Africa, Professor D. C. Krogh of the University of South Africa and an expert witness before the World Court, said: "The optimal solution lies in a policy that treats a less developed people or territory as though it were an independent unit in some respects and as an

202

integrated part of a more advanced unit in some other respects. In other words, a third political arrangement lying between the opposite extremes of colonialism on the one hand and independence on the other is called for. Only in this way can the people or areas in question be developed to the utmost."[10]

The *Rhodesian* question boils down to this. Now that Britain has handed over the Rhodesian question to the United Nations and now that the Security Council has voted for mandatory sanctions to be applied against Rhodesia, will the latter survive what can only be described as a United Nations sponsored economic war against her sovereignty?

Before going into the implications of this question, it is necessary to appreciate three important factors: (i) the White Rhodesian population, including the majority of the Black people, are now solidly behind the existing regime[11]; (ii) according to a judgement of the Rhodesian High Court, the Smith Government may be illegal but it is firmly in control of affairs and seems settled for life; (iii) the Rhodesian case for independence and the effect of its constitution on the development of the country's internal political situation is sound and promising.

A study of this case and a summary of its principal features is *essential* to understanding the direction of political development and future of race-relations in Rhodesia.

What Rhodesia has been trying to get across to the world at large is that her Constitution is perfectly fair, and that in terms of that Constitution, the sky is the limit for anyone – regardless of race, colour or creed.

There is nothing, right now, to prevent the country's Black people claiming the vote in ever-increasing numbers. As things stand, non-Whites are virtually guaranteed a minimum of fifteen seats in Parliament. It lies in their power to fill these seats with people of any race they choose.

And the fifteen seats are only a *minimum*.

There is nothing to stop them making a Constitutional bid for every seat in the House. The way is wide open to them if they care to take it. At present there are fourteen non-White members in the

10. *Africa*, May-June, 1965.

11. *The Rhodesian Crisis*, Report of the American Security Council, December 19, 1966.

House and a fifteenth seat was won on non-White votes by a European. Every one of the remaining fifty seats could be contested by non-Whites.

There is nothing to stop a majority of non-Whites obtaining the vote – if they care to make no more effort to do so, then Europeans have to.

Under Southern Rhodesia's present Constitution non-Whites are *not* barred from the vote. Non-Whites can stand for Parliament. Measures to thwart at the outset any proposed racially discriminatory legislation are part of the law of the land. The entrenched clauses of the Constitution – including the anti-discriminatory measures cannot be altered without the approval, established by referendums, of each of the four main racial groups.

It is frequently asserted that the Black nationalist leaders such as Joshua Nkomo rejected the existing constitution. The truth is that at the time they loudly and publicly claimed the credit for it. When the original Constitution was agreed upon in 1961 at a conference (convened by the Southern Rhodesia Government) at which *all* races and *all* political parties were represented, Mr Nkomo said: "We are to have a new Constitution which is an achievement resulting from the pressure of the National Democratic Party – a thing never before thought of in this country. We feel that the new provisions have given us a certain amount of assurance that the country will not pursue policies which mean that Africans would perpetually be unable to control their country."

In other words, Mr Nkomo publicly made the very point that, in terms of the new Constitution, there was (and is) no limit to non-White political advance. It depends entirely on the non-Whites themselves. And that position still pertains to-day. The Constitution has been honoured completely.

The fact that Mr Nkomo and other African Nationalists subsequently went back on their word, organising a non-White boycott of the new Constitution, does not alter the position.

All applicants for the vote, whatever their colour, are required to conform to minimal standards. *But these standards have not been set impossibly high.* They have only been set so as to ensure that in a country of peoples comprising the most primitive to the most sophisticated, only *responsible* people who appreciate the meaning and significance of a vote shall have the privilege of voting.

The extremists realised that the new Constitution – notwithstanding the original agreement by African Nationalist leaders that it was fair – would deprive them of the weapons on which they had relied on so long. With its many built-in safeguards, the new Constitution was obviously going to make it much more difficult to enforce a one-party, fascist state, and equally it was going to make it much more difficult for the extremists to bludgeon their way to power by terrorist methods.

In terms of this system, African Nationalist leaders could not expect to walk into the seats of power overnight.

They wanted shortcuts, and so they invented various "catches" in the new Constitution. For example, it was suggested that there were not enough opportunities for non-Whites as a whole to improve their position up to the franchise standards . . . The answer here is that Rhodesia devotes more to non-White education than to any other service (and has, indeed, the best record in this respect in the whole of Africa) so that there is no "catch" in this either!

Rhodesia's so-called "White settlers" (whose roots in this country actually go back the best part of 100 years) and the vast majority of non-Whites who have made common cause with them, have honoured the 1961 deal in toto. *All that the 1965 Constitution added was to free Rhodesia from the last few vestiges of British rule.*

Britain's attitude in the Rhodesian question will baffle historians for years to come. *Burma* which not only *declared* her independence but on top of that quit the Commonwealth, hardly caused a ripple in London by this action. *She also continued to receive substantial tariff advantages in Britain.* There have also been at least six ex-British colonies who *negotiated* their independence with Britain and within a few years so changed the constitution (to obtain a one party state such as in Ghana, Uganda and Tanzania) that the present Rhodesian situation looks enormously respectable.

Political progress in Rhodesia to-day is certainly based on merit and nothing but merit and was this not the slogan coined by the former British Prime Minister, Harold Macmillan, as he presided over the dissolution of the once mighty British Empire? Would Britain have adopted the same attitude if Rhodesia had negotiated independence on the basis of the 1961 constitution and then changed it? Closer to home the vacillating British stand (or is it only Mr Wilson's personal stand?) and the double standard in dealing with

Rhodesia becomes even more vivid. Although for example the *majority* of the Irish people favour a Republic, Britain has promised to keep Ulster (Northern Ireland) as an integrated part of the United Kingdom. If majority rule cannot be applied to Ulster then it is wrong in Rhodesia.

Prime Minister Wilson's insistence on changing the constitution to one which would guarantee "majority rule" seems incredible considering that such a state of affairs would most surely lead to the same chaos and loss of individual freedom suffered by the people of Ghana, Nigeria, Tanzania, Uganda and the Sudan. These countries also started off immediately with "majority rule", or, as the cynics put it, "instant democracy" despite the fact that democracy is really wholly alien to Africa. The vast majority of Black Africans do not even have the abstract terms in their languages to grapple with the philosophical ideas that underline democratic principles.

What the Rhodesian Prime Minister is being asked to do is to grant to the African majority a form of parliamentary democracy *every* African government, once free to do so, has repudiated.

As long as the present Rhodesian government is in power, it can be safely predicted that the constitution will be honoured and that merit alone will be the cornerstone of political rights. Rhodesians are convinced that it is immoral to have majority rule now if the consequences of it are to create a worse government, incipient chaos, corruption and finally a Black military government.

There is now an increasing tendency on the part of Britain to surrender to the demands of extremist elements in Africa.

In spite of the security wraps placed on economic statistics, the impartial observer who looked through the cloud of British propaganda began to see that Rhodesia was maintaining its own in the economic war. There was a slowing down of the economy in certain sectors, and even hardship, but in general, Rhodesians and the Rhodesian economy were showing remarkable resilience in the face of the war of British sanctions, and in some respects were doing even better than in previous years. This is borne out by the findings of a team of observers which the South African *Financial Gazette* dispatched to Rhodesia at the close of 1966.

After a year of U.D.I. the Commonwealth Sanctions Committee had to report that Britain's economic war against Rhodesia was not going to bring down the Smith Government. On September 6, 1966,

Mr Wilson played host to the Commonwealth Prime Ministers and came under strong fire from most of the Black leaders for not using force against Rhodesia. He managed to avoid having to give such an assurance but on November 10, 1966, the Afro-Asians rammed through a resolution in the Trusteeship Committee proposing that Britain use force.

By then the verbal war had reached a new crescendo and when the first year of U.D.I. was celebrated in Rhodesia with confidence running high, Mr Wilson's mind was made up and the conference on board the cruiser H.M.S. *Tiger* off Gibraltar was arranged.

Mr Smith and his cabinet rejected the British demands for "a return to legal government" according to which the Governor Sir Humphrey Gibbs would have assumed full legislative powers and control of the armed forces and police. The nineteen point British "proposal" – which really boiled down to demands – had either to be accepted or rejected. While it did make provision for the nomination of Mr Smith as Prime Minister, his new Cabinet had to include five members who would be "independents".

The Rhodesian Cabinet rejected the British demand (or "offer" depending upon which way one looks at it) for basically the following reasons: The British government could have changed the Governor at whim and appointed an extreme left winger to run the country, perhaps someone like Sir Hugh Foot; Rhodesia would, constitutionally speaking, have become a colony, once again completely at the mercy of a Prime Minister whose mercurial approach to the question was by then only too well known; it was incomprehensible to expect that the new Cabinet could function when five of its members were not even Members of Parliament and would probably oppose Mr Smith's policies; finally, there was no guarantee that the Governor, in control of the armed forces, would not dismiss the government and appoint a new Cabinet – he could also, with the powers at his command, introduce a brand new constitution based on one-man-one-vote.

Rhodesia interpreted the British "proposals" as a request for unconditional surrender and to revert to abject colonial control.

Hereafter abdication of British responsibility for Rhodesia became a rout. The Government, after the most heated debate in Parliament since Suez, slammed the door on further talks with Rhodesia and took the matter to the United Nations. Here Britain was in trouble at the outset. The African states got their way and an *oil embargo* was included with the other items on which the Security Council slapped an embargo on December 16, 1966.

December 16, 1966 will go down in history as Mr Wilson's day of total surrender to the demands of Black African extremists.

Much opposition was immediately apparent to the Security Council's approval of the British list of sanctions. Portugal indicated that it would refuse to abrogate its trade pact with Rhodesia; Switzerland refused to comply with the decision; Malawi, Lesotho and Botswana said that they would and could not give any effective support; in both Germany and France there is stiffening resistance.

But the biggest headache to the United Nations and Britain was caused by South Africa who indicated in no uncertain terms that it was not going to be used as an instrument of the United Nations to crush a fellow Western government and would continue "business as usual". Britain went out of its way to assure South Africa that it was definitely not going to get involved in a trade war with South Africa to force it to comply with the sanctions list. Mr Wilson on two occasions publicly stated that Britain could not afford, under any circumstances, to escalate the sanctions war against Rhodesia into a confrontation with South Africa. Britain has made it quite clear that it will not use force against Rhodesia and cannot force a constitution upon the Rhodesians, but will the British Prime Minister now stand back and see force used by the United Nations against people of British descent? In any event, after the United Nations' record against the rag-tag army of Katanga and its virtual bankruptcy as a result of it, can it tackle the far superior Rhodesian armed forces? Any United Nations "action" against Rhodesia in a military sense would involve an operation calling for vast logistic support and a big disciplined force, none of which can be supplied by the African States. In the end the United States or Russia will have to provide the resources. In view of the American commitment in Vietnam which has aroused bitter feelings in the United States, it appears unlikely that the United States will undertake this task. At the same time the Americans or the British would hardly like to see Russians in the blue helmets of the United Nations setting up shop in Rhodesia.

What are the chances then of a *sanctions* war against Rhodesia bringing the Smith government to a fall?

On the home front Rhodesia has benefited from a year of sanctions – the experience has been put to intelligent use. Zambia, on the brink of economic ruin because of transportation problems with its copper, anti-White racism (which is driving skilled White workers from the country and causing an alarming decrease in production in key industries) and losses incurred in the economic war against Rhodesia, may take a more pragmatic attitude towards Rhodesia and give her own economy preference over the war against Rhodesia. For the latter there will be a drop in overall economic activity, exports will greatly fall, national income will sag, some factories will close shop and unemployment will increase. However, *and this is the crux of the matter,* although there will be these difficulties, personal hardships and some migration, the economy will probably not deteriorate to the extent that Rhodesians are forced to surrender.

Some of the reasons for this have already been stated but adaptation and diversification of local industries, normal trade with South Africa, Angola and Mocambique as well as Portugal, a year's experience in how to fight the bite of sanctions at home, and determination to stick it out and fight for a cause which virtually every White man and woman and the majority of Blacks support, are the most important ones.

Consider for one moment that whatever "majority rule" means in theory, in Africa it has meant one man rule and in most cases utterly irresponsible rule such as in Guinea, Ghana and the Congo. The fate of White and Black under majority rule would be infinitely worse than sanctions could ever impose upon them. Most Rhodesians are not at all concerned about the *moral* aspect of their case. They know that thirty-seven nations at the United Nations have governments based on fake elections and *minority* rule while another twenty-five are wide open to suspicion in this respect. In fact, the majority of the world's population are governed by minority groups or factions so that any reference to "world opinion" on this subject is likely to receive a most cynical reception in Salisbury.

Rhodesia is a small country with a total population less than that of one of the four top cities of the United States yet the people have a strong belief in the victory which their country will ultimately achieve over the vastly more powerful Britain. On March 31, 1967 the subscription lists for a R15,000,000 ($21,000,000) Government loan (five per cent for three years) opened in the morning at 9 a.m.

and promptly closed – the loan having been oversubscribed by some fifty per cent – despite the fact that the British Government had warned the previous day that the loan was illegal and that everyone supporting it would do so at his own risk. There seem to be a lot of people therefore who have far greater faith in Rhodesia's future than the British Government has.

Sanctions will not succeed unless Portugal and South Africa comply and the chances of that are very slender. South Africa and Portugal have already indicated that they will not heed the United Nations' call for sanctions but will continue their normal trade with Rhodesia. If the United Nations decides on a blockade of Angola, Mocambique and South Africa, or to apply sanctions against these countries, it would be considered an act of war and the Rhodesian affair would escalate into a dilemma which would most certainly break the United Nations. However, in view of the French attitude to United Nations "expeditions" in Africa, a veto would most likely be forthcoming long before this state of affairs could arise. In view of the inability of the United Nations to agree on the South West Africa issue during 1967, agreement (and action) on the prickly Rhodesian case is even more unlikely.

In the interim Rhodesia will continue to move closer in orbit to the other states of the Third Africa, particularly South Africa and Mocambique. Rhodesia's relations with its neighbours Malawi and Zambia are not as critical by far as they are made out to be in the press. Dr Hastings Banda of Malawi, for one, has no intention of letting relations deteriorate to the point where there is no contact between the two states. The fact of the matter is that he is anxious to have the best of both worlds, the ideological comfort of the Black north and the economic friendship of the powerful south. Rhodesian government representatives were at the independence anniversary celebrations of Malawi in 1965. Mr Banda has thus achieved the rare status of being on speaking terms with both White and Black states in Africa. He has refused to allow the emotional demands of African nationalism in the north to dictate his policy towards Rhodesia which has been one of ideological differences and economic co-operation.

The *general picture* which emerges would indicate that the Third Africa is set for years of political tranquillity and considerable economic expansion and that the Black states in this region,

Malawi, Zambia, the former British Protectorates and South Africa's Bantustans can look ahead to a decade of continued and ever increasing prosperity.

Opportunities for economic co-operation on a scale not dreamed of five years ago are opening before the people of the Third Africa.

The massive Cabora-Bassa hydro-electric and irrigation project in Mocambique is an excellent example of the type of regional project which would benefit not only one particular country but virtually the entire Third Africa. Dr H. J. van Eck, South Africa's top industrialist and Chairman of the powerful Industrial Development Corporation, dealt with this subject in a speech before the South Africa Club in London on October 25, 1966. For one, he said, it means a power grid within the next decade which would run from Zambia's copper belt a distance of over 2,500 miles through Rhodesia, Malawi, Swaziland and the entire Republic down to Cape Town, linking up with the Kariba and Orange River hydro-electric power grids.

The difficulty is that Mocambique on its own has not developed sufficiently to absorb Cabora-Bassa's giant capacity. South Africa's chief of the Industrial Development Corporation, however, felt that the power produced by Cabora-Bassa could be utilised by South Africa, making it possible to begin the giant project now. *Newscheck* reports that in discussions with the Portuguese and during a visit to the Cabora-Bassa site early in 1966, Dr van Eck worked on this insight. His calculation was that power could be delivered into the growing South African electricity grid or network at a point near Middelburg and that this could be done at a competitive price. Zambesi power will save the Republic of South Africa treasured water. By obviating the building of another 2,000 mw. thermal station, it can save the thirty million gallons of fresh water which such a station soaks up each day.

South Africa is both water and power hungry. Its growing industries have a seemingly insatiable demand. Already the country has a higher per capita consumption of electricity than either Japan or Italy, and the Electricity Supply Commission reports that demand is rising by about eight per cent a year, so that by the early Seventies the Republic will be using double the amount of power it needs now. To cope, Escom has embarked upon a R400,000,000 ($550,000,000) expansion programme which will boost its output from 23,000m kwh in 1965 to 31,000m kwh by 1971 – and this excludes power expansion undertaken by other authorities in the country.

In the interim, however, bringing in Zambezi power makes excellent sense. So it was with reason that Escom chairman, Rheinhard Straszacker, said in Lourenco Marques that the Republic could look to a feed-in from Mocambique. Still, the good sense does not stop there. The van Eck logic of employing the Republic's purchasing power to help African neighbours grow faster, applies equally to Kariba. Following the Cabora-Bassa plan, Zambia's President Kaunda could ironically gain his independence from Rhodesian south bank power at Kariba fairly soon. If electricity were sold to a South Africa that can pay (again via high tension DC lines), Zambia would be in a position to develop its own north bank station speedily and even its R50,000,000 ($70,000,000) Kafue scheme to boot.

Yet Cabora-Bassa's message is more then merely electric. Recognising similar possibilities for Zambia and Kariba, and looking as well to the Kunene as a further power source, van Eck's reasoning begins to have meaning on a far wider scale. It implies a closely knit Southern Africa, and it implies too a signal contribution by an outward-looking Republic to all the African countries clustered in the south. Malawi, Angola, Zambia, Rhodesia and Mocambique can all benefit by South Africa being used as a first-stage buyer of power that they for the moment cannot consume. Later the Republic will not need that power, and they will use it more and more as their own requirements expand. In this way all the lands of Southern Africa will help each other to advance. As *Newscheck* quite rightly observed, out of mutual development, mutual friendship must grow.

The heat of Black African nationalism has been lowered through its contact with a strong and sobering White nationalism. Stability, sound governmental relations, the expansion of communications and trade and internal economic growth have now assumed at least as great an importance as the need to exercise one's nationalism. Under these circumstances the development of Swaziland, the last remaining British Protectorate, to independence will probably take place without any untoward incidents.

In a decade the southern tier of Africa will have matured constitutionally, except for the Bantu states in South Africa whose development towards independence will be slowed down by the insistence of South Africa that experience in self-administration, economic viability and educational achievements of a very high order (compared with the rest of Africa) precede self-government.

For these and other reasons, outlined in the chapters dealing with unifying factors, the stage is set for a closer look at the late Dr Verwoerd's key plan for a "common market" for Southern Africa and the motives behind it.

In all of the countries of the Third Africa the late Prime Minister's proposal stirred a public debate on the subject and governments, White and Black, either requested more information or urged further study of the subject. In Botswana Members of Parliament urged the government to accept the proposal since South Africa is the only country from whom Botswana could expect sizeable investments and, if this should be followed by a trade agreement giving "favoured nation" treatment to Botswana, the territory stands to gain enormous benefits in such a market.

In Lesotho, Swaziland and Rhodesia the arguments have been basically the same, while Angola and Mocambique, though already part of the Portuguese Common Market, nonetheless favour much closer economic co-operation.

On the part of Rhodesia there have been vigorous protagonists for economic integration with South Africa. A lengthy report by a team of investigators of the South African *Financial Gazette* reported on February 25, 1966 that the sophisticated Rhodesian business community is all set for this move. They are expected to extoll the virtues of a common monetary unit for Southern African trade, a complete revision of the import control and exchange control legislation, and entire re-thinking of the industrial and agricultural needs of an economically integrated community south of the Zambesi. Rhodesian financial men also see a closely interlocked banking system by the two central banks working in a junior and senior (South African) partnership. Rhodesians are set for a switch to decimal currency closely linked with the South African unit, the Rand (R1 = $1.40), and coins are already so stamped. The Rhodesian unit will be known as the "Rhode" and is also worth R1.00.

In South Africa itself the plan was received with much enthusiasm and a spate of articles appeared in periodicals, magazines, newspapers and technical journals urging support for the Prime Minister's plan. The establishment of the Bank of Lisbon in South Africa in partnership with a big South African financial company was seen as a concrete step in this direction and given wide publicity.

In every single case the necessity to include countries such as Malawi and Zambia was clearly recognised as well as the fact that it would require much contact on a governmental basis between Black and White officials and, in the economic sphere, between Black and White economists.

No one in South Africa gave any indication that this co-operation with Black states would be unnatural, forced or irritating. Professor C. Schuman, one of South Africa's leading economists, pointed out that such a common market programme would not only call for increased trade between countries but go hand in hand with a massive development programme for the various states.

The countries forming part of the Third Africa already enjoy an inter-area trade of R551,000,000. In 1963 this was calculated to be about seventy per cent of the *total* recorded intra-African trade.[12]

As a stimulant the Southern African Common Market would have the Republic of South Africa, the continent's economic and industrial giant. Its *per capita* income is nine times that of the most advanced African state in Equatorial Africa, it produces twice as much electricity and six times as much steel as the entire continent put together; it is by far the biggest importer and its R1,430,000,000 ($1,990,000,000) imports in 1966 represented fifty per cent of all Western exports to Africa. More than fifty per cent of Africa's railway rolling stock and automobiles are here. In addition, it has a population exceeding that of Chad, Dahomey, Gabon, Gambia, Libya, Mauritania, Niger, Rwanda, Sierra Leone, Somalia and Togo put *together*. Its manufacturing industries, chemical concerns, industrial programmes and technical resources dwarf that of the rest of the African continent combined.

In 1965 the plan for a common market was given official impetus when the South African Minister of Planning, then Mr Jan Haak, addressed an international conference in Johannesburg on this

12. Source: United Nations: *Economic Bulletin for Africa*, January 1963. No comprehensive figures for North African intra-trade are available. Furthermore much of the intra-trade in Black Africa which takes place across land frontiers and by coastal shipping is not recorded so that this percentage is only an estimate, and could be 10-20 per cent out either way. Cf. African Institute, Pretoria: *Africa, Maps and Statistics*, No. 9, October 1964, page 177.

subject and the possibilities for closer economic co-operation between the countries of the Third Africa.

Mr Haak pointed out that more and more countries were becoming aware of the benefits that can be derived from inter-regional marketing arrangements. "This," he said, "is borne out by the European Common Market, the European Free Trade Area, the Central American Common Market and the contemplated Common Market of Equatorial African countries and the Cameroun, planned to operate from January 1, 1966. The motive behind this move is to secure the advantages of regional specialisation, larger markets and to accelerate the rate of economic growth."

This need for inter-regional co-operation manifests itself in Africa in particular, as most of these states have only recently obtained their political independence and are now confronted with the problem of achieving economic development in the face of serious problems arising from an acute shortage of trained and skilled manpower, a lack of managerial skills and entrepreneurship, scarce capital resources, balance of payments difficulties, inadequate infrastructures and obstacles in regard to agriculture – on which their economics are mainly based – such as pests, long distances, droughts, etc.

Despite the necessity for closer economic co-operation in Africa, various obstacles, which cannot be ignored, hamper the realisation of such a goal, the Minister said. He added: "The African countries, having nearly all been colonies of the European powers at one stage or another, had and still have close trade and financial links with the metropolitan countries. Their international trade was directed to these metropolitan countries which also provide their development capital. Few deliberate efforts were made to foster inter-African trade. The countries of Africa also belong to various payments and trade systems. For instance, the Portuguese provinces in Africa form a free trade area with Portugal and are administered as an integral part of metropolitan Portugal; the British Commonwealth countries in Africa, again, share in the system of Commonwealth preferences, whereas the former French possessions are associate members of the European Common Market."

These traditional links between various African states and countries in Europe in the fields of trade and payments tend to perpetuate the old established trade exchanges between Europe and

Africa and to act as a deterrent to inter-regional trade co-operation in Africa, the Minister pointed out. Moreover, the fact that the states of Africa are, with minor exceptions, still predominantly producers of primary commodities which few of them can usefully import to any significant extent from the others, clearly imposes rigid limitations on the scope for increased trade between them. The inter-African port and communication systems are also poorly developed. Cognizance has furthermore to be taken of the substantial differences in the level of economic development of the various countries in Africa.

Perhaps most important of all, is the necessity for a sincere desire on the part of the various countries to co-operate in economic matters; for this purpose the participants must be willing not only to share in the benefits that accrue from such an association, but also to shoulder the burdens which this entails.

"The term common market for Southern Africa was used by the Prime Minister of the Republic some time ago deliberately in order to indicate, by means of reference to a well-known concept, the Republic's willingness to co-operate and as an invitation for closer economic co-operation in Southern Africa," observed Mr Haak. "The actual framework of such co-operation can, by the nature of things, only be drawn up by mutual consent and after thorough negotiation."

"Contrary to the Common Market in Western Europe, where the ultimate goal of economic co-operation is political unity, the Republic seeks economic co-operation as a means of maintaining or achieving political independence for the participating states in Southern Africa. Thus we favour the principle of political independence and of economic interdependence with countries in Southern Africa," the Minister said.[13]

South Africa has unquestionably taken the lead in adopting the attitude that a closely knit economic regionalism need not be incompatible with the aspirations of nationalism or the proponents of a strong political independence. It was more than a year later that President Johnson of the United States made a similar statement to African Ambassadors in Washington on June 5, 1966. The President said: "The world has reached the stage where some of the

13. *Verbatim* text issued by Department of Information, Pretoria, 1965.

most effective means of economic growth can best be achieved in large units commanding large resources and large markets. We have learned in this generation that most nations are too small, acting alone, to assure the welfare of all their people. This does not mean the loss of hard earned national independence. It does mean that the accidents of national boundaries do not have to lead to hostility and conflict or serve as impossible obstacles to progress."

Only in the Third Africa is there tangible evidence of such an attitude. In fact, these sentiments are clearly evident in the joint statement issued by Prime Minister Jonathan of Lesotho and Prime Minister Vorster of South Africa after their January 1967 meeting in Cape Town.

In his Johannesburg address the South African Minister of Planning made several other important points which are particularly valid in the light of current attitudes in Southern Africa. "In favouring closer economic ties in Southern Africa," he said, "South Africa believes that her aid to developing countries will have to be over and above the foreign aid schemes already in force. Furthermore, South Africa believes that aid to developing countries should be directed to the promotion of trade. Due to the smallness of the domestic markets in Southern Africa, foreign aid should thus be aimed towards the fostering of exports as a means of creating a sound base for further economic growth. South Africa feels that closer economic ties with these countries should be based on the principle of *trade* rather than *aid* in order to ensure a regular flow of foreign income which is so essential for stable domestic development."

"An analysis of the economic structure and existing trade patterns of the countries in Southern Africa, reveals that these countries produce products for which the Republic can offer a market, whereas in turn South Africa can provide in their import requirements to a larger extent. South Africa would also be favourably disposed towards assisting these countries to improve their infrastructures," the Minister said.

Officially South Africa is taking a cautious approach, since she has no intention of undertaking a one-sided foreign aid programme. In addition she realises that ideological disputes and political friction between countries need to be cut to a minimum before such a market can be made to operate successfully. Nonetheless the intention, willingness to co-operate and the need for such a market is given full recognition. The South African government has also taken the lead in translating its policy of closer economic co-operation into tangible terms. At a press conference in Vienna at the beginning of 1967, the Republic's Minister of Economic Affairs said that South Africa was prepared to enter into a customs agreement with the two Black states of Malawi and Zambia. He said South Africa was also prepared to negotiate trade pacts with any state in Southern Africa. In his policy statement to the House of Assembly in February 1967, South Africa's Foreign Minister also indicated that the green light has now been given for co-operation with neighbouring Black states on an unprecedented scale.

At the official farewell luncheon offered to the visiting three man Cabinet delegation from Malawi the South African Minister of Economic Affairs again spelled out South Africa's policy towards Black Africa for the future. He said:

"Since I have spoken at some length about closer co-operation between South Africa and other states in Africa (and particularly between ourselves and Malawi), I would like to define more precisely what we mean by such co-operation. Our basic approach to this whole concept of fruitful co-operation is that South Africa, as part of the African Continent, has a deep consciousness, an intimate knowledge and a wide measure of practical experience of an immense variety of problems peculiar to Africa. We ourselves live with, and have to seek solutions for these problems from day to day.

"We are prepared to share with other African states our ability to find practical solutions for these problems which will amply take care of the conditions and circumstances peculiar to Africa. We would like other African states – regardless of their political philosophies or domestic policies – to feel free to approach us whenever they are in need of advice, guidance or technical assistance in connection with any problem or matter which affects the welfare of their peoples. South Africa's interest in the well-being of other nations in Africa is deep and enduring – and we are always prepared to help these nations in as constructive a manner as possible towards the solution of difficulties which may be impeding their progress.

"However, there are two very important qualifications to our readiness to help other African states.

"Firstly, we regard it as our duty to help them in such a manner that they will never have reason to regret having asked us for assistance. Any country receiving assistance from us will never have cause to accuse us of being neo-colonialists – in other words, of abusing our willingness to assist them as a means of securing any form of control over their economic or political destinies. We want the other states in Africa to know that we have not now, nor will we in the future entertain any intentions inconsistent with a full and proper regard for their economic and political sovereignty. On the contrary, we would rather lend our support to measures that may serve to maintain and strengthen the political and economic sovereignty of any country recognising this principle.

"The assistance we are prepared to render them, must totally conform to the rigid standards of conduct we have set for ourselves in this particular field. But equally important is our firm belief that such assistance must be given in a form which will generate real productive development, and will produce concrete results in the form of a lasting expansion of output in these states so that their inhabitants may derive real benefit from our help in the form of increased incomes, as well as higher living standards.[14]

On April 28, 1967 the South African *Financial Gazette* issued a twelve page supplement "Southern Africa Common Market" which contained articles by the Minister for Economic Affairs; by Professor J. A. Lombard of the University of Pretoria on the system of economic co-operation which would precede such a market; by Dr H. J. van Eck on the role electricity can play in welding together the Southern African "community"; by Mr N. Cambitzi, Chairman of the Rhodesian Industrial Development Corporation, on the part Rhodesia would play in the common market; by Professor C. Verburgh of the Department of Transport-Economics of the University of Stellenbosch on how the expanding transport system in Africa is breaking down barriers and opening up Southern Africa; by Mr W. T. Passmore, General Manager of the Standard Bank of South Africa on how the banks could assist commerce in a free trade area; by Professor D. J. Smith, Head of the Department of Agricultural-Economics at Stellenbosch University on how agriculture will feature in the structure of the common market; by Dr G. M. E.

14. *Verbatim* text issued by Department of Information, Pretoria, January, 1967.

Leistner of the Africa Institute on how the common market would benefit Malawi; by the Portuguese Ambassador on closer co-operation with the Portuguese provinces and by Mr R. Whyte, General Manager of Barclays Bank D.C.O. on how the Republic of South Africa can lead the way on the road to a free trade area.

From the list of contributors it is obvious that some of the best economists in the country and foremost financiers and planners are backing up the official attitude on closer economic ties in Southern Africa; in fact, they have gone much further in propagating the idea of a Common Market for Southern Africa by spelling out the various steps to be taken, difficulties, advantages, the amount of planning required, existing services and relations between the different countries, resources, etc. It was clearly obvious that no one any longer thought of Southern Africa in terms of watertight compartments, and that political differentiation and economic co-operation can indeed go hand-in-hand.

It has been indicated in this chapter (and the ones dealing with unifying factors) that the Third Africa seems to be heading for a consolidating period in so far as constitutional development is concerned, and for closer economic co-operation, while there has been a lowering of the flame in matters of race relations.

There remains the ever important question of domestic politics and the extent of supra-national political integration which a successful common market may spark. This touches upon the question of the rights and wrongs of domestic policies currently applied in the Third Africa and the need (if any) for a change in extra-territorial policies.

Assuming that the domestic policies of the various states present them with no insurmountable problem during the next two decades, and *assuming* that some form of common market becomes a reality. What chances are there that the various Bantu states in South Africa, Lesotho, Swaziland, Botswana, Rhodesia and the other territories of the Third Africa would move towards political union either through a Council of Ministers as in Europe or through a Federation?

The answer at this stage is a decided "nil".

There will be no political integration in South Africa in the fore-seeable future and there will be no federation or political integration between any of the constituent members of the Third Africa.

There are many reasons for this. One very important and out-standing reason is the simple fact that there has never been a successful federation or political union between different nations and races enjoying an unequal distribution of economic power and where the numerical superiority of the one group is overwhelming.

The dream of a great Atlantic Community, the United States of Europe, uniting five hundred million of the world's most civilized and advanced people with a trillion Rand economy now seems shattered. *The trend is back to nationalism.* In the European Common Market the six members may have travelled a long way towards economic union but this was always only intended as a means to achieve political union. Progress on the political front has come to a standstill over the past three years. The smaller members have been nervous from the outset that it would be dominated by France and Germany. This has indeed happened as General de Gaulle's efforts to change the shape of the Atlantic Alliance, the exclusion of Britain, and his attempts to create a Franco-German alliance begin to bear fruit.

In his book, dealing with the history of attempts at European Unity, René Albrecht-Carrie points out that nationalism has been the strongest force opposed to European unity. In the same way nationalism has been the strongest force in Africa opposed to a Federation of weaker states. The best example of course, is the Central African Federation. As Elspeth Huxley pointed out in 1964, economically the Federation was doing fine and in the first five years of its life the national income went up by forty-five per cent, exports by seventy-five per cent and gross domestic product per head by a full third. "In other words," she said, "the Federation did not die from economic causes." What killed it was African nationalism. Dr Hastings Banda, the Prime Minister of Malawi, went on record that he'd rather his followers starved in rags on the streets than waxed fat in a Federation ruled by Whites.

Dr Banda's attitude is not unique, nor the collapse of the Federation. Britain also once had high hopes of forming a South Arabian Federation, which could absorb some twenty-four troublesome sultanates, sheikdoms and emirates now under British protection.

As a Federation Nigeria is fast approaching the stage of dissolution.

Scandinavia once used to share its kings. After eighty years of war, the Norwegians and the Swedes decided that territorial "apartheid" was after all, the best thing.

In many ways the short stormy history of Malaysia and the reasons for Singapore leaving the Federation are also the same which led to Nyasaland and Northern Rhodesia leaving the Central African Federation. It is also in many ways a vindication of South Africa's policy of separate development of different ethnological groups.

The conflict on the island of Cyrpus is another example. Despite a liberal constitution and safeguards for the Turkish minority (as well as a wealth of advice on the "Brotherhood of Man" and "Human Rights" from the United Nations and the liberal left) in the end it became a simple question of Greek versus Turk.

If ever there was a Federation which should have come into being and which ought to have had a reasonable chance of success, it would have been the East African Federation of Kenya, Uganda and Tanganyika. Nationalism, national aspirations and suspicions between Black and Black killed off this hope in a matter of a year or two. A decade of British preparation for this Federation, including a common currency, a common university, equal tariffs etc. went down the drain.

The list of failures of political unions and Federations during the post war period is a long one. In addition to those mentioned, the Ivory Coast saw to it that the West African Federation never got off the ground; Gabon killed off the Mid-African Federation; Jamaica decided to get out of the West Indian Federation. The Federation of Mali and Senegal endured only for a few months during 1960, and the Union of African States (Ghana, Guinea, Mali) fared little better.

Pakistan and India is another good example, so is Rwanda and Burundi.

The fact is that whenever different races forming disparate communities (culturally and ethnologically) have been thrown together, the end result has been a separation of the ways. In most cases it was preceded by violence such as in Pakistan and India.

There is, therefore, a mountain of realism behind South Africa's apartheid programme, which recognises the multi-national character of the country and prepares to avoid a conflict of cultures by establishing avenues for separate political and cultural development.

It may also be that Canada, long a critic of the theory of apartheid, will soon be forced to apply a liberal measure of apartheid to solve the problem of the French-Canadians. What the French-Canadian right wing is asking for, i.e. a largely autonomous state where the French language would be respected, is no more, no less what the Xhosas of South Africa are asking of the White South African government – and getting.

In the Sudan, the government has had to launch full scale army action to quell southern violence in a deepening split with the Black African separatists. According to the *New York Times* thousands of people have been killed in daily incidents in the south. The wave of guerilla fighting has been almost uninterrupted since it swept over the country in 1963. "The conflict is not an ideological one," observed the *New York Times*. "Authorities say that there is virtually no communism in Southern Sudan. The trouble is deeper than that – it is the great ethnic dividing line of the Islamic Arab north and the Pagan-Christian centre of Africa. There are differences in culture, languages, level of education, way of life and religion that go back into history and run deep into societies."

No one in Southern Africa would, of course, quarrel with this summary of the state of affairs in the Sudan. The fact is that the Arab government of the Sudan wants to convert the Bantu Southerner into a Black Arab and this is being resisted. The Black Southerner on his part is anxious to be ruled by a Black man in a Black country, according to the Black man's customs. Precisely the same circumstances of race and differences between people apply to South and most of Southern Africa. In the words of the late Dr Verwoerd: "What has to be realised is that the White man does not regard the Bantu as an inferior being, but as a different being – with his own background and his own way of life which has been developed through the ages and which should be considered when a future is planned for him."

Even to the avowed Black nationalists in South Africa, separate development, apartheid, is seen as the only way out. The Chief Minister of South Africa's first Bantu State (the Transkei), Mr Kaizer Matanzima, told students of Rhodes University in Grahamstown in 1965 that it was his contention that representation of the Bantu in a predominantly White parliament was "doomed to failure", as such representation "is not the expression of the autonomy of my people, or of the self-determination of the country which is ours, the Transkei, or, for that matter, any other Bantu homeland in South Africa." Speaking to the university's World Affairs Society on "Why I am in favour of Separate Development", Mr Matanzima said that the integrated nature of such a system of representation nullified the opportunity for the Black man to propagate the specific economic and cultural demands of his people. "Any Government of the Republic of South Africa which allowed a mixed Parliament signified by such an act its resolve to merge the races of the subcontinent into one conglomerate, where the identity of the several or numerous nations living in South Africa would be dissolved and a new hybridised community created," he said. "It would be the silliest imaginable thing to attempt this, as it will not only create endless conflict in our heterogeneous community in South Africa, but it would bedevil the peaceful progress of all races, and the country, in such a way that it would be more of a retrogressive than a progressive step to take.

"The Bantu race in South Africa and, for that matter, in the whole of the African continent is proud of its own heritage and does not regard it as an unblemished and unmixed blessing if, and when, the White politician condescends to invite him to integrate with the White community, politically and socially. It must be a very ignorant Bantu who does not realise that such integration with the White people will call for the sacrifice of those national and cultural possessions that are more precious to him than any questionable and temporary elation he may experience at being able to indulge in everything the White man can indulge in his own areas. On the other hand, it must be a very ignorant and foolish White man who does not realise that such integration, while being unpalatable to him in the first instance, will demand from him the sacrifice of those national and cultural attributes which he cherishes as much as the Bantu does his."

The Chief Minister said that political integration would, in the long run, mean nothing less than the "total demolition" of both White and Black in South Africa, and the creation of a coloured race in which the worst characteristics of both White and Black might quite often merge into the national character of a new community without a culture of its own. The cultures of both Black and White would either get lost in the process of "hybridisation", or would be impaired beyond recognition, declared Mr Matanzima.

The situation in Southern Africa is thus one which combines all the difficulties which once faced the proponents of political unification for Europe, for Pakistan and India, Malaysia, Rwanda-Burundi, etc. The chances that a multi-racial community with a liberal constitution protecting the rights of the minority White and Asian groups would ever replace the existing complex of countries must be ruled totally unrealistic.

The chances of a consortium or a community of independent states meeting in absolute equality to discuss matters of regional importance such as trade, tariffs, communications, agricultural problems, scientific development, grants in aid or loans are, however, infinitely better.

No government in Lesotho, Swaziland, South Africa, Rhodesia, Malawi, or Zambia, etc. would object to politically independent states in Southern Africa meeting annually to discuss the matters mentioned above. *This is the concept of community and it may well assume the form of an Organisation of Southern African States.*

It also appears to contain several contradictory and disrupting features – separate sovereignties (most of them but newly-won), separate nationalisms, different races and opposed attitudes towards race relations – more or less the same features to be found in, for example, the Organisation of American States. Yet the notable fact is that these very features are being revealed as working towards a loosely-knit yet organic whole. The explanation – perhaps only dimly sensed at present – is that political independence may make a stronger cement between different kinds of people than formal union; common recognition of the right of each to its own sovereignty and ways may well bind them faster than a common constitution.

South Africa who is often considered to be the fly in the ointment in matters of this nature, is far ahead of the other countries in the public debate on the future of the Third Africa. Many newspapers have gone to great lengths to educate their readers to the fact that South Africa now has to deal on equal terms with Black statesmen and governments not only within South Africa's borders (the Transkei, Swaziland and Lesotho) but also with other states such as Zambia, Malawi and Botswana.

Perhaps the most important function which such a Commonwealth or Organisation of Southern African States could immediately fulfill would be to make a combined attack on the three age-old scourges of Africa, viz. poverty, illiteracy and disease.

Hunger is one enemy which the states could combat simultaneously and in close co-operation. Racialism and disputes of ideological nature are automatically ruled out in such a conflict. "The war on hunger," said President Kennedy of the United States in June 1963, "is truly mankind's war of liberation . . . There is no battle on earth or in space more important (for) peace and progress cannot be maintained in a world half fed and half hungry."

Statistics show that every day of the week for the next few years, some ten thousand people will die of malnutrition or starvation. In India alone, some *fifty million children* will die of malnutrition in the next ten years. More than half the world's three billion people live in perpetual hunger.

In a recent interview distributed by North American Newspaper Alliance, Professor René Dumont of France's *Institute d'Estudes Politiques*, a world authority on African agriculture and adviser to half a dozen French African regimes, predicted that Black Africa faces a very real threat of starvation within fifteen years and that the recent epidemic of coups d'etat has a bearing on this situation. He is convinced Black Africa already is on the road to economic and political ruin which only a "revolution" in the thinking of both Africans and outsiders can avert. He is not optimistic that such a "revolution" will come about.

Dumont ascribes the series of military take-overs to discontent among the "privileged classes" of the new states. These he identifies as the higher and middle bureaucracy and the army and police officer groups.

"In every case," he says, "the privileged elements saw their material advantages in danger of being whittled away, either because of the regime's inefficiency, or because some half-hearted attempts at reform were about to take place. Even those army men who quite sincerely regard themselves as crusaders against corruption have consistently acted with the approval and support of a threatened elite."

As a result he holds out little prospect for military juntas in countries like Nigeria, Ghana, and the Congo being able to strike at the roots of those lands' fundamental troubles. They may, he says, succeed in eliminating some of the most blatant corruption, but that is all.

"What is needed is to awaken the enthusiasm of the mass of people in these countries and instil in them a desire to work hard for the future of themselves and their children," says Dumont. "Right now, this is lacking for the good reason that they see no point in it. If they work and accumulate a surplus, they are robbed of it, one way or another, if only through inflation. So what is the use?"

Since 1958, the average population increase in the newly independent sub-Sahara states has been 2.5 per cent annually. But food production has risen only 1.5 per cent, and in several cases has actually fallen below what it was a decade ago. Despite the vast sums poured into Africa, there is no sign of an improved trend. If anything, it is getting worse.

"The prognosis is for general famine by 1980," said Dumont. "And it will be on a scale outside suppliers won't be able to check."

With the resources at their disposal and their relatively sparse population, the countries of the Third Africa have a better chance than any other region in the world to produce far more food than its population can absorb, and to provide for millions living in less fortunate circumstances abroad. Surely this is a goal worth striving for? Beginning with hunger, the states of the Third Africa can also make a successful effort to eradicate illiteracy in the next two decades and from there proceed to tackle the economic advancement of the lesser developed units.

Provided the Third Africa can effectively oppose or shut out the disrupting forces of Communism, notably China and Russia, and accept each other's *bona fides* and integrity, it will show the world that harmonious race relations are indeed possible on the basis of separate political development, with economic interdependence. South Africa has studiously refrained from leading its Bantu people into political quicksand, and she has done this by preaching political *evolution* instead of *revolution*. Unlike the Black African states South Africa has learned much from the "winds of change".

The White man in Southern Africa can still save the Bantu in this area from the fate of the Black man in Nigeria, Ghana, the Sudan, Burundi, etc. by continuing to build and to improve on the basis that the only lasting political benefits which man has derived from history are rooted in evolution and not in revolution.

The rule of law, the vote, government by Congress, in fact, all the basic tenets of democracy came about by a slow evolutionary process, not by revolution.

In many respects the Third Africa is not "in step" with the rest of the world or "in the main stream of world opinion". It can even be said to be heading "upstream", but in that way it may avoid going over the waterfall for which the protagonists of "world opinion" and "one world – one government" are heading with their cry of immediate majority rule.

In the Utopia of one-world-one-government and one-man-one-vote, will the people of for example, America, really subject themselves to rule by the Chinese peasant majority?

The Third Africa is the only area in Africa where the basic interests of the people are paramount to abstract ideologies; it has the space, the human and rich mineral resources and, above all, the creative ability and drive to turn this part of the continent into the Europe of Africa.

10. South Africa and Africa: Evolution vs Revolution

The winds of change are still blowing over parts of Africa, but it has become an ill wind. It has been blowing ever since *world opinion*, as expressed at the United Nations, decided that the time for the independence of Africa's many races and nations was now, not tomorrow or next year, but now. It was thought that it would blow away the evils of "colonialism" but as the dust began to settle a picture emerged which shows that it has caused widespread havoc which all the drawbacks of colonialism could never match.

Following the independence of India and Pakistan just after World War II political pundits, newspaper editors, columnists, professors of political science and governments of the West and East urged the European colonial powers to "set free the oppressed masses of Africa".

The formula for this independence crusade had a strange uniformity and was basically very simple: eliminate colonialism, set the African nations on the road to independence – not when they are ripe for it but when they demand it – teach them the values of one-man-one-vote and of a two-party Parliamentary system but, above all, treat them as equals in the councils of the world. Africa would then surge ahead to provide a better life for all its peoples, irrespective of race, religion and nationality.

In the aftermath of Africa's grisly march to independence, very few of the crusaders are in the mood to study the editorials of the great newspapers and magazines of the West during the period 1945 to 1960. *The New York Times, Pravda, The London Observer, The Guardian, The Spectator, Le Monde, Die Welt, Dagens Nyheter* had all diligently applied this formula in their editorial columns. In addition articles in political science magazines, lectures at university and radio talks, all reflected "mankind's" hope for Africa once "freedom" had been achieved under one-man-one-vote and colonialism rooted out.

The pressure was put on colonial governments – the French, the British, the Belgians and others. They fled in such haste before the hot wind of "world opinion" that some newly independent states were left standing on their own political feet with only 30 miles of roads, a per capita income of R2 per month and three university graduates.

All that is history now.

What has not yet been chronicled are the changes which one-man-one-vote, "uhuru", instant democracy, call it what you may, have brought to Africa and what hope is held out for the future.[1]

To allege that this flashback is a form of gloating is simply untrue. Only the depraved can gloat over the butchery of some 4,000 children in Rwanda and Burundi during January 1964, not to speak of the tens of thousands of adults killed in that country's insane outbreak of genocide. But it will help to open the eyes of those people in Africa, Europe, Britain, America and most of all in South Africa, who believe that the same liberal and idealistic policy of one-man-one-vote should also be applied as a solution to the problems in Rhodesia, South Africa and South West Africa. It may help to show the proponents of a policy of gradualism in political integration, with political equality in a unitary state as the ultimate objective, that the risks are too great even for such a policy and that failure would be too disastrous to contemplate.

Above all it is to show that the turmoil and ruin is almost exclusively confined to the areas *outside* the Third Africa and therefore serves to illustrate, better than anything else, how much this area differs from Black and Arab Africa.

To understand the immediate past history of conflicts between independent states in the north, of subversion of neighbouring governments and of civil war in countries where there are no longer "White colonials" to blame, is simply to better appreciate the good relations which exist between the countries of the Third Africa.

1. The details of events in Black and Arab Africa in the post-independence era are based on reports obtained from: *U.S. News and World Report; Chicago Daily News; New York Times;* London *Daily Telegraph; Bulletins* of the Africa Institute, Pretoria; *Africa Report* of the African American Institute; Thomas Molnar, *Africa A Political Travelogue,* Fleet, N.Y.; *National Review,* N.Y.; Smith Hempstone, *Africa Angry Young Giant*; Associated Press and Agence France Press reports; Reports of the Africa News Service of the Johannesburg *Star* and other sources.

For the Third Africa there is a future beckoning, for the other two Africas little hope.

The indications are that there will be a further explosion between Black nationalism and Arab socialism in the Sudan.

By the end of 1966 Nigeria was tottering on the brink of civil war. In a special message to the people of America published as a full page advertisement in *The New York Times* on March 10, 1967 the Government of Eastern Nigeria said: "The truth is that Nigeria is on the brink of disintegration. Since May 1966 political upheaval, rioting and murder have left Nigeria a house divided by dissent and suspicion."

There have been large scale outbreaks of barbarism in many parts of Black Africa. Political stability has become a rarity and no less than seven governments were toppled by mutinous armies in as many months during 1965-1966 alone. A complete break with democratic government is evident in the far greater majority of African states. Grandiose schemes, corruption and gross mismanagement have landed the economies of all but a handful of countries in dire straits.

The optimist (one of a decided minority) who predicts that Black and Arab Africa will survive its current political turmoil, economic retrogression and cancerous outbreaks of barbarism bases his prediction on innumerable *ifs*. On the other hand those who predicted and foresee further strife and chaos for Africa in the coming decade have ample evidence to back their forecasts.

Of thirty-eight African states which have become independent since World War II, more than twenty-six have been wracked by severe economic and political convulsions ranging from bloody civil war in the Congo to bankruptcy in Ghana, from armed conflict between Ethiopia and Somaliland to the assassination of a President in Togo and two Premiers in Burundi. The politically planned murder of Prime Ministers Balewa and Ironsi of Nigeria, Africa's most populous state, came as the worst shock since this was the country in which the West had invested most of its hope and faith.

It has been argued that Europe underwent worse convulsions during the birth of its various nation-States when cannon and cavalry cut a bloody swath through the flower of the people of that age. This may be so, but, had Africa the trained soldiers of Bismarck, Cavour and Napoleon instead of its rag-tag armies, or weapon industries supporting the political intrigue of African leaders, the "dark continent" would have had to be renamed the "red continent". Furthermore, the large numbers of people senselessly slaughtered in a dozen different states were killed over a period of only five to seven years. The 20,000 Watusi senselessly slaughtered in Rwanda and Burundi in 1964 were killed by hand and spear with the number of dead equalling the fallen in some of the most famous battles fought in Europe in the 18th and 19th centuries. If cannon, guns and cavalry were available instead of clubs and spears, the Watusi dead may have exceeded 100,000. In February 1964 a World Council of Churches reception centre reported that it was sheltering twelve survivors from a massacre of 6,000; and, in another centre, 2,500 out of an original community of 15,000 persons.

In North Africa the immediate past saw President Ahmed Ben Bella of Algeria in open conflict with Morocco. Ironically Ben Bella had to throw in forces which he had been training to help "liberate" Angola and South Africa to save his own skin. Shortly thereafter he himself was toppled in a coup d'etat. In the Sudan open rebellion broke out. Tens of thousands of refugees have escaped from the Southern Sudan to Ethiopia, Uganda, Kenya and the Congo, leaving in their wake twenty-three burning cities and towns – all because the Arab government was trying to impose Islamic culture on Black Africans with African traditions and thought patterns.

One of the most incredible acts of savagery took place in Cameroun where tens of thousands of people were killed during 1962-1964.

People who could tell you offhand the loss of lives and wounded in the Sharpeville tragedy probably do not even know that Cameroun is an independent state in Africa. Lloyd Garrison, the Africa correspondent of *The New York Times* reported on September 10, 1964, that some 70,000 had lost their lives in civil strife in Cameroun yet this news received less prominence than the execution of two Black men in South Africa who were found guilty of murdering a witness.

There is a thread of deep grief and terror through most of Black Africa. The Organization of African Unity reported early in 1965 that towards the close of 1964 there were 100,000 refugees in Uganda, including Congolese, rebels from the south of the Sudan, and Watusi driven from their ancient homelands by Bahutus in Rwanda. President Milton Obote of Uganda maintains that there are over 200,000 refugees in his country adding that in spite of the help he was getting, they were draining Uganda's resources. In Burundi, the Organization for African Unity reports, there are 80,000 homeless, destitute fugitives, mainly Watusi; and in the Congo there were said to be 40,000 more. Congolese refugees are also in Tanzania and Zambia. In Zambia, so the O.A.U. reports, there were 30,000 refugees, mostly Congolese. Another 25,000 refugees from the Congo and Rwanda were in Tanzania. Of the Rwandans, half were said to be Watusi and the other Bahutus driven out of their country by fellow tribesmen.

From January 1966 to January 1967 the number of refugees in Africa increased by 110,000 to 740,000.[2]

According to the officially published figures of the Government of Eastern Nigeria (March 10, 1967) more than 30,000 men, women and children living in the country's Northern region were murdered. Some *two million* refugees fled the North for Eastern Nigeria. Another two million were maimed, orphaned or widowed and driven from their homes. Their return, said the report, has caused monumental problems of feeding, housing and rehabilitation.

In a matter of weeks after independence, Kenya's Kenyatta swallowed the parliamentary opposition to turn his country into a one-party state; Kaunda of Zambia warned that any criticism of him would be regarded as "conspiracy against the state"; Ben Bella set up military courts to try his own political opponents (no defence counsel or appeal allowed) while his United Nations representative literally howled at South Africa for the public trial of Black men (with counsel and the right of appeal) on charges of sabotage and premeditated murder.

In the Congo White mercenaries have been fighting Red Chinese-backed savages intent on the wholesale massacre of fellow Blacks. Uganda's President Milton Obote in an incredible coup d'etat took over all the powers in his country. In Cairo some four thousand people were arrested between July 1965 and February 1966 for plotting to assassinate President Nasser.

In October 1965 eighty six people were executed in public after an abortive coup in Burundi. The former Prime Minister was

2. United Nations High Commissioner, Geneva, Press Statement, February 22. 1967.

233

assassinated. A hundred other people were shot and tribal warfare has since led to a further five hundred people losing their lives with many thousands rendered homeless. Three months after the abortive coup, newspaper reports said that all the elected members of both legislative houses were *executed*.

So much for "freedom" in Burundi and these are the sort of grisly tragedies which the Secretary General of the United Nations, U Thant, dismissed as unworthy of United Nations action. "Teething troubles", he said.

In Dahomey which became independent in August 1960 there was violence and bloodshed at the time of the first election; in 1961 the Opposition was banned; in October 1963 a general strike followed; in the same month (October 27) there was a coup d'etat; in 1964 the politicians in power were thrown out by fellow politicians and the constitution suspended and in November 1965 army general Soglio deposed President Apithy – the *third* occasion since independence that the government was removed by force.

Elsewhere in the continent, in the words of the late Robert Ruark, "there has been blood and rebellion, assassination and attempted assassination and mutiny, looting and rape . . . a return to cultist violence and a breakdown of facilities and communications . . ." Economies have wasted; poor Africans have become even poorer, their new Black masters richer and more powerful, more arrogant and dictatorial, and riding roughshod over their rights in a fashion no White colonial administrator would ever have dared.

Dictatorships and one party states have become the rule and the countries where a Parliamentary opposition survived are few and far between. With it has gone incredible graft and corruption.

An army of civil servants consume two-thirds of Senegal's entire budget. Imagine the public service in South Africa consuming R700,000,000 ($900,000,000) in salaries alone! In the Central African Republic the rate of literacy is *less* than eight per cent but the army of civil servants total 50,000 out of a total population of some 1.7 million. President Nkrumah's downfall in Ghana was followed by a thorough investigation of the use of state funds. It soon became clear that millions of Rand went into the pockets of the President, his Cabinet and party officials.

Lack of self-determination and colonialism has been blamed for Black Africa's slow development but in Ethiopia, a Black state which was independent two thousand years before South Africa and which has received R150,000,000 ($208,000,000) in aid from America alone since 1952, ninety per cent of the people are still illiterate. Fifty per cent suffer from diseases caused by malnutrition. In the capital, Addis Ababa, the population still live largely in mud huts without a water borne sewage system. Some 40,000 people die every year from malaria, a disease virtually eradicated in South Africa which Ethiopia (in common with the other states with equally miserable conditions) would like to "liberate". Yet Emperor Haile Selassie possesses a private fortune estimated at R600,000,000 ($800,000,000) invested all over Europe. One third of the country's revenue annually disappears before reaching official state coffers. This absolute monarch travels in an air-conditioned yacht worth nearly three million Rand ($4,000,000) – donated by the United States Government.

Another pet theory of the uninformed Westerner but more particularly the Black African politician is that without colonialism the African states would have been in a much better state to-day, economically, socially and otherwise, than they were before the advent of colonialism. "The colonies were raped for the benefit of the European powers," said ex-President Nkrumah of Ghana. "British sucked the blood of Kenya during her colonial administration," observed President Kenyatta of Kenya.

The question of *what* the African states had exactly achieved or were in the process of achieving in the socio-economic field or in the realm of "human dignity and freedom of the individual" *before* the advent of colonialism of course, begs an answer. The short reply would be "nothing". A more detailed reply would take in the despotic powers enjoyed by each African King or tribal chief, the internecine warfare (if the Europeans had not arrived on the scene in South West Africa the Namas and the Herero would have written "finish" to the history of the human race in that part of the world), the complete lack of anything but a subsistence economy; the disease, total illiteracy, high infant mortality, ritual murders, etc., *ad infinitum*.

But what happened in the ten, fifteen years *after* the colonial powers had departed? Were there any signs of *recovery?* After all, with the aid of the Marshall plan, Europe was lifted from the ashes of an all embracing war and after fifteen years was well on the road to prosperity. With foreign aid, Japan managed to build entire cities and a flourishing economy where once there were only blackened ruins and a few rice paddies left.

If the Black African argument is correct, then the record should show general improvement in Africa over the past ten years. After all, the amount of money which East and West pumped into Africa in the form of foreign aid adds up to a stunning amount. America *alone* provided a total of R1,160 *million* ($1,612,000,000) during 1948-1964.

According to Sir Geoffrey de Freitas, British High Commissioner, *Kenya* had received more than R200,000,000 ($280,000,000) in British aid since the war, apart from the millions thrown in by Russia, China and the United States. Despite this generous aid, the number of children in school is dismally low, there is still only one hospital bed for 660 people compared with one in 250 for Rhodesia. The Revised Economic Plan for Kenya 1966-1970 pointed out that in the majority of cases the production of farms now run by Blacks, has dropped by *eighty* per cent.[3] Children are still being sold in slavery.

The picture elsewhere is distressingly similar.

Ghana started off with foreign reserves totalling R500,000,000 ($700,000,000), (about what prosperous South Africa has during boom conditions) but within the short period of nine years Ghana's finances and economy were in ruin. In April 1966 the reserves stood at R500,000. The shocking part is that apart from her reserves Ghana has also received and squandered over one billion Rand in direct and indirect aid from other countries.

For all this money, Ghana has nothing to show that is of any real value to the people.

The *Congo* which was once one of the most prosperous of African countries is now a ruin. (During the colonial period the standard of living was rising, the schools were packed and the future bright.) "The financial, social and economic situation is catastrophic," said President Mobuto in 1965 and the country is running at an annual loss of R120,000,000 ($167,000,000).

In *Tanzania* which has received some R90,000,000 ($125,000,000) from Britain since 1945, the pace of economic development is

3. Cf. Blaine Littell: *South of the Moon*, Weidenfeld & Nicolson, London, 1966.

still that of an ox-wagon and far below the level of pre-independence.

Guinea has been receiving aid the past five years, to the tune of R180,000,000 ($250,000,000) per year from Russian, Chinese, American and other sources. The budget however, has never balanced. This can be readily understood when administrators order enough screwdrivers at one time to supply Guinea for 200 years at present rate of development! An order was also put in for the delivery of cement, in paper bags and during the rainy season. There is now a mountain of solid cement as a monument to Guinea's immaturity!

Enough porcelain toilets were ordered in one month to supply the country for decades!

Despite this record, Black politicians in Southern Africa are not going to promise their people anything less than "freedom and independence" and "one-man-one-vote" in their lifetime. If he does not do so he will not be a politician for long. In promising the political kingdom he is not going to talk in terms of generations or even decades. The banned African National Congress cannot accept a platform calling for gradual integration and "majority government" by the year 2,000 even though there are thousands of White South Africans who will accept such a platform. At least one important Johannesburg newspaper has said that such a platform is not only wise but is inevitable. But the African National Congress and the Pan Africanists are not prepared to wait that long. They want to achieve this "government by majority" while *they* are still fit and alive to run the show. Thus they are caught in a pincer – between their promises and their ability to deliver. The resistance of the White people has little to do with this, it is simply that the educated Bantu community, despite South Africa's heroic efforts at universal education, will not be strong enough (perhaps not for decades) to run an industrialised country such as South Africa.

This is one of the vital factors which the West seems unable to grasp.

In one African country after the other, where power has been given into the hands of a few educated politicians, they have been unable to cope with the pressure of the masses demanding the miracles they were promised. Coupled with the Black Africans' record of nepotism, graft, corruption and tribal enmity as well as incompetence, this generates revolution and a more extreme set takes over.

The underlying conditions in Africa can have no other result *until the populace matures*. It took England some 2,000 years.

Stable government, *democratic* government, requires the solid basis of an informed electorate, free of tribal enmity and with tutelage in terms of generations. Nelson Mandela, Albert Luthuli, Robert Sobukwe or, for that matter, any other consortium of Black politicians cannot achieve such a state of affairs among the Bantu in Southern Africa, not in a decade or in four decades. So the problem of 1966 will still be there in 1999. At the same time the record of failure of democratic institutions in Africa is such that little hope can be held out for the re-installation of that precious heritage. *Tribalism is still the crucible of the Black African's mentality*. Only centuries of benevolent colonialism such as the Roman occupation of a barbarous Britain can instil the deep rooted belief in democracy and law and order which the White people of the West have in common, and the chances of colonialism ever returning to Africa is close to nil.

When the reserved *Christian Science Monitor* published its first "political and ideological map of the world" in 1964 it came to the conclusion, not surprisingly, that the Republic of South Africa was the only democracy left in Africa.

While the immediate past history (1945-1966) of Africa reveals a pattern of violence, corruption, political turmoil and distressing economic retrogression, the eminent American geographer, Dr George Kimble, believes that there is even less hope for the future. Addressing the American Geographical Society on December 6, 1962 he observed that most of the new African states do not have enough people, land or resources *ever* to become viable states. (Of the twenty six states which became independent between 1957 and 1962, only four had a population larger than South Africa's). The Somali Republic has less arable land than there is (or was) on New York's Long Island. Its economy rests almost solely on bananas; that of Senegal on peanuts; Rwanda and Burundi on coffee; the Sudan on cotton – all commodities in little demand abroad but indispensable as export crops for the physical survival of the people of these countries. What all this means, he said, is that they must work with tin-cup budgets. Uganda has a budget the size of Indiana University's; Somalia that of a week's "take" at Sears Roebuck.[4]

4. A large American chain store.

Most budgets can hardly provide for any increase in schools, let alone roads and hospital services (in Ethiopia, Africa's oldest state, there is one doctor for every 102,000 people) which leaves nothing for military installations, embassies and dues for international organizations.

The only way in which the budgets can be increased, said Kimble, is by handouts from wealthier friendly nations. (From this one can deduce that they are left at the mercy of Russian, Chinese or Western "neo-colonialism" and forced to sell their support to the highest bidder – a state of affairs described by one U.N. civil servant as "international prostitution.")

There is also the growing inability of the African physical environment to sustain the burdens put upon it. Thus the topsoil is washing away faster than it is being replaced, water levels are dropping, other forms of erosion are common-place, animals are being indiscriminately slaughtered, and the soil fertility exhausted through over-grazing and primitive farming methods.

Significantly the U.N. recently predicted savage famine in the Far East and Africa unless production of the food is doubled in the next ten years.

Dr Kimble also points to the growing gap between the African's own personal needs and his ability to supply them, and the growing gap between those in power in the one-party states or dictatorships (such as Somalia, Ethiopia, Uganda, Kenya, etc.), and the common man. Summing up, he predicts that only six of the recently established states have the faintest hope of survival, while in the others revolution will follow revolution as the naive, primitive and gullible have-nots (99 per cent of the people) jump to the tune of whoever promises them the most – Russian or Chinese – not knowing that they intend to give little.

These populations, he concludes, are doomed to suffering, to a life of impotance and debt. He could also have added exploitation, mismanagement and misuse of state funds urgently needed to cure the ill, feed the poor and educate the ignorant.

In their scramble to leap the centuries and to emulate the industrialized West, the most astounding events occur. There are canning factories in the Sudan with nothing to can, the East German Printing Press in Guinea operates at five per cent capacity, while the Russians have sold the same country a large number of snowploughs!

The winds of change have brought bitterness, misery and despair to the average Black man and the face of Black political power, far from being democratic, has assumed an ugliness and irrationality which differs little from the brutal despotism of the Zulu kings of the early 19th *century.*

The transition in Black and Arab Africa was a *revolutionary* one. As in the case of virtually all revolutions which were instigated from outside and which did not rest on widespread and deep rooted popular discontent, the end result brought only more misery and turmoil.

Imagine, by contrast, an area in Africa almost twice the size of Europe firmly committed to a regional economic alliance – a non-political common market containing mineral riches and strategic materials vital to the future development of the entire West – with its people living under conditions of exceptional stability and order.

Imagine further that ideologically the region is neither "uncommitted" nor "neutralist", but pro-Western, militantly anti-Communist and devoted to the principles of free enterprise.

Bearing in mind the state of affairs in Black Africa presented in the foregoing pages, one can imagine the influence such an area could exercise on political and economic development in Africa.

The *potential* development of this area, both in terms of human resources and capital goods, cannot be described in anything but superlatives.

Such an area exists in Africa. It exists in the Third Africa.

It is not yet economically unified. The "Common Market" has been established, as yet, only between some of the states, but all the basic ingredients for a larger market are there.

The first public proposals for establishing a "Common Market" have been made by economists, the first official pacts have been signed, the first policy statements recorded by leaders of White and Black controlled states expressing desire for closer political and economic co-operation. Some of these were made in defiance of other power blocs and pressures on national and international levels and are, therefore, worth so much more.

The stability is there, stability unthinkable in Central and North Africa, or in Asia and Latin America.

The purpose is there, the wealth, the determination is there.

In this area are the only territories and states in Africa with booming economies,[5] sound agricultural programmes, adequate communication systems, industries, and where the eradication of poverty, illiteracy and disease is proceeding at a truly satisfactory pace. In this area is the only state receiving tens of thousands of immigrants from Britain and Europe annually. Moreover, events in Central and North Africa are bringing about a blurring of animosities between Black and White scarcely imagined five years ago.

This is the Third Africa, an area as distinct from the usual conception of "Africa in turmoil" and as different from the two other Africas, Black Africa and Arab Africa, as Japan is from the other strife-torn, poverty-stricken countries of Asia.

Here in Angola, Lesotho, Botswana, Mocambique, Rhodesia, South West Africa, the British protectorate of Swaziland and the Republic of South Africa, forces are at work to create a new multinational giant which could become the most successful economic region outside Europe and North America. To these countries may later be added Malawi and perhaps even Zambia, adding 336,000 square miles to the Third Africa and seven million people.

This transition in Southern Africa is not of the revolutionary kind.

While political strife and corruption are overtaking the new states of Black and Arab Africa, followed by economic ruin, dictatorships (euphemistically called African one-party states) and military governments, the principal territories in the Third Africa remain stable, prosperous and, far from gravitating to the East, are becoming increasingly pro-Western. Whether under Black or White control, or part of metropolitan Portugal, they are increasingly and militantly anti-Communist. The early success of Red China in Africa, in brazen competition with their Soviet counterparts, was not at the expense of the states of the Third Africa but occurred largely in the so-called "neutral" Arab and Black states in Africa.

The story of how these important developments were and are still being unknowingly, mistakenly as well as deliberately obscured, talked away, twisted and misrepresented is a tale of cold-blooded political expediency, ignorance and misplaced sympathy.[6]

5. Except for the Ivory Coast.
6. For a detailed examination of the way in which positive developments in South Africa are being obscured and misrepresented and a thorough exposition of the reasons for this state of affairs, the reader is referred to *The Paper Curtain*, published by Voortrekkerpers, Johannesburg in 1967.

11. The Paper Curtain

For the past decade most political and socio-economic developments in the Third Africa which are of real interest to the West, have been so obscured by the racialist news required for mass consumption, that even the details presented in the previous chapter are likely to be considered by the average European or American as, at best, wishful thinking, at worst, outright imagination.

South Africa and Rhodesia provide two of the best case histories.

Most people – particularly those who like to convey the impression that they are deeply concerned about the state of affairs in Africa – glibly refer to the "lack of democracy" in Rhodesia, the "plight" of the people in the Portuguese "colonies", and the "tyranny of apartheid". In actual fact they have little understanding of the real meaning of these concepts and even less knowledge of developments in Southern Africa.

This point was clearly brought out in the testimony of the military writer General S. L. A. Marshall before the sub-committee on Africa of the Committee on Foreign Affairs of the House of Representatives which conducted hearings on US policy towards South Africa in 1966. Referring to an editorial in the *Detroit Free Press* which said that Rhodesia declared independence "so that they can maintain a white autocracy" whereas the American colonists declared independence "so we could be free", General Marshall said: "I thought to myself: 'How hypocritical can you get?' The declaration of independence did not free a single Negro slave. The Bill of Rights did not lift up the position of one Indian or save one Indian's life. It took us more than half a century to work towards the position where we could move toward forming the genuinely good society based on a brotherhood of man in line with our declarations. We did so only after one of the bloodiest strifes in history. As to the white autocracy bit . . . in the period following the Revolutionary War only 6 per cent of the white people of the United States had the vote . . . we were a white autocracy."[1]

What Americans generally consider to be the state of affairs in Southern Africa is simply a caricature, not only of people, places and policies, but of countries. South Africa, for example, wears the face of "apartheid". This is either defined as an attempt by a lot of White "settlers" with a "master race" complex to keep the real owners of the country, "the Blacks", in perpetual serfdom, or it is identified as a particularly severe brand of American deep south segregationism. If told that (a) the Whites in South Africa, far from being *settlers*, are a nation so rooted in the African continent that they speak an Indo-Germanic language not spoken outside Africa; (b) have a greater moral, legal and historical right to their country than the colonists had to North America; (c) that there are not one, but several distinct Black *nations* in South Africa, mostly unable to communicate with each other because of different languages and (d) that under the "apartheid" policy, Blacks have become judges, doctors, professors, cabinet ministers in their own states, etc., while some are paying millionaire income tax on their business enterprises – the hearer generally either expresses astonishment or, in spite of the facts, remains unconvinced.

Sometimes this state of affairs borders on the incredible. New York's Channel 13 (supposedly dedicated to *educating* the public) in 1965 shot a 15-minute television interview with South Africa's Director of Information in New York. After the film had been screened to the programme director, he called the South African official and requested permission to cut the four points mentioned above "since this would confuse the viewers".

There in a nutshell, is the reason for labelling this chapter "The Paper (or Celluloid) Curtain".

The T.V. station (almost to its credit) recognised that a certain image had been built up about South Africa but in order not to "confuse" its viewers, nothing had to be televised which did not fit in with their existing views on the subject.

To the T.V. audience or the average newspaper reader, to the student who has not read any books on South Africa, except those

1. *Hearings before the Subcommittee on Africa*, 89th Congress, Second Session, Part II, pp. 326-327.

prescribed by his professor, the clergy in the pulpit and those members of organisations active in "civil rights" and other similar movements, the real tragedy in South Africa (so they believe) is to be found in the denial of "human rights" to the Bantu, the lack of a "free society" symbolised by one-man-one-vote, lack of "opportunities", absence of a policy according to which "not colour but only merit" will count. The absence of these rights they believe makes it impossible for the Bantu to fulfil his destiny in a Christian society and crushes his spirit.

Journalists, students, businessmen and statesmen who have *paid frequent visits to South Africa* call this sort of talk "sentimental slush" for there is so much naïveté entangled in the analysis of African affairs that it is positively alarming. Writing in the *New York Herald Tribune* in 1964 columnist John Crosby observed pointedly that there has been *little* except nonsense written about Africa anywhere in the Western world. "Unless the facts are stated without sentimentality," he observed, "our policies, our actions and our consciences are going to be clouded for a long time to come."

The main question, however, which neither he nor the others have so far asked, is "Why?" Why has there been so much nonsense written about Africa in general?

One reason is certainly American idealism – which, in international affairs, has always wreaked more harm than good – and of course sheer ignorance; ignorance of the fact that concepts such as "freedom" United States style cannot be transplanted to Africa. "Freedom" in most African states has merely been a licence to the small educated core to enslave, to imprison and to kill those who oppose their tyranny. Ignorance also of basic facts. The well known American columnist Roscoe Drummond, who paid a very brief visit to Africa during 1965 wrote in one of his dispatches that the countries of the Third Africa presented the gravest "threat to peace". The reason? The Black man is denied an effective *voice* in the Government. His article, widely published in the United States, was written in Nairobi some 4,000 miles from the Third Africa (which he has never visited) and *after* Bechuanaland, Swaziland and Basutoland had their first general elections on the basis of one-man-one-vote. This is an example of generalities based on ignorance. Moreover, in those states the victorious parties all ran on a platform which included political and economic co-operation with South Africa.

These facts destroy any merit Mr Drummond's article could possibly have.

Many Americans see it as their country's mission today to reform the world in terms of American experience and American concepts. As a result, their diagnosis of distant situations and the solutions they seek to apply are often grossly at fault. This opinion was expressed by the CBS correspondent Eric Sevareid in an address to a joint session of the Massachusetts State Legislature at the beginning of 1967. American idealism, he said, brought only unrest to Africa because its innovations struck no response among the Native people and the preparatory work for independence, the planning for democratic institutions and economic processes were "all blown to pieces" when independence came.

Idealism and ignorance are two of the most important explanations but they are not the only ones, nor can the present state of affairs which has even led churches in the United States and the United Nations to attempt to excommunicate South Africa, Rhodesia and Portugal "from the community of man", be explained in those terms. It is largely a question of *multiple causation* but much of it is also the result of deliberate planning. This is analysed in detail in the next chapter, The Foreign Crusade, which traces the roots of distortion, exposes the outrageous double standard employed in evaluating the South African and Rhodesian situation as well as the almost fanatical obsession with which some persons and organisations are conducting a hate-South Africa "crusade" – to the exclusion of all other social ills in the world. As far as it is possible in a single chapter, it also dares to define the *specific* reasons for this attitude towards South Africa, Rhodesia and the Portuguese provinces.

The present chapter is confined *inter alia* to the many examples of suppression of news of positive developments in Southern Africa, of double standards and falsehoods. It is also an indictment, a bitter indictment, of those in the free world who have refused or neglected to present the South African, Rhodesian and Portuguese point of view and who have thereby grossly flouted their own principles.

It matters not here whether a full if belated presentation of South African views and a thorough study of the situation merely serves to confirm the point of view now held by so many people in Britain and America. Some may well reason that the situation is too "obvious" for comment. Apart from reflecting a closed mind and being a groundless presumption on its own, it flouts one of the main principles on which our western civilisation rests, namely the right of a man to speak in his own defence.

So many people (particularly those in the robes of the church) declare that "South Africa has been brought before the bar of world opinion and found guilty of misconduct". However, is their case so weak that they dare not present South Africa with the opportunity to defend itself – an opportunity which even an uncivilised Black man accused of the rape of a White woman receives in South Africa, not as a favour, but as a *right* and as a mark of Christian civilisation and the rule of law? And if he cannot afford counsel for defence the State appoints a barrister to do so.

If it was merely a matter of "opinion" no one would have been unduly concerned by the fact that the *Washington Post* once published the shooting of a handful of Black men in South Africa on its front page but relegated to its *entertainment* page the shooting of ten times that number of people in India (plus some two hundred wounded). But the fact is that news on South Africa is carefully selected and deliberately magnified. A dozen people arrested on charges of promoting Communism in South Africa is splashed in *The New York Times*. The arrest of eight thousand in India gets three paragraphs (9.1.64). A law passed to improve Government control of obscene and subversive literature receives the close attention of editorial writers and is declared to be "further evidence of police state rule" in South Africa. However, when Burma (home of U Thant, United Nations Secretary-General) was declared a one-party state, the same newspaper devoted about four inches of space to the news (29.3.64).

Some organisations and movements[2] have seized on this double standard in news coverage of Southern African affairs as a means of drumming up funds to "finance an army of liberation" against South Africa, to obtain popular support for a blockade of South Africa and the boycott of its trade.

Such steps are far removed from the arena of legitimate public protest for it involves physical action against another country.

2. The Organization of African Unity, the United Nations, The American Committee of Africa; Christian Action in London etc. The Carnegie Endowment for Peace saved these would be violators of international law a lot of expense by helpfully sponsoring a study of the possibility of a blockade – an act of *war* against South Africa.

When this happens it also involves other governments and ultimately the United Nations. The South African case, in particular, has already been the subject of a number of Security Council debates and resolutions by the General Assembly of the United Nations to the effect that the situation posed a "threat to world peace", etc.

Any possible threat to world peace is obviously a matter for serious consideration, thoughtful study and a frank and fair analysis of all points of view. As far as South Africa is concerned this has not happened.

Take the case of its administration of the territory of South West Africa, the former German colony. On several occasions in the General Assembly of the United Nations South Africa's presence there was declared to be a threat to world peace. In October 1966 *Foreign Affairs* published a lengthy article by Ernest Gross (who was Chief Counsel for Liberia and Ethiopia when they fought their unsuccessful case against South Africa on the South West Africa issue before the World Court during 1962-1966) in which Mr Gross suggested that the World Court's decision in favour of South Africa was unfairly taken and in which he cast unsubstantiated slurs on the fairness and common sense of the Court and its procedures. An article by the South African Chief Counsel, advocate D. P. de Villiers, correcting his mis-statements was then submitted to *Foreign Affairs* in the hope that it would be published in the interest of fairness and objectivity and in pursuit of the journal's stated objective of affording hospitality to divergent ideas. The Editor, Mr Hamilton Fisch Armstrong, declined to publish the article and in his reply proceeded to criticise the contents of Mr de Villiers' manuscript. The practical result is that the wrong impression left with the readers could not be corrected through the medium by which they were conveyed because of the barely disguised partisanship of the Editor.[3]

The same applies to Rhodesia.

In 1966 a four man team of the American-African Affairs Association went to Rhodesia to investigate the situation. The four included a Congressman, a publisher, a Negro educator and a columnist-author. What they wrote in their findings is the following:

3. See *Reuters* report, Washington, May 23rd, 1967.

"American policy on Rhodesia represents the triumph of ideology over actuality. To excuse American intervention in what should be the purely private conflict between the British Government and Rhodesia, it is argued that the chain of circumstances leading to Rhodesian independence was improperly motivated – the result of a racist philosophy and a uniquely selfish economic interest. This position is based on a profound ignorance of the forces at work in Rhodesia – as well as in the rest of Africa.

"Since that country has been significantly in the news for many months, it might have been expected that the American press would have sent numerous able reporters to Salisbury, the capital city, to report developments there at first hand. Instead, news reaching the United States has come almost exclusively from British circles taking their lead from Labour Party publicists. Dubious sources at the United Nations have added their mite to the muddle of misinformation.

"Certainly, it is no secret that Assistant Secretary of State for African Affairs, G. Mennen Williams, has used what influence remains at his disposal in Washington to discourage on-site inspection by responsible legislators and newspaper correspondents who believe that United States foreign policy should lead from the strength of knowledge rather than the fanaticism of a *priori* judgment. Important publications have been told that the Rhodesian government is not admitting accredited journalists – a totally false charge. In actual fact, the Rhodesian government is not only willing but anxious to open its doors to those able to report what their eyes and ears register. 'We have nothing to hide,' Prime Minister Smith told our Mission when asked if he would receive a Congressional delegation."[4]

In short, Americans have not been provided with all the facts on the Rhodesian situation and it may be justifiably inferred that they have been deliberately withheld.

4. The report is available at the address of the organisation, 550 Fifth Avenue, New York City. Early in 1967 an independent three-man mission went to Rhodesia consisting of Professor Walter Darnell Jacobs of the University of Maryland, the nationally syndicated columnist James Kilpatrick and Rene Wormser, an author of several books on international law. Their report read into the Congressional Record by Representative John Ashbrook of Ohio on April 13th, 1967 reiterated the finding of the four investigators sent to Rhodesia by the American African Affairs Association.

Events in 1964-66 vindicated a variety of South African attitudes and predictions concerning Africa and the advancement of all backward peoples. For one thing, another year passed without the "time bomb" in South Africa exploding. At least a dozen correspondents who have been plying this story for the past fifteen years retired. Editorial writers who, fifteen years ago, predicted that bloodshed on an enormous scale was imminent in South Africa, that Whites would flee the country as Black nationalism flooded southwards, that trade would dry up and the economy collapse, have gained several extra grey hairs and no personal satisfaction. Meanwhile South Africa is enjoying economic growth unmatched by any country in the free world, including Japan; money, investments and foreign companies are flowing into the country; immigration from Europe is at an all time high; foreign reserves are at their highest ever; building plans are triple that of three years ago; Black people from a dozen foreign African countries continue to stream to South Africa for work, education and free health services. Even the staunchest critics of the country admit, wryly, that South Africa is now wealthier, stronger and more self-sufficient than ever. What is more, the outlook is for a doubling of immigrants from Europe to South Africa and for continued growth and prosperity.[5]

It would be reasonable to expect people under these circumstances to ask three simple but key questions; *one*, whether it is possible to attain such prosperous conditions under a policy of suppression and slavery, *two*, whether South Africa could possibly be right about Africa and the Black man and the rest of the world wrong and, *three*, whether this situation could possibly be equated with a "threat to world peace".

Such questions are indeed asked by knowledgeable people who frequently travel to South Africa and it may even be asked by the average newspaper reader or student at university.

The problem is that *question one* is never fully dealt with at universities or in the press. In fact it is avoided like the plague. As this book has shown the principle of the policy is hardly one of slavery.

As for the *second question*, the answer supplied by *Die Burger*, South Africa's leading morning newspaper, is as follows: "Yes, certainly – as it would be if it were asked if the Eskimos could be right about the

5. Cf. Noel Mostert in *The Reporter*, May 4th, 1967.

frozen north of America and the rest of the world wrong. There is no mystery about this and no cause for surprise; it is a straightforward matter of experience. Unlike the Eskimo, other people have had no need to make homes from snow and ice, or food, clothes, blankets and candles from seals. Through the generations the Eskimos have learned to live with their environment, and the South Africans with theirs. The Eskimo's environment has been one of hostile natural forces, the South African's, one of complex human relations. It may take many a year for an Eskimo to know just how to build an igloo. How long does it take for a White man (say from New York) to know a Zulu, Xhosa or Pondo in South Africa? South Africa is the only White nation in the whole of history to have had its home on a predominantly Black continent; and it would be remarkable indeed if South Africans were wrong about Africa and Americans, say, right."

For generations Britain was a colonial power in Africa, but Africa was not her home. In October 1964, the *Times*, London, wrote: "The leaders of opinion in Britain – in Parliament, the Churches, the intelligentsia and the Press – are generally unfamiliar with the practical awkwardness which arises when different cultures are thrown together . . ." The most authoritative newspaper in Britain was saying, in effect, that Britain does not know what race relations are all about. And if Britain does not know, is it reasonable to suppose that Sweden does, or the United States? Have these two countries really heard or digested the South African point of view on race relations – or its views on co-operation with Black Africa, its belief in the potential of the Black man, etc?

South Africans, Rhodesians and the Portuguese are not alone in believing that news about South Africa is frequently exaggerated, slanted, mostly devoid of real substance through the omission of points of view contrary to those held by the reporter and, what is worse, often deliberately falsified. They are not alone in believing that it is this state of affairs which has poisoned public opinion abroad.

Addressing the annual meeting of the Netherlands-South Africa Association in Amsterdam in 1966, the former Netherlands Ambassador to South Africa, Dr Jan van den Berg, said that the Dutch people were being "flooded with lies about South Africa" which "made great play with high sounding sentiments such as the declaration of human rights". He referred to the many "untruthful publications" in Holland which, he pointed out, must have a serious effect on Dutch-South African relations.

Writing in the West German *Industriekurier* Carlheinz Reese said that newspapers "expected unfavourable and slanderous reports from their correspondents in South Africa and the politicians and clergymen who have never visited South Africa even grasp at 'completely fabricated arguments' to substantiate their hostility towards South Africa. Their motto is: 'I have already decided. Don't bother me with the facts'."

This is the distressing picture which one finds in so many countries. Exaggerations, lies, half-truths, misleading statements, fabricated arguments, etc. *ad nauseam*.

In reaction to this situation the editor of the influential *Dines Newsletter* (Dow Jones & Co.) wrote: "Criticism of South Africa in the American Press is so incredibly one-sided as to make anyone suspicious. We have never seen a positive fact printed about that country and there must be some."

Professor Wilhelm Röpke,[6] professor at the Graduate School of International Studies, Geneva, Switzerland, expressed his views on this subject very strongly in an article in the Swiss magazine *Schweizer Monatshefte* in 1964: "With absolutely no idea of the falsification and distortion of which they are victims, countless people are letting themselves see in South Africa an *odium generis humani* merely because it must solve an internal political problem unknown in other countries. They do not seem to wonder if they have been caught in the coils of unremitting and cleverly slanted propaganda. They appear to have forgotten the principle that it is both irresponsible and unworthy of an intellectually mature man to judge the politics of Dr. Verwoerd and his party, which are backed by the majority of South African voters, without first making a real study of the country."

The distortions to which Professor Röpke referred are very often the direct result of an organisation's or newspaper's approach to a local problem. The *New York Times*, *The London Times* and other newspapers have often maintained that they must show un-equivocal support for the non-White cause in their own countries

6. Deceased in 1966.

and that they cannot apply one standard for South Africa and one for Alabama or Nottingham. Their reasoning is a dangerous form of monolithic thinking.

This uniform, monolithic approach to world problems by liberals is also shaky on one other ground, namely, the personal prejudices of the people who hail this approach.

The case of Israel and South Africa is a good example.

Few newspapermen in the United States or Britain, and this applies to politicians as well, give serious consideration to the Arab view of the State of Israel as an "imperialist and capitalistic invention financed by Wall Street." The reason for the existence, and the necessity for the continued existence, of the State of Israel is hardly ever in doubt. There is no question here of pro- or anti-Semitism, on the contrary, simply one irrefutable fact; America and Britain realise that the only factor uniting the Arab states is their common hatred of Israel. Exactly the same situation is to be found in respect of "Pan Africanism" and South Africa. Black Africa is only united in its hatred of the White man and their determination to rid the continent of the White men in South Africa, Rhodesia, the Portuguese territories. All other problems – poverty, illiteracy, disease, the collapse of law and order in some states, economic ruin, civil war and wholesale slaughter of human beings such as in Burundi, are of secondary importance. One can almost say that if South Africa had not existed, Black Africa would have invented such a state, for without this unifying factor the various countries (as pointed out in Chapter 1) are continually at each other's throats, in the same way as the Arab states bicker among themselves when the Israeli question is not on the agenda.

The Israelis base their right on continued existence as a European orientated state in the Arab hemisphere largely on religion, and lately, nationhood. South Africa bases its claim to continued existence as a European nation in Africa on far less subjective grounds. Yet vigorous attempts by its official spokesmen to get this case published in most leading British and American newspapers, magazines and journals have thus far failed. On the other hand, the views of the Israelis have been well and truly presented.

White South Africa claims that its policy represents no more, no less, than a human *desire* to protect its identity and nationhood and the soil to which it lays claim by right of first occupation. It is firmly convinced that its Western Christian society would be swallowed up and destroyed through a policy of one-man-one-vote with the huge mass of non-Christian, non-Western Bantu.

This *attitude* on their part, *not* the merits of the case, but the very fact that they adopt this *attitude*, is immediately denounced as "arrogant racism" an "anachronism" in this "enlightened" age, the expression of a "master race" complex based on hatred for the Black man. Yet in 1965 the 26th World Zionist Organisation's conference in Jerusalem employed the same argument without calling upon their heads the wrath of the liberal press. The Zionist President, Dr Nahum Goldmann, stated as follows:

"The No. 1 problem of Jewish life in the Diaspora, the problem of the survival of three million Jews in the Soviet Union, is the most dramatic example of the tendency of a powerful state not to prosecute its Jews in the usual meaning of anti-Semitism, *but to deny them the right to live their own life religiously, nationally and culturally and to maintain their identity as Jews.*"[7]

Safeguarding the identity of the White nation *and* the various Black nations is one of the cornerstones of the South African racial policy.

The point is not whether Israel is right or wrong in its attitude – the vast majority of informed people in South Africa believe that the Israeli case can stand on its merits and is politically, culturally and morally sound – the point is that many newspapers in Britain and the United States not only print the views of Dr Goldmann and other Jewish leaders in full, but are also prepared to uphold it in argument. On the other hand, should these views be expressed by a White South African (particularly a member of the governing party) it is termed "obnoxious and racist". In the few cases where the South African government point of view has been presented, it has been so diluted as to be almost unrecognisable. This is done by squeezing the government point of view into a few leading paragraphs and then devoting twenty paragraphs to criticism by the opposition parties, exile groups, terrorists and others. In contrast, the views of anti-South African groups are very often published in full without any attempt to balance this by even one paragraph of

7. Italics mine.

government comment or comment by organisations and newspapers sympathetic to the government's views.

It is also a fact that by and large, the liberal press, publishers, notably university publishers such as Frederick Praeger, and "intellectual" journals such as the *Saturday Review*, *Harpers*, etc., not only deny the South Africans the opportunity to express their views – but deny that they have any point of view to express!

In the highly rated *Quarterly Review* of the United States Council for Foreign Relations, several South Africans have had their say, all of them either bitter critics of the present regime or self-styled political "refugees". The magazine has also been the platform for statements of policy by African Heads of State, African Ambassadors and others. However, an attempt by the South African Ambassador or Foreign Minister to have his views published in this magazine has less hope of success than Mao Tse Tung applying for citizenship in the United States.

Leader in this group is *The New York Times* which now, despite the lesson of Castro, maintains that Black and White Communists (Party members and self confessed Communists) sentenced to life imprisonment in South Africa for attempting to overthrow the government are *not* Communists or terrorists but "freedom fighters", or as *The Times* put it "the Jeffersons and Washingtons of South Africa" – again despite mountains of evidence proving their Communist affiliations.

The liberal press, with some notable exceptions, applauded the United Nations for getting Belgium out of the Congo – in such a hurry that the Congo remains a real threat to world peace to-day, years after Belgian withdrawal. The liberal press, by and large, idly stood by while Katanga – the one stable, prosperous, anti-Communist and pro-Western government – was overrun by United Nations military forces, extra-territorial troops, while Katanga's own troops – called "mercenaries" – were branded "a threat to world peace". Today the same mercenaries are being quietly blessed for having saved the Congo from a Red Chinese take-over.

To rely on the liberal press *in general* for a proper perspective of developments in Africa is to imperil one's own rationality. There have been notable exceptions who deserve full credit for refusing to ape the majority, but by and large reporting about South Africa has been demonstrably inadequate, one-sided, tendentious and has often been in the nature of hate mongering.

The liberal element in the United States which controls the communications media and dominates the universities and publishing houses[8] has reacted to *reports* on sporadic events in Africa (in themselves misleading because they are fragmentary and often slanted by omission of other points of view) in the same way as if these events had taken place in America. This contributed to the illusion so rudely and brutally shattered in a dozen African states that all Africa's ills would be cured by uprooting "colonialism" and instituting a "truly democratic system based on one-man-one-vote".

Those who believe that distortions, unbalanced reporting and misconceptions could not take place in the twentieth century or be committed by such respected newspapers as *The New York Times* or *The Washington Post* and others simply do not have the courage to face the truth. They will find the material contained in the rest of this chapter doubly revealing.

The fact is that some of the most famous writers of this decade have on occasions been pulled up for inaccurate and libellous reporting. During the past five years Dame Rebecca West and later Mr Ian Macleod (very nearly a Prime Minister of Britain) and his highly respected newspaper *The Spectator* were sued in British courts, on different occasions, by two South African Judges for writing reports which were not only erroneous but malicious and slanderous. In both cases the accused not only had to publish a public apology but also had to pay substantial damages for libel[9]. The question arises: if people of *their* calibre are capable of such conduct, can one expect persistent honesty, integrity and objectiveness from the bulk of correspondents whose newspapers more often than not are only interested in sensation ("Send me blood and guts," a Canadian newspaper, the *Toronto Globe and Mail*, cabled its correspondent in South Africa) and whose on the spot reports are, also more often than not, rewritten by the editors back home. Reports and personal statements about South Africa in liberal newspapers in most cases would not stand up to scrutiny in court. For example the allegations by petitioners from South West Africa (which have been accepted

8. Cf: Stanton Evans: *The Liberal Establishment* and James Burnham: *Suicide of the West*, Regnery Inc., Chicago.
9. Cf. *Rand Daily Mail*, Johannesburg, 9.12.1965.

by the United Nations as gospel truth) dared not be put to the test of cross examination at the World Court. The South African side not only brought up fourteen expert witnesses who did testify but also offered to pay the fares of the petitioners to come to the World Court. The offer was declined.

America to-day finds itself increasingly in the same position vis-a-vis the press in Africa, the East and even Europe and Latin America. For the first time leading newspapermen and leading citizens are beginning to write and complain loudly about the often *deliberate* distortions of United States actions, of the *twisted* United States image and misleading reports of United States objectives abroad. *Time*, referring to the United States and Belgian efforts to save the lives of Black, White and Brown in the Congo wrote as follows: "The joint United States-Belgian paratroop action was completely understood in the West as humanitarian and if anything, more cautiously carried out than necessary. The 'non-aligned' and Communist worlds (i.e. virtually the entire Communist and Afro-Asian Bloc at the United Nations) through a well-organised propaganda effort made it sound as if the Americans and Belgians, not the Simbas, had committed the atrocities of Stanleyville – *a dizzying and infuriating perversion of the reality.*"

Here was recognition of two vital facts, *firstly* that there *is* such a thing as a deliberate well organised propaganda effort to distort certain actions and *secondly* that reality can be twisted beyond recognition.

The crucial question is, can this only happen where United States interests are at stake, or can it happen where Rhodesian and South African policies and programmes are concerned?

South Africa knows the perversion of truth by the Afro-Asian countries only too well. What is far worse is that though they complain to the editors of *Time* against the most elementary factual inaccuracies or the most glaring misconceptions in that magazine, it is as far as they will get. When propaganda and distortions are debated, *Time* has one standard for the United States and another for South Africa.

The foregoing is but one *example* of distortions to which America itself has lately been subject. Yet how often have newspapers such as the *New York Times*, *The Christian Science Monitor*, *The London Times*, etc., elevated to martyrdom and respectability people in South Africa who were self-confessed saboteurs, terrorists and Communist-trained infiltrators – ignoring protests from all quarters in South Africa? *The New York Times* for instance recently published a favourable review of a book *The Rise of the South African Reich* by one Brian Bunting. It was pointed out to them that in 1949 Bunting was considered by the United States Government as one of the world's 500 leading Communists and was *at the time of the review* actually employed by the Russian Government, but, despite the facts, *The Times* refused to name the author as a card-carrying Communist, in fact refused even to publish a letter to this effect.

In February 1967 National Educational Television distributed a programme by Ruth First to all its outlets across the country. In this programme Miss First related her experiences in prison in South Africa. (It was written up by the *New York Times* on February 28, 1967.) The fact of the matter was that both the B.B.C. who first presented the programme and N.E.T. stated that her background was of no relevance when the programme was offered to them. But Ruth First, of course, was no ordinary critic. She was and still is an official member of the Communist Party and was even thrown out of Kenya for conspiring with the deposed Communist Vice-President Odinga Odinga. One wonders whether N.E.T. or the B.B.C. would accept a programme made by one of Mao Tse Tung's staff on the treatment of Vietcong prisoners, and if they did so, whether the fact that it was a piece of outright Communist propaganda would also be considered irrelevant.

In Rhodesia the picture is the same.

Liberal newspapers in Britain and the United States are bent upon elevating Joshua Nkomo and Ndabaningi Sithole to the status of "freedom fighters". But do they realise that both are being lavishly financed from Moscow and Peking? Sithole has been a regular visitor to China to review his sabotage squads undergoing training (photographs of his visits are available) while Nkomo's political spokesmen were warmly welcomed in Communist North Korea and Moscow. How many Londoners know that Sithole and Nkomo's followers are guilty of petrol bombings, the stoning of schools and school children, extortion and daylight murder . . .? Their victims, let it be carefully noted, are *not* Europeans but Black Africans who suffered this fate because they wished to continue their fruitful and harmonious relationship with the White man.

The Zimbabwe African Peoples Union (ZAPU) headquarters in Lusaka (the movement was banned in Rhodesia because of its terrorist activities) wrote to the *Daily Express*, London: "We cannot compromise with any White government, extreme or liberal, or agree to multi-racial nonsense. We are determined to destroy all vestiges of white civilization. The rivers of Zimbabwe are to turn red with the blood of white tyrants and their children." The barbaric threats despite, ZAPU representatives are assured of the red carpet in America and should they come to power, messages of goodwill to this new "enlightened" majority regime will no doubt pour in from other "majority" governments such as Britain, Canada and Sweden.

Such is the state of the "Truth Curtain" that two African criminals in Rhodesia responsible for murder of fellow Black men, supported by Moscow and Peking, are hailed as the type of leaders preferred to the existing Government which upholds the values of Christian civilisation.

The story is repeated in Portuguese Mocambique.

From across the border in Zambia a terrorist movement has been striking at border settlements in Mocambique. Their leader, Paulo Jose Gumano openly boasts that he aims to recruit major Chinese support to drive out the Portuguese. He is hailed as a "liberator" and "freedom fighter".

For years the allegation has been rubbed under South Africa's nose that it was completely "out of step" with *world opinion*, "flouting" *world opinion* and that its policies were an "insult" to *world opinion*. This is not the place to analyse in detail the myth of world opinion. Sufficient to say that South Africans do not believe in world opinion or in a so-called "international community" and more and more people overseas are apparently beginning to share that view. Not just anyone. The United States Secretary of State, Dean Rusk, is one who has also lately discovered that "world opinion" needs to be taken down a peg or two.

Analysing what he termed this shift of United States attitude on "world opinion", the well known columnist Arthur Krock wrote in the *New York Times* of March 25, 1965: "The Secretary of State who declined to-day to budge an inch under the barrage of foreign criticism of this Government for the employment of chemical warfare in South Vietnam hardly seemed to be the same official who so often made world opinion the principal consideration in shaping United States positions in the United Nations. Although the determination that the views of a majority of the members of the United Nations General Assembly reflected world opinion was the flimsiest of bases for this calculation, Secretary Rusk accepted it as the guide of our United Nations policy in both the Kennedy and Johnson Administrations . . .

"But to-day the Secretary of State, whose conduct of foreign policy has been founded on that speculation gave it short shrift indeed. This Government, he said, would not be swayed by any foreign criticism or propaganda from its decision to equip the Vietnamese with non-lethal gas to prevent Vietcong infiltration, the coercion and murder of Vietnamese villagers and the imperilling of both United States and Vietnamese military groups. The sincere critics of this practice, he comfortably prophesied, were influenced by a misunderstanding of the facts that would be cleared away when these were made clear to them."

Writing in *The New York Times* magazine early in 1965, former United States Secretary of State, Dean Acheson, also analysed the subject of world opinion and concluded: "The short of the matter is that world opinion, whether thought of as fairy light or hobgoblin, to beguile or frighten us, is, like them, pure fancy . . . no more substantial a ghost than the banging of a shutter, or the wind in the chimney." He also made one or two other relevant observations. "A country half slave . . . or all slave . . . to foreign criticism cannot stand, except as a mental institution . . . our image will take care of itself, if we get on with what we have to do." He further pointed out: "World opinion simply does not exist on the matters which concern us. Not because people do not know the facts – facts are not necessary to form an opinion – but because they do not know that the issues exist."

People in countries other than the United States, are also beginning to have serious doubts about the way newspapers are pandering to the myth of world opinion.

Towards the end of 1964 Alberto Lleras Camargo, former President of Colombia and Chairman of the Editorial Board of the Colombian newspaper *Vision*, said: "The United States press reporting on Latin America is bad because American papers are catering more to what interests the public than what Americans should be aware of." He asked that the newspapers of North America as well as those in the southern parts of the hemisphere "abandon the now obsolete criterion of giving the public only what interests it." Now that radio and Television bring news quickly to millions, Camargo said, newspapers must awaken to their new role of being "a commentator upon already familiar news" by presenting the "full background, all possibilities of development and all the refinements that should be added to the event."

What Carmago said of Latin America applies equally well to the countries of the southern tier of Africa, for example Angola.

In his latest book, *Africa: A Political Travelogue* (Fleet Inc., New York), Professor Thomas Molnar observes: "While Angola is 'newsworthy' in a hundred and one respects, the only kind of news items that reach the world's readers refer to Holden Roberto's rebellion. To report on events connected with it is not a journalistic invention; but to report on them exclusively, is a *distortion by silence*. We may derive from our three examples an ominous warning; reporters, journalists, editors, news agencies, etc., and therefore the readers at the end of the line of information, are irresistibly drawn by and submerged in brutal highlights and sensations. Racial or religious riots, spectacular yet flimsy achievements of industrialisation in under-developed countries, displays of misery and hunger – foreign aid, United Nations operations, Peace Corps – such are the usual news items with which they try to catch the public's attention; they represent the state of world events as the latter are understood and digested by the average reader. Yet, in the eyes of the traveller these aspects are often not even like the visible parts of icebergs; one knows in their case that the larger part, although invisible, is there under the sea-level; but in the case of most of popular news reporting, what actually gets printed is, strictly speaking, neither true nor false; it is mostly irrelevant. So many qualifications would have to be added to make a particular news item resemble a full-bodied *fact* that very few reporters can be expected to, (1) dig them out; (2) present them skilfully; (3) risk the home editor's wrath by presenting the truth instead of its attractive or repulsive mask."[10]

10. Stuart Cloete recently wrote a profile of South Africa's Prime Minister for *Life*. He was paid for the article but it was never used because it was too pro-South African.

The extent of the Paper Curtain will appal all South Africans, irrespective of whether they support the government or not and it should certainly be cause for great concern among responsible Americans.

In the United States more liberal newspapers such as the *St. Louis, Post Dispatch, The New York Times, The Washington Post, The Baltimore Sun* and left-wing organisations such as the American Committee on Africa have long held that South Africa is an embarrassment to the West, has an "evil" government bent on the permanent subjugation of the Black man in a state of near slavery, is "obnoxious", an insult to all intelligent and enlightened men, etc. The same refrain can be found in England's *Manchester Guardian, The Observer, The London Times*, in *Le Monde* (France) or *Die Welt* (Germany).

It is true that there has been a great number of prominent American newspapermen, politicians, economists, lawyers and students of political science, who returned from South Africa with impressions differing vastly from those of the aforementioned individuals, journals and organisations.[11] However, the crux of the matter is that their statements never appear in the newspapers mentioned above – the ones claiming the copyright to "world opinion" – their books are not prescribed to students, nor are they invited to speak at universities or to appear on Television panel shows and radio programmes. Evidence hereof is on record – it cannot be disproved. What they have stated after visiting South Africa, is so contrary to what normally appears in print, in the books written by so many political scientists and on television, that one cannot escape the conclusion that South Africa truly has two faces – one held up by most newspapers and television stations and the other revealed to visitors who have taken great pains to learn at first hand South Africa's problems.

The question is not so much that people have visited South Africa and returned with different impressions. That is news in itself, no doubt, but the emphasis here is on the extent of their differences. Their opinions were in effect *vastly* different and in some prominent cases *diametrically opposite* to those held forth by the United Nations and leading citizens, professors and clergymen in Britain and the

11. Cf.: *Some American Comments on Southern Africa*, Edited by Frank Meyer, American African Affairs Association, New York, 1967.

United States. After all, when one refers to a police state where the non-Whites are denied the most fundamental human rights and where the tension is such that it is a positive threat to peace on the African continent, it does not leave much room for doubt. There are no "buts" and "ifs" involved. A respectable journalist or industrialist who returns from South Africa with glowing reports about the way apartheid is helping the Bantu to develop to nationhood, about his education, the increase in his living standard, about the booming economic conditions and the stability and prosperity being enjoyed all round, can therefore, most decidedly, not be accused of "misreading the signs" or of "lack of perspective".[12] He is either reporting what he saw, or experienced, or he is deliberately misleading the world.

If an American newspaperman returned from Haiti and wrote a glowing report about President Duvaliers' government, he would probably be ridiculed or shunned by his journalistic colleagues. There is, therefore, some solace in the fact that the many newspapermen who have reported in generally favourable terms on South Africa have not been so treated; they have only had their views played down or ignored.

To thinking people, however, it must raise grave questions about the basic integrity of so many of our important communications media.

Most visitors who have condemned South Africa on returning to their own homes, have spent less than a week in the country, some of them never moving out of Johannesburg. The most objective reports, from a South African point of view, came from those staying at least a month to three months, visiting all parts of the country. In 1963 Dr E. F. Flohr of the West German Geographical Association spent three months in South Africa studying race relations. His report stated that South Africa was busy carrying out a programme of self-help for the Bantu which must succeed and will serve one day as a lesson to Black Africa. "If I lived in South Africa," he said, "I would have been an enthusiastic supporter of the policy of differential development for the disparate Black groups." He believed that it was the only healthy experiment in

12. Cf.: *The Journal of Commerce*, New York, South African Supplement, May 1967 and *Fortune*, December 1966, p. 180.

Africa to uplift the backward and primitive Bantu to civilisation as quickly as possible, but even then it was a process which would take generations.

In a formal report submitted to the French Senate in 1963, the four member Commission of Cultural Affairs of the Senate reported after their visit in 1962 that in all of Africa it was difficult to find achievements of a more satisfactory nature favouring development for the Bantu, than in South Africa.

Abroad, delegates of Black African countries have on occasion been shocked into silence by the views of *non-Whites* from South Africa.

At the International Labour Conference in Geneva in 1962, Afro-Asian delegates listened in disbelief as a Coloured man, representing the workers of South Africa (under the constitution of the I.L.O. he is not nominated by the Government but by the labour unions) delivered a speech which amounted to an oblique defence of apartheid. At the 1966 conference of the World Executive of the Y.M.C.A., Mr Harrison Skosana, a Bantu delegate, also shocked delegates from Afro-Asian countries by telling them that South Africa is a better country for non-Whites to live in than any other African state.

"This was the first time many delegates at the World Executive meeting had met an educated African from South Africa," he said. "Their impression had always been that non-Europeans in this country were an ignorant, illiterate lot. They were surprised when I told them I had a son at university studying for a B.Sc. degree. They were also surprised to find that we were running a Y.M.C.A. programme on the same lines as those in other parts of the world and that I was the head of an autonomous Y.M.C.A. with the normal constitution and all the usual facilities and amenities."

The list of foreigners who have expressed favourable opinions on South Africa is a mile long and includes newspaper editors, heads of faculties at various European universities, American political scientists, economists, newspapermen, statesmen and politicians from twenty different countries. Some, such as America's Clarence Randall[13] and the military writer General S. L. A. Marshall,

13. One of the first recipients of President Kennedy's "Freedom Medal", and economic adviser to Presidents Kennedy and Eisenhower.

expressed the firm opinion that South Africa is a country destined for tremendous progress "provided it be left alone to sort out its problems". Others, such as the Whaley Eaton Foreign News Service in Washington (which sent out Editor Stanley Shaw to have a first-hand look at South Africa) expressed their views more forthrightly: "In the entire African continent there is only one country, South Africa, which can hold up its head in the company of modern free nations," the editors wrote on Christmas Day 1962. "Indeed it is one of the most prosperous, aggressive, self-sufficient countries in the world to-day. And it is that way entirely because, under White leadership, it has undertaken and is carrying out a programme for separate development of its racial groups. Yet no country is excoriated so severely by ignorant do-gooders and self-appointed and wrongly informed critics." And the views held by this body are by no means exceptional.

These were basically the same sentiments expressed by Lord Colyton, the former British Minister of State for Colonies, by the Pulitzer Prize winning journalist, Hodding Carter, and others such as Professor Ernest van den Haag of New York University and Professor Richard Logan of the University of California. The Editor of the *N.Y. Journal of Commerce*, Stanley Ferguson, the Editor of the Austrian *Kurier*, Dr Hugo Portisch, André Villiers of *Europe Magazine*, T. H. Ram of *Het Financiele Dagblad* in Holland, and other editors have also expressed distinctly positive opinions on developments in South Africa. Publishers such as Waldemar Schutz of West Germany, authors such as America's Thomas Molnar (*Africa: A Political Travelogue*), Britain's John Creasy, France's Paul Giniewski (*The Two Faces of Apartheid*, Regnery, Chicago) and American columnists such as Holmes Alexander, Arthur Veysey (*Chicago Tribune*), Syndicated columnists Ralph de Toledano and Russel Kirk, Jameson Campaign (Editor of the *Indianapolis Star*), Robert Hallet (*Christian Science Monitor*), Smith Hempstone of the *Chicago Daily News*, Thomas Gephart of the *Cincinatti Enquirer*, John Davenport of *Fortune*, Stephen Kann of *Industrial World*, and many others have come forward with reports on developments in South Africa which are at complete variance with what the American, British or French public *normally* have to digest on South Africa in the vast majority of newspapers. The same is true of other western countries, such as Australia, West Germany, Canada and New Zealand.

To a certain extent, the scope of which depends on a multitude of factors, the South African press itself and the peculiar socio-political set-up of the country have contributed to the Paper Curtain.

The division between political parties in South Africa is largely along language lines. Thus the Afrikaans press, almost to a man, supports the party in power, the National Party, and the government's policy of separate development of the races. On the other hand, the English language press, some of it controlled by outside interests, is opposed to the government and supports either the United Party or the Liberal and Progressive Parties. A striking example can be found in Johannesburg: The *Rand Daily Mail* (English language morning paper) supports the Progressive Party which advocates a one-man-one-vote policy based on qualifications. On the other hand *Die Transvaler* (Afrikaans language morning paper) supports the National Party and the Government's policy of separate development. A foreign visitor capable of understanding both languages would be right in observing that by reading only the *Rand Daily Mail* one is impressed by the fact that the Government in power is just about the worst thing that could ever have happened to South Africa and that the country is going "down the drain". The same visitor, reading only *Die Transvaler* would come to more or less the opposite conclusion, namely that the Government in power has committed no errors and is incapable of making any errors – irrespective of the fact that to err is human and irrespective of whether errors were made under pressure of circumstances over which the government may have had no control.

This pattern of conflicting opinions can be traced all over South Africa. However, since Afrikaans is a language spoken only on the African continent and in South Africa, the chances of an American or British visitor being able to read and understand Afrikaans is almost nil. In addition, the English language press in South Africa not only outnumbers its Afrikaans counterpart by far, but its circulation is perhaps triple that of the Afrikaans press. (This incidentally is not a reflection of political opinion, for the National Party has thirty per cent more voter support than the principal opposition party.) The reason for this is to be found in the wide-spread bilingualism among the people, particularly the Afrikaners who read both English and Afrikaans newspapers.

The problem of misconception arises when foreign students,

professors and newspapermen arrive in South Africa for a short stay. No one visiting a country such as France for a short period is going to pick up more than a smattering of French, much less Afrikaans which is a language restricted to South Africa instead of being like French, one of the three principal foreign languages in the West. The visiting journalist is therefore naturally inclined to the English speaking journalists at English language newspapers, exchanges views with them in English and reads the *Rand Daily Mail* and other English language newspapers. He has no time to arrange for translations from the Afrikaans press and relies on what he can find in English newspapers for an interpretation of the Afrikaans point of view. Because of the political schism this point of view is not always fairly reported. The result is a report which is so one-sided that Afrikaans speaking editors, nine times out of ten, have found reason to object strenuously to its contents.

The journalist representing a big British or American newspaper invariably finds offices in the *Rand Daily Mail* or some other English language newspaper building. He stays in South Africa for a year or so and never learns Afrikaans – only a few European correspondents, mostly German, Dutch or Swiss ever did so. The line of his cabled reports reflects the view of the United, Progressive or Liberal Parties, as published by the English language press but hardly ever the National Party view. If a report consists of ten paragraphs the chances are good that two would be a condensation of the Government's viewpoint and eight that of the Progressive, United or Liberal Parties.

In many cases stringers simply "lift" the story from the local English language newspaper and presto – the next day it appears in the *Sydney Morning Herald* (Australia), *The London Times*, *The New York Times*, *The Toronto Globe*, etc.

Journalists of the South African Information Service who have spent many years abroad (their status is the same as that of journalists employed by the United States Information Agency or the British Information Service) can vouch that as a result of this state of affairs reports published abroad on political developments in South Africa in most cases are a reflection of the views of the United (opposition) Party with the splinter parties such as the Progressive and Liberal Party sometimes getting a disproportionate share.

On the other hand the number of reports "lifted" from the

Afrikaans press during the past ten years are just about nil. The number of overseas correspondents who had offices in one of the Afrikaans newspapers is nil. The number of American newspapers who have Afrikaans language newspapers as their representatives in South Africa is almost nil. There are one or two exceptions. Whatever the case, the fact is that in so far as it originated at home, *the mirror of political opinion in South Africa held up to the world is largely that of the opposition parties.*

The language barrier has had the same result in books published abroad. Take a look at the books on South Africa prescribed at most American universities – books by Loewenstein, Gwendoline Carter, Huddleston, Ruth First and Gowan Mbeki (both Communists), Leslie Rubin (a political exile), de Kiewiet, McKay, Leo Kuper, Sheila Patterson, Edward Roux (a Communist) John Hatch, Hoernlé, Bunting (an active Communist) and Phillip Mason. The chances that they have listed works in the Afrikaans language as sources of information are negligible. On the other hand studies in the Afrikaans language by writers such as Cronjé, Rhoodie, Scholtz, Kruger and others contain an impressive bibliography of English books which they have consulted.

South Africa is, of course, not altogether unique in being saddled with an inbuilt barrier to a fair press abroad. Canada finds itself in the same position. The average Canadian, unless he was born in Quebec, does not speak French and cares little about French-Canadian grievances. He does not understand the French speaking Canadian viewpoint and because the majority of the newspapers are English language newspapers, the world at large does not understand it. The result is often a "shocker" such as occurred when the separatist movement to establish a French state began in Quebec. Another shocker was when the Royal Commission on Bilingualism and Biculturalism tabled a report in the Canadian Parliament in 1965 to the effect that Canada was in great danger from this cultural conflict. Here is further substantiation of the contention that South Africa's poor image overseas is partially the result of a language barrier. For what other reason was the French movement in Canada so readily understood in France? The average Frenchman does not read English, consequently whatever was received in the mail, or cabled by French journalists during a hasty trip to Canada, was taken from the local French language

267

newspapers in Canada or based on interviews with the French speaking population.

No thinking South African would ever accuse his country's English speaking journalists of *deliberately* misrepresenting the facts or *knowingly* obscuring positive developments. The English language press which opposes the government in power has a duty to its readers. They will and should continue to be outspoken about government affairs. South Africa has always had a free press and the vigorous debate on public affairs touched off by this press has been to the benefit of the country. As a result no one can accuse South Africa of being politically stagnant. Things are constantly humming and there is strong preoccupation with affairs of the day; politics, sports and race relations. This is good for a developing country. Nonetheless because it is hostile, partisan and sectional, the by-effect of this language barrier, not on the resident South African, but on visitors, students from abroad, authors of political surveys and the foreign press has been to the general detriment of the country.

It needs to be emphasised that no one expects the opposition press to change its views to suit the government. The opposite would be true if the Afrikaans press suddenly found themselves supporting a party out of power. However, *and here is the crux of the matter*, whatever criticism they may raise of the new Government in power has little chance of being freely, automatically and easily relayed to the overseas world through the medium of cabled reports, books and pamphlets (as currently happens when the opposition press loosens a broadside against a government act or programme) simply because Afrikaans is an unknown language abroad.

What could be done about this state of affairs is not the subject of analysis here, what is important is to recognise the practical effects of it on the Paper Curtain. The sound developments, achievements and victories which the Afrikaans language press held up to its readers contributed to the National Party increasing its votes at each successive general election since 1948, until to-day only a political landslide could oust the party. This "good news" to which they gave preference, for purely political and many other obvious reasons, did, however, *not* find its way abroad while the "bad news" to which the English press gave preference and prominence, also for purely political and other equally obvious reasons, *did* find its way into overseas newspapers through the processes described earlier.

The curtain against truth which obscures vital developments in South Africa (such as the granting of the franchise to three and a half million Xhosa men and women to elect their own legislative assembly in the Transkei with wide ranging powers including the right of taxation, control over education, the courts, etc.) is nowhere more striking than in the United States of America.

For two decades (up to 1964) there was not a *single* book published in this country or even imported from South Africa which could remotely be considered as presenting the White majority point of view in South Africa. Until MacFaddens published Eric Louw's speeches at the United Nations in 1963 under the title *The Case for South Africa*, not even a paperback could be purchased. A few such books did exist in Britain but not in America. Up to 1967 not a single hardcover book by a South African supporting and explaining apartheid had been published in the United States.

Yet, on the other hand, literally dozens of books written by people varying from clergymen to dyed-in-the-wool Communists such as Brian Bunting (*The Rise of the South African Reich, Penguin*) could be found in any bookshop. Every manuscript or outline of a book which was sympathetic towards the White South African point of view was turned down flat by important American publishers, usually in fear of being accused of "promoting an unpopular point of view" and "in fear of retaliation on the part of Civil Rights demonstrators in the United States", as the Longmans Green representative put it. These also included Praeger, Macmillans, McGraw Hill, Penguin and others. During 1963-1964 Penguin published three books on South Africa: *South Africa – The Peasants' Revolt* by Gowan Mbeki, *South West Africa* by Ruth First and Bunting's *Rise of the South African Reich. All three* are known and self-confessed Communists. All three books are prescribed to students by the Foreign Service Institute of Washington, not because they are examples of Communist propaganda, but supposedly for background information on South Africa!

To South Africans this action of the Institute smacks off insanity. The Doubleday Company's spokesman clearly implied that since he was personally opposed to apartheid, manuscripts explaining the policy had no hope of getting past him. This extreme treatment was not accorded even the most vicious dictatorships in all of Africa. Ghana's Nkrumah, who considered even unwritten criticism of his policies a crime worthy of five years in prison without trial (irrespective of the fact that the critic may be a legally elected Member of Parliament) has not only had his own book published in America by Praeger but also books by his Foreign Minister, his Ambassador to the United Nations and others. South African officials, on the other hand, could hardly get an *appointment* with Praeger and several other respected American publishers. The Secretary of the respected Council on Foreign Relations in 1964 flatly refused to see the South African representative in New York since he could see no point in any discussion with him!

During the past decade *The New York Times* in its Sunday Magazine has published (at a quick count) some forty articles referring to South Africa directly or obliquely. Of these, only *one* presented South Africa's point of view – an article by its Foreign Minister dated June 7, 1964.

Not only in the publishing world and the newspapers, but also in the world of magazines and television do we find this same Paper Curtain. Lord Bertrand Russell can count on any magazine in the United States to publish his views on South Africa – which happen to be severely critical. Lord Russell is the same man who, without having as much as looked at the Warren Commission's Report of the assassination of President Kennedy and within hours after it had been issued, branded it "a sorrily incompetent document" which "covers its authors with shame". As *The New York Herald Tribune* pointed out in its editorial of September 29, 1964, his letters to the press show "a disregard for facts and an increasing reliance on tendentious assertion". The question is: would any liberal newspaper in the United States dare criticise Lord Russell's views of South Africa for the same reason? Or is there a double standard applied – one for critics of the United States and one for those of South Africa?

There has never been a single instance where a pro-South African spokesman, official or otherwise, has been invited to appear solo on a major television programme in the United States or Britain to state his country's views. Yet every conceivable sort of critic, from terrorist leaders to outright Communists (the card carrying type) have had their crack at South Africa through this medium.

South Africa has been found guilty by these self-styled experts, sentenced and condemned without either being able to speak for itself or allowed to designate someone to speak on its behalf.

At universities in Britain and America one symposium after the other has been studded with speakers from the left, by Communists, self-confessed terrorists and saboteurs – lately called "refugees" to give them respectability.

Speakers who could and would defend South Africa are simply not invited.

To the wildly idealistic organisers of most of these meetings it is not a question of examining both sides of the question in South Africa but rather how to get rid of the government and its supporters. On the other hand, speakers from one-party dictatorships in Black Africa, states bogged down in poverty, corruption and racked by internal unrest and bloodshed (while their "leaders" languish in air-conditioned apartments in New York) have had a field-day at universities, ladies' clubs, on television and radio. Their speciality is – not the misery of their own people or problems in undeveloped countries – but apartheid in South Africa and what to do about it – exactly as if apartheid was a germ causing civil war in Nigeria, illiteracy in Ethiopia and genocide in Burundi. As the Editors of *Life* caustically pointed out in 1966: "The African politician would usually rather talk heatedly about liberating Angola, for instance, than about collective efforts to guarantee foreign investments, to sponsor health programmes, etc. . . ."

The Carnegie Foundation Library in New York in 1964 held a "seminar" on South Africa at which the Ambassador of Ghana was the main speaker[14]. South African attempts to attend this meeting failed. The organisers made it quite clear that they were not interested in hearing South Africa speak for itself. A light hearted "counter-proposal" that a symposium be held on government integrity in Ghana at which the South African Ambassador would be the main speaker was described by the Carnegie spokesman as "a strange request"!

14. Shortly afterwards *The New York Times* observed editorially that Ghana has written itself out of the society of civilized nations.

271

It is of no avail claiming that the preceding statements are not in perspective or true. The record is there for anyone to consult. South Africa (as well as Portugal and Rhodesia) could simply say "show me", and what would there be to show?

Thus in a country where freedom of speech is said to be almost as sacred as the Bible, South Africa is effectively silenced.

The irony of the whole matter is that those responsible for Acts of State in South Africa are accused by the very same journals, newspapers and television stations which deny them their say, of deliberately ignoring world opinion and of deliberately isolating themselves.

That an informed public opinion is a prerequisite to an intelligent and realistic foreign policy is a truism. Yet the fact that America recently voted with the Russian and Afro-Asian bloc for the study of an embargo against South Africa and subsequently announced (as did Britain under its Socialist Prime Minister Wilson) that it was curtailing sales of military equipment to South Africa, is the best example of how uninformed and, what is worse, misinformed officialdom can contribute to the problem of the West.

The only arms South Africa requires are for external purposes and to defend the strategic Cape of Good Hope sea-route.

It needs to be emphasised that this arms embargo (a punitive gesture aimed at South Africa's domestic racial policy) is directed against the same nation whose pilots were shot down in American aircraft over Korea, whose pilots flew in the Berlin airlift and who fought on the side of the Allies in World Wars I and II. On the other hand weapons are sold to many other African and Asian nations, hardly friends of the West and who promptly use them on their own people or against other sovereign states. The recent Middle East war is a good example.[15]

The tragedy of this is that as long as liberal American and British newspapers, political science professors and well-meaning politicians remain in some sort of intellectual vacuum as regards the subject of South Africa (and, for that matter, the whole southern part of Africa) the danger remains of a catastrophic miscalculation based on this misconception and ignorance of developments in South Africa

15. Other examples are Indonesia against Malaya, Ethiopia against Sudan, Egyptian forces in Yemen and India against Pakistan.

and its neighbouring states. Such a miscalculation would dictate support for the Afro-Asian dominated United Nations against South Africa or failure to get the United Nations to stop the Organisation of African Unity (which has sworn to "liberate" South Africa, Angola, Rhodesia and Mocambique by force of arms) from sending trained saboteurs and terrorists into those territories, disrupting trade and communications and killing innocent men, women and children. This is what the Red Chinese managed in the Congo and what the Viet-Cong are perpetrating in Vietnam.

It was a miscalculation of the first degree which caused the United States to call off the shore leave of the battle weary crew of the US carrier *Roosevelt* (ex Vietnam) after the ship had already docked in Cape Town, and after shore arrangements had already been accepted by the local United States representative, on the grounds that the crew would be subject to "apartheid". The net effect was to upset the entire city of Cape Town, offend the South African government and turn the ship into a disgruntled vessel. Within a few months after this proud vessel had been used for this ideological broadside against apartheid, the Middle East War closed the Suez Canal and American supply ships *en route* to Vietnam were forced to use Cape Town harbour to obtain fuel and supplies. It was done with the minimum of fuss for fear of spotlighting the rather embarrassing situation the United States authorities had landed themselves in. The mind boggles at the situation America would have found itself in had the southern tip of Africa now been in the hands of a "neutral" African state with its harbours closed to the vast traffic of ships diverted from the Suez round the Cape of Good Hope.

This chapter has illustrated how South Africa – and this applies as much to Angola and Rhodesia – is being isolated from the world not through its local policies but by a wall of often deliberately created misrepresentations and misconceptions which, for lack of a more suitable term, one can only call a "Truth Curtain". However, since in ninety per cent of cases, access to these views are gained through the printed word (the newspapers, magazines and books) a better definition undoubtedly is the "Paper Curtain". This Paper Curtain differs in one important respect from the Russian "Iron

Curtain", East Germany's infamous "Wall" and Red China's "Bamboo Curtain" in that it is being drawn *not* by the people held responsible for all the "evil deeds" of "apartheid" but by the very people who claim that they wish to introduce sanity and reason into South Africa, Rhodesia or Portuguese Africa.

12. The Foreign Crusade

Not since World War II (perhaps never in peace time) has any other country in the world been subjected to such a barrage of vehemently hostile criticism and so many attempts to force a change in its domestic policy as South Africa has. To unravel and discover all the conflicting emotions and motives for this course of events is exceedingly difficult.

Foreign criticism (with attempts being made to bring the government to a fall) differs from domestic criticism not only in its intensity but in its ultimate objective. The stock phrase is that South Africa must be saved from a racial conflict which may embroil the entire continent by forcing it to apply a policy of one-man-one-vote. The same objective is held to be true for Rhodesia (with its policy of gradual franchise for the Black man in a common political set-up) and the Portuguese territories with their policy of racial assimilation.

The student is, therefore, confused at the outset.

How could completely opposite policies have the same effect, a racial war? How can one be hostile to so-called "segregation" in South Africa and equally hostile to racial "integration" in Angola?

During the last five years, perhaps because so many clergymen have overnight managed to become experts on Africa with the conviction that they have the solution to its ills, South Africans began to refer to this hostility from abroad as the "Holy Crusade".

There is, however, more than just religious fervour involved in this crusade. Too many things are obviously wrong here and recently more and more statesmen, economists, students of political science and journalists have attempted to unravel the trend of the crusade. Far from being an attempt to "save" South Africa from the oft predicted racial conflict (although some people do earnestly and sincerely hold this belief) it now appears increasingly to be a question of using South Africa as a pawn in international politics and of "saving it for ourselves".

There is an inherent danger in any selfish approach to South African affairs, for a miscalculation on the part of the West could lead to a disastrous turn of events in Southern Africa from which the free world would emerge as the real loser. For this reason many South Africans have made a close study of foreign attitudes. If they did not like them at least they would try to understand them. In brief their principal thesis is as follows: Fear of a nuclear holocaust and a combination of strident international issues *together with a set of clearly identifiable racial and political factors* have created a state of affairs and tension which most organisations, institutions and individuals concerned with developments in Africa have been unable to cope with.

The result is often an unbelievable hostility against anything South African, or the application of an outrageous double standard in evaluating South African policies, a one-sided inflammatory dialogue or a fanatical obsession with South African affairs to the exclusion of all other injustices and problems in the world.

The set of identifiable racial and political factors which have caused so much confusion (by their interaction) in the evaluation of developments in Southern Africa include the following: (1) Anti-White racism at the United Nations as exemplified by Black Africa's reaction to the United States-Belgian paratroop lift in the Congo; (2) the distortion of the Charter of the United Nations by the Afro-Asian Bloc into an anti-colonial dictate; (3) the exploitation by the Communists of racial problems in the West; (4) an identification of racial problems "at home" for example in the United States, Britain, Canada, New Zealand and Australia with racial problems in Southern Africa; (5) the egalitarian fever quietly foisted on the West by Russia as a means of levelling frontiers and forcing an amorphous society on the world where there would be no frontiers to hinder the spread of Communism; (6) the direct propaganda campaign against the southern tier of Africa by the Communists to create chaos and disorder so as to pave the way for a left wing take-over and, finally (7) the deliberate efforts by the socialist and racially orientated dictatorial states in Africa (Ghana, Algeria, Uganda, the U.A.R., Mali and others) to mount a military and ideological campaign against the South in order to annex the riches of South Africa and to drive the White man out of Africa.

It is not as if individual aspects of this state of tension are not understood by interested parties but that the interaction, the sum total, of all these cross currents has created a turmoil in the minds of men and in the arena of international politics and race relations which bedevilled a cool realistic appraisal of almost any situation, more so one so complex as in South Africa. It has also meant that by assisting one nation or bloc of nations caught in the maelstrom created by the interaction of these factors, the benefactor may be allowing a more worthwhile country or cause to sink into the depths. Katanga is a possible example and some maintain that in helping "neutral" India to arm itself, pro-Western Pakistan was left to drift towards China.

The net result again is a distortion of values, moral hypocrisy and a blurring of perspectives which often manifests itself in the most outrageous double standards. It reveals itself in a blind refusal to even consider the views of those in disagreement on a particular issue or to accept *prima facie* the integrity of their leaders. Quite often in such a dispute the accused nation is as guilty as the accuser, some suspecting but none daring to concede that both may be victims of this maelstrom of racial and political forces.

For the Third Africa, the most important aspects are (1) the growing realisation abroad that behind much of the anti-South African, anti-Portuguese crusade is a set of entirely reprehensible objectives; (2) the double standard which is beginning to reveal itself to an increasing extent all over the world; (3) the absolutely racist and almost imperialist nature of the Afro-Asian campaign against South Africa, Rhodesia and the Portuguese provinces; (4) the way in which the United Nations has been drawn inexorably into this crusade against a member state and (5) the broader aspects of the East-West struggle as it affects South Africa.

Analysing the advocacy of United Nations sanctions against South Africa, Dr Stephen Enke of the Institute of Defence Analysis in Washington, observed in an article in *Optima:*[1] "There is also a lot of envy and hate behind the sanctions clamour. Some Governments of backward countries want chaos in South Africa because it is embarrassing that Africans there should enjoy higher living standards than their own people. Others simply want to undermine the Whites in South Africa, regardless of how much more badly

1. Johannesburg, March 1962, p. 1.

other races are injured in the process." Dr Enke who made a careful study of the problem including a lengthy visit to South Africa was not just giving vent to his imagination when he stated that behind the clamour (crusade) was much more than a desire to see South Africa conform to "world opinion". He is also far from being alone in his evaluation of the situation.

In the authoritative journal *Europe Magazine* (Brussels), André Villiers wrote: "Behind the international crusade against South Africa was much more than the so-called abhorrence of apartheid." Selfish motives, he observed, are a far stronger motive than the loudly proclaimed international concern over "human rights" in South Africa. "If international hypocrisy and selfishness could create such chaos in the Congo in the name of anti-colonialism, human rights and democracy, it is understandable why the crusade against South Africa is so outrageous," he stated.

Through the carelessness of an African diplomatic mission in London, photographic copies of a secret document issued by an organisation known as *Interform* fell into the hands of the *London Daily Telegraph*, in December 1966.[2] The documents revealed Interform to be an organisation with headquarters in Zurich, Switzerland and affiliated offices in New York, Washington, Rome, Paris, London, Frankfurt and Brussels. This organisation which is said to be financed by an American Foundation (in February 1967 it became widely known in the United States that the Central Intelligence Agency had been secretly channelling funds through foundations to well known international organisations who are trying to condition popular opinion for military action against South Africa and Rhodesia) and by several African nations has launched a secret political and propaganda campaign against Rhodesia and South Africa with the avowed object of eliminating the existing and constitutionally elected governments of these two countries. Subsequently further documents and letters were uncovered by the newspaper. One document explains Interform's methods as ". . . firmly based on the principle that all techniques used must be unobtrusive and that results achieved must appear to stem naturally from a concensus of informed opinion which cannot easily be identified with any direct source of propaganda." Under-

2. *The Daily Telegraph*, London, December 19th, 1966, p. 1 and back page.

standably the existence of a secret organisation bent on the overthrow of governments with whom the Swiss Government enjoys
good relations created consternation in Switzerland. The most
important fact which emerged from all the documents of Interform
was that much of the so-called public reaction against the policies of
Portugal, Rhodesia and South Africa is artificial and much of the
detrimental reporting in European and American newspapers (as
well as public statements made by politicians and government
officials) can be traced to the efforts of Interform. This organisation
is therefore in effect trying to establish a completely false state of
crisis.

Enke and Villiers are only two investigators who now believe that
behind the foreign crusade against Southern Africa there is also
hate, envy and greed. The list of other people who have investigated
this state of affairs is long.

In an editorial early in 1965, *The Times*, London, observed that
Russian and Czech members of the United Nations "expert committee" investigating the possibility of sanctions against South
Africa avoided facts and figures and merely demanded "sanctions".
Their aim, the paper said, goes beyond discrediting British and
American motives in African eyes. "They know that if sanctions
were attempted, they would lead to war. The African Communist
objective is not limited to inducing the South African government to
repeal their unjust laws; it is to bring on a full scale revolution."

This is clearly one of the reasons why the Communists take such
an active part in anti-South African movements. The anti-Apartheid
Movement in Britain, a loosely federated front of twelve organisations, is a good example. As the former Chairman of the South
Africa Society in London, Blyth Thompson, pointed out in 1966:
"Every single one had a salaried Communist on its management
committee."

Apart from such sinister motives behind the international crusade
against South Africa, there is also increasing recognition of an
outrageous double standard being applied in the analysis and
presentation of South African affairs.

The following examples should be sufficient to allay even the
worst case of scepticism.

In *Haiti* political opponents of President Duvalier are simply lined
up against a wall and shot without any trial. In reprisal for a rebel

attempt to overthrow his government, Duvalier in 1964 had ninety political prisoners executed by his personal army of bodyguards in the infamous Fort Dimanche Prison in Port-au-Prince.[3] In *Algeria* opponents of erstwhile President Ben Bella, including some of the men who helped him to power, were tried in secret military courts without the right of counsel and without the right of appeal. In *Russia* executions of political prisoners are commonplace. People advocating or found guilty of practising capitalism have been shot. Between May 1961 and August 1963 Western observers counted 179 *executions* for political crimes in Russia. Among those executed were a deputy minister of commerce, a departmental chief in the Soviet Ministry of Finance and several women. In *Indonesia* offenders were heard in secret by President Sukarno's judges and sentenced in secret. The sentence was also carried out in secret. In several Middle East countries (for example Yemen) opponents of the Government in power are shot out of hand or beheaded in public – few of them ever get to see a courtroom, much less a jury, judge or defence counsel. The fourteen *Moroccan* nationalists executed in Morocco early in 1965 were also tried by a military court behind closed doors.

In *South Africa*, on the other hand, a person accused of sabotage or treason may obtain legal counsel from anywhere in the world, is tried in public with the press and judges of foreign countries invited to sit in on the proceedings; the accused are tried by a Supreme Court Justice (who is not the nominee of a political party, as in the United States, or appointed by the Head of State as in Ghana) and have the right of appeal. He is not tried for "opposing" the Government (there are hundreds of thousands of people and perhaps a dozen newspapers "opposing" the Government every day) but for a *specific crime*. This includes dynamiting of a Post Office or power station (sabotage) or smuggling of arms from abroad, training of terrorist troops to assist in an armed attempt to overthrow the government, etc.

Clearly there is a tremendous gap between established Roman Dutch Law and court procedures in South Africa compared with the "justice" existing in Haiti, Russia, Indonesia, Yemen, Algeria, Morocco and literally dozens of African, Arab, Latin American and

3. Latin American Correspondent, *The New York Herald Tribune*, 20.9.1964.

Asian states. Yet not *one* of those states has ever been singled out in a public statement by, for example, the Presbyterian or Methodist Church of America for "political trials" nor condemned in a resolution by the General Assembly of the United Nations for "executing political prisoners", or editorially lambasted by, say the liberal *London Observer* to the extent South Africa has been.

The mind boggles at the absurdity of the United Nations Commission on Human Rights which decided in March 1967 to establish a special group to investigate allegations of cruelty against prisoners in South African jails while in Saudi Arabia, according to the Anti-Slavery Commission's latest report to the United Nations, slaves are still sold in Mecca at the *Dakkat Al Abeed* slave market in public. Although King Feisal of Saudi Arabia in 1962 issued a decree abolishing slavery the Society insists that wealthy members of the Royal family, high government officials, rich merchants and other individuals still hold some 100,000 slaves. The only step which the Human Rights Commission of the United Nations has so far taken in response was to sponsor an international convention (ten years ago) which prohibited slave trade. However only 70 of the 122 members of the United Nations have signed the convention and 40 members did not even bother to reply to a recent questionnaire about the subject of slavery.

The island of Ceylon provides a classic example of how the Afro-Asian world views with calm equanimity what goes on in one of their own countries that would be the signal of a storm of protest if it happened in South Africa. It concerns the fate of more than a million non-nationals, the majority of whom are Indian Tamils. For ten years they have become a human shuttlecock of Indian-Ceylonese politics. Nobody wants them and they have remained stateless with no political or constitutional rights in India or Ceylon. The "problems" of the half-million Asians in South Africa who enjoy citizenship, travel under protection of a South African passport when abroad, freedom of religion, free education and hospital services and enjoy a per capita income six times that of their brethren in India, pale into insignificance compared with the fate of the Tamils in Ceylon. Yet since the late 1940's the Afro-Asian states (including, ironically Ceylon and India) have been belabouring South Africa at the United Nations for its "inhuman treatment" of people of Asian descent.

This is another example of the double standard tolerated by the West and the majority of its newspapers.

An even worse case recently occurred in Burma from which the Secretary General of the United Nations, U Thant, hails. In 1964 *Time* published a lengthy (uncontested) report on the persecution of Asians in Asia. Since January 1964, the article said, nearly nine hundred thousand people have fled across the borders to escape *religious* persecution in Pakistan and India. Their fate, however, cannot be compared with the fate of the five hundred thousand Indians in Burma. Ship and plane loads of refugees have been arriving in Madras and Calcutta – with only the clothes on their backs. Caught up in the wave of nationalisation and Premier Ne Win's drive towards socialism in Burma, the Indians who had no citizenship, and were not permitted ownership of property or government jobs, were literally thrown out of the country. At the airports and docks Indian women and children were stripped of all gold and jewellery while many Hindu women were forced to give up their gold and black *mangal sutra* necklaces worn as a symbol of marriage.[4]

While the "plight" of Asians in South Africa is a perennial issue before the United Nations and the South African "treatment" of Asians is attacked in every book written on the subject and at almost every meeting of international church organisations, not a whisper of the Burmese problem has been heard in the United Nations, on college campuses, in church or elsewhere. This is a particularly glaring example of the double standard, more so since South Africa's programme to repatriate the Asians included free passage home and compensation for loss of business. The Asians have so far refused *en masse* to return to India, a wonderful example of how meaningless the slogan "people always prefer freedom in poverty to riches in slavery" really is. The entire Afro-Asian bloc accuse South Africa of "slavery" but the half-million Indians on the spot seem to prefer "riches in slavery" to "freedom in poverty" in India.

Laws have been passed in dozens of countries in the world to eliminate discrimination on grounds of race, religion and culture but these laws are not worth the paper on which they are printed.

4. *Time,* July 17th, 1964.

Time recently conducted a survey of discrimination and discord in Asia and found that in practice religious hatred, caste systems, racial discrimination and abuse continue as before the introduction of such legislation. In fact the situation is so grave that the Editors of *Time* concluded that hatred among peoples, classes and races still represents the greatest single cause of turmoil in Asia.[5]

The lesson to be learned from this is quite plain: simply because an Asian state passes a law forbidding, say, a caste system, does not give that state the moral right, or any other right, to sit in judgement on racial affairs in Rhodesia or South Africa.

The West realises this but by remaining silent they are condoning and encouraging the double standard and international hypocrisy which has riddled the United Nations.

Security legislation in South Africa, Portugal and Rhodesia has been the subject of the most intense criticism by bar associations and newspapers in Britain and the United States. It has also been the subject of Security Council debates in the United Nations. (Ironically, while those debates were dragging on people were being slaughtered like cattle in Burundi.) It was alleged by the West German newspaper *Industriekurier* that similar, in fact, worse, legislation existed in Germany[6]. The British Act on North Ireland, has also never been challenged in the United Nations or by the International Commission of Jurists.

When South Africa introduced stringent security measures to prevent sabotage and subversion (and to outlaw Communism) *The New York Times* and other liberal newspapers in the United States and Britain almost had editorial heart failure. The "Anti-terror" decree passed in British Guiana however, received one five inch report on the inside pages of *The New York Times*[7] and that was that. Similar legislation in Ceylon, Ghana, Indonesia, Malaya, Pakistan and a host of other countries is yet to be *mentioned* let alone *attacked*.

South Africa, faced by a real threat[8], imposed preventive detention (ringed round with legal safeguards) yet she alone has incurred world wrath.

5. *Time*, April 9th, 1965.
6. April 4th, 1964.
7. February 28th, 1965.
8. Terrorists trained in Russia and China for the Organization of African Unity.

Strangely the newspapers which insist that White, Black and Yellow should be treated with equality in Southern Africa, apply a double standard themselves in this respect; one for the Afro-Asian nations, one for the European states. A "rebellion" in Malawi during which one-hundred and thirty rebels were caught and three killed, rates a three paragraph report in *The New York Times*[9]. Events of far less significance than this, occurring in South Africa, have filled columns in the same newspaper.

The world has still to witness one member of the United Nations denounce President Duvalier's barbarous rule in Haiti, or a single church organisation raise its voice in objection. Not a single picket has been seen outside the offices of the Haiti Mission to the United Nations. Haiti, in short, may just as well not exist.

Whether Duvalier kills one or a thousand political opponents apparently does not make the slightest difference to the world at large. But until this state of affairs is put in its proper perspective, South Africans of all colours and creeds will have a right to accuse the churches of condoning murder elsewhere in the world while protesting not the murder of an innocent man, but the trial of his murderers in South Africa. They will have a right to accuse the United Nations and the Secretary-General of gross impropriety and of maintaining a double standard of the most outrageous kind.

One could almost say that this double standard is primarily racially motivated.

This brings one to the crux of the matter.

"World opinion" requires of South Africa to discard all feelings of prejudice against non-Whites and to eliminate all laws affecting people of different colour. Whether it is to protect them or not is immaterial. It is an attempt to introduce into South Africa the credo of a colourless and "equal" society. Yet the very same people who advocate this philosophy set an example of racialism (anti-White racialism) by ignoring crimes of Black against White and Black against Black.

Even Western Governments who should be keenly aware of the double standard practised by the Afro-Asian world have elected to follow the same line.

9. March 2nd, 1965.

284

President Johnson, speaking of South Vietnam at the University of California in February 1965, said that "terror and violence, directed and supplied by outside enemies press against the lives and liberties of people who seek only to be left in peace . . . those engaged in external direction and supply could do well to be reminded and to remember that this type of aggression is a deeply dangerous game."[10]

It has been clearly established that the "terror and violence" in Angola, Portuguese Guinea and Mocambique has been and still is directed from across the northern border. Trained guerillas are openly moved across international boundaries, for example from Tanzania into Mocambique. If the statement of the President is true in respect of South Vietnam, it is equally true in reference to the Portuguese provinces in Africa. The political status of these territories remains a matter for the nearly five million people in Angola and the six and a half million in Mocambique to determine for themselves and not by outside alien insurgent forces.

British newspapers were quick to defend the actions of certain White students at the University of Rhodesia who had apparently made a spirited defence of Britain's right to control the destiny of Rhodesia, but there was a deafening silence on their part when at a court case in Salisbury during the week of February 26, 1967 it became known that these same university lecturers and students were the brains behind a network of Moscow trained spies, African terrorists with instructions to murder White men, women and children, and an attempt to recruit an army of 600 terrorists and the smuggling of a large amount of Russian arms and ammunition into Rhodesia. Behind their so-called "protest" against U.D.I. was a story of violence, sabotage, gun running and Egyptian, North Korean and Moscow intelligence agents and saboteurs.

The declared objective of the Organisation of African Unity is to "liberate" South Africa by force of arms. The training of an "army of liberation" and the official commitments by member states to raise funds for the campaign is scarcely a secret to Washington. Yet there has been no official American denunciation of these aggressive plans. On the contrary in 1966 President Johnson sent a special message of goodwill to the O.A.U. praising its work in Africa. It is

10. *The Chicago Sun-Times*, February 21st, 1965.

a valid question whether the President's views on aggression are applicable only to United States operations in Vietnam.

At the opening session of the 1964 NATO Ministerial Committee, held at The Hague, Dean Rusk, American Secretary of State, said: "It is essential for the security of the free world for aggression to be eliminated. I mean aggression *anywhere* and of *any* kind, including subversion, terrorism, the infiltration of men and weapons and guerilla warfare."[11] To prove that the Organisation of African Unity (or Ghana under Nkrumah) is guilty of every single crime mentioned by Mr Rusk, is not difficult at all. Nor have the O.A.U. bothered to hide this fact; indeed, they boast about it, it is written into their constitution.

Yet the United States Secretary of State has not warned the Organisation of African Unity that they are threatening the peace of Africa and the world.

The American government in 1964 finally went so far as to halt the sale of arms to South Africa. Since it knows full well that South Africa can manufacture all the weapons necessary for the maintenance of law and order, it is only depriving the country of arms required to meet the external aggression, posed by the O.A.U., and of the means of fulfilling its role as the guardian of the vital sea route around the Cape of Good Hope.

Faced with this double standard, South Africa can only assume that political expediency has become a virtue and respect for international law an evil. However, in the event of a future East-West conflict one can safely assume that America and Britain will suddenly find it politically expedient to arm South Africa to the teeth – in the interests of its "global responsibilities" of course. Apartheid had been South Africa's policy for many years before the Korean war began. There was no moral or political objection *then* to arming South Africa. South African pilots were showered with United States decorations. Thus the whole tragic business would be at times almost ludicrous were it not so deadly serious.

The vendetta which the Afro-Asian bloc has been pursuing against South Africa and the Portuguese provinces in Africa escalated from mere threats, the severance of diplomatic relations (even where they did not exist) to trade boycotts, denial of overflying rights to pas-

11. *The New York Times*, May 12th, 1964.

senger aircraft, closing of ports to shipping from these countries and a campaign at the United Nations to expel South Africa from that organisation. All these efforts have failed and the vendetta has now become a desperate face saving operation. Attempts are being made all over the world to drum up public and government support for the use of force against South Africa (and Portugal and Rhodesia) as part of a crusade "to liberate the people of South Africa from the oppressive heel of the Nazi government in power" as it was expressed by a delegate at the meeting of the Organisation of African Unity in 1966.

In order to fully appreciate the emptiness, the naked racism and the barely disguised Black imperialism motivating this particular foreign crusade, it is necessary to examine in some detail what it is that the African states really fear in Southern Africa and what would happen if they failed in their attempts to "liberate" the Portuguese provinces, Rhodesia and South Africa.

In these crucial years of shifting alignments between West and East, the obviously profitable course for the Afro-Asian states to follow is to perpetuate what instability and uncertainty there may be in Southern Africa while remaining "neutral" or "unaligned" in the East-West dispute. In this way the smallest of countries, such as Gabon and the Ivory Coast, and backward countries such as Ethiopia and Mali, can play a role in world affairs completely out of proportion to their population, national income, power, civilisation and experience in world affairs. Playing both sides against the middle is such a well-known pastime, particularly among the African states, that the statement hardly requires substantiation.

While it pays the African states to keep the Sino-Soviet leaders and the West guessing as to their true alliance, they fear the long range implications of the increasingly cordial relationship between Rhodesia, South Africa and the Portuguese territories on the one hand and "Black states" such as Zambia, Malawi, Botswana, Lesotho and Swaziland on the other. If left "unchecked" the growth of a stable pro-Western consortium and, worse from their point of view, a closely knit complex of Southern states in a friendly if loose co-operation with White-ruled South Africa would soon put an end to their game of "non-alignment" and "neutralism".

Political stability and social order are built on rational economic co-operation; and a prosperous regional association in the Third

Africa would replace the "neutralism" that has been held up to be, up to now, the only solution for those who do not care to be pro-Moscow but who have not been permitted to be pro-Western.

The Third Africa possesses the key to a regional alliance and economic pact which threatens to upset the plans of these would-be African Caesars. These territories are clearly moving (cautiously but nonetheless distinctly) in the direction of exactly such a regional alliance as feared by the African states and the Communists.

At the *maximum*, territories in the Third Africa not only comprise forty per cent of the African landmass but between them would constitute such a powerful economic market that the West may simply prefer to come to terms with this market, leaving the rest of the African states out on a non-aligned limb. This would leave them without any real influence at the United Nations. The flow of foreign aid would come to a standstill. Unable to do anything about the south, chances of a split between the French-speaking states (which have hitherto shown more responsibility in international relations) on the one hand and the more irresponsible ex-British colonies and Arab states on the other hand would be good, while the Organisation of African Unity would have to close its doors.

With the information set out in the preceding chapters, it is less difficult to understand why Portuguese Angola, Mocambique, Rhodesia and South Africa between them present such an obstacle to (a) Black African imperialism as expounded by ex-President Nkrumah, (b) the success of a Sino or Soviet bridgehead in Africa such as in Tanzania, (c) profitable "neutralism" á la Haile Selassie and (d) Arab imperialism of the cut of ex-Prime Minister Ben Bella of Algeria.

Writing in *Foreign Affairs*[12], Charles Manning (Emeritus Professor of International Affairs, London School of Economics) observed that the thinking South African may be sure of one thing: "The hostility of the non-White world can be explained without reference to the merits of the apartheid programme. Indeed, for Afro-Asians the possibility that it has any merits can scarcely arise. It is the policy of White men governing Black; and the only good thing that White men still wielding authority in Africa can do is to abdicate in favour of the non-White majority. Anything else they may think

12. Published by the Council on Foreign Relations, New York, 1965.

to do is by definition bad. In the eyes of the Bandung confraternity, South Africa ought never to have existed and ought now no longer to exist. It is not a question of whether she is meeting her responsibilities with humanity, wisdom or even a measure of self-abnegation. What in their eyes is wrong is not what South Africa may do, but the fact that she should continue in a position to do anything at all. King Ahab, in the Old Testament story, was not interested in how Naboth was administering his vineyard. Hitler was not really much concerned with what Benes might be willing to do for the Sudeten Germans. The Addis Ababa powers are not interested in South Africa's current policy of home rule for all. If those powers have not consciously adopted Hitler's language, it must at least be admitted that Hitler did anticipate some of theirs.''

This unconfessed fear at developments in the South on the part of the majority of African states has been deliberately translated into a loudly proclaimed "fear" that developments in the South are "threatening the peace" – without specifying what kind of peace it is that has led 32 African countries into mass murder (Burundi), dictatorship (Algeria), secession (Biafra from Nigeria) and economic ruin (Ghana) as examples. They simply seized upon the policy of apartheid as a *cause célèbre*.

This "fear" has affected the United Nations to such an extent that the organisation, in permitting itself to be used in a shockingly partisan way, has itself launched a crusade against South Africa and may well founder (shades of the League of Nations) as a result of it.

It is ironic that in the six or seven weeks, when tension in the Middle East had built up to such a degree that the United Nations simply had to notice it and had to realise that the worst could happen, the Organisation was wasting its time with a special emergency session on South West Africa, struggling with the phantoms and ghosts of its imagination.

This took place in spite of the danger growing in the Middle East. The only contribution from the United Nations was to withdraw the task force which had been placed in the Middle East for the very purpose of maintaining peace, and in the midst of this U Thant, Secretary General of the United Nations, kept himself busy working out plans to appoint a commission to take over South West Africa, which would inevitably lead to violence.

To crown it all U Thant was going to attend a picnic of militant African States and guerilla "freedom fighters" in Dar es Salaam to discuss the overthrow of the South African regime by violence.

Who are being "threatened" by South Africa, Rhodesia, Portugal and exactly how they are being threatened, the world has yet to learn. The facts are not being investigated, for facts do not favour the case that the Afro-Asian states are building up in the United Nations with the assistance of Secretary General U Thant. One of those facts is that a war of conquest against member states of the United Nations by other members is being openly *advocated* and planned in Africa. South Africa, Rhodesia and Portugal are not guilty of this offence but the Organisation of African Unity is.

In the American hemisphere, the Organisation of American States made short shrift of Cuba, which was found guilty of *aggression* on the grounds that it provided guerilla forces to fight in Venezuela, broadcast propaganda to that country urging the people to rebel, smuggled in saboteurs and arms. This, the Organisation of American States said, was against the Charter of the Organisation. (For punishment the Charter provides everything from a rebuke to a blockade and even invasion.) Many African states are guilty of the same crimes against Portugal, Rhodesia and South Africa, but as far as these acts of aggression are concerned Black Africa's staunchest supporters, the liberal press in Britain and the United States, remain tongue tied. The United Nations which should act to prevent this breach of international law, seems oblivious of what is taking place.

The question is, can the liberal press say anything except to admit that the United Nations itself is guilty and has now become nothing but an anti-colonial (anti-White) platform for the Afro-Asian bloc because it enjoys a two-thirds majority in the General Assembly? So they remain silent, fearful of admitting the truth to their readers, fearful because a newspaper once suspected of *knowingly* coddling the truth, cannot survive.

Not the invaders but the defenders are being accused by the United Nations of threatening world peace. Meanwhile members of the United Nations, such as Uganda, Tanzania and Ethiopia, which brazenly flout all rules of international law (and the Charter of the United Nations) by making their soil available for attacks on Portuguese territories in Africa and helping the attackers with arms, money and men, go scot free. Those who *defend* themselves are called the aggressors.

Here, then, is an example of what is meant by a deliberate crusade: an illogical fiction is created by the General Assembly of the United Nations, acting on the instructions of the Afro-Asian majority, but it never is permitted to become a public issue. The open attacks against Angola across international borders are shrugged off. Only the Afro-Asian line fills the columns in "public opinion-forming" media and so the illogical fiction becomes, for many people, an undisputed fact.

A war is being waged in Africa – by Black nationalism, Black imperialism against the White communities and, as always in war, truth is the first casualty. What matters it if South Africa was an independent state for forty years before Ghana was even born. Dr Nkrumah was reported to have said that South Africa should be "liberated" so that Africa could use its industrial power and its gold to develop the whole of the continent. He was never repudiated for so overtly aping Hitler's ideas of "liberation".

South Africa has perhaps suffered more as a result of the foreign crusade than either Portugal or Rhodesia. Why this should be so, even allowing for the fact that the Afro-Asian bloc at the United Nations is using that organisation as an anti-South African weapon, is really not difficult to understand.

South Africa wants to create opportunity for its Bantu (Black people) and to assist them to develop into full nationhood, and therefore conditions of equal human dignity, in their own homelands. At the same time it wishes to secure the continued existence of a White nation, with a nationalism fifty years older than that of any Black nation, in the White part of South Africa.

Opposed to this endeavour, there is a threefold "world opinion".

In the first place there is the Afro-Asian group which is actuated (as far as South Africa is concerned) almost solely by racialism and, as Professor Manning observed, will not be satisfied with anything less than immediate non-White domination in Rhodesia, the Portuguese provinces and the whole of South Africa. Their charge is that South Africa's programme for separate political freedoms (also described as a balkanisation of the country into several politically independent states) is based on the White man's belief in the inferiority of the Black man. They believe that the Whites have no rightful place in Africa except as *individuals* in a Black state.

In the second place, there is Soviet Russia with her satellites who support the Afro-Asians because they want to end the stabilising influence of White people in Africa. Even the most anti-Western state in Africa would privately concede that stability in the Congo is only guaranteed by the presence of the 20,000 White people. This is part of their systematic endeavour to weaken the West and remove its strategic bridgeheads.

And *in the third place* there is the group of Western powers which, partly under pressure from their own Leftist politicians who believe that nationalism is dead and that "one world" government is the cure to all human problems[13] and partly for opportunist diplomatic reasons, or vote catching at the United Nations, wants to retain the favour of the non-White states of the world. This they must do, so it is claimed, in order to prevent them from leaning towards the anti-colonial, anti-White line being pursued by Russia and Red China. They must, therefore, show unequivocal support for non-White peoples wherever they may be – irrespective of the White man's claim to nationhood and to his land.

This is particularly true of the United States where the Negro vote is so vital in national elections and where the Negro political movements have actively concerned themselves with United States policy towards South Africa.

For these and other reasons, the Western States join its detractors in censoring a fellow Western nation – a nation which was good when it jumped in twenty years ago to assist them in maintaining themselves against the Axis powers, but is now condemned because it wants to maintain itself.

A diplomat at the United Nations, faced with these circumstances, must set his sights on votes and not on the merits of the issues involved. Horse trading in votes is one of the more generally acknowledged and recognised evils of the United Nations. Consequently, a two-thirds vote against South Africa or Portugal at the United Nations reflects a solid majority of "world opinion". This in its turn, is echoed in the press of the world, analysed in books, discussed at symposiums, presented in articles, until the world is

13. See Burnham, James: *Suicide of the West.*

convinced that South Africa is an outcast because her policies are contrary to "world opinion".

In this way the foreign crusade takes shape.

In 1962 South Africa's Foreign Minister, Eric H. Louw, addressed the General Assembly of the United Nations and pointed out how the Black people of South Africa were better educated, better fed, better housed, better cared for in old age and illness and how they were being prepared to govern themselves in a far more democratic way than any Black people in the world outside the United States. In final proof he pointed out how thousands upon thousands of Blacks from other independent states were migrating to South Africa. Rather than face the formidable task of challenging his facts and comparing conditions in their own states with South Africa, the African states led by Ghana (whose parliamentary opposition was then in prison) charged that the entire speech was "fictitious and erroneous". The General Assembly then voted overwhelmingly to censure Eric Louw for daring to make such a speech and to have it erased from official United Nations records.

In this way the truth curtain was let down on facts which could not be argued away, while the West stood by and made only half-hearted points about "freedom of speech".[14]

The Paper Curtain shielding the world from the true state of affairs in all of the Third Africa is thus to a large extent dependent on the United Nations and Afro-Asian crusade against South Africa.

It was in recognition of these facts that the highly respected American financial paper *Barrons* launched a stinging attack on the United Nations in 1964. It was so much to the point and so evidently "inspired" (if this is possible) by the naked double standard at the United Nations and the unreasonable crusade against South Africa, that most of its readers probably thought they had received a South African newspaper by mistake. The editors did not mince their words:

"What is perfectly clear is that the time has come for a critical reappraisal of the widespread hostility toward the free world's leading source of gold. By word and deed alike, enemies of the Republic (formerly Union) of South Africa – a formidable array that includes journalists and playwrights, statesmen and winners

14. See Louw, E. H.: *The Case for South Africa*, McFaddens, N.Y.

293

of the Nobel Peace Prize – for years have assailed its policies and sought its downfall. The United Nations General Assembly pays courteous heed to butchers like Cuba's Che Guevara and to passionate defenders of the murderous Congolese rebels; however, when the delegate from South Africa rises, many of his colleagues in the Parliament of Man (where other points of view, no matter how obnoxious, are granted a hearing) invariably take a walk . . .

"Hence for years the Verwoerd government, with scarcely a dissenting voice, has been subjected to the same kind of calumny as that aimed at Chiang Kai-Shek, Fulgencio Batista and Ngo Dinh Diem – and toward the same end. In the glass house on the East River the campaign of hatred has run riot. In a mockery of parliamentary procedure, delegates from Black Africa have refused to participate in discourse and debate with spokesmen from Pretoria (which was one of the United Nations original founders). Disregarding the United Nations Charter, which acknowledges the right of a sovereign state to defend itself, the General Assembly has passed a resolution calling for an arms embargo against South Africa, a lawless plea to which the United States and the United Kingdom have given disgraceful assent. Now the Afro-Asian bloc, to the applause of certain peace-loving American sympathisers, are beating the drums for a 'massive' economic boycott.

"Unlike other observers of the African scene, one hardly knows at this point whether to cry or to laugh . . .

"As a so-called potential threat to peace, South Africa to-day scarcely compares with its accusers, who recently defended the savage Congolese rebels and assailed the Western rescue operations around Stanleyville in language which struck even tolerant Adlai Stevenson as irrational, irresponsible, insulting and repugnant."[15]

The banner headline to this report appropriately read: *The United Nations' Crusade Against South Africa is a Disgrace.*

The remaining aspect of the foreign crusade is of a more subtle nature, not so much because of its objectives but because of the inner workings and overlapping of well meaning, honourable interests with that of a more sinister kind. To some people it is known as "the struggle for the minds of men", others refer to it simply as "the cold war". To a third group it is the crusade for egalitarianism,

---

15. *Barrons*, Dow Jones Co., New York, December 28, 1964.

the struggle for "the rights of man" and freedom of the individual, liberalism. To others it is a clever communist crusade, a cold war onslaught dressed up in liberal language. However the crux of the matter is that race relations and racism has become so involved in this crusade (or struggle) that it can no longer be distinguished as a single motivating force. It has led to a confused terminology, a blurring of values, a complete recasting of the meaning of "human dignity". It has led to the establishment of artificial values and concepts such as *neutralism, positive non-alignment* (as if non-alignment could be negative or positive), *world opinion*, "liberation" of countries already independent, *international standards of justice* and the *international community*.

In this state of affairs people have been led to support a movement which has a noble sounding declaration of principles but whose real objectives are distinctly shady.

Mr Sean McBride, Chairman of the International Executive of Amnesty International – an organisation receiving wide support because of its dedication to the release of political prisoners all over the world – in March 1967 made a scathing attack on the society's activities when it became known by word of Miss Polly Toynbee, daughter of the historian and an Amnesty official, that the funds for Amnesty's work in Rhodesia were being made available by the British Government. This of course cast serious doubt on the noble objectives of the society.

The same state of affairs has led people to believe in slogans instead of common sense, to contribute financially to the work of persons claiming to be working for the less privileged, but not realising or knowing that the authors had in mind a much more sinister objective. They are blind to the possibility that people could callously exploit the dilemma of others to boost their own status in the eyes of the local community. Many Communist front organisations have names such as the Society for a Peaceful World, the Society for the Promotion of Human Rights, etc., and count among their members respectable and well meaning citizens.

There has been a virtual explosion of these Societies, Leagues, Fronts, Committees and Associations all over the globe. They find themselves in the mainstream of the foreign crusade against South Africa.

The theoretical and political background to this state of

affairs has been the subject of much thought and discussion in South Africa.

The key to this whole situation, South Africans believe, is at least partially the prevalent trends in international relationships, not the least of which is the struggle for the minds of men (if not their souls and countries). It explains such phenomena as last year's plea by some members of the Council of British Churches for a blockade against South Africa, to be followed by an invasion and the destruction of apartheid. The watered down plea later adopted still puts the Church right back into the age of the Crusades when entire villages were massacred for the sake of a "Christian" objective.

The disturbing element, observed Cape Town's *Die Burger*, is not the armed aggression advocated by members of the Church or any new danger which this poses to the already beleaguered Southern Africa. It is contained in the incomprehensible indifference that it seems to reflect with regard to the future of the Christian mission and civilisation in Africa. The fact is that, in so far as it concerns governments, the exodus of colonial administrations from Africa has gone hand in hand with an equally fast and equally complete eclipse of Christian influence on this continent. In the Congo, savagery and cannibalism have reappeared. In Algeria the whole Christian community as such has disappeared. In the Sudan they have been bitterly persecuted. There and throughout most of the rest of the continent, Mohammedan and heathen administrations have taken over.

In the Sudan, a Christian to-day carries a special pass in much the same way as the Jews wore their star in Nazi Germany. There are territories that have openly become springboards for godless Communism or where Communism is busy digging itself in. In others such as Ghana, Black leaders have been put on an equal footing (and with more enthusiasm) with God Himself.

In the Congo numerous missionaries have been murdered, nuns raped, abused and dishonoured in the most terrible and shocking ways.

Thus all over Africa *except in the Third Africa*, values other than Christian ones are taking root creating conditions which should give grounds for the gravest concern on the part of the Church. But it is not this aspect of Africa that is keeping Church leaders occupied. In fact there is no evidence that it enjoys even the passing attention

of the various churches. Certainly there have been no public protests, no solemn warnings from the pulpit, no marches through the
cities of London or New York, no petitions to the United Nations.
What they are doing, on the contrary, is to offer their allegiance to
the Communists, Mohammedan and heathen attackers of South
Africa and Portugal to destroy with force the one stronghold of
Christianity left on the continent.

Where in Africa is the Bible still the best selling book – except in
the Third Africa? Where can missionaries work unhindered except
in Rhodesia, Angola, South Africa, Mocambique, and other parts
of the Third Africa? Which Church in Africa spends more per
capita on bringing the Bible and Christianity to the heathen
population of South Africa, even to heathens outside the borders
of that country, than the Churches of South Africa?

For a body of men supposedly representing the spirit of Christ on
earth, the action of some churches appears decidedly un-Christian
but it is caused by forces beyond the control of individual men and
women except where it has been deliberately promoted by fanatics
in the guise of clergymen.

The action of the Commission on Race of the United States
Presbyterian Church in issuing a statement in Atlanta in 1964
condemning South Africa for having arrested and executed three
men for "their opposition to apartheid" is an example of how easily
gullible men can be led by the nose – so to speak. At the time when
the Presbyterian Church adopted this statement with all the pomp
and ceremony at its command, the defendants, far from being
executed, were still facing trial for having wilfully and brutally
murdered another Black man. So does the church condone murder
for political ends! Attempts to get the Church to retract its stupendous error met with no success. As it turned out the statement was
largely the work of one Kenneth Carstens, a bitter, self-exiled
clergyman from South Africa, now operating as a professional
anti-apartheid speaker in America, receiving his thirteen pieces of
silver after each public attack on White South Africa.

The actions of Churches, the statements by various politicians, the
voting at the United Nations and the open aggression being per-
petuated against countries in the Third Africa are all aspects of the
power struggle between the Sino-Soviet forces and the West, and
the whole question of race which has swept through the world in

297

an uncontrolled outburst of passion, hate and prejudice, ignorance and obsession.

Both Russia and America are painfully aware that a large-scale nuclear war would result in the destruction not only of their respective countries but the entire Northern hemisphere. Hence they employ all possible means to avoid this ultimate catastrophe. The result is that psychological indoctrination (whereby the morale of the enemy is undermined), subversion, infiltration of the enemies' institutions of power and communications media to weaken resistance to "threats" from abroad, sabotage, etc., have come to play a much more important role than ever before.

Anyone who was not convinced about deliberate efforts in the United States to condition public opinion for the leftist attacks on South Africa, probably has had much food for thought since it became known in February 1967 that the Central Intelligence Agency had been financing various organisations who were bitterly and violently opposed to the governments of South Africa and Portugal. For example, we find that the *American Society of African Culture* has been regularly obtaining money from the CIA through a conduit foundation. The same society sponsored a huge conference in Washington in March 1965. The gathering under the title of "The National Conference on the South African Crisis and American Action" discussed ways of bringing an end to the sovereignty of the South African government! Another example is the *African American Institute*. This is the leading organisation in the United States dealing with African affairs. Its President, Waldemar Nielsen, and its main publication, *Africa Report*, have always been severely critical of the Portuguese and other White people in Africa. Everyone thought that Nielsen's was an independent judgement and that the views of the magazine were based on genuine research. Yet it is now known that at one time the Institute was getting *half* of its funds from the CIA. Mr Nielsen's articles have appeared in *Harpers Magazine*, *The New York Times*, *The New Leader* and other liberal journals. According to *The New York Times* the Africa Institute has also aided one of the leaders of the terrorist movement in Portuguese Mocambique. No information on this political role of the Institute was ever leaked to readers of *Africa Report*. And can anyone now believe in the independent thought of Mr Nielsen, *Africa Report* or the African American Institute? May not people fairly conclude that the CIA dictated the anti-White editorial comments of the Magazine and its contributors?

In his book *The Strategy of Subversion*, Paul Blackstock[16] pointed out that the dark and obscure field of "covert political warfare" forms one of the greatest dangers to the peace in an age of international tension and nuclear deterrence. To-day, nations throughout the world – most notably the United States and Soviet Russia – place increasing reliance on subversive techniques to influence the internal affairs of other countries. The conclusions from the book are inescapable; the great powers have opened a Pandora's box of explosive techniques which threaten the peace. While these nations cannot fully master their operations, the newly emerging and more inexperienced governments are imitating the principles of subversion, and South Africa is one of the principal targets.

Seen in the context of man's fear of a nuclear holocaust and the confusion created by the set of circumstances outlined earlier, well-meaning people, organisations, newspapers and governments have made statements and revised their honoured standards all in an effort to silence those considered an "obstacle" to a proper "solution" to the world's ills.

The Communists have seized upon this fluid situation and through fellow travellers and front organisations launched their post-war campaign at world domination. Caught in this powerplay are a few small countries with microscopisms of the world's ills – such as South Africa.

To understand this world wide confusion and tension is to understand the pressure being put on South Africa. To grasp this new psychological war is to appreciate the foreign crusade to "solve" South Africa's problems.

During the past few years the Russians have been glibly talking about "peaceful co-existence" but their activities in South America, Africa, East Asia and elsewhere leave no doubt that their ultimate objective remains unaltered. The American Bar Association's Standing Committee on Education Against Communism, in a recent study of Communist statements and actions *after* the Bay of

16. A former intelligence specialist of the United States government and now Professor of Political Science at the University of South Carolina.

Pigs disaster in Cuba, declares: "Communist actions and Communist words prove that Communist goals are unchanged. The danger may well be greater now in our moment of one-sided relaxation than in the tense days of Stalinism . . . Moscow and Peking agree that capitalism and human liberty are still the primary targets. Both subsidise class war, ideological war and guerilla war while debating with each other as to whether we are a paper tiger or a nuclear lamb."[17]

In the short run, the Association found, polycentrism in the Communist world means that we are now menaced by the two competing strategies; (1) the revolutionary violence of Chinese orientated Communists in Afro-Asia and Latin America; and (2) the more sophisticated Popular Front subversion of Russian-aligned Communist factions.

In any case, is there a government still so naive as to believe in Communist peaceful co-existence after the Red Chinese and Russian support of the barbaric, cannibalistic rabble (the so-called "liberation movement" of Christopher Gbenye) which butchered White, Black and Yellow in the senseless killings in the Congo in November 1964? If there are, then the chances are good that those governments participated in the so-called *Tri-Continent Conference* held in Havana, Cuba, during January 1966. Although the Soviet Union was represented by a forty-member delegation, the chief result of the conference was to foster the Chinese thesis of Communist seizure of power in countries allied to the free world. The new liberalist camp and its newspapers such as the *New York Times* make much of the so-called "split" between Russia and China but the unanimity of the delegates on Chinese tactics for "wars of liberation" points out the futility and danger of this argument. The resolutions approved by the Russian delegation were clearly a strident call for "hot" and "cold" war subversion and sabotage of the free world.

The other alarming significance of the conference stems from the scope of participation. There were delegations from eighty-two nations and many of the delegations were officials in high government positions, for example from Syria, the United Arab Republic, Tanzania, Guinea, Ghana and Algeria. The conference set out in

17. *Peaceful Co-existence* – American Bar Association, West Publishing Company, 1964 – pp. XVI-XVII. Cf.: Editorial on Peaceful Co-existence in *Pravda* – September 18th, 1965.

detail the aggressive designs of world Communism and in this the Chinese and Russian delegates disagreed only on tactics and timetable.

There are many reasons for Russia and Red China's aggressive attitude towards South Africa which need not be analysed here. Sufficient to say that editorials in *Pravda* and I*zvestia* and the official Communist Party statements do not even attempt to disguise their objective of destroying the White Government in South Africa and of substituting a Socialist "People's Republic" in its place.

Two of the methods which Russia in particular has applied with resounding success are (a) its so-called drive to "eliminate racial discrimination" and (b) its "anti-colonial posture". In both instances South Africa has been the pawn and – in the ideological battle with the West – the victim.

The Communists maintain (and this was Marx's credo) that to create a better world, not racial warfare but class warfare is required. The labourers all over the world must and will re-volt against their capitalist bosses and exploiters. *Acknowledgement of racial differences was to be vigorously opposed.* Except for outward racial differences, nationalism or regionalism was not to be tol-erated.

This was the beginning of the school of egalitarianism.

Idealists all over the world apparently found its *philosophy* (as distinct from Communist institutions) very attractive.

The greatest injustice may however, result from the uncritical acceptance of this unproved idealistic doctrine. Thus if in the United States of America, Canada, New Zealand and elsewhere the principle of non-discrimination had been rigidly applied and if no special provision had been made for the Indians, Eskimos and Maoris in these countries they would not have survived as ethnic groups – indeed the result would have been genocide. This also applies to the Bushmen and the Bantu of South Africa. Land reserved for the lesser developed Black man in South Africa would long since have become the property of the Whites should they have been allowed to compete freely with the less economically astute Bantu in buying and selling land.

The meek acceptance of a highly contentious Communistic philosophy on race by influential journals and policy forming individuals in America and the West has not only been most

301

advantageous to Russia but has resulted in an alarming breach in the Western line of defence.

Russia has been allowed to choose the psychological battle-ground and has not only effectively put her enemies on the defensive *but also in the position where they believe they must sacrifice some of their allies in order to contain Communism.*

In Africa the West has supported the worst kind of dictatorships such as in Ghana, Algeria, Guinea and Mali, with handouts and aids, and ignored their unlawful and immoral attacks on South Africa, Britain, Belgium and Portugal, all in an effort to show that it was pro-Black.

The attitude of the United States, Britain and France in the United Nations towards emerging Black nations was largely in reaction to the Communist call for the "liberation of Africa". The net result is that a conglomeration of tribes, led by a few educated but unscrupulous men, have been propelled into the world as nation states generations before they had developed sufficiently to become viable and stable communities. Ethiopia, which had been an independent kingdom long before the Norsemen discovered America 1,000 years ago, has yet to reach the overall state of development (in terms of its economy, science, literature, etc.) enjoyed by mid-Eastern states during Biblical times.

What earthly chance then have such artificially created states as Rwanda, Burundi, Guinea, Chad, Gambia, Mali which only saw the light as "nation states" a bare six years ago to exercise any responsibility in the current psychological war?

Liberals in the United States in fear of seeing their country accused of "racism" or of being anti-Black (with the reaction to German "racism" fresh in the minds of men) threw overboard caution, commonsense, logic and experience in order to outdo the Communists in anti-colonialism and to show the world (and their own Negro voters) that it was as pro-Black as man could be.

Perhaps one of the more easily distinguished effects of this state of affairs (further contributing to the confusion of international values and objectives) is the way in which two principal countries of the West, Britain and the United States, have identified racial problems at home with those in South Africa and Rhodesia even though an intelligent investigation of the scene would have con-

302

vinced the interested parties that there can, in effect, be *no* comparison whatsoever.

The day before he left South Africa after his visit there in 1965, General Lauris Norstad, former Supreme Allied Commander, Europe, and Commander in Chief of United States Forces, said that the racial problem in the United States was *more critical* than in South Africa "as it had already reached its crisis and was in full swing." He felt that South Africa's problem was different and more of a long range nature. He was impressed by its magnitude and complexities. "It is greater than I realised but it is still not as acute as the American one. South Africa's leading citizens are making a sincere and honest effort to solve the problem."[18] General Norstad therefore underlined a very simple fact, viz. that people in South Africa are not blind to the gravity of their problem or incapable of doing anything about it although the Liberal press is trying hard to create this impression. It was also evident from his statement that, unlike the liberals in America, he himself did not believe that racial problems all over the world were the same.

The South African who has read extensively about the racial situation in the United States and who has lived in the country for an appreciable length of time, long enough for him to visit the South or the slums in Chicago and New York would be the first to observe that the United States has a truly *racial problem*. To the South African, the Negro is an American, a Black American. He speaks American, he acts American and history shows that he has laid down his life for America. It is presumed that he loves America – if not all its people. The average Negro has never heard the languages of Africa or Europe; the chances even his grandfather knew them or ever set foot on African soil are equally small. Clearly the problem in the United States is how the Administration should proceed to provide opportunities for the Black Americans to find a rightful place in their own society – the American society, the only society which they know, the only culture, the only physical environment.

When White Americans, newspapers, clergymen, politicians and students observe how Black men are deliberately being prevented in other states from enjoying their constitutional rights, they are upset and when this prevention is accompanied by violence as in

18. *The Pretoria News*, Johannesburg *Star*, 1.4.1965.

Selma, Rochester and Alabama, they are outraged. To say that the United States is to-day generally incensed about the racial situation is to put it mildly. The number of racial riots, killings, boycotts and demonstrations which have wracked the nation are countless. In cities such as New York, Chicago and Los Angeles, racial animosities are positively electric. Detroit is a city of fear. The incidents at Little Rock, Rochester, Harlem, Watts, Birmingham and Selma have brought clergymen, students and private citizens from all over the country to demonstrate. Newspapermen have been abused, shot at, killed and assaulted.

To expect a cool appraisal of South African *objectives* in this atmosphere is asking too much of human nature. That much South Africa understands. But, that the situation in South Africa and the United States is so often *equated* by responsible people and organisations with a severe brand of Southern segregation is inexcusable. The necessary proof of the differences is not even below the surface; it is there in the open for everyone to see.

The basic situation in South Africa is that different nations, Black nations differing from each other, and a White nation have been forced together in one country through an act of war – the Anglo-Boer War and British colonial history.

In South Africa the divisions between White and Black are the same which have prevented the Scandinavian, European and Asian nations from all becoming one Scandinavian, one European or one Asian nation. White and Black find themselves in South Africa not by freedom of choice but by force of history. If integration were impossible in the case of Belgium and Holland, Norway and Sweden, Pakistan and India, for Indians and Negroes in Guinea, for Greeks and Turks in Cyprus, Malays and Chinese in Malaysia, or, for that matter, for Spaniards and Portuguese on the Iberian peninsula, it would be even more impossible in South Africa where, in addition, differences between White and Black on the scale of western civilisation are so great as to be almost insurmountable for the next ten generations.

Oblivious of these differences, people and organisations in the United States fight against the policy of separate development of the nations in South Africa with the same zeal and on the same premise as they are battling segregation in Alabama and Mississippi.

Encouraged by the success following their crusade against "racial differentiation" and "racial discrimination" the Communists launched a second crusade against "colonialism", although perfectly aware that they themselves are guilty of the most severe and tyrannical form of colonialism. Here again South Africa and Portugal have been the butt of their propaganda.

With boundless exuberance, exceeding that of the early crusades, the West responded to the appeal of the Communists, without anybody suggesting that the crusade might appropriately start in Latvia, Lithuania, Poland, Hungary, Bulgaria or Czechoslovakia.

In the United States, Russia had its greatest success.

Religious bodies, welfare societies, powerful philanthropic foundations, newspapers and many other public organisations are still only too eager to become allies in this crusade. It has, after all, a noble objective, and it is perhaps above all, fashionable.

The enslavement of Eastern Europe was conveniently forgotten by the West and attention concentrated on Africa. "Liberation" of the Eastern European states may have precipitated the nuclear war which everyone dreaded and was, therefore, too risky.

Except that the West is trying to outdo and outplay the Communists at their own game, it is difficult to find any other logical explanation for the "crusade" of Western nations against "colonialism". In this crusade Rhodesia, Angola, South West Africa and South Africa are usually listed as "the remaining colonial problems". That the result of decolonisation in Africa has brought political slavery, hunger, dictatorships, chaos and even cannibalism to the erstwhile colonies, is apparently beside the point. Betrayed into doing Russia's work in Africa in establishing a large number of unstable, weak nations ripe for exploitation while ignoring the old captive nations in the Communist embrace, the West merely guarantees that Russia gets more votes in the United Nations. Meanwhile Russia is sowing chaos in Africa, and moreover, gets the West (the United States of America and Britain) to pay for it. The moment the Americans heard the African cry of Uhuru (freedom) they saw in their mind's eye the Boston Tea Party. The insincerity of the United States in supporting this role is exemplified by the fact that it votes side by side with Russia in the United Nations for free African elections with universal suffrage when Poland and Hungary do not have it.

The "fall-out" from this state of affairs directly affected South

Africa for, except for the informed student and government official, South Africa was seen in the West as just another "colonial spot" with a "White settler problem" which could be solved (Uhuru fashion) in the same manner as the "problem" in Kenya and Tanganyika.

It has been suggested in London and Washington that Algeria provides a pointer to the future of South Africa. This suggestion can only have merit if the most elementary and most important consideration is totally disregarded. As Professor Charles Manning pointed out: "The fact overlooked is that the vital decisions on Algeria were made in Paris and in Evian, and were not made by a White community in Algiers. But in South Africa, which has long been self-governing, the relevant decisions must be made in Pretoria or Pretoria and Cape Town. If the *colons* of Algeria have indeed been expended, this was not of their doing. The liquidation of White South Africa would require, constitutionally, an act of collective submission – a manifestation, perhaps we should say, of that sacrificial love which is the very essence of Christianity. But, if it is only by such collective self-immolation that a people can reveal itself as Christian, never since the coming of Christianity has there existed a Christian people, as distinct from a people composed in part of Christian individuals."[19]

The Communists are far better equipped than their opponents to grasp the significance of the Third Africa. They realise that it occupies a very strategic position, but from their point of view it is of the utmost importance to confuse the world regarding developments there.

Communist agitators and saboteurs are held up by left wing sympathisers not as criminals or enemies of law and order, but as "freedom fighters" and sooner or later this propaganda finds its way into liberal newspapers in the West. Professor Charles Manning pointedly observed: "In few cases, if any, can a Communist-encouraged, if not necessarily Communist-inspired, campaign of systematic mood-engineering have met with comparable success in the Western world. Whether, for instance, the Communists should be described as having joined with the Western democracies in condemning the suppression of saboteurs in South Africa, or whether

19. In *Foreign Affairs*, Council on Foreign Relations, N.Y., 1965.

it is the democracies that should be said to have toed the Communist line, may seem an academic point. But it is not from Western propaganda that the Communist countries will have learned their hostility to a capitalistic South Africa. Who shall say that the converse is equally true? Is it the democracies that have deliberately set themselves to create chaos in South Africa? They may well appear to have been doing so; but it is hard to believe that they really have. Whereas, if the Communists have been striving to avert chaos, their efforts have been remarkably well disguised."

Writing in *The Cincinatti Enquirer* (October 1963) William L. McGrath, Chairman of the Board of Cincinatti's Williamson Company and an expert on Communist propaganda said: "The Soviet Union has launched a major propaganda offensive against the Republic of South Africa for the sole purpose of appending that gold producing area to the Soviet bloc." He added "In their South African campaign, as in most of their other efforts to gain dominance around the world, the Russians have found a false issue. In this instance it is apartheid, the system whereby the Government is seeking to build parallel White and non-White societies."

Lord Milverton, the former British Governor of Nigeria (also of Jamaica, North Borneo, Gambia and Fiji) observed during 1964 that "the encouragement of unrest over apartheid was a Communist interest". As a prominent Member of the British Government whose sympathies are decidedly not with South Africa, Lord Milverton obviously had no interest in anything except the unpalatable truth.

The Communist interest in economic sanctions against Rhodesia, Angola or South Africa is obvious. As Dr Stephen Enke of the Institute of Defence Analysis in Washington pointed out in an article in *Optima*[20] economic sanctions, to be effective, would have to be supplemented in time with an armed blockade. "But armed blockade, envolving into war in other ways, could bring widespread war to the most economically developed and most staunchly anti-Communist nation in Africa." The Communist objective is only too clear. From such an adventure, Dr Enke pointed out, the anti-Communist countries, which need a stable government in that strategic part of the continent, would ultimately emerge as the losers.

20. Johannesburg, March, 1962, p. 1.

Finally there is the role played by prominent individuals in the Foreign Crusade.

It is not the purpose here to analyse the character of those learned individuals in the academic community who also glibly refer to the South African and Portuguese presence in Africa as "a threat to peace" and are now going to extreme lengths to marshal "world opinion" against these two countries.

What is generally evident is that they see the problem in South Africa in its simplest form: man and race, and apply to this a hypothetical solution which is *theoretically* and academically quite logical, accurate and valid, viz. equality "for all human beings" and one-man-one-vote. Where they fail is in considering man only in his most perfect state, i.e. an individual or nation incapable of prejudice, fear or selfishness, devoid of his or their herd instinct or their belief in nation and mother tongue. Their hypothesis has only academic value in man's life and struggle, for its most important premise, the state of man as an individual, is negated by history, culture and anthropology. Had their premise been true, people would have been interchangeable like pieces on a chess board, whereas history teaches us that an influx of one race or nation into the residential area of another group, race or state, invariably leads to problems not overcome after centuries, despite goodwill between leading figures in the respective groups. Of this America, India, Burma and Ceylon are good examples.[21]

Individual clergymen and politicians who will stage a public march on the South African Embassy at the merest suspicion of a mis-step on the part of South Africa, quite often are also prisoners of their own personalities whose bitter frustration at not being able to get a small country to conform, sometimes leads to the most extreme and unreasonable attitudes. Their unreasonable pre-occupation with South Africa causes them to ignore infinitely worse problems elsewhere – including countries where atrocities on an appalling scale have been committed. To them South Africa has become an obsession. Among them are many who advocate a physical invasion of South Africa. They do not seem to care whether sanctions can be applied effectively, about the dangerous chain

21. Cf.: Ardrey, Robert: *The Territorial Imperative* and Possony, S.: "Nationalism and the Ethnic Factor", *Orbis*, Foreign Policy Institute of the University of Pennsylvania, March, 1967.

reaction which would follow, or about the dangerous precedent it would set. They are fanatics bent on disaster, who care neither for the consequences to all the people of South Africa nor, in the final analysis, mankind in general. In a way their thinking is similar to that of the Red Chinese, sharing Peking's iron indifference to the deaths of millions because they are hypnotised by the idea that the confrontation of South Africa by force is inevitable.

To fear for South Africa to-day is to fear for the world, for in a certain sense and through no special evil or arrogance on South Africa's part, the world has made South Africa the symbol both of its hope and its despair. But it must be prevented from turning South Africa into the anvil of genocide.

In the end the "foreign crusade" has simply led to a greater cohesion between different political groups in South Africa. There has been a closing of the ranks. Old animosities have been buried. In seven years (since 1960 when the crusade went into top gear) the foreign crusade has done more for the political unification of the country than any Prime Minister could have dreamed of achieving in fifty years.

A crusade aimed at highlighting the differences between the political parties would have had infinitely better hope of success – up to 1958. To-day such an attempt would have even worse luck. Politicians in South Africa who, after 1958, turned their coats to the hot wind blowing from the United Nations and the Winds of Change from Number 10 Downing Street, London found themselves blown out of every position of influence in Parliament, in fact, blown out of political influence altogether.

Regretfully the foreign crusade also had the effect of making South Africans cynical of the values and opinions expressed by other nations, whether by their leaders or newspapers.

An intelligent low-keyed exchange of opinions and views concerning political and social problems cannot be anything but beneficial to world order. But as this chapter has shown the employment of a double standard, political expediency and hypocrisy of the worst kind on the part of most Western states have all but destroyed the hope of such a dialogue – at least for the near future. The average South African who is well read and well travelled, whether businessman, politician or diplomat, finds himself in complete agreement with this evaluation. This will for a long time seriously impair the hope of the "intelligent dialogue" with South Africa which some governments, statesmen, newspapers and churchmen are now belatedly calling for.

The one point to bear in mind is that the American idealist as well as the South African idealist pursue more or less identical goals, namely freedom and progress for all, and that a meaningful debate can take place only after the identity of those goals has been accepted. Given this identity of purpose the debate, logically speaking, must deal with methods of implementation. Unfortunately, the methods which have been proposed by American writers have not been thought through systematically and have rarely reflected more than a sloganised understanding of the major and complex difficulties in Africa.

The chances are that the South African image in the world (and the same applies to Rhodesia and Angola) will also, as Dean Acheson remarked about the American one, "take care of itself". It will improve not because South Africa *argued* its case effectively but because concrete results at home speak louder than a million critical articles or a million delegates at the United Nations.

The leaders in the foreign crusade refuse to acknowledge that the vast scope of illiteracy, poverty and disease existing in Africa plus the threat of large scale famine, represent a far more crucial problem than apartheid. *They* will, of course, *live* to regret their pre-occupation with race relations in South Africa. But millions of Black men elsewhere in Africa will *not* live to appreciate the actions of their would-be benefactors in London and New York.

13. Conclusion: by Professor Stefan Possony,

Director International Political studies Programme,
Hoover Institution on War, Revolution and Peace,
Stanford University, California

Before an American – almost any American – sits down to read a book by a South African on South Africa, he better begin by making a secret confession: that he knows next to nothing about that faraway land; that almost all of what he thinks he knows is false; and that most of the rest is misinterpretation based upon unwarranted generalizations of American experiences. This writer must confess that he, too, was sure about South Africa years before he ever departed on his first trip. For many long semesters he tormented a student whose dissertation was to prove the policy of separate development was economically unfeasible. The poor man was forced to recalculate his statistics four or five times before I finally understood that *a priori* reasoning cannot refute facts.

The African states who, under the guidance of a foremost American international lawyer and former high State Department official, were suing the Republic of South Africa before the International Court of Justice considered their case irrefutable. They discovered that they had swallowed false information and that their "evidence" did not hold up. They admitted as much and substituted for their concrete case against oppression an abstract case based on an alleged norm of international law. The American press was so surprised it did not find this development newsworthy.

On the assumption which he uncritically accepts, that South African policies are "racist", the average American opposes them across-the-board: By punishing South Africa, Americans tend to satisfy their own bad conscience about past and present attitudes in American life and to support demonstratively recent American policies designed to advance the progress of the American negro. In the continuing conflict of the American conscience, South Africa has been playing the role of a surrogate scapegoat.

The United States, since its founding, has been championing the principle of equality. Between 1941 and 1945, the United States fought the Nazis and their policies of racial oppression and genocide. In 1945, the U.S. was one of the principal founders of the United Nations. Little does the average American remember that South Africa also has a long and proud tradition of fighting for political freedom. South Africa, too, was fighting the Nazis, and it was one of the co-founders of the U.N. South Africa has been taking its obligations under the U.N. Charter as seriously as the U.S.

There has arisen a widespread conviction in the United States that the principle of equality means more than that all persons are equal before the law, all voters are equal in the voting booth, and all sinners are equal before God. Never too clearly expressed and usually just hinted at by implication, many American writers profess to believe that all or most individuals are materially equal in their talents and their mental and psychological make-up; hence, given equal "opportunities", all men will be equal in their drives and accomplishments. Just about everybody can be a Euclid, a Mozart or an Edison!

In U.S. administrative practice this doctrine often is expressed by the cliché that one "warm body" can be substituted for any other "warm body" and that any man is as good as any other. I am not sure this doctrine has been proved with respect to insects. I know it is inaccurate with respect to cats, dogs and horses. It is highly inaccurate with respect to Americans – or why have aptitude tests and elections? Somewhat incongruously, the belief is held simultaneously that "diversity" has been one of the roots of American success. In any event, it is quite impossible to equalize conditions and opportunities.

There is, of course, the American experience that people from many lands have succeeded in creating a single "integrated" society. If immigrants from many stocks were unable to co-operate, intermingle, intermarry, and develop a new cultural synthesis, America would have been forced to restrict immigration severely, the American economy would have moved at far slower pace, and the country hardly would have risen to world leadership. Small wonder, then, that the United States has considered itself to be the anointed champion of the "melting pot" philosophy and has pressed its viewpoint before the entire world.

Unfortunately, many official and unofficial spokesmen of this philosophy have been inclined to overlook the near-uniqueness of the American condition and often have presented an overly simplistic interpretation of the American experience. The melting-pot functioned effectively only with persons of European descent;[1] its boiling speed was slow; and not all elements were melted down into a uniform slag. During the 19th century, immigrants tended to live together in ethnically marked parts of cities, countries and states; they upheld their linguistic and cultural traditions for generations; and they married within their own ethnic circle. Because of a fast growing population and economy, a steady move from farm to factory, the settlement of the entire vast country, and a mandatory public school system that served the purpose of Americanization, the integrative processes were accelerated during the 20th century. Nevertheless, even today after countless inter-marriages between Jewish and Irish, Italian and English, German and Spanish, French and Russian families, the ethnic identities of the original settler or immigrant groups have not been completely lost. There remains a widespread desire to preserve at least minimal ethnic ties.

Integration has occurred but the process requires *at least* three generations and presupposes people who, in terms of cultural levels, attitudes to life and work, aptitudes, and numerous additional traits are similar *ab ovo*. There were several keys to this American success: First, integration happened in response to overpowering social and economic forces; these forces themselves emerged from the pre-existing similarity of the integrating groups. Second, integration was brought about without political coercion, though by no means without political trouble (especially in periods of national crisis). Third, the range of integration extended principally to people of the White race. Fourth, Americanization involved immigrants and their descendants who had no original roots in the country, but instead were eagerly searching for new identities and attachments. There was *no* "melting pot" merging ethnic groups with distinct racial characteristics and living at clearly distinguishable "higher" and "lower" cultural levels. There was marginal inter-breeding and partial adjustment to the higher culture, but the various groups remained apart from one another. In particular, the integrationist philosophy did not work with the American Indians. The Alaskan

1. Note that in Canada, where some of the conditions are different, the British and French elements could not be mutually assimilated.

Eskimo continues to lead his own separate life. The Mexicans have not been assimilated. The Puerto Ricans live mostly outside the American society, although the white educated Puerto Ricans have found it easier to overcome the barriers than purely European immigrant groups. In Hawaii, the race relations between Whites, Chinese, Japanese, and Hawaiians are almost ideal. Yet, essentially, the four racial groups are living side by side, with only limited inter-breeding. The Nisei and the third and fourth generation Chinese-Americans have risen to high cultural levels in recent years and have been freed of ostracistic practices, but for the most part, they too continue to live within their own ethnic milieu. The American negro remains in a status of merely attenuated segregation.

The United States has been employing *different* empirical methods to handle ethnic groups which, for one reason or the other, are hard to assimilate. Segregationist practices against Jews have been, more or less successfully, voided by legislation – and by Jewish professional accomplishments. The Indians were placed under a protective regime, after more than a century of *laissez-faire* policies through which their ethnic integrity was weakened gravely and vast tracts of land were lost. As a result, many tribes disappeared or survived merely in small remnants. The statute worked out by the Hoover and Roosevelt administrations assigned to the Indian tribes their own "reservations", or homelands, from which Whites are excluded. Following this reform, some Indian tribes began to recover. At present, two-thirds of the Indians live in their "reservations". About one-third of the Indian population live in cities, i.e. within the American society, but many of those Indians ultimately return to their homeland and only few become detribalized.

This Indian regime has not escaped criticism but generally has been hailed as a progressive measure. It shows many similarities with the South African policy of separate development, notably the basic concept of tribal homelands. However, some dissimilarities between U.S. and South African practices are worth noting. The African natives have preserved territorial continuity for many generations, while the Indians moved, or were moved, from one area to the other: only a few small reservations are in the area of the original homeland. The South African government is making a far stronger effort to help the native groups to preserve and develop their own culture. Both governments stress education and economic development, but the South Africans have been comparatively more successful.

The American Indians could not be assimilated, despite the fact that they were a very small and divided group which, if it had intended to give up its identity, could have been submerged within a few generations; but the Indians wanted to survive *as a group*. In South Africa, the Bantus are more numerous than the people of European origin. Rapid merging of the Bantus with the Europeans is impossible, while the merging of the Europeans with the Bantus would entail the destruction of a modern economy (thus result in a substantial reduction of population) and also result in the destruction of a highly advanced culture.

It is superfluous in this context to evaluate the desires – or the consent – of the "warm bodies" that would be thrown into the White-Bantu "melting pot".

There is not much point comparing vastly different situations. But if the present U.S. statutes regulating the lives of the Indian tribes are deemed to be "progressive", then Americans have little ground to criticize South African policies, which would have to be considered to be still more progressive.

By and large and with appropriate modifications, the United States applies its Indian policies to the Eskimos and the various populations on the island possessions and trust territories. Some U.S. administrating authorities have failed to see to it that the native language be used as an initial language of instruction or be taught in school at all. There usually was no opposition against the native "dialect" but there never has been more than mere toleration. There have been no instances of American authorities trying to develop a native language.

It is by no means easy for Pacific natives to move to the United States; in fact, the immigration of these people is regulated. I just record the fact, without criticizing it. Hawaii and Alaska are states of the Union, and therefore, their citizens enjoy free mobility within the entire U.S. Hence Hawaiians and Eskimos are free to go to the mainland. Likewise, mainland Americans are free to move to Hawaii and Alaska, which they are doing in increasing numbers. Hence the native populations are gradually deprived of their way of life and within a few generations may have vanished altogether – they did lose self-government long ago. It is said that the Hawaiians are enjoying it all, because the Japanese are running the business, the Chinese are doing the work, and the Americans are paying. Perhaps, this is better left open.

The United States adopted a different solution to Puerto Rico. The Puerto Ricans still have their own land and their self-government, which they greatly strengthened; but they also are over-populated and need free access to the American labour market. They chose "association" within a "commonwealth" with the U.S. This form of independence provides the advantages of self-reliance without the normal disadvantages resulting from independence (or, conversely, statehood within the Union). The U.S. was able to go along with the commonwealth arrangement, because the numerical ratio between Puerto Rico and the United States (about 1:100) is such that even the immigration of all Puerto Ricans into the U.S. would not make much difference. Moreover, Puerto Rican immigrants often have skills and can be usefully employed. Puerto Ricans (as well as Puerto Rican exports) are allowed into the United States without restrictions; and American industries and business firms have been moving to Puerto Rico, where they enjoy tax and wage advantages. A portion of the large Puerto Rican immigration to the United States ultimately returns to the island and virtually all immigrants preserve strong ties with their relatives who remained home. The arrangement was confirmed on July 23, 1967, in a plebiscite, in which the proponents of full independence polled barely any votes (·5%). Indeed, the commonwealth arrangement is highly advantageous to Puerto Rico which, with a per capita income of $1,149, is by far the most affluent country of Latin America.

The "separate development" of Puerto Rico has been institutionalized in a manner similar to some of the solutions which the South Africans have in mind. The main difference is that free migration would not be practical between the ethnically different parts of South Africa; indeed, free immigration into the American mainland was not precisely an overwhelming success in the U.S.-Puerto Rican case. But the association of two separate and independent states, and their mutual collaboration in the areas of economics, foreign policy and defence, is the essence of the concept: it has proved workable because of the strength of the American economy. *Mutatis mutandis*, this sort of American solution is applic-

316

able to South African conditions, but Americans are astounded when South Africans talk in those terms.

Most Americans, once they reflect upon U.S. arrangements and do a little research on nationality policies, will discover that the concept of separate development has its origin in the science of anthropology and in European socialism. The Nazis did not envisage separate development but forced labor for the more or less "acceptable" groups, and expulsion or genocide for the "undesirable" ones: moreover, they were considering forced breeding with select non-German women in order to increase *German* demographic strength. By clear contrast, the inviolate integrity *and the development* of the ethnic group is the starting point of South African policy.

At this point, the critics like to argue that in the U.S. the individual Indian, for example, is free to leave his reservation whenever he so chooses, to live anywhere in the United States, and to become a member of the American society, just as the Puerto Rican can go freely to the U.S., live anywhere, and assimilate. Yet the South Africans control population movements from and to the native reservations. This argument is correct in abstract legal terms, and it can be said in favor of both the American and African solutions that they are responsive to concrete circumstances: there are just a handful of Indians, the Indian-White ratio being 1:400, while the Bantu-White ratio in South Africa is approximately 3.6:1. No other differences need to be mentioned to prove the requirement of non-identical solutions.

The American Indian usually goes to live in towns which are not far from his reservation. He lives together with other Indians, or in urban or rural sectors with a significant Indian population, and he makes his living in professions typically exercised by other Indians. Since the influx of Indians always has been small, the government employment service has been able to supply the jobs. No regulation of migration, therefore, was required. Naturally, there was no real need to legislate against White influx into Indian reservations.

The Puerto Rican usually goes to New York or a few other big cities, and virtually always lives in areas inhabited by Puerto Ricans and vacated by non-Puerto Ricans. If he is White, he "assimilates", often on a bilingual basis. If he is dark, he is anxious to differentiate himself from the American negro but he experiences many of the same tribulations. Since unlimited immigration plus welfare payments resulted in numerous difficulties, including unemployment and crime, regulation of Puerto Rican immigration would have been a method more satisfactory to the immigrants, their settled predecessors, and the host population. In the end, the market regulated the migratory movement with considerable brutality. If Puerto Rico had become a fully independent state, it would have been treated like any other South American country and the would-be emigrants would have been kept on the overpopulated island. The U.S. has not adopted a free immigration policy vis-a-vis Mexico, for example, but metes out rather harsh treatment to the migrant farm workers who live in camps and after the harvest must return to Mexico.

The United States maintains very strict immigration laws which originally were inspired by economic as well as ethnic-racial considerations (including some which were rather untenable). The present immigration law ostensibly departed from the old scheme. In reality, by making it more difficult for unskilled foreign labor to migrate to the U.S., the new law just continues the old system, albeit under egalitarian figleafs. The policy, whether avowed or not, still is to prevent the "racial balance" being upset by immigration. Moreover, this American policy results in a "brain drain" from Europe and is considerably more utilitarian than egalitarian.

These specific American experiences and models may be compared, approvingly or critically, with the measures controlling native migratory moves within the Republic of South Africa. There is, however, little justification in claiming that U.S. practices are praiseworthy, while the South African practices must be condemned on principle. This writer, being an immigrant himself, is in favor of freedom of migration; but he is also in favor of orderly process and he does not believe that any ethnic group or settlement area is obligated to tolerate an unsolicited mass influx which, inevitably, will have demographic-ethnic consequences. After all, unrestricted immigration, especially if it is influenced or controlled by foreign agencies directing the immigrants, ultimately becomes tantamount to invasion and threatens the integrity of the recipient state and people. Hence regulation of immigration is an inalienable prerogative of sovereignty.[2] No one ever operates on a different basis.

The "melting pot" philosophy has broken down in the case of the American negro. If we consider the whites as a single group, the American negro is by far the largest minority within the United States. Even if the white group were divided by ethnic origin (i.e. into "British", "Germans", etc.), the negroes still would remain one of the largest groups. The exception therefore is highly significant and by no means trivial: it does prove that there are, or have been so far, clearly drawn limits to the "melting pot" technique of racial or ethnic cohabitation.

There have been few organized attempts to apply the "melting pot" philosophy to the solution of the American negro problem. The term "integration" does not, in American usage, refer to race mixing – this subject has remained utterly taboo. "Integration" refers, *inter alia*, to equal treatment in public places, fair employment, school desegregation, better housing, etc.[3] Those who favor this circumscribed sort of "integration" tacitly assume that the intimate closeness of the two races will not result in a significant increase of the miscegenation rate. Those who oppose desegregation derive the emotional strength of their opposition, not from fear of better negro education or housing, but from the expectation that miscegenation, on an ever larger scale, will be an inevitable by-product of common housing, desegregated schooling, and a joint social life. For the most part, this fear is expressed in private conversation only, while public objections are raised on different grounds; but the private fears and attitudes regulate behavior, and the public language serves to veil the reality.

A small number, mostly intellectuals, believe that it doesn't matter whether race-mixing takes place; a still smaller number alleges that miscegenation would be useful. Rightly or wrongly, the majority seems to be convinced of the contrary. Few people give

2. The question of political asylum must be distinguished from that of immigration.

3. A typical American definition by Carl F. Hansen, former superintendent of schools in the District of Columbia, reads: "Integration . . . is the capacity of people to be together without being conscious of race – the appreciation of each other regardless of race or economic status or religion."

much thought to the problems posed by combined racial and cultural mixing.

A different group assumes that desegregation in housing and schooling would not result in closer social intercourse but in sharper social cleavage; and also that, while some forms of school desegregation may be permanent, desegregation in housing will not become significant. In general, those observers anticipate that the desegregation ruckus will result in increasing racial strife – and the facts, so far, seem to bear them out. The statistical facts are, incidentally, that race-mixing, though it is virtually unimpeded, occurs only on a small scale. However, this extent of mixing would be enough to ensure the disappearance of the American negro within 200 years or so. As a by-product, negro heredity – sooner or later – would be dispersed all over the American society. History need not and usually does not conform to such calculations. It is far more probable the American negro will *not* disappear, but his genes will be propagated more widely: this heredity may be absorbed or extruded by various biological processes. Widespread "assortive mating" between whites and near-whites, and the mating trends within the negro population, may result in three instead of the present two groups: the whites, as well as the light and the dark negroes.

The American situation differs from South African patterns in that the American negroes include only a relatively small number of pure-blooded "Africans". The overwhelming majority of American negroes are mulattoes, many of whom are descendants of "aristocratic" (i.e. slave-owning) white families in the South. The entire group possesses about one-third "white genes". A substantial percentage – from 15 to 20% – are predominantly white but culturally belong to the negro community and are visually recognized as "negroes". A small but not insignificant number "passes" regularly into the white society. Little is known about their fate.

How can the negroes be drawn fully into the American society? It does not seem as though this self-imposed and perplexing task is soluble; surely, it is not soluble in the short run and clearly it is not soluble through the assimilationist method. In the absence of plausible or convincing proposals, there does not seem to be much basis for rejecting divergent approaches. The American moral and sometimes inquisitional fervor is the more astounding since the U.S. adopted the assimilationist policy toward the negroes only recently and merely in a declaratory, not in a real sense. This policy which dates from the Supreme Court's desegregation decision of 1954 did not result from adequate scientific preparation but from deductive ideological reasoning, as well as from deliberately "suggestive" and selective evidence.

The South African government has derived its policies from the recognition that the majority of the groups within the Republic want to co-operate, while preserving their ethnic integrity. The United States government, in the face of a social reality of segregation and lack of interest in close togetherness both by the whites and the American negroes, has announced the dogma that these groups simply must intermingle because they are holding identical citizenship. The U.S. policy is inspired by the entirely praiseworthy – and belated – objective to eliminate all artificial burdens placed upon American negroes and to accelerate their progress. But the implementation of this American policy has been an exercise in *inverted racialism* because the existence of problems more fundamental than "intolerance" or "prejudice" was denied.

What has been the result? Virtually all school administrations have attempted to comply with the Supreme Court desegregation order of 1954. The battle-cry was that negro education would improve through desegregation and that in addition some negro psychological traumas would disappear, thanks to the desegregated schools. Enormous agitation was undertaken for "racially balanced schools", to the point that in order to achieve "balance", children must be transported ("bused") to the other side of town. Thereupon, a boom for private schools occured, the quality of education in many public schools deteriorated dramatically, the whites moved from the big towns, negroes moved into the cities, and segregation came back, in fact, it became more severe than it had been before. The urban "ghettos" grew larger, the tax problems of the cities became ever more severe, and violence erupted all over the country. Withal, hardly 10% of the negroes entering the labor market at 18 have received "an education reaching the job-producing standard of education for white Americans", to quote Joseph Alsop, the well-known American columnist. Yet the purpose was precisely to provide better education and improved job preparation.

The old segregated system was unsatisfactory: it provided inadequate education, though the question is not altogether cleared up whether the main fault was with the system or with the educability and the attitudes of the pupils. Be that as it may, desegregation was the predictably wrong method because, among other reasons, desegregation is an aim, not a remedy, to quote Alsop again. Whether it is a good or bad aim, it is apparent that the proponents of segregation backed the wrong method of implementing their objective, because they did not want to admit that the educational requirements of whites and negroes are *not* equal. American pragmatism lost to emotional ideologizing.

The much maligned South African policy prescribes a more realistic approach to education in a multi-racial society. At the very minimum, the South Africans deserve a fair hearing, and Americans who made a mess out of "segregation" and "desegregation" might do well to listen and to suspend their preaching.

1. In virtually all important aspects, the negro problem in the United States is fundamentally different from the problem of African populations in the Republic of South Africa. First of all, in terms of numerical relationships, the American negro does not constitute a serious, let alone a survival threat to the American white, except through the real or imaginary dangers arising from race-mixing. Disregarding the possible dysgenic effect on the whites, there is a distinct survival threat to the American negroes who, because of gradual miscegenation, may not survive as a group. By contrast, virtually all conceivable types of integration policies would gravely threaten white survival in South Africa. American theoreticians may not be disturbed by the disappearance of the American negro[4] – but their "so what" attitude, even if it were to persuade those American negroes who reportedly suffer from self-hatred, is hardly relevant to South African whites who *do* want to survive as a group. For that matter, the often evoked respect for the dignity of the American negro surely presupposes a commitment to his survival.

2. The African natives are by no means uniform. There are several Bantu groups, all speaking different, though sometimes related languages. These African peoples have enjoyed historical continuity (which the American negro lost), and all are living in

4. In fairness it should be added that the sermonizers hardly have given consideration to the possible long-range effects of their proposals.

more or less clearly delineated areas which have been their home-lands for many generations. Very small tribes may be absorbed. Some of the Bantu tribes may ultimately merge into larger Bantu peoples. A few groups are basically hostile to one another and must be expected to oppose "merging" for a long time. There are in South Africa nine Bantu peoples (or tribes) who are numbering over 100,000. The Xhosa, Zulu, South Sotho, Tswana, and Sepedi have each a population of 1 million or more, and are growing rapidly.

3. In addition to the Bantu or negro groups, there are remnants of Bushmen and Hottentots who are the true "natives" of the area. (There is in South West Africa a small white-Hottentot group, the Rehoboth Basters, who have had their own ethnic history for about three hundred years.) There are furthermore Asian Indians; and there is, notably in the Cape, a strong "coloured" group, mostly composed of a mixture between whites and Malays. All groups have their particular physical features, their own social institutions and religious traditions, and their specific psychological dispositions and abilities. The "coloured" group may not be interested in group survival, but perhaps it would be safer to say that no one really knows. The Indians do not want to mix. The Hottentots and Bush-men need and want protection of their freedom and way of life. Note that their culture is of stone-age vintage and that they have not yet progressed from the large family group or clan to the tribal type of organization.

4. Among the American negroes, there are few, if any, traces left of their tribal origin. The original languages have disappeared, without leaving any significant traces. All American negroes speak English, though many speak it with a distinct sound. Some African social and religious traditions survive, but in a strictly "Ameri-canized" form. American literature often refers to the "disorganiza-tion" of the negro family – the frequency of mother domination, of illegitimacy, of children by different fathers, and of vanishing fathers with a weak urge to work. To be sure, this sort of family life may be called "disorganized" in an American context; but it should be apparent that the American negro family exhibits many of the characteristics of matriarchal African customs. In virtually all other social aspects, the American negroes have been assimilated to the American culture, although they are deemed to have developed a

"sub-culture" of their own. They all are Christians or ex-Christians, and though large numbers still live in the Southern states and in the so-called "ghettos", they have no territorial roots and are highly migratory.

5. Unlike the American negro, the native groups in South Africa have had, without interruption, their own social, political and judicial institutions, and their own tribal self-governments. The American negro, by contrast, never had his own political structure. His recent history is not identical, but it gravely overlaps with the history of the American white society. The American negroes are socially highly stratified (which the Bantu are not), but their own social institutions, to the extent that they exist outside overall American institutions, are rudimentary and fragmented. Although American negroes have served as policemen, lawyers, judges and elected officials, the negro group as such always was subject to the white judiciary, the white legislator, and the white political executive. To be elected, a negro must be chosen jointly by negro and white voters: he must represent the "people" as a whole, and not merely his own ethnic group which, *qua* group, has no political representation. Few Americans ever reflect on this important point.

6. It would be wrong to compare the African Bantu who is living in the big South African cities to American urbanized negroes. The fundamental difference is that regardless of how many years or generations the Bantu has been living in a predominantly modern town, the "urbanized" Bantu still is not detribalized. Instead he considers himself as a full-fledged member of his tribe, with whom he maintains close contacts and whose language he speaks, although he is also fluent in Afrikaans or English. This characteristic is attributable to the fact that the Bantu societies continue as going and growing concerns, while the urbanized American negro does not hail from a distinct negro society.

7. In the United States, the differential between white and negro cultural levels is quite conspicuous. Negro "cultural deprivation" often is considered as one of the effects of segregation. Nevertheless, even at the level of the unskilled laborer, the American negro is using the same tools as the American white; he is living within the money economy; his professional life is intertwined with that of American whites; his career is dependent, in the main, on the same

factors which control the careers of whites; more often than not he is literate in a meaningful sense; and he practises the American "way of life". In South Africa, the cultural differentials are far more pronounced. Most of the Bantus still live, more or less, in a subsistence economy and within the framework of their native culture. Modern tools, practices, and techniques are coming into use, more than half of the Bantu are now literate, and an increasing number of natives are being drawn into the ambit of modern economy. But the two types of culture remain fundamentally different and wide apart, they overlap only to a limited functional degree, and while modern tools and techniques are absorbed, the native culture, despite rapid change, retains its continuity. The native outlook on life, native costumes, and the native value systems remain entirely distinct and in many ways *sui generis*.

For these reasons, and many more, even if American methods for the solution of the American negro problem were beyond argument, these methods would not be applicable to South Africa. It is theoretically conceivable that in future American methods may become more pertinent than they are at present. It is more likely that the United States, which has the excellent tradition of learning pragmatically from its own experiences, will change its current approach. It is most probable that in view of their dissimilarity, the two countries will fare best by solving their problems each in its own way.

In any event, if it is conceded that South Africans are just as highly motivated as Americans, it would seem self-evident that while indubitably the former could learn, positively or negatively, from the American experience, so just as indubitably the latter could learn from the South African experience.

At this point, the typical American ideologue usually insists that the South Africans are "racialists" who oppose the principle of equality and who want to oppress the natives. If the principle of equality is to be implemented in a realistic and not in a purely legal manner, it calls for "unequal" measures. If two persons are to be given equal opportunities, and if one person is handicapped while the other is not, equal opportunity exists only if the handicapped individual is helped more amply and by qualitatively different means. Furthermore, the principle of equality does not apply only to

325

individuals, but also to groups of individuals like ethnic groups. Thus, if one group is "behind" or handicapped while the other is not, the trailing group must be helped more amply; and if the two groups are different in attitude and aptitude, they require differential types of assistance. Legislation that distinguishes between groups does not, because of those distinctions, violate the equality principle but may implement it: e.g., a progressive tax is unequal treatment for a strictly egalitarian objective.

In a multi-ethnic state, a policy of oppression would require differential legislation, just like a policy aiming at the constructive development of all groups. To decide whether there is oppression or assistance, a mere finding that there is differential treatment is not enough. The intent of the legislation, the legislation itself, and its implementation, must be studied to determine whether the system helps or hinders progress and sustains or violates human rights.

As to the presumed South African desire to "oppress" and "exploit" the natives, it merely needs to be said that such an allegation could not be substantiated before the International Court of Justice. I think it is fair to say that even some of the judges who voted against South Africa, while they did not agree with the South African approach, nevertheless disregarded the more extreme accusations which, for that matter, were dropped by the applicants themselves. Since it would be inappropriate in this text to refute in detail the various allegations of oppression, I refer the incredulous to the voluminous pleadings before the Court. I merely wish to add that South Africa never contended its policy of separate development does not entail hardship cases, like *any* policy must that anybody can devise to handle a complicated situation. South Africa *did* show that its policy allows reasonable flexibility to handle exceptional cases and to adjust rules to changing circumstances.

The concept of "exploitation" which is bandied about frequently is derived from dubious Marxian economics. The American economy, which is the most prosperous in the world, was built upon the experience that rising wages and rising labor productivity are among the main prerequisites of economic progress. By contrast, mere subsistence wages and static labor productivity delay or preclude progress and instead of enriching the "exploiters", keep them poor. For example, the unprofitability of forced labor was

326

recognized in all societies practising such a system: only recently, after Stalin's death, the Soviet Union abolished most of the labor camps holding political opponents and slowing down Soviet economic growth. The South Africans are excellent businessmen and industrialists. They are fully aware of the need, in their own interest, to improve labor productivity and to increase the wages of the native labor force; and indeed both factors have been progressing impressively. The economic development of the native societies constitutes an enormous advantage, not a disadvantage, to the "interdependent" white society. This point does not imply that there could be no exploitation in a factory or on a farm: people everywhere tend to abuse other people. The point is that (a) an effective industrial or agricultural producer prefers high to low labor productivity; (b) the policy of the South African government is *not* to legalize exploitation but to prevent and suppress it; and (c) the South African objective is to foster the economic development of *all* groups inhabiting the Republic, not the development of one group at the expense of the others.

But what about "racialism"? Let us face this issue squarely. It is an experience as old as mankind that distinct ethnic groups who are in close contact often harbor mutual animosity. If the distinction is not merely ethnic but also racial, the animosities tend to be more virulent and more permanent. Whether such animosities are inevitable in each case; whether through suitable psychological treatment of individuals or through mass propaganda, such animosities can be prevented, reduced, or overcome; whether those animosities are ever strong enough to prevent sexual inter-group relations; and whether the antagonism always must result in hostility and violence, all this does not greatly matter. Ethnic-racial animosity exists ranging from simple lack of empathy to outright murderous hatred. It does not exist always and everywhere, but it occurs often enough and must be taken into account, if only, because a crisis rarely fails to activate it. Unfortunately, group behavior is, or in any event has been, beyond the control and even the influence of social psychologists. Tension may be reduced by skilful policies or be increased by primitive hate appeals, but such policies or "psychological treatments" merely succeed in limited alterations of existing attitudes, like a melody that is played *fortissimo* or *pianissimo*. Note that ethnic-racial tensions have been particularly low in South Africa, a country of minimum violence.

When one group, through slavery or serfdom, could avail itself of cheap labor, mostly agricultural labor, it tended to concoct theories to justify its iniquitous behavior. During the 19th century, negro slavery often was justified in the United States on the basis of alleged racial inferiority; but it was just as often, if not more frequently, defended on the basis of a twisted interpretation of the Gospels. When slavery was abolished, the fatuous arguments which supported it were forgotten, but beliefs in racial inferiority and *Untermenschentum* continue to be imputed to political opponents by some partisans of integration and race mixing. The basic situation of racial tension or lack of mutual empathy can be easily misinterpreted and every difficulty or dispute can be inflated by racialist overtones and by "scapegoating" of individuals. There are, indeed, individuals who hate the other group: this hate is primary, while the theory to "prettify" the hatred is merely apologetic. It is the "otherness" which provokes the original emotional reactions; the various hate "isms" are derivations from those emotions and serve as tools in the political power struggle.

Policy is racialist if it preserves and promotes racial antagonisms; it is invertedly racialist if it ignores existing antagonisms and animosities; and it is anti-racialist if it seeks to prevent the haters from doing damage, to circumscribe the scope of inter-racial hatred, and to remove its causes; not merely by preaching but by well thought-out political and socio-economic action.

Be it added that I did not see much evidence of race hatred in South Africa; I did see full and friendly awareness of otherness and of the mutual advantages of distance.

But for incessant "whipping boy" references, it should be unnecessary to discuss the so-called nazi race doctrine in this context. However "bad" the South Africans may be, the nazi shoe does not fit them. The nazi doctrine was applied by one white group against other white groups, not between different races. The Jews, the chief target of nazi oppression, were regarded as being good only for genocide but not suitable even for exploitation. The Jews were alleged to be a "race", but they were identified, not on the basis of racial characteristics, but on the basis of current and ancestral religious affinity. Anti-semitism was not a purely spontaneous phenomenon, but it had been cultivated over the centuries, with the basic animosity springing from a medieval religious cleavage. During the 19th century the content of anti-semitism was altered in direction of complaints about economic competition.

The decisive point is this: the nazi doctrine did not create anti-semitism, but exploited and organized pre-existing inchoate anti-semitism and intensified it to the point of extreme and criminal absurdity. If there had been no pre-existing anti-semitism, the nazi race doctrine would have had no impact. This pre-existing anti-semitism was not considered strong enough to require governmental action. In retrospect, the Weimar democracy should have taken steps to prevent the explosion. It was a mistake to ignore the problem officially until Hitler took over in 1933 and then exploited artificially inflated anti-semitic sentiments for destructive purposes. But any recognition of anti-semitism, albeit for the purpose of combating it, would have been regarded as a special kind of anti-semitism: ignore the trouble, and it will go away. Unfortunately, emotional problems are stubborn.

Policy can be designed to take advantage of hate emotions to gain power or economic advantage, or it can aim at minimizing such emotions as a hindrance to peace and progress. If the destructive policy is rejected, no constructive policy can succeed if, explicitly or implicitly, it is based on the naive assumption that inter-ethnic antagonism has no real meaning.

The recent American approach has been to deny that there are fundamental racial cleavages or to argue that those cleavages are purely artificial and manageable by educational means. The South African approach has been to accept the existence of human divergency, to recognise the overwhelming character of "otherness" – which in South Africa is fourfold, namely racial, ethnic, cultural and social – and to embark upon a course of action which is designed to forestall the further development of sentiments of animosity and politics of antagonism.

In both countries, incidentally, there have been ample experiences to show that white and black man can work together, provided the personal and private spheres of life are kept apart. This sort of "apartheid" is natural between social strata and classes: the rich and the poor, as well as educated and uneducated groups, spontaneously segregate. Hence segregation comes even more naturally if the social difference is paired with ethnic and racial distinction. One may deplore this universal human attitude and one may elect it as a target for "reconditioning"; but this attitude exists. A forceful assault on such an ingrained trait would lead to conditions similar to those brought about by the American prohibitionist experiment; even the most convinced foes of drinking no longer recommend prohibition and have reconciled themselves to the fact that most humans remain committed to the devil of alcohol.

Neither country must assume that the cleavages necessarily border on, or are identical with, hatred: not all countries could be so optimistic. But the otherness remains and so does the reluctance of the several distinct groups to mingle. The South Africans have taken this reluctance, or resistance, as the starting point of their policy. The United States has chosen instead the notion of "color blindness" which is applicable to inter-personal but not to inter-group relations and which negates the social reality of "race" (however defined in the halls of academe).[5] In fact, the U.S. presently puts great stock in the nonsensical cliché that race is merely "skin-deep" and a matter of color (i.e. a visual impression in the mind of the viewer). This may be so – but even purely ethnic differences, which lack the color distinction, are not any less real because a few professors do not regard them as "meaningful".

The recognition that there *is* race as a social reality and that in multi-racial states race is a significant factor, is not racialism.[6] The denial of race and of its potential and actual social significance is

5. Some American scientists tend to argue against the "race concept" on the grounds of scientific biology. Whatever the need for a scientific definition of race; whatever the choice between alternate and possibly mutually exclusive definitions; and assuming even that "race" may not be a useful concept for the biologist: *in social life* race is an important reality. It is quixotic to argue that race is nothing but a scientific "myth", when every observer in the street experiences the facts of race. The deductions drawn from "naive" observation may be right or wrong, or even "mythical", and if so, should be criticized; but we are in cuckoo-land when we describe common and easily verified observations as "myths".

6. Likewise, no one would argue that the recognition of the existence of social classes involves a commitment to the "class struggle", or to communism, or to the conviction that classes and class-distinctions must always be of overriding importance and necessarily exclude social peace.

nothing but upside-down racialism. It is also the denial of a fact which, as such, is "neutral".

The recognition of the fact that various races display smaller or larger numbers of trait differences is not racialism. The denial of such differences, or of the fact that most people in contact with individuals from other races are experiencing racial differences subjectively, is nothing but racialism turned upside-down.

The recognition of the fact that racial groups living in close contact with one another may have mutual or one-sided feelings of animosity which, even if dormant, may become activated during crisis situations, is not racialism. The denial of such emotions, as well as the underestimation of their frequency and possible intensity, is nothing but upside-down racialism.

The recognition of the fact that, on the statistical average, different races display different aptitudes and attitudes is not racialism, especially if those differences have been determined by the best objective methods presently available. The denial that such distinctions exist and may be (but not necessarily are) economically and politically significant, is nothing but inverted racialism.

A policy which takes racial differences into account and which aims at the co-operation and mutual interdependence *and* independence of the various racial groups is not racialism.

By contrast, racialism is a policy of fostering hostility toward the other race and of exaggerating the significance of race phenomena beyond their reasonable limits. Racialism is the denial of similarities between races (which exist in addition to dissimilarities) and the rejection of the common-sense proposition that effective co-operation between dissimilar races is possible, desirable, and necessary for the survival of all. Racialism is the denial of the right of independent group development, the imposition of artificial handicaps and hindrances, and the refusal to help in the solving of given difficulties.

But racialism *also* is the denial to any group, be they South African whites, to live their own lives in their own homeland and to be protected against eviction, swamping by massive immigration, and domination by a numerically overpowering and racially alien "majority".

Far from being racialistic, the South African policy is an attempt to get rid of racialism and to prevent and reduce antagonism and strife which arise because several races are living together. It is this very point which American observers find particularly difficult to grasp. American observers are fascinated by minor incidents or by "small apartheid" which they mistake for the South African purpose and reality. The South African "blueprint" is not yet complete; many procedures and solutions must be tested experimentally, some situations are unique and others unpredictable, there are officious bureaucrats who interpret regulations by the letter instead of by common sense, there are persons who lay traps to make the policy look ridiculous – and, yes, there are defects. Moreover, each and any policy has its costs and penalties. There is every reason to criticize mistakes, because criticism is the first step on the road to improvement. But the criticism is not valid unless it is derived from full comprehension of the overall facts. The part cannot be criticized effectively if the whole is not seen, let alone understood.

Let us probe the proposition that those who recognize the importance of race differences usually believe one cohabitating race is superior to the other, and more particularly that the "white race" is superior to all others. In order to prove such a hypothesis it would be necessary to measure 200 or more basic human traits, such as stamina, intelligence factors, and will-power. If in most or all of those measurements group A performs significantly better than group B, there exists superiority in the traits measured. If there is no overlap between the curves, so that the highest performers of B always perform below the lowest ratings of group A,[7] superiority could be considered as an established fact.

Thus, the term "superiority" has two possible precise meanings:

1. Of two groups most of whose relevant traits have been measured, most of the higher medians are achieved by one group, while the other group achieves the majority of the lower medians. 2. The measurement curves of most of the relevant traits of two groups show no overlap, with one group achieving most or all of the higher curves.

No extensive measurements of something like 200 traits have been made in comparative studies of race characteristics. The

7. There are, indeed, one or two Pygmy tribes whose tallest members are shorter than the smallest members of some Nilote tribes. This lack of overlap is entirely exceptional.

measurements which are available show, almost invariably, that there is overlap between the curves. It is most unlikely that even if all necessary trait measurements were available, all or most of the medians of group A would be below the medians of group B. It is far more likely that each group has its own characteristic share of higher medians and that many variations between medians indicate no statistically significant difference. However, the medians and several other characteristics of the curve usually differ between distinct and distant ethnic and racial groups: on the basis of the measurements accomplished to date, this statement can be made with considerable confidence.

Thus, the measurements, once made, probably will not prove across-the-board superiority of one race, but *hic et nunc* superiority of one group with respect to particular traits. There is little doubt that they also will show differential performance between several ethnic groups *within the same race*.

The measurements will confirm the observation of daily life that, statistically, the various groups differ from each other in significant traits. But the term "statistical" means that the "low" group includes high performers and the "higher" group low performers. The low performers of A and B would be "equally low" (i.e., in an intelligence test, the low performers of *all* groups range from 0-70 I.Q.), but B would have a larger number of low performers than A (e.g. 30% against 12%). Similarly, the high performers of A and B would be equally high (e.g. 120-180 I.Q.), but A would have more high performers than B (e.g. 5% against 1%). Thus, both A and B can have "geniuses" but given the same size of population, A would have higher frequency of genius (e.g. 1,000 per generation against 10).

Even if a majority of A's traits were found to be "superior", it would not follow that the present situation will be permanent and that A cannot decline or B cannot rise. Historical experience proves that the performance of ethnic groups is variable: elites may be killed or may decline, and new elites with new talents may take over. Consequently, it would be racialism to assume that current handicaps or advantages are permanent instead of being more or less temporary. It would be equally racialist to deny that traits – or performance capacities – are, within limits, subject to constructive or destructive action. Yet it is inverted racialism to refuse to admit differences against persuasive evidence of their existence and significance.

Finally, it is racialism if existing differences, whatever their nature, are used to justify aggressive policies and the withholding of political rights. Regardless of its size, talents, characteristics, and attitudes, each ethnic and racial group is entitled to live its own life, to maintain its independence, and to govern itself. By the same token, if group A wants to live with group B, but B does not want to live together with A, then the desire of B must necessarily have precedence. If both A and B want to intermingle, such a decision is within their rights also. However, such a desire must not be postulated apodictically.

The American confusions about ethnic problems are hard to explain. After World War I, the United States championed the rights of national minorities. On January 20, 1919, President Wilson asked all members of the League of Nations to obligate themselves to uphold minimum standards of minority protection. Yet on May 3, 1919, he agreed to change the relevant clause of the Versailles Treaty and to substitute protection of individuals for the protection of groups: the term "communities" was replaced by "inhabitants". The change was motivated by a desire to help newly created states in Eastern Europe to consolidate. Minority protection was weak during the 1919-1939 period; this weakness and the incessant troubles of several minorities were among the roots of World War II.

During the Pan-American conference in 1938 at Lima, the United States accepted Resolution XXVII which stated: "The system of protection of ethnical, language, or religious minorities cannot have any application whatsoever in America, where the conditions characterizing the groups known as minorities do not exist." The theory was that emigrants deliberately abandoned not only their homeland but also their original language and culture, and voluntarily opted for the culture and language of the country of their choice. If immigrant states were to make special provisions for minority groups, they could never forge national unity, or become brand-new nations composed of a new "mix" of populations, or protect themselves against internal subversion.

Granted the security interests of immigrant states, it remains doubtful to which extent an immigrant is able to abandon his heritage: there are obvious and narrow limits to re-culturation regardless of how fervently the identification with the new group may be desired. Given the fact that a non-Portuguese or non-Spanish European immigrant to South America, unless he arrives as a very young child, will retain his accent and his original language for the rest of his life, and probably will remain a cultural European, minorities of immigrants actually do come into existence and may require protection. The immigrants also need protection for the activities they want to pursue as the people they actually are. It is not implied that there has been much persecution and it is not denied that the building of immigrant states is a special task. But ignoring the reality of ethnic problems is not going to strengthen the security of any state, including an immigrant state.

Still more significant, it would seem as though the drafters of the Lima Resolution never heard of the Indian peoples or of the large negro minorities in Latin America. They must have been ignorant about Indian-negro antagonisms, the difficulties of the Asian groups in Latin America, the various newly mixed races and their tribulations, the manifold policies designed to protect and help the Indians *as groups*, and for that matter, the differences between theory and practice, creed and accomplishment even in countries which like Brazil have been highly successful with their integrationist policy. The fact blindness of the Lima Resolution is amazing and frightening.

In 1942, the doctrine was propounded by the U.S. government that the proper protection of human rights *ipso facto* would guarantee the protection of minority groups, i.e. only the individual really exists. Hence if all individuals are given their rights, the group of necessity must be in good shape. This view overlooks the need for institutions and group activities, and it neglects the complex problems of political representation.

During the Paris Peace Conference of 1946, an American representative wondered why any state should want to protect minorities instead of absorbing them. In the subsequent discussions about the Genocide Convention, the United States suggested eliminating a clause forbidding "cultural genocide", such as the suppression of language or the dispersal or absorption of ethnic groups. Yet precisely this type of crime occurs far more frequently than the (more severe) crime of physical genocide.[8]

By contrast, in 1949 an American delegate to the U.N. strongly supported international protection of minorities. On October 8, 1951, the U.S., together with Britain, submitted a draft resolution on the protection of minorities which included the right to preserve the language. But in the 1952 discussions about the right of self-determination, the United States turned around and refused to combine provisions for self-determination with protection of minority rights. The United States turned again in 1956 and took the position that immigrant groups, like all other minority groups, are entitled to preserve their language and culture: it would be a violation of fundamental human rights if this were not allowed. On American insistence a sentence, to the effect that immigrant groups are not entitled to consider themselves as minorities, was dropped from a draft resolution on discrimination in education.[9] These frequent shifts hardly would have occurred if the U.S. had had a thoroughly considered policy on the subject.

American practice at home has been very liberal and, as a matter of course, has tolerated all activities which the minority groups wanted to organize and finance themselves. There was no active support, except by and large for the Indians and negroes, but there was full toleration and in recent times ample opportunity to benefit fully from the welfare state. However, in many of its activities within the United Nations, the U.S. has taken the rather reactionary line of arguing for the absorption of minority groups. Certainly, there are situations where such absorption is feasible and desired by all the groups concerned. But the American experience has demonstrated that assimilation is not feasible in every case; and that assimilation is a protracted process even under optimal conditions. Other experiences have shown that assimilation aborts if

8. There also is a crime of "psychological genocide" – operations to change the psychological make-up of a group by breaking its continuity; the crime does not consist in the introduction of new communications and techniques but in suppressing existing traits, instead of allowing them to adjust spontaneously to new conditions and achieve a new synthesis. Slavery, abduction, and disruption of tribal cohesion resulted in something close to psychological genocide of the American negro.

9. See Heinz Kloss, *Das Nationalitaetenrecht der Vereinigten Staaten von Amerika*, Wien-Stuttgart, Braumueller, 1963, pp. 319-326.

coercion is applied. It is certainly also true that there are situations where minorities may endanger the unity and security of a state. If so, the minority cannot be absorbed anyway, and the real question is whether the multi-ethnic state must be transformed into a federal structure or be partitioned, or whether the troublesome minority should be resettled.

The notion that entirely different and even antagonistic groups can be merged rapidly into a new and stable "nation" completely misses the nature of ethnos and nation: every state has a population but not every state population is a nation.[10] American authors tend to defend centralized states ruling multi-ethnic populations. But they usually are ignorant of the ethnic facts. If they support unitary rule over multi-ethnic diversity, their argument runs counter to the American philosophy of federation.

Assimilation through the subtle forces of education and economic division of labor may work in those instances where the "distance" between the groups is short, where the consciousness of ethnic identity is weak, where the groups are socially and culturally not cohesive, and where they do not enjoy a territorial contiguity but are intermingled. However, the longer the "distance", the more time is needed. At the end of the process, all involved groups would be changed: the weaker groups would be fully absorbed, whereas the stronger "surviving" groups would be merely modified. For the willingly absorbed groups assimilation means geno-suicide. If assimilationist policies are pursued against resistance, and against the obstacle of very great cultural and biological group "distances", such a policy is tantamount to an attempt at cultural genocide, that is the wilful destruction of an ethnic group *as a group* but not as a set of individuals.

In terms of outcome, it does not matter much whether the process is one of brute force or whether more imperceptible methods are

10. U.S. practice of talking about the "nations" of Ghana, Tanzania or the Congo won't change basic ethnic facts: these and other black African states are inhabited by numerous and different ethnic groups; there are no such nations, let alone nations composed of incompatible ethnic groups; most African states are artificial and cannot possibly be or become "nation-states"; and most of them are in the hands of one or a few predominant ethnic groups which, usually, are oppressing the weaker groups and are trying to "assimilate", i.e. absorb and dissolve those tribes. In the long run, many of the "unitary" black states will not survive, because they do not correspond to ethnic realities.

used. To be sure, in the milder processes the individual would be preserved, and his heredity may linger on. But members of dying communities are denied the right and opportunity to pursue their happiness. One well-known, very "liberal" American anthropologist writing about the Bushmen calmly anticipated their disappearance: they just don't fit the modern world. But who says so? Even if they do not fit the pattern – or precisely because they don't – do they not need protection? The treatment of the American Indian, who did not fit the modern world either, was one of direct force plus indirect force like corruption and economic trickery (e.g. the buying of Manhattan for 60 guilders). It entailed the destruction of Indian peoples, including the most talented ones, who might have had a great future. The "new deal" put the Indians on their feet again. But this lesson has not been learned and it has not been applied to the handling of the negro problem and to American foreign policy.

It is self-evident that Americans and the U.S. government do not desire or tolerate genocide in any form, shape or manner, and are justifiably incensed when their moral purposes are doubted. There is no intent whatever to question, let alone deny, American moral integrity. By the same token, Americans must learn not to question, largely on *a priori* doctrinal grounds, the moral integrity of the South Africans. Americans also must familiarize themselves with the contradictions, implications and dangers of the policies they are preaching all over the world. A matter like genocide, even if unintended, cannot be ignored or argued away with rhetoric. The duty is to foresee and to prevent.

The South African policy of separate development is based on the following fundamental propositions:

1. The deliberate destruction, through integrationist policies or as a by-product of uncontrolled development, of ethnic groups, their identities and cultures is a form of genocide and therefore unacceptable.

2. There is no obvious advantage which the integrationist or assimilationist approach offers to the groups concerned, provided they do not – all of them – want to lose their ethnic identity. The protection of human rights does not require assimilation. On the contrary, deliberate integration may violate basic human rights.

3. A policy of mere ethnic toleration within the framework of human rights is not adequate as a method of group protection. Instead of mere toleration, ethnic policy must be aimed at the strengthening of ethnic identity, the stabilization and survival of ethnic entities, and the activation of the cultural and economic development of ethnic groups as such.

4. Like any ethnic group anywhere in the world, the ethnic groups living in South Africa have – all of them – the unquestioned and inalienable right to live their own lives, to survive, and to grow on the basis of their own traditions and desires. Many of these South African groups can be expected to accomplish considerable progress and to modernize their own cultures.

5. Each ethnic group is self-governing and the scope of its responsibilities grows together with its development. If one or the other group does not want to remain within an overall multi-ethnic state, but become entirely independent, or merely wishes to preserve loose associational ties, South Africa would interpose no objection.

6. Each individual is a voter within, and only within, his own ethnic group, just as an American only votes as an American. Similarly, a Zulu has no voting rights among the Sothos, a Xhosa cannot vote within the white community, and a white is not a voter in the Transkei. The completion of the present effort of creating "Bantustans" will give real substance to this system of self-government.[11] To vote the voter need not be in his homeland but can vote, like Americans can, through absentee ballot. This fundamental principle is eminently sound, even if there are confusions and rough spots in execution, such as difficulties of classifying urbanized individuals as to their proper ethnic affiliation. The system, ultimately, would seem to require an overarching multi-ethnic legis-

11. The slow development of the "Bantustans" often is criticized and sometimes interpreted as a symptom of "bad faith". Actually, the speed of the progress is underrated and goes largely unreported, e.g. the establishment of the Transkei was barely mentioned in the U.S. press and but for one South African "ad" in some key newspapers might have passed entirely unnoticed. The speed of orderly development depends (a) on the level reached by the native group, (b) on resources available, and (c) on the speed of the preparatory planning which, for many material reasons, cannot be accelerated too fast. Precipitate development precludes orderly process.

lature and genuinely joint executive organs to provide for the common functions.

7. The assimilation of the different ethnic and racial groups living in the Republic of South Africa is not practical in the present situation, nor – probably – in the distant future. Even if all the groups concerned were to agree on integration in some form, many generations and centuries would elapse before the cultural levels would be substantially equalized and a still longer time before the "melting pot" could finish its work. In the meantime, the cohabitation of the disparate groups must be regulated for their mutual benefit.

8. Each group must be protected *qua* group and community, as though it must be preserved for a splendid national future as a modern nation.

9. The right of each ethnic group to live its own life and to survive is entirely independent of the size of that group. This right of group survival is inalienable, whether the group is only 1,000 head strong or forms a large people. It applies to the Bushmen who have not yet reached the tribal stage; to the Bantus some groups of whom may merge into nations; to the Asian Indians who probably will remain local minorities; and to the whites who have grown into a solidly structured nation of the Western type.

I shall skip consideration of the fact that some African political movements, especially those with communist sympathies, advance "integrationist" slogans for South Africa in order to conquer the country and drive out the white South Africans.

In brief, active development of each group is the distinguishing hallmark of the South African policy. This policy goes beyond the tradition of "granting" self-determination[12] in that it protects and strengthens the various ethnic groups, enables them to become truly

12. Although "passive", the American policy is quite generous as the Puerto Rican example shows. The Puerto Ricans are free to choose full independence, or commonwealth association status, or statehood in the Union, except that the U.S. Congress may reject statehood and cancel association. Under the commonwealth status, the Puerto Ricans do not have voting representation in Congress and do not vote for President. They enjoy the enormous triple advantage of free immigration, no federal income taxes, and eligibility for receiving federal subventions; in addition they levy their own import duties. The Puerto Ricans have the best of two worlds – the case cannot therefore serve as a model that can be universally imitated.

independent, prepares them for a genuinely free choice of their political status, and during this transitory period systematically provides for their participation in economic and cultural progress. The objection has been raised that the preservation of separate ethnic groups must result in "balkanization" and necessarily precludes the emergence of strong centralized states. This is the same type of thinking which denies that there should be minorities in immigrant countries; the same argument also serves to justify expansionist policies. Ethnic diversity is not incompatible with effective statecraft, provided the state is non-aggressive. Even if diversity were to lower governmental efficiency, is the requirement of a uniform state overriding? Must such a requirement be satisfied at the cost of direct or indirect genocide? Must the uniform state necessarily be a large state? Must the large state necessarily be a uniform state?

Obviously, the state must be fitted to the community to which it belongs. A large group will have a large state, a small group a small state, and a dispersed group must be politically organized in a different way from a group living together in a contiguous area. A tribe needs a political structure that differs from the structure of a proto-nation which, in turn, differs from that of a stabilized nation. An area populated by several groups which have not stabilized yet, needs more flexible and diversified political arrangements than an area inhabited by fully formed nations.

Some areas, like the entire African continent, are characterized by enormous ethnic diversity. The twin concepts of the unitary-large state and the nation-state therefore remain inapplicable.

During recent years, the rights of small and very small states have been strengthened. If the dwarf state has a reason to exist, the small ethnic group has a still stronger right; both small states and small ethnic groups are capable of independence. Naturally, independence is not the only objective an ethnic group or a state must pursue. The people also must be able to live and prosper, and for this purpose they must have access to resources and export and labor markets. Mankind has been smart enough to invent solutions to take care of such problems – solutions which range flexibly from various forms of autonomy via federation, confederation, association, protective treaties, and customs unions, to common markets. There are dozens of methods by which disparate ethnic groups of

341

various sizes can join together within one state structure especially designed to handle the peculiar problems of the particular area. Within such an overarching state, each group must be allowed to use its own language, preserve and develop its own culture, inhabit its own territory, or in case of dispersal practise its autonomy – all enjoying self-government, all collaborating economically, and each citizen possessing his political, civil and human rights.

In some instances, an overarching common state is desirable and practicable, in others desirable and impracticable, and in still others undesirable. The self-governing ethnic groups should be able to join and also to secede; and each group needs suitable representation and protective institutions. The policy of separate development which calls for an effective and mutually satisfactory combination of ethnic self-government, inter-ethnic co-operation, cultural continuity, and structural flexibility embodies a concept that is far more suitable to the African continent than the fictions of African "nations", African "nation-states", "negritude", cultural assimilation, and political integration on the basis of electoral systems that work only under conditions of ethnic uniformity. U.S. policy toward black Africa would be far more successful if it were to give the ethnic factor its full weight.

The recent battle cry in the United States for "black power" should make this entire complex increasingly comprehensible to the American observer. This slogan had initially a clearly revolutionary and violent meaning; and some foolish young people still are trying to incite American negroes to take up arms against the whites.[13] But

13. Some of the spokesmen for negro violence are clearly Maoist in orientation. One speaker for the Black Panther Party talks this language:
"It was explained to the brothers that they as youth who have been resisting oppression across this country must develop a tactic and unite around something practical, and that the only practical thing that a people can unite around to win their liberation is the gun." The Black Panther Party "understands the necessity of uniting around the gun, arming ourselves in self-defence in all areas of racist oppression . . . We must use strategically applied tactics with the gun, and let this racist white power structure know . . . that we intend to change the adverse conditions that we are subjected to." The speaker then gave his definitions of black power. "Political power comes through the barrel of a gun." (This is an exact quote from Mao Tse-tung.) The speaker added: "If we organize and use gun power in a strategic fashion against a racist power structure, the power structure then becomes aware of the fact that we have been correctly educated on the true

gradually a new meaning of the slogan has been emerging. Despite the groans from the integrationists and many others who misinterpret the concept of "America, one and indivisible", "black power" – in the non-violent and constructive sense – is not at all alien to the American tradition.

The truth of the matter is that the American negroes, more than 22 million of them, have been quite powerless and have been unable to defend their rights and interests effectively. The U.S. government has established and supported special universities for negroes. Despite all the desegregation talk those universities, which have fine traditions, have not been abolished. Higher education creates "black power" and negro doctors, lawyers, engineers, businessmen, artists, journalists and writers constitute "black power". "Black power" could have been created under a system of school segregation if those schools had been designed to develop the negro potential. This might have happened if the negro community had organized itself to run and supervise the educational activities of concern to themselves. Had such school control organizations become effective, they could have formed the nucleus of "black power" in the communities. Conversely, desegregation does not necessarily create "black power": it rather points in the opposite direction. Desegregation certainly will not strengthen the negro community if it is not accompanied by qualitatively better education – which so far it is not.[14]

understanding of politics." "Now if we want to exercise black power, we do not go out and have a lay-in in this kind of situation . . . We do not have a ride-in, we do not have a roll-in or step-ins. All these 'ins' have been exhausted. The only thing that we can do now, brothers and sisters, is get our guns organized, forget the 'ins' and shoot it out. Organize with the tactics to be taught by the Black Panther Party for self-defence. It would be practical to start getting our guns right away so we can defend ourselves righteously . . . And while we are surviving every day in our struggle, remember when you rip something off, steal from the white man, snatch whatever you can, you are dealing with real politics." (*San Francisco Examiner*, July 21, 1967, page 12.) Considering the disparity in strength, Maoist-type violence does not seem to be very promising for the American negro.

14. In the school district of Washington, D.C. which has been desegregated since 1954 (and which, for this very reason, had 91% negro pupils in 1967), teaching was offered along four "tracks". This arrangement, an American adaptation of a system used almost universally, served to provide maximal educational benefits to the "slow learners" *and* to the "fast learners", and also prepared talented pupils

343

Despite current misinterpretations of the U.S. constitution, there is nothing wrong with the idea that negroes should live together with other negroes, and whites with other whites. The ethnic groups tend to live separately, anyway. Under the American system, freedom of choice should be guaranteed both to those who desire togetherness and to those who don't. It is entirely true, however, that negro housing and slums are deplorable. Is this exclusively the result of poverty, as it is asserted often? The U.S. negro has a higher average family income than virtually all Europeans and the Japanese. Is this the fault of white exploitation or neglect, as the "civil rights leaders" never tire to affirm? The white racists, by contrast, blame the negroes for self-neglect and believe the slums were created by the negroes themselves.

Those simple answers are unsatisfactory: there are more general and complex causes.

For example: there are no negro construction firms; there are very few negro house-owners and few landlords; and there are only a few negro real estate firms and mortgage banks. The negro community could and should have made itself "independent" from the white real estate structure. Since there is no structured or organic negro community and only a "sum" of negro individuals, the federal and state governments, partly for the purpose of community building, should have helped in the development of negro business. To the extent that such business had come into existence, it would have constituted "black power".[15]

An old Frisian proverb has it: "If everybody sweeps in front of his own door steps, certainly the whole town is clean." But negroes often don't sweep before their own front doors, because their housing is not owned by them and their sense of private property has not been aroused, because their business and credit relations are not

for college. This sensible system was abolished in 1967 by court decision. It had been opposed by many negro "civil rights leaders", yet since those "leaders" never won an election, no one knows whether they really speak for the negro community. In any event, this quixotic action hurts the negroes.

15. The South African government is helping Bantus to establish their own businesses – the program is quite effective and proves that negroes can become successful businessmen. The U.S. government, instead of expecting wonders from "protests" and demonstrations, should learn this lesson and help negro business in a businesslike fashion.

344

with other negroes, and because the negroes don't have their own political community organizations which would enforce discipline. Unlike the Chinese who are administering their communities without incorporating them as public bodies, the negroes never got organized as communities and never elected their own spokesmen – and the American authorities never encouraged such a development.

It was inevitable, therefore, that negro housing was not improved, that new houses and government-provided low-rent quarters deteriorated speedily, that many types of community facilities never were provided, that crime became ever more rampant, and that rabble-rousers, demagogues, homegrown and imported revolutionaries have achieved undue influence over the American negroes, despite the fact that those people are fundamentally conservative and in their majority desire to lead an orderly life.

There has been a great deal of negro unemployment and it is very true that the unemployment rates for the negro are far higher than for the American white.[16] The solutions that were attempted to take care of this problem, notably "fair employment" legislation and pressure on business firms to hire negroes whether they need them or not, cannot possibly work. The Chinese understood the economic aspects of "discrimination" and set themselves up in such a way that they were not overly dependent upon business cycles and upon the whims of white hiring and firing personnel. The many Chinese restaurants, tailors, laundries, food stores, truck gardens, and the numerous firms which are exclusively serving the Chinese community, not to mention cultural enterprises, radio stations and even banks, plus the Chinese insistence on learning, education and manners, have made that community self-reliant and protect it against discrimination in employment.

The American negroes have not created, or are merely at the beginning of creating, businesses of their own. If there were many

16. American unemployment figures are not based on actual counts but on "samples" and tend to be inflated. Against this high unemployment, the comparatively higher public contributions to the negroes must be taken into account. There were in the U.S. during 1966 7.3 million persons on relief, including 3.5 million children and their 900,000 mothers and 150,000 fathers (of whom two-thirds are incapacitated). A racial breakdown is not available but the figures suggest that, at a very minimum, 10% of negro mothers are on relief and are using motherhood as a source of income.

negro firms, there would be "black power". If there were structured negro communities, there would be ever more negro business; and if there were more business, there would be stronger communities and a real capacity for self-help. After all, in terms of population and income, the U.S. negro group is "equivalent" to Belgium and Holland combined. But unlike the South African government, the U.S. government has not contributed much to the development of a negro entrepreneurial class. Such an effort falls outside the sphere of the fashionable cliché.

In summer of 1967, the "Congress of Racial Equality" (CORE), which had been a "multi-racial organization", reconstituted itself as "a mass membership organization to implement the concept of black power for black people."[17] CORE called for negro business in negro neighbourhoods, for black labor unions, and for a negro political party. It is useful to quote the new CORE philosophy:

The civil rights movement of ten years ago no longer exists. Black people recognize that access to lunch counters doesn't solve their larger problems. In order to enjoy full citizenship, black people must participate actively in the economic and political life of the nation. To do so, they must organize. That organization must be their own.

In the past, there was pressure from black people demanding their rights as citizens – with occasional accommodation by whites. Misguided attempts were made by well-meaning people to moderate even this minimal pressure, in order to disrupt the system as little as possible. There has been virtually no initiative on the part of the whites.

Where were the whites who recognized the injustice of the situation of the black man in hard, realistic terms? Where were the white parents organized to provide equal educational opportunity for

17. Floyd B. McKissick, National Director, CORE, in a letter to the *New York Times* of July 18, 1967, tried to explain this turn away from multi-racialism: "The CORE constitution is years old and needs revision. A constitutional convention is being called later this year for that purpose. One provision, as heretofore interpreted, required chapters to have a multi-racial membership. New chapters are now being organized in ghetto areas where black people are likely to be the only applicants for membership. It would be ridiculous to deny affiliation to these chapters because they don't have a token white member." This is unconvincing because white members can be easily recruited.

black children? Where were the white unions organized to end discrimination in employment? Where were the white housing experts and home-owners' associations organized to create quality integrated housing and end illegal slums? Where were the white organizations formed to create a welfare system consonant with the high-flown principles so frequently addressed to us?

With rare exceptions, these white organizations have not existed. Where they have existed, they have been tiny and largely ineffective minorities in the white power structure ... Since the initiative rests with the black community, the aims of the present movement and its policies must be controlled by that community. Too often in the past well-meaning white people have attempted to exercise policy functions in the movement. Through lack of understanding and divergence of aims, much of their effort was misplaced.

The Irish, Jews and Puritans all developed their own movement and their own leaders. Black people in America are developing theirs ... The days when the movement was controlled by white college boys, great as they were, are over.

The new CORE policy was described as a "backward leap toward segregation" and was held to be as unreasonable, among other reasons, because a negro political party could succeed only in a few counties.[18]

This is true enough, and CORE took, at least partly, the wrong road, especially since they did not draw a line against violence. Yet the argument that negroes should not establish their own political party because they cannot win elections is singularly obtuse: of course they can't, *but only* because the American electoral system was built for a "uniform" society and does *not* function well for the purposes of a multi-ethnic society. A uniform system necessarily and inevitably suppresses the ethnic minority. For this very reason, a multi-ethnic society needs electoral provisions to ensure the repre-

18. There is now operating a Mississippi Freedom Democratic Party "which will not support a white candidate who does not openly offer concessions to negroes." There also are negro candidates for office in predominantly negro counties in Mississippi. But they are running into the difficulty that "some negroes don't think other negroes are capable of holding office." (The *Washington Post*, July 17, 1967, p. A7.)

sentation of minorities and to prevent majoritarian tyranny.[19] This is the main lesson of innumerable national struggles, which the U.S. affects to ignore.

To be sure, the U.S. electoral system is what it is and it would be very difficult and time-consuming to change it. Yet those are no reasons why the American negroes, a clearly marked separate ethnic group, do not need their own negro representation. They definitely need their own political structure and their own leadership whom they can trust, especially in a time of crisis.[20] With a little imagination, insight and goodwill some sort of negro self-government could be arranged without upsetting the basic American system but providing it with more flexibility. It is now widely recognized that "communications" must be kept "open to all minority groups so problems can be solved as they arise",[21] instead of piling up. But who should communicate with whom? The negroes have no elected spokesmen. This fact, too, begins to dawn on some people, as an editorial in the *Washington Post* of July 17, 1967, clearly shows. This editorial is particularly remarkable since the *Washington Post*

---

19. This principle, in its territorial application, is the *raison d'être* for the American Senate and is underlying the system governing elections to the Senate. (Note that there are barely any attempts to find out, for example through opinion polling, what American negroes are thinking).

20. The big riots during July 1967 in Newark, N.J., took place in a town about half of whose population is negro. The city is considered the most integrated town in the U.S., with negroes holding high positions in the city government, easy "communications" about grievances, and a large and growing negro middle class. Yet it also has a population density of 18,000 per square mile, overcrowded schools, 15% negro unemployment, and 99% of its policemen allegedly are white. Self-styled negro leaders asserted that the city's negroes "all are fed up with broken promises and do-nothing attitudes existing for so many years." A negro prominent in civil rights and poverty programs, acknowledged "there has been constant dialogue with the city administration prior to the unfortunate events of the past few days. But nothing, nothing, nothing ever came from it," he said, pounding his desk. "It was entirely sterile and only heightened the feeling of hopelessness and frustration". It took 2,000 National Guardsmen, 200 State troopers and 1,400 policemen to subdue the rioters who fought under the battle cry: "Kill white devils." (*U.S. News and World Report*, July 24, 1967, p. 6; and *San Francisco Examiner and Chronicle*, July 16, 1967, Section A, p.4). Casualties were 27 dead and more than 1,200 wounded. There were 1,316 arrested and more than 15 million dollars in property damage. (*San José Mercury News*, July 23, 1967, p.3F.)

21. Editorial in *San José Mercury*, July 19, 1967, p. 14.

has been in the forefront of the integrationists and of the anti-South African front:

The remedy begins, of course, with the restoration of order, and the strengthening of social programs to do what they can. But it will also require, no doubt, changes in the style of city government in this country. Highly centralized, impersonal government does not work to the benefit of the slums; the governments of the big cities will now, if they are wise, consider the advantage of very substantial decentralization. The present theory of political representation appears to be defective; for the people who have rioted in Newark, and dozens of other American cities, clearly feel themselves utterly unrepresented and impotent in their city governments. These rioters differ from most rioters throughout history in that they believe themselves harmed little by the worst of defeats and benefited little by the best of successes. The expression of this despair is a highly unusual style of riot that becomes not only wantonly destructive, but profoundly self-destructive.

The troubles created by current policies are best illustrated by "a self-portrait of Newark taken from the Model Neighbourhood Program of the Department of Housing and Urban Development":

Among major American cities, Newark and its citizens face the highest percentage of substandard housing, the most crime per 100,000 of population, the heaviest per capita tax burden, the sharpest shifts in population and the highest rate of venereal disease, new cases of tuberculosis and maternal mortality. In addition, Newark is second among major cities in population density, second in infant mortality, second in birth rate, seventh in absolute number of drug addicts and has a rate of unemployment persistent enough and high enough to make it one of only five cities in the nation qualified for special assistance under the Economic Development Act . . . Three out of every four public school children in the city are either negro or Puerto Rican . . . the percentage of negroes now living in Newark is an open and active question. Estimates range from a low of 40 per cent to a high of 60 per cent . . .

Here is what Newark's Model Neighbourhood application had to say about the city's school:

A yearly turnover rate of 44 per cent, a cumulative 1962-66

dropout rate in grades 9-12 of 32 per cent,[22] one-half of the pupils in the sixth grade reading 18 months below the national average, one-third of new pupils each year being new arrivals to Newark . . .

Tom Wicker, a reporter for the *New York Times*, explained that: Newark has not ignored these problems. It was one of the first cities to get and use anti-poverty money. It has pushed hard for public housing and urban renewal projects and has a good statistical record in these fields. It has one of the few welfare work experience programs in the nation and established the first Neighbourhood Youth Corps . . . But Newark's negroes, who hold the balance of political power, have not exercised it because of a lack of unity and effective leadership; only two negroes sit on the board of nine councilmen and when another ran for mayor last year, he came in third. The lack of negro leadership has allowed a basically white political structure to remain in power . . . As a result, the majority of the populace feels itself ignored and abused in the city's management as well as its economy and society . . . Newark's leaders tried to meet its problems, but they did not really understand its people, and that ought to be the lesson for every other city trying to avoid Newark's tragedy.[23]

On their part, the negroes drew quite different lessons. Meeting in torn-up Newark, a four-day National Conference on Black Power, attended by more than 1,000 delegates representing almost every faction of the negro community, adopted a series of resolutions of a militant "separatist" character. No whites were permitted at any of the sessions.

A deep distrust of white society was evident as the delegates cheered through proposals to set up permanent contacts with African nations; independent, black-controlled political parties or voting blocs, and gear the products of negro artists and professionals more closely to the need of black people . . . "Black people do not

---

22. To keep balance it may be mentioned that in 1967 15 out of 1,000 American negroes attended college and university, against 11 in 1963. Average European university enrolment is 7 out of 1,000. (*U.S. News and World Report*, July 31, 1967, p. 84f.) Since there are no "colleges" on the continent, the figures are not comparable and the extent of European education is understated.

23. Tom Wicker, "Newark made a Try, Misunderstood People", *San José Mercury News*, July 23, 1967, p. 2F.

wish to be absorbed into the white community. Our interests are in conflict."[24]

Many delegates argued against accepting American culture for the negro.

The Conference did not place much stock in federal aid but emphasized what the negroes can do for themselves. The various resolutions called for a "black university", a "black national holiday", black financial institutions, refusal to accept birth control programs, a school for black political organizers, a political force independent of the major parties, and "a black militia" to train black families in all aspects of self-defence and racial survival.

I will disregard resolutions dealing with the Vietnam war and also ignore the obvious "people's war" aspects of others, not to mention resolutions of an outspokenly anti-Christian character. To Americans the most surprising resolution was one which called for "starting a national dialogue on the desirability of partitioning the United States into two separate nations, one white and one black."[25] This resolution was enthusiastically supported.

If this is not acceptance of "apartheid" by the most advanced negro group in the world – what is it? It should be observed, however, that there are numerous reasons to consider the partition idea as utterly impracticable in the United States. Nor is it necessary to give to autonomy a predominantly territorial meaning. It is entirely feasible to set up autonomy, or some sort of ethnic self-management, on a personal instead of territorial basis. The concept was developed and successfully tried at the beginning of the century in Austro-Hungary but has remained unknown in the United States.

This is not the place to discuss and evaluate solutions to the problems besetting the American negro. Suffice it to say that the bankruptcy of the old clichés is becoming painfully obvious. In the face of some 60 "black rebellions" between July 1964 and July 1967[26] and an "unpublicized listening post" in the Justice Department to

24. *San Francisco Examiner*, July 24, 1967, p. 8.
25. According to another version, America is to be partitioned into a "homeland for black Americans and a homeland for white Americans." (*San José Mercury*, July 24, 1967, p. 2).
26. *San Francisco Examiner*, July 21, 1967, p. 12.

provide an "early warning system" on "ghetto violence",[27] the assimilationist prescription is found sadly wanting.

Is looting the main purpose of the lawlessness? The editorialist of the *Washington Post* describes it as the "most curious aspect" of negro slum riots that, to an "extraordinary extent" they have been "not revolutionary or homicidal, but purposeless and suicidal." Roy Wilkins, a negro and executive director of the National Association for the Advancement of Colored People, explained: "The people who actually take part in it (the riots) do not expect to gain anything that way. They only want to call attention to the problems." Wilkins opposes rioting. Negro psychologist Kenneth Clark (whose one-sided testimony impressed the Supreme Court in 1954) said seemingly "suicide" riots by negroes in their own neighborhoods were an attempt to show that they want their ghettoes destroyed. "I would suggest the hypothesis that in some unconscious, or maybe not so unconscious, incoherent way the rioting people are saying, we want this destroyed. See? They're saying, you know, it's the only way that we'll get change." He added the "horror" of the riots was that society was so arranged that "the only way they could seem to get some thrill out of living was by destruction."[28]

U.S. Attorney General Ramsey Clark called the "idea of an internal racial war . . . an exaggeration" but admitted "the threat of widespread conflict between negroes and whites is very serious and must be dealt with."[29] Pathetically, negro Charles Evers, an

---

27. *San José Mercury*, July 15, 1967, p. 24. This post also is referred to as a "situation room" and "war room". The "systematic collection of riot data" was expected to "show a pattern that would make the flashpoint incidents predictable. It didn't." "The potential for riots . . . is present in almost every big city." The "situation" in the U.S. might be confronted with a statement by Anglican Bishop C. Edward Crowther who was deported from South Africa. The *Washington Post* (July 17, 1967 p. A6) reported Bishop Crowther as saying "that since there were no peaceful democratic means for non-white South Africans to better their circumstances, he could not be optimistic about the avoidance of bloodshed. When asked if there were any indications of possible violence, he said we have only to look at history to see that an oppressed group will eventually use what means it can for change." In other words, he could not help but admit that there is no bloodshed in South Africa.

28. The *Washington Post*, July 17, 1967, p. A9.

29. *Ibid.*

352

organizer of NAACP, whose brother Medgar was slain by a negro-hater, expressed the innermost utopian wish of most American negroes: "They say I want to become a member of the white man's world. Of course, I do – that's what my brother died for."

The polarization of negro thinking is thus complete. It cannot be gainsaid that *both* the proponents of passing into the "white man's world" and of black power are in part motivated by self-destructive urges. The situation is not only unfortunate but fraught with extreme danger. It is naive to assume that the enemies of the United States will not try to explode a social fission bomb that is handed to them free of charge. I am not pessimistic and I do not believe that catastrophe is unavoidable. But it is necessary to think about race and ethnic problems in a fresh way.

Since thinking is disarrayed, how could society not be in disorder? Edmund Burke left us this wise counsel: "Never, no, never, did Nature say one thing and Wisdom say another."

Appendix

TABLE 1 Southern Africa Inter-African Trade

Southern Africa: Matrix of Merchandise Imports and Exports, 1964—(R1,000)

Export / Imports	Rep. of S.A.	Rhodesia	Malawi	Zambia	Angola	Mocambique	Botswana	Lesotho	Swaziland	S.W.A.	Rest of World	Total
Rep. of S.A.	X	59,894	1,089	32,312	2,153	18,286	4,665	15,210	15,770	126,000	863,036	1,138,415
Rhodesia ..	21,955	X	14,459	81,465	451	2,335	3,964	7	96	120	169,366	294,218
Malawi ..	1,561	3,262	X	915	—	248	6	—	9	1	18,140	24,142
Zambia ..	20,263	10,793	972	X	14	62	102	—	4	34	317,174	349,418
Angola ..	1,308	112	7	925	X	2,137	—	—	—	—	154,613	158,436
Mocambique	7,083	2,754	460	52	2,465	X	—	—	150	—	69,197	82,161
Botswana ..	4,069	658	—	311	—	—	X	—	—	—	5,135	10,173
Lesotho ..	4,940	3	—	—	—	—	—	X	—	—	257	5,200
Swaziland ..	9,759	130	—	95	—	74	—	—	X	—	12,637	22,695
S.W.A. ..	75,483	112	—	43	—	—	—	—	—	X	87,235	146,773
Rest of World	1,519,167	143,672	11,477	42,586	122,195	98,115	592	1,683	2,971	13,845	X	1,956,303
Total	1,665,488	221,390	28,464	158,038	127,278	121,257	9,329	16,900	19,000	140,000	1,696,790	4,203,934

1. Source: Dr G. Leistner, in Tegnikon, March 1967, p. 22.

TABLE II *Expenditure on Social Services*

Expenditure by Some Africa Authorities on Social Services[1]
In Rand,[2] per head of the population[3]

NATURE OF SERVICE	South Africa	Kenya	Ma-lawi-	Ni-geria	Ugan-da	Sudan	Tan-zania
	1964/65	1964/65	1965	1962/63	1964/65	1964/65	1964/65
	R	R	R	R	R	R	R
Education	2.07	1.38	1.04	1.13	2.06	0.98	1.68
Health	6.19	.57	0.25	0.45	1.09	0.75	0.63
Housing	1.86⎫	0.71	0.16	0.56	0.39	2.17	0.54
Other social services	3.58⎭						
Total	13.70	2.66	1.45	2.14	3.54	3.90	2.85

1. The particulars of the other African states have been calculated from official budget figures which appear in the U.N. statistical yearbook for 1965. It is clear that South Africa's per capita expenditure is the highest in all respects. The Republic's total expenditure on social services (R13.7 per head) is more than nine times as high as Malawi's, and more than three times greater than the Sudan's (R3.90), which is the highest of the other countries shown above.

2. 1R = $1.4

3. Only the Bantu population has been included in the case of South Africa but the total population in the case of other countries.

TABLE III *Earnings of Foreign Bantu in South Africa*[1]

Country of birth	Sector of employment/Form of renumeration								
	Agriculture		Mining‡		Other industries		Total		
	Cash	In kind	cash	In kind	Cash	In kind	Cash	In kind	Total
Lesotho	4,914	2,495	12,213	10,827	10,832	434	27,959	13,755	41,714
Botswana	1,560	792	3,737	3,337	3,539	141	8,836	4,270	13,106
Swaziland	546	277	1,179	1,049	1,312	128	3,037	1,454	4,491
Sub-total: Former High Commission Territories..	7,020	3,564	17,129	15,213	15,683	703	39,832	19,480	59,312
Rhodesia	624	317	2,322	2,093	1,676	211	4,622	2,621	7,243
Zambia	234	119	1,327	1,196	670	84	2,231	1,399	3,630
Malawi	1,170	594	4,312	3,887	2,807	352	8,289	4,833	13,122
Mocambique	1,950	990	17,358	15,900	1,598	175	20,906	17,065	37,971
Other	234	119	6,027	5,606	157	6	6,418	5,731	12,149
Sub-total Other foreign countries..	4,212	2,139	31,346	28,682	6,908	828	42,466	31,649	74,115
Total	11,232	5,703	48,475	43,895	22,591	1,531	82,298	51,129	133,427

1. Source: G. M. Leistner, "Foreign Bantu Workers in S.A.", South African Journal of Economics, March 1967, p. 51.

TABLE IV *Population Growth in Africa*

POPULATION GROWTH IN AFRICA	Population Mid. 1966 est. (millions)	Yearly increase 1958–1964 per cent	Number of years to double	Birth rate per 1,000	Mortality rate per 1,000	Population Estimate 1980 (millions)
SOUTHERN AFRICA						
Angola	5·2	1·4½	50	—	—	6·0
Botswana	·6	3·1	23	—	—	—
Lesotho	·8	1·7	41	—	—	1·0
Malawi	4·1	2·8	25	—	—	6·1
Mocambique	7·0	1·3	54	—	—	9·1
Rhodesia	4·4	3·3	21	46–53	—	7·1
South West Africa	·6	2·0	35	—	—	0·9
South Africa	18·3	2·4	29	—	—	26·8
Zambia	3·8	2·9	24	49–54	—	5·7
REST OF AFRICA						
Algeria	11·4	0·9	78	46–50	—	—
Burundi	2·9	2·5	28	—	—	4·2
Cameroons	5·3	2·1	33	44–52	24–30	—
Central African Rep.	1·4	2·2	32	42–50	26–32	6·4
Chad.	3·4	1·5	47	45–50	25–31	—
Congo (Brazzaville)	0·9	1·6	44	43–51	—	1·1

POPULATION GROWTH IN AFRICA	Population Mid. 1966 est. (millions)	Yearly Increase 1958–1964 per cent	Number of Years to double	Birth rate per 1,000	Mortality rate per 1,000	Population Estimate 1980 (millions)
Congo (Leopoldville)	16·0	2·1	33	40–48	—	21·5
Dahomey	2·4	2·9	24	47–55	20–26	3·0
Egypt	30·4	2·7	26	41–44	16–18	46·8
Gabon	0·5	1·6	44	32–40	—	0·5
Gambia	0·3	2·4	29	—	—	—
Ghana	7·9	2·7	26	47–54	—	12·3
Guinea	3·6	2·8	25	53–57	33–35	5·0
Ivory Coast	4·0	3·3	21	49–56	—	—
Lybia	1·7	3·7	19	35–43	—	—
Liberia	1·1	1·4	50	—	—	1·2
Madagascar	6·6	3·1	23	42–50	17–21	—
Mali	4·7	2·3	31	55–63	26–32	6·4
Morocco	13·7	2·8	25	44–50	—	22·4
Mauritania	0·9	2·2	32	—	—	—
Mauritius	0·8	2·9	24	35·5	8·6	1·1
Niger	3·4	3·3	21	49–57	24–30	4·5
Nigeria	58·7	2·0	35	47–55	—	91·2
Rwanda	3·2	3·1	23	—	—	—
Senegal	3·6	2·3	31	40–47	23–29	4·4

361

POPULATION GROWTH IN AFRICA	Population Mid. 1966 est. (millions)	Yearly Increase 1958–1964 per cent	Number of Years to double	Birth rate per 1,000	Mortality rate per 1,000	Population Estimate 1980 (millions)
Sudan	13·9	2·8	25	48–55	—	19·3
Somalia	2·6	3·5	20	—	—	—
Tanzania	10·7	1·9	37	42–51	—	14·6
Togo	1·7	2·8	25	50–59	26–32	2·3
Tunisia	4·8	2·0	35	45.1	—	6·5
Uganda	7·7	2·5	28	42–48	—	10·0
Upper Volta	5·0	2·5	28	46–52	27–32	6·3

TABLE V *Education in Africa*

SOUTHERN AFRICA	Universities and Colleges	Secondary Schools	Primary Schools
Angola	3	103	2,019
Botswana	–	8	241
Lesotho	1	67	928
Malawi	14	136	2,280
Mocambique	3	63	4,172
Rhodesia	43	97	3,099
South Africa	89	1,042	9,382
South West Africa	–	30	430
Swaziland	1	36	268
Zambia	14	88	1,876
REST OF AFRICA			
Algeria	1	429	2,495
Burundi	4	9	130
Cameroun	1	101	4,012
Cape Verdi Is.	–	8	243
Central African Rep.	8	27	555
Chad.	–	20	389
Comoro Is.	–	2	56
Congo (Brazz.)	1	40	495

REST OF AFRICA	Universities and Colleges	Secondary Schools	Primary Schools
Congo (Kin.)	139	290	9,477
Dahomey	3	30	587
Egypt	46	419	8,697
Ethiopia	3	56	1,278
French Somaliland	–	8	26
Gabon	1	–	601
Gambia	–	14	77
Ghana	46	85	9,714
Guinea	7	31	1,665
Ifni	1	1	6
Ivory Coast	1	69	1,698
Kenya	37	230	5,150
Liberia	4	125	700
Malagasy	15	210	3,019
Mali	9	175	672
Mauritania	1	7	268
Mauritius	2	112	358
Morocco	3		
Niger		18	513
Nigeria	273	1,362	15,090
Port Guinea		22	164

REST OF AFRICA	Universities and Colleges	Secondary Schools	Primary Schools
Ruanda	9	9	118
Sao Tome, Principe		3	30
Senegal	1	523	4,001
Seychelles	1	11	31
Sierra Leone	2	37	586
Somalia	1	40	233
Spanish Guinea	–	3	159
Spanish Sahara			39
St. Helena		1	11
Sudan	24	416	2,542
Tanzania	25	85	3,715
Togo	1	14	74
Tunisia	6	132	1,941
Uganda	34	622	2,422
Upper Volta	6	31	700

Countries of Africa

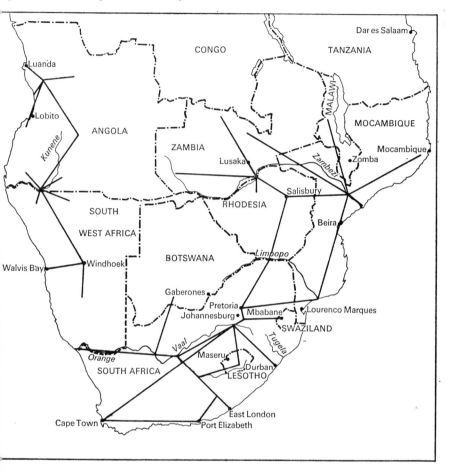

Rail Net-Work and Sea Routes of the Third Africa

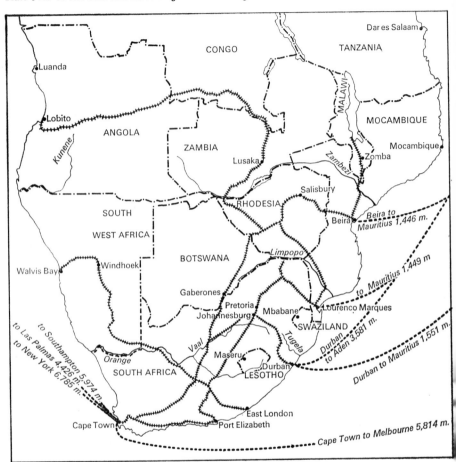

South West Africa
Proposed Development

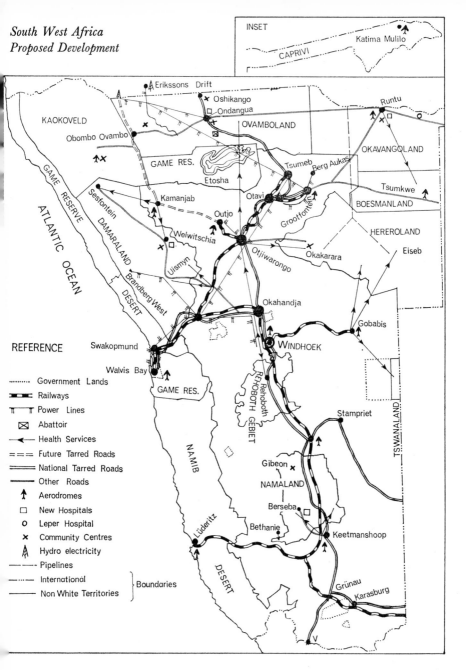

INSET

CAPRIVI

Katima Mulilo

Erikssons Drift

KAOKOVELD

Oshikango

Ondangua

OVAMBOLAND

Runtu

Obombo Ovambo

OKAVANGOLAND

GAME RES.

Tsumeb

Berg Aukas

Etosha

Tsumkwe

Kamanjab

Otavi

BOESMANLAND

Sesfontein

Outjo

Grootfontein

HEREROLAND

Welwitschia

Okakarara

Eiseb

Uismyn

Otjiwarongo

Brandberg West

DESERT

Okahandja

Gobabis

Swakopmund

WINDHOEK

Walvis Bay

GAME RES.

Stampriet

NAMIB

REHOBOTH GEBIET

Rehoboth

TSWANALAND

Gibeon

NAMALAND

Berseba

Lüderitz

Bethanie

Keetmanshoop

DESERT

Grünau

Karasburg

ATLANTIC OCEAN

GAME RESERVE

DAMARALAND

REFERENCE

.... Government Lands

■■■ Railways

ᴛ ᴛ Power Lines

⊠ Abattoir

◄— Health Services

=== Future Tarred Roads

=== National Tarred Roads

— Other Roads

↑ Aerodromes

□ New Hospitals

o Leper Hospital

✕ Community Centres

Ѧ Hydro electricity

----- Pipelines

-···- International

— Non White Territories

} Boundaries

Bibliography and List of Sources

A. *Books and Reference works* (Alphabetically by author)

Adam, T. R.: *Government and Politics in Africa South of the Sahara*, Random House, New York, 1962.
Africa Institute, Pretoria: *Map Series*, Nos. 1—9, 1963—1965.
Allighan, Garry: *The Welensky Story*, Purnell and Sons, Johannesburg, 1962.
American African Affairs Association: *Red China in Africa*, New York, 1966.
American African Affairs Association: *Some American Comments on Southern Africa*, New York 1967.
American Bar Association: *Peaceful Co-existence*, West Publishing Company 1964.
Anti-Slavery Society, London: *Report to the United Nations*, 1967.
Blackstock, Paul: *The Strategy of Subversion*, New York, 1965.
Bruwer, J. P. van S.: *South West Africa – The Disputed Land*, Nasionale Boekhandel, Cape Town, 1966.
Brzezinski, L.: *Africa and the Communist World*, Standard University Press, 1963.
Burnham, James: *Suicide of the West*, Regnery, Chicago, 1965.
Cockram, B.: *Problems of Southern Africa*, South African Institute of International Affairs, Johannesburg, 1963.
Culwick, A. T.: *Britannia Waives the Rules*, Nasionale Boekhandel, Cape Town ,1964.
Da Gama Publications: *State of South Africa*, 1960—1967.
de Villiers, H. H. W.: *Rivonia*, Afrikaanse Pers, Johannesburg, 1963–1966.
Evans, Stanton: *The Liberal Establishment*, Regnery, Chicago, 1966.
Frank, Thomas: *Race and Nationalism*, Fordham University Press, New York, 1960
Frankel, S. H.: *The Economic Impact on Underdeveloped Societies – Essay on International Investment and Social Change*, Oxford University Press, 1953.
Giniewski, Paul: *Livre Noir, Livre Blanc – Dosier du Sud-oest Africain*, Berger-Levrault, Paris, 1966.
Giniewski, Paul: *The Two Faces of Apartheid*, Regnery, Chicago, 1965.
Griffiths, Sir Percival: *The Changing Face of Communism*, Bodley Head, London, 1962.
Hailey, Lord: *An African Survey*, Oxford University Press, London, 1956.
Harrigan, A.: *Red Star Over Africa*, Nasionale Boekhandel, Cape Town.

Haw, Richard: *No Other Home*, Stuart Manning, Bulawayo, 1961.

Hempstone, Smith: *Africa, Angry Young Giant*, Praeger, New York, 1963.

Holloway, J.: *Apartheid, a Challenge*, Afrikaanse Pers, Johannesburg, 1964.

Institute of World Affairs: *Yearbook of World Affairs*, London, 1966.

Kimble, George: *Tropical Africa* (Two Volumes), Anchor Book Company, New York, 1962.

Lessing, P.: *Only Hyenas Laugh*, M. Joseph, London, 1966.

Lessing, P.: *Africa's Red Harvest*, John Day, New York, 1962.

Levinson, Olga: *The Ageless Land*, Tafelberg Uitgewers, Cape Town, 1961.

Louw, E. H.: *The Case for South Africa*, MacFaddens, New York, 1963.

Ludi, G. & Grobbelaar, B.: *The Amazing Mr. Fisher*, Nasionale Boekhandel, Cape Town, 1966.

Macmillan, Publishers: *The Statesman's Yearbook*, London, 1961—1967.

McKay, V.: *Africa in World Politics*, Harper & Row, New York, 1963.

Meyer, Frank S.: *African Nettle*, John Day Co., New York, 1966.

Millin, Sarah & Others: *White Africans are Also People*, Howard Timmins, London, 1966.

Molnar, Thomas: *Africa, A Political Travelogue*, Fleet, New York, 1966.

Murdoch, G. P.: *Africa, Its People & History*, McG. Hill Book Co., 1964.

Nqubane, J.: *An African Explains Apartheid*, Praeger, New York, 1964.

Pich, Anthony: *Inside Zambia and Out*, Howard Timmins, Cape Town, 1967.

Rhoodie, E. M.: *The Paper Curtain*, Voortrekkerpers, Johannesburg, 1967.

Rhoodie, E. M.: *South West: The Last Frontier in Africa*, Voortrekkerpers, Johannesburg and Twin Circle Book Publishers, New York, 1967.

Rhoodie, N. J.: *Apartheid and Partnership*, Academica, Pretoria, 1967.

Sampson, A.: *The Principle of Apartheid*, Voortrekkerpers, Johannesburg, 1966.

Soref, H.: *The Puppeteers*, Tandem Books, London, 1965.

South Africa Foundation: *South Africa in the Sixties*, Central News Agency, Johannesburg, 1964.

Steward, Alexander: *The Challenge of Change*, Howard Timmins, London, 1965.

Stillman, J.: *Africa in the Modern World*, University of Chicago Press, 1966.

Texeira, A.: *The Fabric of Terror*, Devin-Adair, New York, 1965.

Timmins, Publishers: *Yearbook and Guide to Southern Africa*, Cape Town, 1963—1966.

Van Der Merwe, H. J. J. M.: *Gebeure in Afrika* (Forty-five radio talks), Dagbreekpers, Johannesburg, 1961.

Van Reenen, T. H.: *Land, Its Ownership and Occupation in South Africa*, Juta, Cape Town, 1962.

Walker, E. A.: *A History of Southern Africa*, Longmans, London, 1964.

Young, Kenneth: *Rhodesia and Independence*, Eyre and Spottiswoode, London, 1967.

B. *Government Publications and U.N. Documents*
(Alphabetically by title)

Africa's Future: The Soviet View: Central African Federation. An abridgement of I.I. Potekhins booklet "Afrika Smotrit V Budushcheye".
The Africans of Southern Rhodesia: Southern Rhodesia. Information Service Publication, April 20, 1961.

Baxter Report on Central Africa, 1951: United Kingdom, 1951.
Blue Book on Relations with the United Kingdom: Rhodesia. C.S.R. 49—1966.

Codicillus, (Law Journal): Special edition on the South West Africa case, University of South Africa, October, 1966.
Communist Propaganda Around the World: United States Information Service, Washington, 1962.

Demographic Year Book: United Nations, 1965—1967.

Ethiopia and Liberia vs. South Africa: Department of Information Official account of proceedings on South West Africa before the International Court of Justice at the Hague, 1962—1966.

Fact Sheet on Botswana: Botswana, Gaberones, 1966.
Federation and Nyasaland: The British Government's Broken Pledges and the Consequences: White Paper, Central African Federation, 1963.
The Federation of Rhodesia and Nyasalamd: United Kingdom, Cmd. 1948, 1963.

Lantern: Journal of Adult Education, Department of Education, issues of 1957—1966.
Legacy of Progress: White Paper: Central African Federation, 1963.

Monthly Chronicle: United Nations.

Progress Through Separate Development: Information Service of South Africa New York, 1966.
Progress of the Bantu People Towards Nationhood: Department of Information, Pretoria, 1966.
Prospects and Progress: Information Service of South Africa, 1966.

Report on the Possibilities of African Rural Development: Food and Agricultural Organisation, U.N. F.A.O., African Survey, Rome, 1962.
Report of the Commission of Inquiry into South West Africa: Odendaal Report No. 12, Government Printer, Pretoria, 1964.
Report on the Strategy and Tactics of World Communism: United States Congress House Document No. 707, Supplement 400.
Report on the Zimbabwe African Peoples Union: Southern Rhodesia, 1962.
Rhodesia in Africa: Rhodesia, 1966.

372

Seminar on the Multi-National Society: United Nations. Yugoslavia, 1965.
South African Digest: Department of Information, Pretoria, 1960-1967.
South West Africa Survey: Department of Foreign Affairs, Pretoria. Government Printer, Pretoria, 1967.
Statistical Year Book: United Nations ,1964-1967.

Year Book of World Affairs: United Nations, 1965—1967.

Various press statements, bulletins and brochures of the Governments and Information Service of the United Kingdom, Rhodesia, South Africa, Angola, Mocambique, Lesotho and Botswana: Hansards, Blue Books, Government Gazettes and Yearbooks of the period 1960—1967.

c. *Newspapers and Magazines*
(By Name)

Africa Report: Washington, D.C., 1961—1967.
The African Communist: Various issues (distributed by Ellis Bowles Inc., London).
African World: London.
The Age: Melbourne, 1957—1960.
Annual Review: Barclays Bank D.C.O., 1962—1967.

Barrons: New York, 1960—1967.
Bulletin: Africa Institute, Pretoria, 1964—1967.
Die Burger: Cape Town.

The Christian Science Monitor: Boston, 1960—1967.
The Constitution: Atlanta, 1960—1965.

Daily Telegraph: London, 1964—1967.
The Daily Express: London.
The Dines Letter: Dow Jones, New York.

The Economist: London, 1963—1967.
The Enquirer: Cincinatti, 1960—1966.
The Enquirer: Philadelphia, 1960—1966.
Editor and Publisher Year Book: New York, 1963—1966.
Europa Magazine: Brussels, 1964.
Evening Echo: Southampton, England.

Foreign Affairs Quarterly: Council on Foreign Relations, New York, 1962—1967.

The Globe: Toronto.

Het Financiele Dagblad: Holland.
The Herald Tribune: New York, 1960—1965.
The Hindustani Times: New Delhi, 1963.

Industriekurier: West Germany.

Journal of Commerce: New York, 1964—1967.
Journal of the African Society: London.

Kurier: Vienna.

Life: 1960—1967.

Monthly and Annual Reviews: Standard Bank, 1963—1967.
The Morning Herald: Sydney, Australia, 1957—1960.

The Nation: New York, 1960—1967.
National Review: New York, 1960—1967.
National Geographic Magazine: Washington, 1960—1967.
The New Statesman: London, 1964—1967.
Newsweek, New York: 1960—1967.
The New Yorker: New York.
The New York Times: New York, 1960—1965.
The New Zealand Herald: 1957—1960.

Optima: (Anglo American Corporation), Johannesburg, 1961—1967.
Orbis: Foreign Policy Institute, University of Philadelphia: Quarterly, 1966—1967.
Orbis: Foreign Policy Institute, University of Philadelphia: Quarterly, 1966—1967.

Perspective: Fleet Street, London, 1964—1967.
The Post: Washington, 1960—1966.
The Post Dispatch: St. Louis, 1960—1966.
The Press: Detroit.
Press and Advertising Year Book: P. N. Barret Co., Johannesburg, 1966—1967.

The Reporter: New York, 1960—1965.
R.S.A. World: Pretoria, 1964—1967.

The Star: Washington, 1960—1966.
The Sun: Baltimore, 1960—1966.
Schweitzer Monatshefte: Zürich, 1964.
The South African Journal of Economics: 1960, 1965—1967.
Southern Africa Review: St. Bride Foundation, London, 1960—1967.
The South African Financial Gazette: Johannesburg, 1963—1967.
The Spectator: London.
The Star: Johannesburg.
The Sunday Times: Johannesburg.

The Tribune: Chicago, 1960—1967.
Tempo: South African Foundation, 1965—1967.
Time: New York, 1960—1967.
The Times: London.
The Times: Canberra, 1957—1960.
Die Transvaler: Johannesburg.
The Tribune: Durban, Pretoria.
U.S. News and World Report: Washington, 1960—1967

374

Vision: Columbia,1964.
Wall Street Journal: New York, 1960—1967.
Washington Report: American Security Council, 1963—1967.
The Worker: (Communist) New York, 1962.

D. *Diverse Sources*

Various press statements, bulletins, brochures and publications of the American Committee on Africa, the African-American Institute (Washington), the Carnegie Endowment for the Study of War and Peace (New York), the National Student Association (U.S.A.), the Anti-Apartheid Movement (London), the International Commission of Jurists (Geneva), The Organisation of African Unity (Addis Ababa), The African Bureau (London), The Movement for Colonial Freedom (London), Students for a Democratic Society (U.S.A.), Amnesty International (London), Christian Action (London), The World Council of Churches, the Congress for Cultural Freedom (Paris), and several other related organisations who are united in their efforts to change the entire social-political structure in Southern Africa, by every means, including sanctions and force.

Index